The

HISTORY

of the

AMERICAN

REVOLUTION

Volume I

DAVID RAMSAY
1749 – 1815

The

HISTORY

of the

AMERICAN
REVOLUTION

IN TWO VOLUMES

by David Ramsay, M.D.

———

EDITED BY LESTER H. COHEN

———

Volume I

Liberty Fund

INDIANAPOLIS

Foreword and editorial additions © 1990 by Liberty Fund, Inc.

Frontispiece portrait of Dr. David Ramsay (1749–1815), oil on canvas, by Rembrandt Peale. Courtesy of the Gibbs Museum of Art/Carolina Art Association, Charleston, South Carolina.

Facsimile title pages for both volumes are courtesy of the Rare Books and Manuscripts Division, The New York Public Library, Astor, Lenox and Tilden Foundations.

Cover art for Volume I is of Paul Revere's ride, by an anonymous artist. Cover art for Volume II is a woodcut illustrating the battle at Lexington, by John W. Barber.

Library of Congress Cataloging-in-Publication Data

Ramsay, David, 1749–1815.
    The history of the American Revolution/by David Ramsay; edited
by Lester H. Cohen.
      p.   cm.
    Originally published: Philadelphia: Printed and sold by
R. Aitken, 1789.
    Includes bibliographical references.
    ISBN 0-86597-078-5 (set).—ISBN 0-86597-081-5 (pbk.: set).
    ISBN 0-86597-079-3 (v. 1).—ISBN 0-86597-082-3 (pbk.: v. 1).
    ISBN 0-86597-080-7 (v. 2).—ISBN 0-86597-083-1 (pbk.: v. 2).
      1. United States—History—Revolution, 1775–1783. 2. United
States—Politics and government—1783–1789. 3. United States—
Constitution. I. Cohen, Lester H., 1944– . II. Title.
E208.R187   1989
973.3—dc20   89-14583

05 04 03 02 01 C 6 5 4 3
05 04 03 02 01 P 6 5 4 3

Liberty Fund, Inc.
8335 Allison Pointe Trail, Suite 300
Indianapolis, Indiana 46250-1684

Contents

CONTENTS

CONTENTS

Foreword

DAVID RAMSAY'S *The History of the American Revolution* appeared in 1789, during an enthusiastic celebration of American nationhood. "Nationhood," moreover, was beginning to take on new cultural and intellectual connotations. The United States had declared its *political* independence more than a decade earlier, and a rising group of "cultural nationalists" was asserting that it was now time to declare *cultural* independence as well. The American people would never be truly autonomous otherwise. "However they may boast of Independence, and the freedom of their government," wrote Noah Webster, lexicographer, historian, and the nationalists' most brilliant spokesman, "yet their *opinions* are not sufficiently independent." Instead of liberating themselves from the influences of English culture, as they had from England's arms and government, the

Americans were continuing to manifest "an astonishing respect for the arts and literature of their parent country, and a blind imitation of its manners." While such "habitual respect" for England was once understandable, even laudable, it had become an impediment to creating an independent American character and therefore posed dangers for the future.[1]

Cultural nationalism was almost inevitable in the aftermath of a revolution that seemed to require Americans to define not only their political identity, but their spiritual identity as well. Such nationalism manifested itself in a variety of ways in literature and the arts, science, and education. In its superficial manifestations, it testified to an American inferiority complex, consisting mainly of defensive protests against the notion, common in eighteenth-century Europe, that the New World was a physically and morally debased version of the Old, and of mushy effusions of patriotic sentiment over any product of American literature, art, or science. Thus one commentator gushed over Ramsay's *The History of the Revolution of South-Carolina* (1785), saying that it "reflects honour on this country, and gives room for hope that her literary will in time equal her military reputation," and Rev. James Madison enthused that the work's "Dress is altogether American." Another reviewer, praising *The History of the American Revolution,* observed that it is a "necessity that the history of the American revolution be written in our own country, by a person of suitable abilities, who has witnessed the incidents attendant on that great event."[2] Thus did patriotism pass for culture, and Ramsay's work obviously measured up.

On a more sophisticated level, some cultural nationalists—Ramsay among them—developed greater insight into the idea of American

1. Noah Webster, *Dissertations on the English Language* (Boston, 1789), pp. 397–398. See Lawrence J. Friedman, *Inventors of the Promised Land* (New York, 1975) and Richard M. Rollins, *The Long Journey of Noah Webster* (Philadelphia, 1980).

2. *Columbian Magazine, or Monthly Miscellany,* 1 (1786): 22–25; Rev. James Madison to Thomas Jefferson, March 27, 1786, in Robert H. Brunhouse, ed., *David Ramsay, 1749–1815: Selections from His Writings,* American Philosophical Society, *Transactions,* New Series, 55 (1965), Part IV, p. 226; *Columbian Magazine,* 4 (1790): 373–377.

cultural identity. These nationalists recognized that, along with the richly deserved celebration and self-congratulation, the new nation needed a strong unifying culture. Without a culture that articulated the fundamental tenets of liberty, constitutionalism, virtue, and simplicity, the principles of the American Revolution would soon become corrupted. Such corruption could come from without, through the people's continued reliance on English cultural values; it could also come from within, through the disintegrating forces already operating to dissolve the new nation into a multitude of disparate fragments. This realization prompted the nationalists anxiously to develop a notion of American identity that rested on two major premises: that politics, culture, and society were inextricably intertwined, so that a change in any one would subtly alter the others; and that culture was a significant force in shaping human consciousness, an idea which offered a powerful incentive to use literature as a means of exhortation.

Like all the historians of the Revolutionary era, Ramsay saw historical writing as a vehicle for fostering nationhood, an instrument for promoting the kind of unity, even homogeneity, that the cultural nationalists desired.[3] Almost all the leading cultural nationalists were also political nationalists, the surest sign of which was that they saw the Constitution as the great vehicle for both creating and preserving American unity. And, although it was possible to be a nationalist culturally while opposing the Constitution for political reasons (as the historian, poet, and playwright Mercy Otis Warren made clear), Ramsay's reasons for writing a peculiarly consensual or national history were intimately tied to his Federalist political views.

Those reasons were motivated by Ramsay's perception that the new nation faced two sorts of danger: on the one hand, the danger of political divisions between the states and within each state, divisions which had already given rise to factions with competing economic interests; and on the other, the threat of social and cultural

---

3. See Arthur H. Shaffer, *The Politics of History: Writing the History of the American Revolution,* 1783–1815 (Chicago, 1975); Lester H. Cohen, *The Revolutionary Histories: Contemporary Narratives of the American Revolution* (Ithaca, 1980), Chapter 6.

divisions among the people of the several states and regions, which could readily lead to insularity and hostility.

Thus, for example, he wrote in political terms about his fellow South Carolinians who put local interests ahead of national unity and opposed ratification of the Constitution. "To write, to speak, or even to think of a separation of the states is political blasphemy," he wrote to Jedidiah Morse. " 'One Indivisible' is my motto."[4] He even postponed publication of his history of the Revolution until the fate of the Constitution had been decided, for "The revolution cannot be said to be compleated till that or something equivalent is established."[5] But Ramsay continued to fear the potential for disunity even after the Constitution had been operating for years. "We should, above all things, study to promote the union and harmony of the different states," he cautioned in 1794. "We should consider the people of this country . . . as forming one whole, the interest of which should be preferred to that of every part."[6]

While it is impossible to separate his political from his cultural motives, Ramsay was at his best when he spoke of the importance of historical writing with his cultural concerns in mind. In fact, in his Federalist pamphlet, "An Address to the Freemen of South-Carolina (1788)," he cast one of his strongest political arguments for the Constitution in cultural terms. He called upon his fellow Carolinians to "consider the people of all the thirteen states, as a band of brethren, speaking the same language, professing the same religion, inhabiting one undivided country, and designed by heaven to be one

4. Ramsay to Jedidiah Morse, May 5, 1813, in Brunhouse, pp. 118–119, 174. See Ramsay to Benjamin Lincoln, January 29, 1788.

5. Ramsay to Benjamin Rush, February 17, 1788, in Brunhouse, p. 119. Ramsay was a staunch Federalist delegate to his state's constitution-ratifying convention; he wrote to Rush, April 21, 1788, exulting: "I hope in my next [letter] to congratulate you on South Carolina being the 7th pillar of the new Government." Ibid., p. 120.

6. Ramsay's "An Oration," for July 4, 1794. Ibid., p. 195. However, Ramsay's was not a naive vision of homogeneity, for he also thought that "Even the prejudices, peculiarities, and local habits of the different states, should be respected and tenderly dealt with." Ibid. He emphasized unity of vision—an intellectual consensus—rather than a bland uniformity of customs or conduct.

people."[7] Ramsay was as sensitive as any intellectual of his era to the kinds of divisions, real and potential, that tended to separate Americans and undermine the unity he sought. Even ratification of the Constitution was less a culmination than a beginning, less a sign of unity than a foundation for it. "We are too widely disseminated over an extensive country & too much diversified by different customs & forms of government to feel as one people[,] which we are," he confided to John Eliot in 1795. But through historical writings, such as Jeremy Belknap's *History of New Hampshire* (1792), "we might become better acquainted with each other in that intimate familiar manner which would wear away prejudices—rub off asperities & mould us into a homogenous people." Belknap's achievement was all the more remarkable, for Belknap had written about a single state, yet his work breathed a national spirit.[8] In short, even in ostensibly local history, it was possible—indeed, necessary—to write of the nation and its character, for such writings tended to unify the people. "I long to see Dr. [Hugh] Williamson's history of North Carolina," Ramsay wrote to Belknap in 1795. "Indeed I wish to see a history of every state in the Union written in the stile and manner of yours & Williams's history of Vermont. We do not know half enough of each other. Enthusiastic as I am for the Unity of our republic[,] I wish for every thing that tends to unite us as one people who know[,] esteem & love each other."[9] In 1809, Ramsay's own *The History of South-Carolina* would join the list of nationalistic state histories.

Ramsay's passion for unity and his fear of fragmentation prompted him to invent a national past characterized by consensus. This is not to say that Ramsay was a dissembler or deceiver who created a past out of whole cloth. It is, rather, to emphasize that for Ramsay, as for all the historians of the Revolution, historical writing was not so much an end in itself as it was a means to cultivate the political

7. "An Address to the Freemen of South-Carolina, on the Subject of the Federal Constitution," (Charleston, S.C., 1788), p. 13; rpt. Paul Leicester Ford, ed., *Pamphlets on the Constitution of the United States, Published During Its Discussion by the People,* 1787–1788 (Brooklyn, 1888), p. 379.
8. Ramsay to Eliot, March 11, 1795, in Brunhouse, p. 139.
9. Ramsay to Belknap, March 11, 1795, in Brunhouse, pp. 139–140.

and moral consciousness of the present and future generations. Sensitive to divisions within America—political, ethnic, racial, religious, economic—Ramsay genuinely feared chaos, and his experience in both state and confederation politics led him to believe that only by generating a constellation of commonly held values and principles could the nation resist the forces that tended to pull it apart. Ramsay did not invent those values and assumptions; he drew them out of the intellectual climate of Revolutionary America and found clues to them in America's past. But he focused upon them and molded them into the story of the new nation, so that his version of the past appeared to be inevitable. Thus, when Ramsay spoke of using history as an instrument of national unity, he meant to incite future generations to commit themselves to the principles of revolutionary republicanism.[10]

Ramsay, even more than his contemporary historians, was experienced in politics, knowledgeable about world affairs, sensitive to the economic and political interests of his compatriots, and had access to a vast number of historical records. He knew that America's past had been marked by tensions that from time to time had erupted into open conflict. Yet he purposefully created an image of the colonial past that diminished the importance of conflicts and portrayed the colonists as revolutionaries—an image of consensus, unity, and an unfaltering commitment to republican principles. In short, he attempted to create a national future by inventing a consensual past—to provide an instant tradition for a revolutionary people.

Ramsay's principal strategy was to establish a republican lineage, an unbroken succession of American generations that were strenuously committed to the principles of revolutionary republicanism from the moment of settlement in the seventeenth century. The colonists' chief characteristic was that they formed an intellectual, even spiritual, consensus on three major principles: they were politically dedicated to an ordered liberty within the context of law and balanced, representative government; they were ethically com-

10. See Lester H. Cohen, "Creating a Useable Future: The Revolutionary Historians and the National Past," in Jack P. Greene, ed., *The American Revolution: Its Character and Limits* (New York, 1987), pp. 309–330.

mitted to the obligations of conscience and the public good, so that social life was simple and felicitous and individual conduct marked by industry and prudence; and they were convinced philosophically that people are free and efficacious beings who are responsible for their actions and for the consequences their actions bring about. It was this constellation of fundamental principles that constituted the American national character as Ramsay depicted it; and it was to this constellation that he pointed when he exhorted members of his own and future generations to develop cultural unity as a bulwark against division.

Again, Ramsay insisted that these principles were not new to the Revolutionary generation; the conflicts between the Americans and the British during the 1760s and '70s had merely called forth the original settlers' character. The complex coincidence of geography, politics, social arrangements, and values in colonial America had "produced a warm love for liberty, a high sense of the rights of human nature, and a predilection for independence."[11]

"From their first settlement, the English Provinces received impressions favourable to democratic forms of government." Colonization generally coincided with the struggles in England between Parliament and the crown, so that the issue of popular government based on consent, as contrasted with the divine rights of kings, was a current topic of debate. The colonists who emigrated to the New World consisted mainly of people who were "hostile to the claims of [monarchical] prerogative." They "were from their first settlement in America, devoted to liberty, on English ideas, and English principles." Crucially, these ideas were not mere abstractions. The colonists "not only conceived themselves to inherit the privileges of Englishmen, but though in a colonial situation, actually possessed them."[12]

By showing that republican principles and practices had been deeply ingrained in the people for generations, Ramsay vivified the image of a revolutionary past so far as to suggest that the colonists

---

11. David Ramsay, *The History of the American Revolution* (hereafter *HAR*), I, p. 26.
12. *HAR,* I, pp. 31, 27.

---

had been *independent* from the beginning. "The circumstances under which New-England was planted, would a few centuries ago have entitled them, from their first settlement, to the privileges of independence." The colonists had set out at their own expense, with no prospects other than hard work, to build homes and plant civilization in a wilderness. They purchased their lands from "the native proprietors" and exerted themselves to reap the bounties of nature. One hardly needed John Locke to make the argument that people who expended their own labor, paid for their own lands, and voluntarily formed their own governments owed no obligations to Britain except those that "resulted from their voluntary assent" as revealed in "express or implied compact." And those were manifestly limited. The people knew that government rested upon contracts freely entered; that taxation and representation were indissolubly joined; that they held and alienated their property only by consent; that the end of government was the happiness of the people; that the people were free to assemble and petition the government for redress of grievances; and that, all proximate means failing, the people had the natural right to rebel against tyrannical rule.[13] Thus did the colonizing generation consist of proto-revolutionaries.

The colonists were not only republicans in politics, they were also dedicated to personal and social practices that conduced to individual happiness and to the public good. "The state of society in the Colonies favoured a spirit of liberty and independence," Ramsay wrote. Here, the "inhabitants were all of one rank. Kings, Nobles, and Bishops, were unknown to them." The people were "unaccustomed to that distinction of ranks" which characterized European society, and they were "strongly impressed with an opinion, that all men are by nature equal." The colonists' religious practices "also nurtured a love for liberty." The majority were Protestants, Ramsay noted, "and all protestantism is founded on a strong claim to natural liberty, and the right of private judgment." There were, of course, numerous sects, but "they all agreed in the communion of liberty, and all reprobated the courtly doctrines of passive obedience, and non-resistance." Nor were the colonists subjected to the pernicious effects

13. *HAR,* I, pp. 334–337, 27–33.

of the luxury and opulence indulged in by the courts of Europe. Instead, "inured from their early years to the toils of a country life, they dwelled in the midst of rural plenty."

Colonial American society, in short, was characterized by simplicity of manners, and habits of industry, prudence, and morality. The colonists' experience thus "gave a cast of independence to the manners of the people" and diffused among them "the exalting sentiments" of liberty.[14]

Given the colonists' ingrained political and social values and their commitment to the principles of liberty and democratic government, it was obvious that the American Revolution was not a sudden upsurge of resentment against particular acts of Parliament. Resistance and revolution were the inevitable and justifiable responses of a people long habituated to such values. "The genius of the Americans"—that is, their original "republican habits and sentiments"— had prepared them to resist encroachments on their rights and to form popular governments during the Revolutionary era. This was the final element in Ramsay's message to future generations: confronted with arbitrary power, the colonists had established a tradition of showing the courage of their convictions, resisting inroads against their liberties, and taking responsibility for the future.[15]

But why should Ramsay have presented this manifestly one-dimensional image of the colonists as strenuous republicans, committed to simplicity, industry, prudence, equality, and natural rights? To some extent he actually did see them as American revolutionaries in the making, for so powerful was the "republican synthesis" in his own day that it shaped his ideas and experience and predisposed

---

14. *HAR,* I, pp. 29–33. Even the colonists' readings, though few in number, "generally favoured the cause of liberty." They included *Cato's Letters,* the *Independent Whig,* and, in New England, histories of the Puritans, which "kept alive the remembrance of the sufferings of their forefathers, and inspired a warm attachment, both to the civil and the religious rights of human nature." Ibid., p. 30. Ramsay, who wrote of the powerful unifying force exerted by New England histories, was no doubt influenced by them in his own writings.

15. *HAR,* I, p. 350.

him to see all of history in its terms.[16] Yet this will not entirely explain Ramsay's over-simplifications, which seem drastic insofar as his history contains little or no intercolonial rivalry, popular uprisings against proprietary governors, political strife among competing interest groups, ethnic tensions, religious intolerances, or class divisions. Even slavery appears in Ramsay's *History* as a mitigated evil, which, while manifestly wrong, at least had produced sentiments of liberty and independence among the masters.[17] If for five or six

16. The major sources are Bernard Bailyn, *The Ideological Origins of the American Revolution* (Cambridge, Mass., 1967) and *The Origins of American Politics* (New York, 1971); Gordon S. Wood, *The Creation of the American Republic,* 1776–1787 (Chapel Hill, N.C., 1969); and J.G.A. Pocock, *The Machiavellian Moment: Florentine Political Thought and the Atlantic Republican Tradition* (Princeton, N.J., 1975). Three excellent historiographical essays are Robert Shalhope, "Toward a Republican Synthesis: The Emergence of an Understanding of Republicanism in American Historiography," *William and Mary Quarterly,* 3d Series, 29 (1972): 49–80, and "Republicanism and Early American Historiography," Ibid., 39 (1982): 334–356; and Linda K. Kerber, "The Republican Ideology of the Revolutionary Generation," *American Quarterly,* 37 (1985): 474–495. I have discussed the impact of republicanism on one historian in "Mercy Otis Warren: The Politics of Language and the Aesthetics of Self," *American Quarterly,* 35 (1983): 481–498.

17. In fact, Ramsay publicly opposed slavery and branded the slave trade an "infamous traffic." [See Ramsay to Rush, August 22, 1783, September 9, 1783, January 31, 1785, December 14, 1785, April 12, 1786, in Brunhouse, pp. 76, 77, 86–87, 94, 99.] According to Winthrop Jordan, moreover, Ramsay was the only Southerner who, upon receipt of a copy of Thomas Jefferson's *Notes on the State of Virginia,* wrote that he thought Jefferson had "depressed the negroes too low." Ramsay was as strong a proponent of the Lockean principle that environment shapes human nature as one could find in eighteenth-century America. He believed that "all mankind [is] originally the same & only diversified by accidental circumstances." [Ramsay to Jefferson, May 3, 1786, in Brunhouse, p. 101. Jordan, *White Over Black: American Attitudes Toward the Negro,* 1550–1812 (Chapel Hill, N.C., 1968), p. 456.] While Ramsay's attitudes toward slavery are beyond the scope of this essay, it is useful to note that his failure to condemn slavery more vehemently in his *History* was integral to his strategy of diminishing the

generations the Americans had held the deeply ingrained political, social, moral, and philosophical principles that Ramsay described and if they had experienced a minimum of conflict, then why did Ramsay have to remind his readers of the American tradition above all else?

The answer contains three parts. First, as noted earlier, there were Ramsay's apprehensions. He feared that disunity would rend the fabric of the new nation—indeed, that without shared assumptions, principles, and values, as well as a federal Constitution, America might even separate into thirteen autonomous states or into two or three regional governments. In either case, it would become prey to the great European powers, even if it did not destroy itself from within.[18]

Second, Ramsay feared that the great tradition, particularly its powerful moral elements, had been badly damaged by the war. Throughout the war years and into the 1780s, Ramsay expressed his doubts whether the people had sufficient moral courage to make a republican experiment work. Within a year of delivering his stirring vision of an American republican future in his "Oration on the Advantages of American Independence" (1778), he wrote to William Henry Drayton that "A spirit of money-making has eaten up our patriotism." To Benjamin Rush he added: "I most devoutly wish for peace. Our morals are more depreciated than our currency, & that is bad enough." By 1783 he was worried that "This revolution has introduced so much anarchy that it will take half a century to eradicate the licentiousness of the people. I wish for the honor of human nature that in these last ages of the world it may appear that mankind are capable of enjoying the blessings of freedom without the extravagancies that usually accompany it." By 1785 the theme of internal corruption had become more insistent and urgent. "I feel

importance of the forces that could tear the nation apart. For a fine discussion of Ramsay and slavery, see Arthur H. Shaffer, "Between Two Worlds: David Ramsay and the Politics of Slavery," *Journal of Southern History,* 50 (1984): 175–196.
18. See Ramsay to Jefferson, April 7, 1787, in Brunhouse, p. 110; "An Oration" for July 4, 1794, Ibid., p. 195.

with you the declension of our public virtue," he wrote to John Eliot. "Liberty which ought to produce every generous principle has not in our republics been attended with its usual concomitants. Pride[,] Luxury[,] dissipation & a long train of unsuitable vices have overwhelmed our country." And within a year he expressed the ultimate fear: "We have neither honesty nor knowledge enough for republican governments. . . . During the war we thought the termination of that would end all our troubles. It is now ended three years & our public situation is as bad as ever."[19]

The third part of the answer is that historical writings, like Fourth of July orations, sermons, and "all the powers of Eloquence" had the capacity to shape thought, and thus historians, like ministers and politicians, had an *obligation* to use their writings "to counter-act that ruinous propensity we have for foreign superfluities & to excite us to the long neglected virtues of Industry & frugality."[20] History, in short, was a moral art. That was why Ramsay praised Belknap's and Williams's histories; that was why he believed that John Eliot's *Biographical Dictionary* "rendered an essential service to the living by holding up so many excellent models for their imitation from the illustrious dead"; and that was why he deliberately omitted conflict and strife in the colonial past.[21] Indeed, Ramsay once drew an instructive analogy between history and fiction: "Novelists take fiction & make it a vehicle of their opinions on a variety of subjects," he observed. "I take truth & the facts of history for the same purpose."[22] Ramsay was well aware that he was using "art" in the service of history and history in the service of morality and national unity. "Had I a voice that could be heard from New Hampshire to Georgia," he said in 1794, "it should be exerted in urging the necessity of

19. Ramsay to Drayton, September 1, 1779; to Rush, July 18, 1779; to Rush, July 11, 1783; to Eliot, August 6, 1785; to Rush, August 6, 1786; in Brunhouse, pp. 64, 62, 75, 90, 105.

20. Ramsay to Eliot, August 6, 1785, in Brunhouse, pp. 90–91.

21. Ramsay to Eliot, April 7, 1810, in Brunhouse, p. 166.

22. Ramsay to John Coakley Lettsom, October 29, 1808, in Brunhouse, p. 163. This analogy raises the issue of "truth" in historical writing, which I have addressed in "Creating a Useable Future," and *The Revolutionary Histories,* particularly chapters 6 and 8.

disseminating virtue and knowledge among our citizens." His histories represented that voice.

RAMSAY'S VOICE WAS, in fact, heard all over America and over much of Europe as well.[23] Between 1785, when he was thirty-six, and his death in 1815, he published three histories—two on South Carolina and *The History of the American Revolution*—that remain significant after two hundred years. He also wrote numerous other works, ranging from an analysis of yellow fever and well water in Charleston, to a eulogy on the death of his friend and mentor, Benjamin Rush, to a memoir of his wife, Martha Laurens Ramsay, to two examples of that distinctively American genre, the Fourth of July oration.

Even in an age dominated by such *philosophes* as Benjamin Franklin and Thomas Jefferson, Ramsay is notable for his fertile and restless intellect. He entered the sophomore class of the College of New Jersey (later renamed Princeton) in 1762 and was graduated three years later at age sixteen. For the next five years he taught school in Maryland and Virginia. Deciding finally to pursue a career in medicine, he enrolled in the newly reorganized medical school of the College of Philadelphia, which boasted an excellent faculty that included the brilliant twenty-four-year-old Rush. Ramsay received his Bachelor of Physic in 1773. On Ramsay's graduation Rush summarized the talents of his young friend, whom he esteemed as "far superior to any person we ever graduated at our college; his

23. *The History of the Revolution of South-Carolina* was, thanks to Jefferson's brokering, translated into French. The fascinating story of Jefferson's efforts is contained in several letters: Ramsay to Jefferson, June 15, 1785; Ramsay to Jefferson, July 13, 1785; Ramsay to Jefferson, August 8, 1785; Jefferson to Ramsay, August 31, 1785; Jefferson to Ramsay, October 12, 1785; Ramsay to Jefferson, December 10, 1785; Jefferson to Ramsay, January 26, 1786; Jefferson to Ramsay, January 27, 1786; Ramsay to Jefferson, May 3, 1786; Jefferson to Ramsay, July 10, 1786; Ramsay to Jefferson, November 8, 1786; Jefferson to Ramsay, August 4, 1786; Jefferson to Ramsay, May 7, 1788; Ramsay to Jefferson, October 8, 1788, in Brunhouse, pp. 88–94, 97, 101, 104, 107, 112–113, 121, 123. *The History of the American Revolution* was translated into Dutch and German, and *The Life of George Washington* was translated into French and Spanish.

abilities are not only good, but great; his talents and knowledge are universal; I never saw so much strength of memory and imagination, united to so fine a judgment."[24]

In 1774, after practicing medicine for a year in Cecil County, Maryland, Ramsay set out for Charleston, where he made his home for the rest of his life. Charleston was then a leading Southern city, with some 12,000 inhabitants, a growing commerce, and a well-defined social hierarchy that divided whites from one another along class lines and whites from blacks along racial lines—clear evidence of the divisions in society to which he was so sensitive and which he deemphasized in his *History*. Yet within a year of his arrival, this outsider from Pennsylvania, the son of immigrants and a Presbyterian in the midst of an Anglican elite, had married Sabina Ellis, daughter of a prominent merchant,[25] and within three years, he was elected to the South Carolina assembly. By 1778 Ramsay had a seat on the state's prestigious privy council. He served in the Continental Congress in 1785, returned to his seat in the state assembly in 1786, served as a delegate to the convention that ratified the South Carolina state constitution in 1788. From 1791 to 1797 Ramsay was president of the state senate. His only disappointment in politics was his resounding defeat by William Loughton Smith for a seat in the first federal congress.[26]

Neither his political nor his medical and scientific careers, however,

24. Rush quoted in Robert Y. Hayne, "Biographical Memoir of David Ramsay, M.D.," *Analectic Magazine*, 6 (1815): 206. I have relied on Brunhouse, pp. 12–48 for biographical material.

25. Ramsay was married three times: first, in February 1775, to Sabina Ellis, who died in June 1776; then in March 1783 to Frances Witherspoon—daughter of John Witherspoon, president of the College of New Jersey (Princeton)—who died while delivering their child December 9, 1784; and finally in January 1787 to Martha Laurens—daughter of Henry Laurens, one of the giants of South Carolina politics and commerce; this marriage lasted some twenty-five years.

26. Ramsay's loss to Smith was almost certainly related to his anti-slavery sentiments. See Shaffer, "Between Two Worlds"; George C. Rogers, Jr., *Evolution of a Federalist: William Loughton Smith of Charleston* (1758–1812) (Columbia, S.C., 1962), especially pp. 162–171.

seemed to satisfy his intellectual curiosity. Ramsay turned to historical writing, he explained to Thomas Jefferson, "when I was in
confinement in St. Augustine in the year 1781 and [it] has employed
my leisure hours ever since."[27] But Ramsay was drawn to history
and to his national vision by his political experience, which convinced
him that state government was, by turns, too timid and too wild to
solve many of the problems that arose in the post-Revolutionary era.
"There is a languor in the States that forebodes ruin," he complained
to Rush in 1786. He also noted the "temporising" of the Southern
states in particular, and feared the disintegration of the United States
if the Constitutional Convention did not produce "an efficient federal
government."[28] Politics and government were no better in South
Carolina; they may have been worse:

> The eight years of war in Carolina were followed by eight years of
> disorganization, which produced such an amount of civil distress as
> diminished with some their respect for liberty and independence. Several
> apprehended that the same scenes which had taken place in England
> in the seventeenth century after a long and bloody civil war, would be
> acted over again in America by a fickle people who had neither the
> fortitude nor the wisdom to govern themselves. . . . Peace and liberty
> were found inadequate to promote public happiness without the aid of
> energetic government.

The state legislature either languished and did nothing or legislated
too much. The best and most courageous act performed by state
officials, finally, was to agree to the Constitution that would constrain
some of their own power![29]

With first-hand experience of the inefficiencies and vacillations of
state government and an urge to cultivate eloquence, Ramsay began

27. Ramsay to Jefferson, June 15, 1785, in Brunhouse, p. 88. Ramsay, along
with other prominent Charlestonians, was arrested by the British on May
12, 1780, upon the capitulation of the city. On August 27 he was exiled to
St. Augustine; a year later he was released.
28. Ramsay to Rush, February 11, 1786 and Ramsay to Jefferson, April 7,
1787, in Brunhouse, pp. 98, 110.
29. David Ramsay, *The History of South-Carolina*, II, pp. 238–240, 83–84.

writing history. He announced optimistically in his "Oration on the Advantages of American Independence" (1778) that the very presence of free, republican institutions was bound to produce an exalted literature. In an oppressive regime, "ignorance," after all, "was better than knowledge," whereas "Eloquence is the child of a free state." America, he predicted, "will produce poets, orators, cricks, and historians, equal to the most celebrated of the ancient commonwealths of Greece and Italy."[30]

Despite his optimism about the prospects of culture in the new nation, Ramsay soon faced a grim reality. Although he became known as America's "Tacitus" and "Polybius," he learned all too quickly that "the trade of an author is a very poor one in our new world." Concerning *The History of the Revolution of South-Carolina,* he lamented to fellow historian William Gordon: "My advances will not be replaced till I have sold 500 copies & my debts contracted and yet unpaid will require the sale of 700 more. The edition has cost me 5,000 dollars. The printers bill is 2500 dollars. The engravings 800[,] the binding 4/10 a copy. In short I have no brilliant pecuniary prospects before me."[31]

Yet despite the financial failure of his South Carolina history, Ramsay immersed himself in *The History of the American Revolution* during his tenure in the Continental Congress. Here he had access to people prominent on a national level and to an enormous archive. He predicted to Rush that "I can write the general history of the revolution with more ease than I have wrote a part of it. Indeed, I have got the facts already collected." He had ready to hand, he said, a great many documents: "from my access to papers . . . and the regularity of records in the offices of Congress[,] I have been enabled to do a great deal in a little time."[32] His facts may have been

30. "An Oration on the Advantages of American Independence. . . ," in Brunhouse, pp. 184–185.
31. Ramsay was referred to as the "Tacitus" of America by J. Kingston, in *The New American Biographic Dictionary* (Baltimore, 1810), and as America's "Polybius" in *Niles Weekly Register,* 11 (October 5, 1816), both quoted in Brunhouse, p. 220; Ramsay to Gordon, January 18, 1786, in Brunhouse, p. 96.
32. Ramsay to Rush, May 3, 1786, in Brunhouse, pp. 101–102. He added:

substantially collected, but Ramsay made the effort to pose numerous detailed questions to several people about various aspects of the Revolution. He wrote to Rush on several occasions; to Elias Boudinot (commissary general of prisoners for the Continental Army and a member of Congress for five years); to Gouverneur Morris (member of the New York provincial congress and for four years an assistant minister of finance under Robert Morris); to Charles Thomson (secretary of the Continental Congress from 1774 to 1789); and to John Adams. He also sent his manuscript to Charles Thomson, who read it, made comments on it, and promised to circulate it among other knowledgeable readers.[33]

No doubt these inquiries made for a better history. But Ramsay fared almost as poorly on this work as he had on the previous one. He had problems with his printer, Robert Aitken, whose work, said Ramsay, "offends against every principle of good printing. The printing[,] the spelling[,] the ink[,] the form of the lines are in many cases execrable." In addition, asked the outraged Ramsay, "What think you of his stopping the work on the pretence of want of money[,] though 760 dollars were advanced in the time of the work[,] the whole of which was only to cost 1200 dollars?"[34] He also complained that he had been "cheated by booksellers & printers," who were taking far too much of the proceeds of the sales in

---

"For some months past I have spent from five to 8 hours every day at this work. The drudgery is nearly done. I have got my facts & I shall put them together in Carolina."

33. Ramsay to Rush, April 13, 1786, September 26, 1786, May 1, 1787, and August 18, 1787, in Brunhouse, pp. 99–100, 105–106, 112, 113–114; Ramsay to Boudinot, April 13, 1786, to Morris, May 12, 1786, to Thomson, November 4, 1786, to Adams, September 20, 1787, in Brunhouse, pp. 100, 102, 107, 114. Thomson's lengthy letter responding to Ramsay's manuscript has been reprinted by Paul H. Smith, *Quarterly Journal of the Library of Congress,* 28 (1971): 158–172.

34. Ramsay to Ashbel Green, October 4, 1791, in Brunhouse, p. 130. Aitken had a very good reputation, and he attempted to explain his procedures to the irate author. See Brunhouse's index for several references to Aitken; Isaiah Thomas, *The History of Printing in America* (1810), rev. ed., by Marcus A. McCorison (New York, 1970).

advertising. Ramsay was eventually reduced to barter: "If my books that are unsold could be exchanged for a copy of your state laws or of the laws of the neighboring states," he wrote to John Eliot, "I would be most pleased. I would exchange them for any good books rather than [that] they should remain on hand." Finally, Ramsay had to swallow the fact that his *History* had been pirated by John Stockdale in London. It was bad enough that "The errors & blunders of Aitkens edition are many and cannot be corrected," he wrote to John Eliot. Worse yet, "Stockdale has printed one in London without my consent & many of the copies of Aitkens edition are yet on hand." Ramsay had not yet seen the London edition in April 1793, nor had he "any knowledge of it till it was nearly executed." Needless to say, he realized no profit on Stockdale's editions or on the several that were based on it.[35]

Ramsay's reputation as a historian was excellent throughout his life and for decades afterwards. *The History of the American Revolution* has enjoyed a resurgence of interest in the last twenty-five years. The only significant dissenting voice in the last two centuries was that of Orrin Grant Libby, who showed that Ramsay had plagiarized portions of both it and *The History of the Revolution of South-Carolina* from the *Annual Register*.[36] Each issue of the *Annual Register,* published continuously from 1758, contained a superb "History of Europe" section which for some years was written by Edmund Burke. This section contained a narrative of the most important events in contemporary English history. Thus, during the years between 1765 and 1783, it was filled with news of American

35. Ramsay to Eliot, October 19, 1789, April 13, 1792, April 7, 1810, and April 12, 1793, in Brunhouse, pp. 126, 131, 166, 135.
36. Orrin Grant Libby, "Ramsay as a Plagiarist," *American Historical Review,* 7 (1901–02): 697–703. Libby also demonstrated that William Gordon had plagiarized from the same source in "A Critical Examination of William Gordon's History of the American Revolution," American Historical Association, *Annual Report* (1899), I: 367–388. Brunhouse has pointed out that two other historians followed Libby's lead: Josephine Fitts, "David Ramsay . . ." (Unpub. M.A. thesis, Columbia University, 1936); and Elmer D. Johnson, "David Ramsay: Historian or Plagiarist?" *South Carolina Historical Magazine,* 57 (1956).

affairs—political, military, economic. Along with the sections known as "State Papers" and "Appendix to the Chronicle," both of which contained the texts of contemporary documents, the "History of Europe" was a comprehensive, beautifully written narrative that had the additional merit of being written from an English Whig (and, therefore, an anti-war or pro-American) standpoint. Each issue of the *Annual Register* went through numerous editions and circulated widely in America.[37]

Ramsay did, in fact, lift passages verbatim from the *Annual Register,* though Libby certainly exaggerated in suggesting that Ramsay "plagiarized a large part" of his book on the American Revolution either from it or from William Gordon's work.[38] But even if all the examples are conceded, they amount to a very small part of the seven hundred pages. More important, the plagiarism has no substantial impact on its value to modern readers; there is no reason for us to agree with Libby's conclusion that, because of the plagiarism, the *History* is "well-nigh worthless."[39]

First, scholarly citation as we know it was not an issue for eighteenth-century writers, who honored the practice, if at all, only in the most irregular and idiosyncratic manner. Second, eighteenth-century American histories were performances, not proofs; they more nearly resemble sermons, which inspire by enunciating principles and applying them to human situations, than scientific or legal discourses, which depend for their cogency and persuasiveness on their marshalling of evidence. Finally, and most importantly, Libby's criticism, which spoke to the advocates of "scientific" historicism at

37. Burke's role on the *Annual Register* is still, apparently, a matter of controversy. See Thomas W. Copeland, "Burke and Dodsley's Annual Register," *PMLA,* 54 (1939): 223–245; Bertram D. Sarason, "Edmund Burke and the Two Annual Registers," *PMLA,* 68 (1953): 496–508.

38. Libby adduced eight examples of plagiarism in Ramsay's *The History of the American Revolution.* Fitts added ten more, Brunhouse six. Ironically, Libby searched only the *Annual Register,* whereas Ramsay himself mentioned that the *Remembrancer,* another English periodical also was available to him. See Ramsay to Rush, May 3, 1786, in Brunhouse, p. 102. Brunhouse lists the examples of plagiarism at p. 219.

39. Libby, "Ramsay as a Plagiarist," p. 703.

the start of the twentieth century, has become largely irrelevant to most modern readers. While we still learn factual information from some of our "ancient" histories—Cotton Mather's *Magnalia Christi Americana* (1702), incredibly rich with detail, leaps to mind—we do not similarly value the factual nature of Ramsay's histories with the possible exception of *The History of South-Carolina* (1809). Hence, we are less concerned with having precise information about Ramsay's sources.

Instead, we learn from Ramsay the *interpreter* of his present and his past. We learn about the intellectual predilections of the eighteenth-century historian: the values, assumptions, principles, and expectations of one who lived and wrote amidst the events he narrated. We learn from the ways in which he *shaped* history: his use of language, his sense of the significance of people and events, his narrative style, his use of history as propaganda, as exhortation, and as fiction. We do not, in short, rely on Ramsay to tell us what happened during the Revolution, any more than we rely on him for medical advice, which included Benjamin Rush's recommended practice: bleeding. In most respects we know a great deal more about what happened than he did, particularly since *we* are now the arbiters of what is significant. We rely on Ramsay not for information, but for the ways in which he reveals the sensibility through which the events of his era were filtered.

Lester H. Cohen
Indianapolis, Indiana
April 1989

LESTER H. COHEN received M.Phil. and Ph.D. degrees from Yale University and a J.D. degree from Indiana University School of Law, Indianapolis. He taught intellectual history and American studies for fourteen years at Purdue University. He currently practices law with the firm of Barnes & Thornburg in Indianapolis.

Bibliography

THE WRITINGS OF DÁVID RAMSAY

MANUSCRIPTS

Ramsay's papers are scattered among almost two dozen repositories. Listed below are institutions with significant holdings:

Library Company of Philadelphia

Historical Society of Pennsylvania

Library of Congress

Massachusetts Historical Society

American Philosophical Society

South Carolina Historical Society

New York Public Library

COLLECTIONS

Robert L. Brunhouse, ed., *David Ramsay, 1749–1815: Selections from His Writings*, American Philosophical Society, *Transactions*, New Series, 55 (1965), Part IV.

PUBLICATIONS

"A Sermon on Tea," (Lancaster, Pa., 1774).
  Reprinted in Brunhouse: 170–182.

"An Oration on the Advantages of American Independence. . ." [July 4, 1778], (Charleston, S.C., 1778).
  Reprinted in Brunhouse: 182–190.

The History of the Revolution of South-Carolina, from a British Province to an Independent State (2 vols.; Trenton, N.J., 1785).
  French translations: London, 1787; Paris, 1796.

"An Address to the Freemen of South-Carolina, on the Subject of the Federal Constitution, Proposed by the Convention, which met in Philadelphia, May 1787. By Civis," (Charleston, S.C., 1788).
  American Museum, 3 (1788): 413–418.
  Paul Leicester Ford, ed., *Pamphlets on the Constitution of the United States, Published During its Discussion by the People, 1787–1788* (Brooklyn, 1888): 371–380.

The History of the American Revolution (2 vols.; Philadelphia, 1789).
  London, 1790, 1791, 1793; Dublin, 1793, 1795; Trenton, N.J., 1811; Lexington, Ky., 1815; Campen, Holland, 4 vols., 1792–1794; Berlin, Germany, 4 vols., 1794–1795.

"Observations on the Decision of the House of Representatives of the United States, on the 22d of May, 1789; Respecting the Eligibility of the Hon. William Smith, of South-Carolina, to a Seat in that House," (New York, 1789).

"A Dissertation on the Means of Preserving Health in Charleston, and the Adjacent Low Country. Read Before the Medical Society of South-Carolina, on the 29th of May, 1790," (Charleston, S.C., 1790).
  New-York Magazine, or Literary Repository, 6 (1795): 514–519, 585–593.

[Supposed Author], "Observations on the Impolicy of Recommending the Importation of Slaves, Respectfully Submitted to the Consideration of the Legislature of South-Carolina. By a Citizen of South-Carolina," (Charleston, S.C., 1791[?]).

"An Oration, Delivered in St. Michael's Church, before the Inhabitants of Charleston, South-Carolina, on the Fourth of July, 1794, in commemoration of American Independence. . . ," (Charleston, S.C., 1794).
   Reprinted in Brunhouse: 190–196.

"A Review of the Improvements, Progress and State of Medicine in the XVIIIth Century" [Delivered January 1, 1800], (Charleston, S.C., 1800).
   Reprinted in Brunhouse: 196–217.

"An Oration on the Death of Lieutenant-General George Washington, Late President of the United States, who Died December 14, 1799. Delivered in Saint Michael's Church, January 15, 1800. . . ," (Charleston, S.C., 1800).

The Life of George Washington, Commander in Chief of the Armies of the United States of America, throughout the War which Established their Independence, and First President of the United States (New York, 1807).
   London, 1807; Boston, 1811; Baltimore, 1814, 1815, 1818, 1825, 1832.
   French translation: Paris, 1809.
   Spanish translations: Paris, 1819, 1825; New York, 1825; Philadelphia, 1826; Barcelona, 1843.

The History of South-Carolina, from its first Settlement in 1607, to the Year 1808 (2 vols.; Charleston, S.C., 1809).
   Newberry, South Carolina, 1858.
   Photo-facsimile of 1858 ed. (Spartanburg, S.C., 1959 – 60).

Memoirs of the Life of Martha Laurens Ramsay. . . (Philadelphia, 1811).
   Charlestown, Mass., 1812; Boston, 1812, 1814, 1824, 1827; Philadelphia, 1813, 1845, 1895; Glasgow, 1818; Chelmsford, 1827.

Historical and Biographical Chart of the United States (n.p., n.d.).

A Chronological Table of the Principle Events which have taken Place in the English Colonies, now United States, from 1607, til 1810... (Charleston, S.C., 1811).

"An Eulogium upon Benjamin Rush, M.D. . . . Delivered . . . on the 10th of June, 1813. . . ," (Philadelphia, 1813).

History of the United States, from their first Settlement, as English Colonies, in 1607, to the Year 1808, or the thirty-third of their Sovereignty . . . Continued to the Treaty of Ghent, by S.S. Smith . . . and other Literary Gentlemen (3 vols.; Philadelphia, 1818).

Universal History Americanized; or, an Historical View of the World, from the earliest Records to the Year 1808. With a particular reference to the State of Society, Literature, Religion and Form of Government, in the United States of America... (12 vols.; Philadelphia, 1819).

A list of Ramsay's articles published in the *Medical Repository*, 1801–1808, is in Brunhouse, *Selections*, 230–231.

SECONDARY SOURCES

The starting point for Ramsay studies is Robert L. Brunhouse, ed., *David Ramsay, 1749–1815: Selections from His Writings*, American Philosophical Society, *Transactions*, New Series, 55 (1965), Part IV. Brunhouse's superb collection includes a biography of Ramsay, some three hundred letters, and reprints of "A Sermon on Tea" (1774), "An Oration on the Advantages of American Independence" (1778), "An Oration . . . on the Fourth of July, 1794," and "A Review of . . . Medicine in the XVIIIth Century" (1800). Robert Y. Hayne, Ramsay's friend and the executor of Ramsay's estate, published a view of Ramsay's life and work in "Biographical Memoir of David Ramsay, M.D." *Analectic Magazine*, 6 (1815): 204–224.

Studies of historical writing in the Revolutionary Era include Arthur H. Shaffer, *The Politics of History: Writing the History of the American Revolution, 1783–1815* (Chicago, 1975), in which Ramsay figures prominently; William Raymond Smith, *History as Argument: Three Patriot Histories of the American Revolution* (The Hague, 1966), which focuses on Ramsay, John Marshall, and Mercy Otis

Warren; and Lester H. Cohen, *The Revolutionary Histories: Contemporary Narratives of the American Revolution* (Ithaca, N.Y., 1980); "Creating a Useable Future: The Revolutionary Historians and the National Past," in Jack P. Greene, ed., *The American Revolution: Its Character and Limits* (New York, 1987): 309–330; and Mercy Otis Warren's *History of the Rise, Progress and Termination of the American Revolution* (Indianapolis, 1988): xvi–xxxvii. Wesley Frank Craven's *The Legend of the Founding Fathers* (Ithaca, N.Y., n.d.) remains a lively and provocative study of the image of the founding of America in the writings of successive generations of American histories.

The best interpretation of Ramsay's historical writings and political thought include Page Smith, "David Ramsay and the Causes of the American Revolution," *William and Mary Quarterly*, 3d Series, 17 (January 1960): 51–77 (this was reprinted in Page Smith, *The Historian and History* (New York, 1960), which rescued Ramsay and his work from the pall cast over them by Orrin Grant Libby); Lawrence J. Friedman and Arthur H. Shaffer, "David Ramsay and the Quest for an American Historical Identity," *Southern Quarterly*, 14 (July 1976): 351–371, and "History, Politics, and Health in Early American Thought: The Case of David Ramsay," *Journal of American Studies*, 13 (April 1979): 37–56; and Arthur H. Shaffer, "Between Two Worlds: David Ramsay and the Politics of Slavery," *Journal of Southern History*, 50 (May 1984): 175–196.

Editor's Note

THIS EDITION OF RAMSAY'S *The History of the American Revolution* is the first to reprint the original 1789 edition printed by R. Aitken and Son in Philadelphia. That was the only edition that Ramsay actually authorized. The others, including the popular London edition of 1793, printed by John Stockdale, were pirated before the promulgation of effective copyright laws.

Aitken's and Stockdale's editions vary only minutely. In numbering the pages, Aitken omitted page numbers 321 and 322 of the first volume, so that the text flows directly from page 320 to page 323. Stockdale did not preserve Aitken's error; we did, in order to conform to the pagination of the first edition. Aitken also rendered page 32 of volume 1 as page "13." We have corrected that error, since it has no bearing on the actual pagination and since preserving it would have no value for modern readers. Stockdale's copy of Aitken's edition, like the one we used here, may have contained a few illegible passages. Stockdale must have interpolated at those points and occasionally misread the text. We have stayed with the wording of the original by comparing it with another printing.

Ramsay was substantially correct about Aitken's "execrable" printing. Aitken's punctuation is wildly irregular and his spelling idiosyncratic. He transposed letters and abbreviated titles inconsistently and, apparently, according to some inner vision. Thus, we were faced with numerous choices. We have tried here to fulfill the ideal of remaining as faithful to the original text as possible while producing a volume that is accessible to modern readers. We have silently corrected the text where errors were obviously the result of the printer—transposed letters, misspelled words—and where to preserve the errors would have no realistic scholarly or aesthetic value. In a number of instances Ramsay's punctuation has been modernized. Most of the time this meant removing dashes erratically placed (by today's standards) and extraneously placed (duplicating a directly preceding or succeeding punctuation mark). In rarer instances, periods and commas were inserted or removed to correct a glaring omission or a usage that strongly clashed with modern conventions of punctuation. As already implied, our policy was to make such alterations in as conservative a manner as possible—and thus a number of the original quirks and errors, which do have the merit of preserving something of the flavor of the first edition, still reside in this one.

We have, in addition, rendered lengthy quotations in block-indented form, rather than run quotation marks down both sides of paragraphs as in the original.

We have preserved the page numbers of the original, which here appear in brackets in the text. We have also preserved Ramsay's and Aitken's marginalia, although we have silently corrected dates appearing in the margins where the originals were clearly erroneous and deleted some of the most redundant of the dates that were repeated. We have added an index for the convenience of modern readers and researchers. Four appendices, interspersed between chapters rather than included together at the end of the book, have been kept in the place originally assigned to them by Ramsay and Aitken.

EDITOR'S NOTE

ACKNOWLEDGEMENTS

In addition to sharing with me his knowledge and writings on Ramsay, Arthur H. Shaffer graciously read an early version of the introduction and offered useful suggestions. I am currently reviewing Shaffer's authoritative biography of Ramsay, the manuscript of which arrived unfortunately too late for me to borrow from as liberally as I would have liked. Upon publication, Shaffer's biography will be as indispensable as Brunhouse's excellent collection of sources. Linda Levy Peck proved again the value of her friendship and her keen eye for bad writing. She favored the foreword with several readings, helping me to eliminate the gaffes that no longer appear. Dan McInerney and Bruce Kahler, two former Ph.D. students, also read this material and made numerous valuable suggestions. Bill Dennis, Barbara Reynolds, and Chuck Hamilton of Liberty Fund were, as always, a delight to work with. They took a chance on publishing two early American histories—first Mercy Otis Warren's and then David Ramsay's—and made the experiences gratifying for me.

In preparing Ramsay's *History* for publication, I had the extraordinary experience of coming full circle. At the beginning of my graduate career in 1966, I was blessed by having Page Smith as my mentor and friend; at the end of my teaching career, there was David Ramsay, whom Page introduced to me, along with his passion for the beauty and deceptive simplicity of narrative. I have always identified the two, David Ramsay and Page Smith, no doubt because Page has always exemplified for me the finest spirit of the eighteenth century. If these volumes were mine, rather than Ramsay's, to dedicate, I would dedicate them with admiration and respect to Page Smith.

L.H.C.

Preface

[to the first edition]

THE MATERIALS FOR the following sheets were collected in the year 1782, 1783, 1785, and 1786; in which years, as a member of Congress, I had access to all the official papers of the United States. Every letter written to Congress by General Washington, from the day he took the command of the American army till he resigned it, was carefully perused, and it's contents noted. The same was done with the letters of other general officers, ministers of Congress, and others in public stations. It was intended to have enlarged the work by the insertion of state papers, as proofs and illustrations of my positions. This I could easily have done, and shall do at a future time, and in a separate work, if the public require it. At present I thought it prudent to publish little more than a simple narrative of events, without introducing my authorities. Several of these are already in my *History of the Revolution of South-Carolina,* and such as are printed may be found in the periodical publications of the day. I have endeavoured to give much original matter at a small expence. As I write about recent events, known to thousands as well as myself, proofs are at present less necessary than they will be in future.

I appeal to the actors in the great scenes which I have described for the substantial truth of my narrative. Intentional misrepresentations, I am sure there are none. If there are any from other sources, I trust they will be found in small circumstances, not affecting the substance.

October 20, 1789

The

HISTORY

of the

AMERICAN

REVOLUTION

Volume I

THE

HISTORY

OF THE

AMERICAN REVOLUTION.

By *DAVID RAMSAY,* M. D.

IN TWO VOLUMES.

VOLUME I.

PHILADELPHIA:

PRINTED AND SOLD BY *R. AITKEN & SON.*

M.DCC.LXXXIX.

CHAPTER I

Of the Settlement of the English Colonies, and of the political Condition of their Inhabitants.

[1] THE EXTENSIVE CONTINENT which is now called America, was three hundred years ago unknown to three quarters of the globe. The efforts of Europe during the fifteenth century to find a new path to the rich countries of the East, brought on the discovery of a new world in the West. Christopher Columbus acquired this distinguished honor in the year 1492, but a later navigator Americus Vespucius who had been employed to draw maps of the new discoveries, robbed him of the credit he justly merited of having the country called by his name. In the following year 1493, Pope Alexander the sixth, with a munificence that cost him nothing, gave the whole Continent to Ferdinand and Isabella of Spain. This grant was not because the country was uninhabited, but because the nations existing there were infidels; and therefore in the opinion of the infallible donor not

entitled to the possession of the territory in which their Creator had placed them. This extravagant claim of a right to dispose of the countries of heathen nations, was too absurd to be universally regarded, even in that superstitious age. And in defiance of it, several European sovereigns though devoted to the See of Rome undertook and successfully prosecuted further discoveries in the Western hemisphere.

1496

[2] Henry the seventh of England, by the exertion of an authority similar to that of Pope Alexander, granted to John Cabot and his three sons a commission, "to navigate all parts of the ocean for the purpose of discovering Islands, Countries, Regions or Provinces, either of Gentiles or Infidels, which have been hitherto unknown to all christian people, with power to set up his standard and to take possession of the same as Vassals of the crown of England." By virtue of this commission, Sebastian Cabot explored and took possession

1498

of a great part of the North American continent, in the name and on behalf of the king of England.

The country thus discovered by Cabot was possessed by numerous tribes or nations of people. As these had been till then unknown to all other Princes or States, they could not possibly have owed either allegiance or subjection to any foreign power on earth; they must have therefore been independent communities, and as such capable of acquiring territorial property, in the same manner as other nations. Of the various principles on which a right to soil has been founded, there is none superior to immemorial occupancy. From what time the Aborigines of America had resided therein, or from what place they migrated thither, were questions of doubtful solution, but it was certain that they had long been sole occupants of the country. In this state no European prince could derive a title to the soil from discovery, because that can give a right only to lands and things which either have never been owned or possessed, or which after being owned or possessed have been voluntarily deserted. The right of the Indian nations to the soil in their possession was founded in nature. It was the free and liberal gift of Heaven to them, and such as no foreigner could rightfully annul. The blinded superstition of the times regarded the Deity as the partial God of christians, and not as the common father of saints and savages. The pervading

4

influence of philosophy, reason, and truth, has since that period, given us better notions of the rights of mankind, and of the obligations of morality. These unquestionably are not confined [3] to particular modes of faith, but extend universally to Jews and Gentiles, to Christians and Infidels.

1496

Unfounded however as the claims of European sovereigns to American territories were, they severally proceeded to act upon them. By tacit consent they adopted as a new law of nations, that the countries which each explored should be the absolute property of the discoverer. While they thus sported with the rights of unoffending nations, they could not agree in their respective shares of the common spoil. The Portuguese and Spaniards, inflamed by the same spirit of national aggrandizement, contended for the exclusive sovereignty of what Columbus had explored. Animated by the rancour of commercial jealousy, the Dutch and Portuguese fought for the Brazils. Contrary to her genuine interests, England commenced a war in order that her contraband traders on the Mexican coast, claimed by the king of Spain might no longer be searched. No farther back than the middle of the present century, a contest concerning boundaries of American territory belonging to neither, occasioned a long and bloody war between, France and England.

Though Queen Elizabeth and James the first denied the authority of the pope of Rome to give away the country of Infidels; yet they so far adopted the fanciful distinction between the rights of heathens and the rights of christians, as to make it the foundation of their respective grants. They freely gave away what did not belong to them with no other proviso, than that "the territories and districts so granted, be not previously occupied and possessed by the subjects of any other christian prince or State." The first English patent which was given for the purpose of colonising the country discovered by the Cabots, was granted by Queen Elizabeth to Sir Humphry Gilbert, but this proved abortive. Soon after she licensed Walter Raleigh, "to search for heathen lands not inhabited by christian people," and granted to him in fee all the soil "within 200 leagues of the places where his people should make their dwellings and abidings." [4] Under his auspices an inconsiderable colony took possession of a part of the American coast, which now forms North-Carolina. In

1578

1584

1585

5

honor of the Virgin Queen his sovereign, he gave to the whole country
the name of Virginia. These first settlers and several others who
followed them, were either destroyed by the natives, removed by
succeeding navigators, or died without leaving any behind to tell
their melancholy story, for they were never more heard of. No
permanent settlement was effected till the reign of James the first.
The national ardor which sprung from the long and vigorous administration of Queen Elizabeth, continued to produce its effects for
some time after she had ceased to animate the whole. Her successor
though of an indolent disposition, possessed a laudable genius for
colonisation. Naturally fond of novelty, he was much pleased with a
proposal made to him by some of the projectors of that age "for
deducing a colony into that part of America commonly called

1606 Virginia." He therefore granted letters patent to Thomas Gates and
his associates, by which he conferred on them "all those territories
in America, which were not then possessed by other christian princes
or people, and which lay between the 34th and 45th degree of north
latitude." They were divided into two companies, the first consisting
of adventurers of the city of London, was called the London company,
the second consisting of merchants of Plymouth and some other
Western towns, was called the Plymouth company. The adventurers
were empowered to transport thither as many English subjects as
should willingly accompany them; and it was declared "that the
colonists and their children should enjoy the same liberties as if they
had remained, or were born, within the realm." The month of April

1607 1607, is the epoch of the first permanent settlement on the coast of
Virginia, the name then given to all that extent of country which
now forms thirteen States. The emigrants took possession of a
peninsula on the Northern side of James-river, and erected a town
which in honor of their sovereign they called James-Town. They
soon experienced the embarrassments [5] which are the usual lot of
new settlers. In a few months diseases swept away one half of their
number. Those who survived were greatly chagrined by the many

1609 vexations incidental to their new and forlorn situation. In 1609, the
Southern or London company surrendered their rights to the crown
and obtained a new patent. There were then added to the former
adventurers, many of the first nobility and gentry. To them and their

successors were granted, in absolute property, the lands extending from Cape Comfort along the sea coast, southward 200 miles, from the same promontory 200 miles northward, and from the Atlantic westward to the South sea. Licence was given to transport to Virginia, all persons willing to go thither. The colonists and their posterity were declared "to be entitled to the rights of subjects, as if they had remained within the realm." The company being thus favoured by their sovereign, were encouraged to proceed with spirit in supporting and extending their settlement, but before this was thoroughly accomplished, a great waste of the human species had taken place. Within 20 years after the foundation of James-Town was laid upwards of 9000 English subjects had, at different times, migrated thither, but diseases, famine, wars with the natives, and the other inconveniences of their new settlement, had made such havoc among these adventurers, that by the end of that period, there remained alive only about 1800 of that large number. The same and other causes continued to operate so forcibly that, notwithstanding frequent accessions from new adventurers, Virginia in 1670, sixty three years after the settlement of James-Town contained no more than 40,000 inhabitants.

Thirteen years elapsed after James-Town began to be built before any permanent establishment was effected in the Northern or second Colony. Various attempts for that purpose had failed, nor was the arduous business accomplished, till it was undertaken by men who were influenced by higher motives than the extension of agriculture or commerce. These men had been called Puritans in England, from their earnest desires of farther [6] reformation in the established church, and particularly for their aversion to certain popish habits and ceremonies, which they deemed sinful from their having been abused to idolatry. Such was the intolerance of the times, and so violent the zeal for uniformity, that popular preachers of this sect, though men of learning and piety were suspended, deprived, imprisoned, and ruined, for their not using garments or ceremonies which their adversaries acknowledged to be indifferent. Puritanism nevertheless gained ground. On experiment it was found that no attempts are more fruitless than those which are made with the view of bringing men to think alike on the subject of religion. The leaders both of Church and State were too little acquainted with the genuine

1620

1620

principles of policy and christianity, to apply the proper remedy for preserving peace among discording sects. Instead of granting a general liberty of conscience, compulsory methods were adopted for enforcing uniformity. An act was passed for punishing all who refused to come to church or were present at any conventicle or meeting. The punishment was imprisonment till the convicted agreed to conform, and made a declaration of his conformity. If that was not done in three months, he was to quit the realm, and go into perpetual banishment. In case, he did not depart within the time limited, or returned afterwards without a license, he was to suffer death. Such is the renitency of the human mind to all impositions on conscience, that the more the Puritans were oppressed, the more were they attached to their distinguishing opinions, and the more did their sect prevail. Several of them suffered death, in preference to purchasing an exemption from legal penalties, by doing what, in their opinion, was wrong. It was afterwards resolved to send others, who had equally persevered in their non-conformity, into banishment. Many chose to avoid these evils by voluntarily exiling themselves from their native country.

A congregation of these Puritans, under the pastoral care of Mr. John Robinson, being extremely harassed for their religious opinions, resolved to elude their persecutors by removing to Holland. They continued there [7] ten years, and by hard labor, earned a living. Though they were much esteemed and kindly received by the Hollanders, they were induced by very cogent reasons to think of a second removal. The morals of the Dutch were in their opinion too dissolute; and they were afraid that their offspring would conform to the bad examples daily before them. They had also an ardent desire of propogating religion in foreign lands, and of separating themselves from all the existing establishments in Europe, that they might have an opportunity without interruption of handing down to future ages the model of a pure church, free from the admixture of human additions. America, the colonising of which, then excited a considerable share of public attention, presented a proper theatre for this purpose. After serious and repeated addresses to Heaven for direction, they resolved to cross the Atlantic. An application on their behalf, was made to their native sovereign King James, for full liberty and freedom of conscience, but nothing more could be obtained than a promise, that he would connive at and not molest them. The hope that, when at the distance of 3000 miles, they would be out of the reach of ecclesiastical courts, induced them nevertheless to venture. They sailed 101 in number from Plymouth, in September and arrived at Cape Cod in the November following. Before landing they formed themselves into a body politic, under the crown of England, for the purpose of "framing just and equal laws, ordinances, acts, constitutions and offices," to which forty one of their number subscribed their names, and promised all due submission and obedience. After landing they employed themselves in making discoveries till the 20th of December. They then fixed on a place for settlement, which they afterwards called New-Plymouth and purchased the soil from its native proprietors. These adventurers were now at the commencement of a long and dreary winter, at an immense distance from their former habitations, on the strange coast of an uncultivated country, without a friend to welcome their arrival, or a house to shelter them. In settling down on bare creation they had every [8] obstacle to surmount that could prove their firmness, or try their patience. The climate was unfavorable; the season cold and pinching. The prospect of obtaining a supply of provisions, by cultivating the stubborn soil, required an immensity of previous labor, and was both distant and uncertain. From the disorders occasioned by their tedious voyage, with insufficient accommodations, together with those brought on them by the fatigues and exertions unavoidable in a new settlement, and the rigor of the season, they buried forty four persons, nearly one half of their original number, within six months after their landing. Animated with a high degree of religious fervor, they supported these various hardships with unabated resolution. The prospect of an exemption from the tyranny of ecclesiastical courts, and of an undisturbed liberty to worship their creator in the way that was agreeable to their consciences, was in their estimation a sufficient counterbalance to all that they underwent.

This handful of people laid the foundation of New-England. From them and their subsequent associates have sprung the many thousands that have inhabited Massachusetts, New-Hampshire, Connecticut and Rhode-Island. The Puritans, to which sect these primitive emigrants belonged, were a plain, frugal, industrious people, who were strict observers of moral and social duties. They held, that the Bible was the sole rule both of faith and practice—that every man was bound to study it and to judge of its meaning for himself, and to follow that line of conduct and mode of worship, which he apprehended to be thereby required. They were also of opinion that no churches or church officers had any power over other churches or officers, so as to control them—that all church members had equal rights and privileges—that the imposition of articles of faith, modes of worship, habits or ceremonies, was subversive of natural rights and an usurpation of power, not delegated to any man or body of men. They viewed church hierarchy, and especially the lordly pomp of Bishops, as opposed to the pure[,] simple, and equal spirit, of christianity. Their sufferings for non-conformity disposed them to reflect on the nature [9] and extent of civil authority, and led to a conviction that tyranny, whether in church or state, was contrary to nature, reason and revelation. There was a similarity between their opinions of government, and those which they held on the subject of religion. Each strengthened the other. Both were favourable to liberty, and hostile to all undue exercise of authority.

It is matter of regret, that these noble principles of liberty ceased to operate on these emigrants soon after they got power into their hands. In the eleventh year after their settlement in America they resolved, "that no man should be admitted to the freedom of their body politic, but such as were members of some of their churches," and afterwards, "that none but such should share in the administration of civil government, or have a voice in any election." In a few years more, they had so far forgot their own sufferings, as to press for uniformity in religion, and to turn persecutors, in order to accomplish it. No better apology can be made for this inconsistent conduct, than that the true grounds of liberty of conscience were then neither understood, nor practised by any sect of christians. Nor can any more satisfactory account of so open a dereliction of former principles be offered, than that human nature is the same in all bodies of men, and that those who are in, and those who are out of power, insensibly exchange opinions with each other on a change of their respective situations. These intemperate proceedings were

1631

overruled for good. As the intolerance of England peopled Massachusetts, so the intolerance of that Province made many emigrate from it, and gave rise to various distant settlements, which in the course of years were formed into other Provincial establishments. Connecticut, Rhode-Island, and New-Hampshire, were in a great measure shoots from the old venerable trunk Massachusetts, and their early growth was much accelerated by her impolitic zeal for uniformity. The country which was subdivided into these four Provinces had been called New-England ever since the year 1614. The propriety of classing them under one general name became more evident from their being settled by the same kind of people, who were [10] strongly connected with each other by blood, uniformity of manners, and a similarity of religious and political sentiments. The early population of this Northern country was rapid. The Puritans, harrassed for their non-conformity in England, passed over to it in great numbers. In the short space of twenty years from its first settlement 21,200 settlers arrived in 298 vessels. About the year 1640, from a change of affairs, the emigration from Old to New-England in a great measure ceased.

Maryland was the third English colony settled in North America, but the first which from its beginning, was erected into a Province of the empire. The first and second colonies were many years governed by corporations, and in a manner subversive of natural liberty, but the third was from its first settlement ruled by laws enacted in a provincial legislature. The first emigration to Maryland consisting of about two hundred gentlemen, chiefly of the Roman Catholic religion, sailed from England in November, 1632, and landed near the river Potowmack in the beginning of the subsequent year. Calvert their leader purchased the right of the Aborigines, and with their consent took possession of a town, which he called St. Mary's. He continued carefully to cultivate their friendship, and lived with them on terms of perfect amity. The lands which had been thus ceded were planted with facility, because they had already undergone the discipline of Indian tillage. Food was therefore easily procured. The Roman Catholics, unhappy in their native land, and desirous of a peaceful asylum, went over in great numbers to Maryland. Lord Baltimore, to whom the Province had been granted, laid the foundation of its future prosperity on the broad basis of security to

1633

property, and of freedom in religion. The wisdom of these measures converted a dreary wilderness into a prosperous colony, because men exert themselves in their several pursuits in proportion as they are assured of enjoying in safety those blessings which they wish for most. Never did a people enjoy more happiness than the inhabitants of Maryland under Cecilius the founder of the Province. While Virginia persecuted the Puritans, her [11] severity compelled many to pass over into this new Province, the Assembly of which had enacted, "that no persons, professing to believe in Christ Jesus should be molested in respect of their religion, or in the free exercise thereof." The prudence of the one colony, acquired what the folly of the other had thrown away. Mankind then beheld a new scene on the theatre of English America. They saw in Massachusetts the Puritans persecuting various sects, and the church of England in Virginia, actuated by the same spirit, harrassing those who dissented from the established religion, while the Roman Catholics of Maryland tolerated and protected the professors of all denominations. In consequence of this liberal policy, and the other prudent measures adopted by the rulers of this Province, it rapidly increased in wealth and population.

The distractions which convulsed England for 25 years preceding the restoration in 1660, left no leisure for colonising; but no sooner was Charles the Second restored to the throne of his ancestors, than it was resumed with greater spirit than ever.

Soon after that event the restored monarch granted a charter to Connecticut, which had been previously settled by a voluntary association of persons, who held the soil by an Indian title, without any authority from England. By this charter King Charles established a pure democracy. Every power, legislative, judicial and executive, was invested in the freemen of the corporation, or their delegates, and the colony was under no obligation to communicate its legislative acts to the national sovereign.

In the year following, a royal charter, with a grant of similar powers, was conferred on Rhode-Island and Providence plantations. These, like Connecticut, had been previously settled by emigrants chiefly from Massachussets, who as an independent people had seated themselves on land fairly obtained from the native proprietors, without any authority from the parent state. This colony was originally

1662

1663

planted on the Catholic principle, "That every man who submits peaceably to the civil authority, may [12] worship God according to the dictates of his own conscience, without molestation," and under all the changes it has undergone, there has been no departure from that broad basis of universal toleration.

Even today R.I. is very liberal and welcoming to all

In the same year a patent was granted to Lord Clarendon and others, comprehending that extent of country, which now forms the States of North Carolina, South Carolina, and Georgia. Carolina though settled originally as one government, was about the year 1728 divided into two. Georgia was, in the year 1732, formed by George the Second into a distinct Province.

1663

In the year 1664, King Charles the Second gave to his brother James Duke of York, a patent which included New-York and New-Jersey. These Provinces had been previously settled by Dutch Colonists, and held as territories of the United Netherlands, but they were easily reduced to the obedience of the King of England, who claimed the country by the right of prior discovery. The Duke of York in the same year, gave a deed of New-Jersey to Lord Berkely and Sir George Carteret.

1664

Seventeen years afterwards King Charles gave to William Penn, a patent for Pensylvania. Mr. Penn some time posterior to this, obtained a farther grant of the land on the Western side of the River Delaware, and South of Pennsylvania, which was formed into a separate Government, and is now the State of Delaware. Notwithstanding these charters Mr. Penn did not think himself invested with the right of the soil, till he had purchased it from the native proprietors. In the charter of Pennsylvania; there was no express stipulation as had been inserted in all other Colonial patents "that the Pennsylvanians and their descendants should be considered as subjects born within the realm." But clauses were inserted, providing that "acts of Parliament concerning trade and navigation, and the customs, should be duly observed." And it was also stipulated, ["]that no custom or other contribution should be laid on the inhabitants or their estates, unless by the consent of the Proprietary, or Governor and Assembly, or *by act of Parliament in England*." The omission of the first clause, the insertion [13] of the second, and the reservation in favor of Parliament, in the last, may have been occasioned by difficulties

1681

which had then arisen about the rights of the Colonists and the power of Parliament over them. Massachusetts had before that time questioned the authority of Parliament to tax them and legislate for them. The general clause that the Colonists should retain all the privileges of Englishmen had already been made, the basis of claims against which some in the Mother Country had many objections. Perhaps the ruling powers of England were sensible, that they had previously delegated too much of independence to their Colonies, and intended to be more guarded in future, but their caution was too late. Had it been seriously intended to control the natural order of events, by the feeble force of words and clauses in a charter, the experiment ought to have been tried from the first, and not reserved for that of Pennsylvania, which was one of the last granted to the Colonies. Near a century after, Dr. Franklin, when examined at the Bar of the British House of Commons explained the matter by saying "that the inhabitants from the first settlement of the Province relied, that the Parliament never would or could by virtue of that reservation tax them, till it had qualified itself constitutionally for the exercise of such right, by admitting Representatives from the people to be taxed."

In the rapid manner just related, was the English North American Continent parcelled out into distinct Governments. Little did the wisdom of the two preceding Centuries foresee of the consequences both good and evil, that were to result to the old world from discovering and colonising the new. When we consider the immense floods of gold and silver, which have flowed from it into Europe—the subsequent increase of industry and population, the prodigious extension of commerce, manufactures, and navigation, and the influence of the whole on manners and arts[—]we see such an accumulation of good, as leads us to rank Columbus among the greatest benefactors of the human race: but when we view the injustice done the natives, the extirpation of many of [14] their numerous nations, whose names are no more heard—the havoc made among the first settlers—the slavery of the Africans, to which America has furnished the temptation, and the many long and bloody wars which it has occasioned, we behold such a crowd of woes, as excites an apprehension, that the evil has outweighed the good.

CHAPTER I

In vain do we look among ancient nations, for examples of Colonies established on principles of policy, similar to those of the Colonies of Great-Britain. England did not, like the republics of Greece, oblige her sons to form distant communities in the wilds of the earth. Like Rome she did not give lands as a gratuity to soldiers, who became a military force for the defence of her frontiers: She did not, like Carthage, subdue the neighbouring States, in order to acquire an exclusive right to their commerce. No conquest was ever attempted over the Aborigines of America. Their right to the soil was disregarded, and their country looked upon as a waste, which was open to the occupancy and use of other nations. It was considered that settlements might be there formed for the advantage of those who should migrate thither, as well as of the Mother Country. The rights and interests of the native proprietors were, all this time, deemed of no account.

What was the extent of obligations by which Colonies planted under these circumstances, were bound to the Mother Country, is a subject of nice discussion. Whether these arose from nature and the constitution, or from compact, is a question necessarily connected with many others. While the friends of Union contended that the King of England had a property in the soil of America, by virtue of a right derived from prior discovery; and that his subjects by migrating from one part of his dominions to another, did not lessen their obligations to obey the supreme power of the nation, it was inferred, that the emigrants to English America, continued to owe the same obedience to the King and Parliament, as if they had never quitted the land of their nativity. But if as others contended, the Indians were [15] the only lawful proprietors of the country in which their Creator had placed them, and they sold their right to emigrants who, as men, had a right to leave their native country, and as subjects, had obtained chartered permission to do so, it follows from these premises, that the obigations of the Colonists to their parent State, must have resulted more from compact, and the prospect of reciprocal advantage, than from natural obligation. The latter opinions seem to have been adopted by several of the Colonists particularly in New-England. Sundry persons of influence in that country always held, that birth was no necessary cause of subjection, for that the subject of any Prince or State, had a natural right to remove to any other

State or quarter of the Globe, especially if deprived of liberty of conscience, and that, upon such removal, his subjection ceased.

The validity of charters about which the emigrants to America were universally anxious, rests upon the same foundation. If the right of the sovereigns of England to the soil of America was ideal, and contrary to natural justice, and if no one can give what is not his own, their charters were on several accounts a nullity. In the eye of reason and philosophy, they could give no right to American territory. The only validity which such grants could have, was that the grantees had from their sovereign, a permission to depart from their native country, and negotiate with the proprietors for the purchase of the soil, and thereupon to acquire a power of jurisdiction subject to his crown. These were the opinions of many of the settlers in New-England. They looked upon their charters as a voluntary compact between their sovereign and themselves, by which they were bound neither to be subject to, nor seek protection from any other Prince, nor to make any laws repugnant to those of England: but did not consider them as inferring an obligation of obedience to a Parliament, in which they were unrepresented. The prospects of advantage which the emigrants to America expected from the protection of their native sovereign, and the prospect of aggrandizement which their native sovereign expected from [16] the extension of his empire, made the former very solicitous for charters, and the latter very ready to grant them. Neither reasoned clearly on their nature nor well understood their extent. In less than eight years 1500 miles of the sea coast were granted away, and so little did they who gave, or they who accepted of charters, understand their own transactions, that in several cases the same ground was covered by contradictory grants, and with an absurdity that can only be palliated by the ignorance of the parties, some of the grants extended to the South Sea, over a country whose breadth is yet unknown, and which to this day is unexplored.

Ideal as these charters were, they answered a temporary purpose. The colonists reposed confidence in them, and were excited to industry on their credit. They also deterred foreign European powers from disturbing them, because agreeably to the late law of nations, relative to the appropriation of newly discovered heathen countries, they inferred the protection of the sovereign who gave them. They also opposed a barrier to open and gross encroachments of the mother country on the rights of the colonists; a particular detail of these is not now necessary; some general remarks may, nevertheless, be made on the early periods of colonial history, as they cast light on the late revolution. Long before the declaration of independence, several of the colonies on different occasions, declared, that they ought not to be taxed but by their own provincial assemblies, and that they considered subjection to acts of a British parliament, in which they had no representation, as a grievance. It is also worthy of being noted, that of the 13 colonies, which have been lately formed into States, no one (Georgia excepted) was settled at the expence of government. Towards the settlement of that Southern frontier, considerable sums have at different times been granted by parliament, but the twelve more Northern provinces, have been wholly settled by private adventurers, without any advances from the national treasury. It does not appear, from existing records, that any compensation for their lands was ever made to the [17] Aborigines of America, by the crown or Parliament of England; but policy as well as justice led the colonists to purchase and pay for what they occupied. This was done in almost every settlement, and they prospered most, who by justice and kindness took the greatest pains to conciliate the good will of the natives.

It is in vain to look for well balanced constitutions in the early periods of colonial history. Till the revolution in the year 1688, a period subsequent to the settlement of the colonies, England herself can scarcely be said to have had a fixed constitution. At that eventful era the line was first drawn between the privileges of subjects, and the prerogatives of sovereigns. The legal and constitutional history of the colonies, in their early periods, therefore, affords but little instruction. It is sufficient in general to observe, that in less than eighty years from the first permanent English settlement in North America; the two original patents granted to the Plymouth and London companies were divided, and subdivided, into twelve distinct and unconnected provinces, and in fifty years more a thirteenth, by the name of Georgia, was added to the Southern extreme of previous establishments.

To each of these, after various changes, there was ultimately granted a form of government resembling, in its most essential parts, as far as local circumstances would permit, that which was established in the parent state. A minute description of constitutions, which no longer exist, would be both tedious and unprofitable. In general, it may be observed, that agreeably to the spirit of the British constitution, ample provision was made for the liberties of the inhabitants. The prerogatives of royalty and dependence on the Mother Country, were but feebly impressed, on the colonial forms of government. In some of the provinces the inhabitants chose their governors, and all other public officers, and their legislatures were under little or no controul. In others the crown delegated most of its power to particular persons, who were also invested with the property of the soil. In those which were most immediately dependent on the King, he exercised no higher prerogatives over the colonists than over their fellow [18] subjects in England, and his power over the provincial legislative assemblies, was not greater than what he was constitutionally vested with, over the house of commons in the Mother Country. From the acquiescence of the parent state, the spirit of her constitution and daily experience, the colonists grew up in a belief, that their local assemblies stood in the same relation to them, as the parliament of Great Britain, to the inhabitants of that island. The benefits of legislation were conferred on both, only through these constitutional channels.

It is remarkable, that though the English possessions in America were far inferior in natural riches to those which fell to the lot of other Europeans, yet the security of property and of liberty, derived from the English constitution, gave them a consequence to which the colonies of other powers, though settled at an earlier day, have not yet attained. The wise and liberal policy of England towards her colonies, during the first century and [a] half after their settlement, had a considerable influence in exalting them to this pre-eminence. She gave them full liberty to govern themselves, by such laws as their local legislatures thought necessary, and left their trade open to every individual in her dominions. She also gave them the amplest permission to pursue their respective interests in such manner, as they thought proper, and reserved little for herself, but the benefit of their trade, and that of a political union under the same head. The colonies, founded by other powers, experienced no such indulgencies. Portugal and Spain burdened theirs with many vexatious regulations, gave encouragement only to what was for their own interest, and punished whatever had a contrary tendency. France and Holland did not adopt such oppressive maxims, but were in fact not much less rigorous and coercive. They parted, as it were, with the propriety of their colonies to mercantile associations, which sold to the colonists the commodities of Europe, at an enormous advance, and took the produce of their lands, at a low price, and, at the same time, discouraged the growth of any more than they could dispose of, at excessive profits. These oppressive regulations were followed [19] with their natural consequences: The settlements thus restricted advanced but slowly in population and in wealth.

The English colonies participated in that excellent form of government, with which their parent isle was blessed, and which had raised it to an admirable height of agriculture, commerce, and manufactures. After many struggles, it had been acknowledged to be essential to the constitution of Great-Britain, that the people could not be compelled to pay any taxes, nor be bound by any laws, but such as had been granted, or enacted, with the consent of themselves, or of their representatives. It was also one of their privileges, that they could not be affected either in their property, their liberties or their persons, but by the unanimous consent of twelve of their peers.

From the operation of these general principles of liberty, and the wise policy of Great Britain, her American settlements increased in number, wealth, and resources, with a rapidity which surpassed all previous calculations. Neither antient nor modern history can produce an example of colonies governed with equal wisdom, or flourishing with equal rapidity. In the short space of 150 years their numbers increased to three millions, and their commerce to such a degree, as to be more than a third of that of Great Britain. They also extended their settlements 1500 miles on the sea coast, and 300 miles to the westward. Their rapid population, though partly accelerated by the influx of strangers, was principally owing to internal causes. In consequence of the equality of fortune and simplicity of manners, which prevailed among them, their inhabitants multiplied far beyond the proportion of old nations, corrupted and weakened by the vices of wealth, and above all, of vanity, than which, perhaps, there is no greater enemy to the increase of the human species.

The good effects of a wise policy and equal government, were not only discernible in raising the colonies of England to a pre-eminence over those of other European powers, but in raising some among themselves to greater importance than others. Their relative population and wealth, were by no means correspondent to their respective [20] advantages of soil and climate. From the common disproportion between the natural and artificial wealth of different countries, it seems to be a general rule, that the more nature does for any body of men, the less they are disposed to do for themselves.

The New-England Provinces, though possessed of comparatively a barren country, were improved much faster than others, which were blessed with a superior soil and milder climate. Their first settlers were animated with a high degree of that religious fervor which excites to great undertakings. They also settled their vacant lands on principles of the wisest policy. Instead of granting large tracts to individuals, they sold the soil in small farms, to those who personally cultivated the same. Instead of disseminating their inhabitants over an extensive country, they formed successive settlements, in townships of six miles square. They also made such arrangements, in these townships, as co-extended the blessings of education and of religious instruction, with their settlements. By these means industry and morality were propagated, and knowledge was generally diffused.

In proportion to their respective numbers, it is probable that no other country in the world contained more sober orderly citizens, and fewer who were profligate and abandoned. Those high crimes which are usually punished with death, were so rare in New-England, that many years have elapsed, in large populous settlements, without a single execution. Their less fertile soil disposed them to a spirit of adventure, and their victorious industry rose superior to every obstacle. In carrying on the whale fishery, they not only penetrated the deepest frozen recesses of Hudson's Bay, and Davis' straits: But pierced into the opposite regions of polar cold. While some of them were striking the harpoon on the coast of Africa, others pursued their gigantic game, near the shores of Brazil. While they were yet in their infancy as a political society, they carried on this perilous business to an extent exceeding all that the perserverance of Holland, the activity of France, or the vigor of English enterprize, had ever accomplished. A spirit of liberty prompted their [21] industry, and a free constitution guarded their civil rights. The country was settled with yeomanry, who were both proprietors, and cultivators, of the soil. Luxury was estranged from their borders. Enervating wealth and pinching poverty, were both equally rare. Early marriages, and a numerous offspring, were common—thence population was rapid, and the inhabitants generally possessed that happy state of mediocrity, which favors the improvement both of mind and body.

New-York adjoined New-England, but did not encrease with equal rapidity. A few by monopolizing large tracts of land, reduced many to the necessity of being tenants, or of removing to other Provinces, where land could be obtained on more favorable terms. The encrease of population, in this Province, was nevertheless great, when compared with that of old countries. This appears from the following statement of their numbers at different periods. In 1756, the Province of New-York contained 83,233 whites, and in 1771, 148,124, an increase of nearly two for one, in the space of fifteen years.

Pennsylvania was at first settled under the auspices of the celebrated William Penn, who introduced a number of industrious inhabitants, chiefly of the sect of Quakers. The population of this country advanced, equally, with that, of the New-England Provinces. Among the inducements operating on foreigners to settle in Pennsylvania, was a most excellent form of provincial government, which secured the religious as well as the civil rights of its inhabitants. While the Mother Country laboured under an oppressive ecclesiastical establishment, and while partialities of the same kind, were sanctioned by law, in some of the American Provinces, perfect liberty of conscience, and an exact equality of all sects was, in every period, a part of the Constitution of Pennsylvania.

Quaker simplicity, industry, and frugality, contributed, in like manner, to the flourishing of that Province. The habits of that plain people correspond, admirably, with a new country, and with republican constitutions. Opposed to idleness and extravagance, they combined the whole [22] force of religion, with customs and laws, to exile these vices, from their society. The first Quaker settlers were soon followed by Germans, whose industry was not inferior to their own. The emigrants from other countries who settled in Pennsylvania, followed these good examples, and industry and frugality became predominant virtues, over the whole Province.

The policy of a Loan-Office was also eminently beneficial. The Proprietaries of Pennsylvania, sold their lands in small tracts, and on long credit. The purchasers were indulged with the liberty of borrowing, on interest, paper bills of credit, out of the Loan-Office, on the mortgage of their lands. Perhaps there never was an institution which contributed more to the happiness of the people, or to the flourishing of a new country, than this land Loan-Office scheme. The Province being enriched by the clear interest of its loaned paper, was thereby enabled to defray the expences of government, with moderate taxes. The industrious farmer was furnished with the means of cultivating and stocking his farm. These improvements, by increasing the value of the land, not only established the credit of the paper, but enabled the borrower, in a few years, to pay off the original loan with the productions of the soil. The progressive improvements of Pennsylvania may be estimated from the increase of its trade. In the year 1704, that Province imported goods from the Mother Country, amounting in value only to £11,499 sterling, but in 1772, to the value of £507,909, an encrease of nearly fifty for one, in little more than half a century.

In Maryland and Virginia, a policy less favorable to population, and somewhat different from that of Pennsylvania, took place. The Church of England was incorporated with the first settlement of Virginia, and in the lapse of time, it also became the established religion of Maryland. In both these Provinces, long before the American Revolution, that church possessed a legal preeminence, and was maintained at the expence, not only of its own members, but of all other denominations. These deterred great numbers, especially of the Presbyterian [23] denomination, who had emigrated from Ireland from settling within the limits of these governments, and fomented [a] spirit of discord between those who belonged to, and those who dissented from, the established church.

In these and the other Southern Provinces, domestic slavery was common. Though it was not by law forbidden any where, yet there were comparatively few slaves any where, to the Northward of Maryland. The peaceable and benevolent religion of the Quakers, induced their united opposition to all traffic of the human race. Many individuals of other denominations, in like manner discountenanced it, but the principal ground of difference on this head between the Northern and Southern Provinces, arose, less, from religious principles, than from climate, and local circumstances. In the former, they found it to be for their interest to cultivate their lands with white men, in the latter with those of an opposite colour. The stagnant waters, and low lands, which are so frequent on the shores of Maryland and Virginia, and on the coasts, and near the rivers in the Southern Provinces, generate diseases, which are more fatal to whites than blacks. There is a physical difference in the constitution of these varieties of the human species. The latter secrete less by the kidnies, and more by the glands of the skin than the former. This greater degree of transpiration renders the blacks more tolerant of heat, than the whites. The perspirable matter, thrown off by the former, is more foetid than that of the latter. It is perhaps owing to these circumstances, that blacks enjoy better health, in warm and marshy countries, than whites.

It is certain, that a great part of the low country in several of the provinces must have remained without cultivation, if it had not been cultivated by black men. From imagined necessity, founded on the natural state of the country, domestic slavery seemed to be forced on the Southern provinces. It favored cultivation, but produced many baneful consequences. It was particularly hostile to the proper education of youth. Industry, temperance, and abstinence, virtues essential to the health and vigor of both mind and body, were with difficulty [24] practised, where the labour of slaves procured an abundance, not only of the necessaries, but of the delicacies of life, and where daily opportunities and facilities were offered, for early, excessive, and enervating indulgences. Slavery also led to the engrossing of land, in the hands of a few. It impeded the introduction of labouring freemen, and of course diminished the capacity of the country for active defence, and at the same time endangered internal tranquility, by multiplying a species of inhabitants, who had no interest in the soil. For if a slave can have a country in the world, it must be any other in preference to that, in which he is compelled to labour for a master. Such is the force of habit, and the pliancy of human nature, that though degrading freemen to the condition of slaves, would, to many, be more intolerable than death, yet Negroes who have been born and bred in habits of slavery, are so well satisfied with their condition, that several have been known to reject proffered freedom, and as far as circumstances authorize us to judge, emancipation does not appear to be the wish of the generality of them. The peasantry of few countries enjoy as much of the comforts of life, as the slaves, who belong to good masters. Interest concurs with the finer feelings of human nature, to induce slave-holders to treat with humanity and kindness, those who are subjected to their will and power. There is frequently more happiness in kitchens than parlours, and life is often more pleasantly enjoyed by the slave, than his master. The political evils of slavery do not so much arise from the distresses it occasions to slaves, as from its diminishing the incitements to industry, and from its unhappy influence on the general state of society. Where it is common, a few grow rich, and live in ease and luxury, but the community is deprived of many of its resources for independent happiness, and depressed to a low station on the scale of national greatness. The aggregate industry of a country, in which slaves and freemen are intermixed, will always be less than where there is a number of freemen equal to both. Nothing stimulates to industry so much as interest. The man who works for another, will contrive many artifices to make [25] that work as little as possible, but he who has an immediate profit from his labor, will disregard tasks, times and seasons. In settlements where the soil is cultivated by slaves, it soon becomes unfashionable for freemen to labor, than which no greater curse can befal a country. The individuals, who by the industry of their slaves are released from the necessity of personal exertions, will be strongly tempted to many practices injurious to themselves and others. Idleness is the parent of every vice, while labor of all kinds, favours and facilitates the practice of virtue. Unhappy is that country, where necessity compels the use of slaves, and unhappy are the people, where the original decree of heaven "that man should eat his bread in the sweat of his face" is by any means whatever generally eluded.

The influence of these causes was so extensive, that though the Southern Provinces possessed the most fruitful soil and the mildest climate, yet they were far inferior to their neighbours in strength, population, industry, and aggregate wealth. This inferiority, increased or diminished, with the number of Slaves in each Province, contrasted with the number of freemen. The same observation held good between different parts of the same Province. The sea coast which, from necessity, could be cultivated only by black men, was deficient in many of the enjoyments of life, and lay at the mercy of every bold invader, while the Western Country, where cultivation was more generally carried on by freemen, though settled at a later period, sooner attained the means of self defence, and, relatively, a greater proportion of those comforts with which a cultivated country rewards its industrious inhabitants.

In the Southern Provinces, the long credit given by British merchants, was a principal source of their flourishing. The immense capitals of the merchants trading to the North American Continent, enabled them to extend credit to the term of several years. They received a profit on their goods, and an annual interest of five per cent on the sums for which they were sold. This enabled the American merchant to extend credit to the [26] planter, from whom he received a higher interest than he paid in Great-Britain. The planters being furnished, on credit, with slaves and every thing necessary for the cultivation of their lands, when careful and industrious, cleared so much more than the legal interest with which they were charged, that in a few years of successful planting, the difference enabled them to pay their debts and clear their capital. By the help of credit, a beneficial intercourse was established, which redounded to the benefit of both parties.

These causes eminently contributed to the prosperity of the English Provinces. Others, besides co-operating, to the same end, produced a warm love for liberty, a high sense of the rights of human nature, and a predilection for independence.

The first emigrants from England for colonising America, left the Mother Country at a time when the dread of arbitrary power was the predominant passion of the nation. Except the very modern charter of Georgia, in the year 1732, all the English Colonies obtained their charters and their greatest number of European settlers, between the years 1603 and 1688. In this period a remarkable struggle between prerogative and privilege commenced, and was carried on till it terminated in a revolution highly favourable to the liberties of the people. In the year 1621, when the English House of Commons claimed freedom of speech, "as their ancient and undoubted right, and an inheritance transmitted to them from their ancestors;" King James the First replied, "that he could not allow of their style, in mentioning their ancient and undoubted rights, but would rather have wished they had said, that their privileges were derived from the grace and permission of their sovereign." This was the opening of a dispute which occupied the tongues, pens and swords, of the most active men in the nation, for a period of seventy years. It is remarkable that the same period is exactly co-incident with the settlement of the English Colonies. James, educated in the arbitrary sentiments of the divine right of Kings, conceived his subjects to be his property, and that their privileges were [27] matters of grace and favour flowing, from his generosity. This high claim of prerogative excited opposition in support of the rights of the people. In the progress of the dispute, Charles the First, son of King James, in attempting to levy ship-money, and other revenues without consent of Parliament, involved himself in a war with his subjects, in which, after various conflicts, he was brought to the block and suffered death as an enemy to the constitution of his country. Though the monarchy was restored under Charles the Second, and transmitted to James the Second, yet the same arbitrary maxims being pursued, the nation, tenacious of its rights, invited the Prince of Orange to the sovereignty of the island, and expelled the reigning family from the throne. While these spirited exertions were made, in support of the liberties of the parent isle, the English Colonies were settled, and chiefly with inhabitants of that class of people, which was most hostile to the claims of prerogative. Every transaction in that period of English history, supported the position that the people have a right to resist their sovereign, when he invades their liberties, and to transfer the crown from one to another, when the good of the community requires it.

The English Colonists were from their first settlement in America, devoted to liberty, on English ideas, and English principles. They not only conceived themselves to inherit the privileges of Englishmen, but though in a colonial situation, actually possessed them.

After a long war between King and Parliament, and a Revolution—these were settled on the following fundamental principles.

> That it was the undoubted right of English subjects, being freemen or freeholders, to give their property, only by their own consent. That the House of Commons exercised the sole right of granting the money of the people of England, because that house alone, represented them. That taxes were the free gifts of the people to their rulers. That the authority of sovereigns was to be exercised only for the good of their subjects. That it was the right of the people to meet together, and peaceably to consider of their grievances—[28] to petition for a redress of them, and finally, when intolerable grievances were unredressed, to seek relief, on the failure of petitions and remonstrances, by forcible means.

Opinions of this kind generally prevailing, produced, among the colonists, a more determined spirit of opposition to all encroachments on their rights, than would probably have taken place, had they emigrated from the Mother Country in the preceding century, when the doctrines of passive obedience, non resistance, and the divine right of kings, were generally received.

That attachment to their sovereign, which was diminished in the first emigrants to America, by being removed to a great distance from his influence was still farther diminished, in their descendants. When the American revolution commenced, the inhabitants of the colonies were for the most part, the third and fourth, and sometimes the fifth or sixth generation, from the original emigrants. In the same degree as they were removed from that parent stock, they were weaned from the partial attachment, which bound their forefathers to the place of their nativity. The affection for the Mother Country, as far as it was a natural passion, wore away in successive generations, till at last it had scarcely any existence.

That mercantile intercourse, which connects different countries, was in the early periods of the English Colonies, far short of that degree, which is necessary to perpetuate a friendly union. Had the first great colonial establishments been made in the Southern Provinces, where the suitableness of native commodities would have maintained a brisk and direct trade with England—the constant exchange of good offices between the two countries, would have been more likely to perpetuate their friendship. But as the Eastern Provinces were the first, which were thickly settled, and they did not for a long time cultivate an extensive trade with England, their descendants speedily lost the fond attachment, which their forefathers felt to their Parent State. The bulk of the people in New England knew little of the Mother Country, having only heard of her as a distant kingdom, the rulers [29] of which, had in the preceding century, persecuted and banished their ancestors to the woods of America.

The distance of America from Great Britain generated ideas, in the minds of the colonists, favourable to liberty. Three thousand miles of ocean separated them from the Mother Country. Seas rolled, and months passed, between orders, and their execution. In large governments the circulation of power is enfeebled at the extremities. This results from the nature of things, and is the eternal law of extensive or detached empire. Colonists, growing up to maturity, at such an immense distance from the seat of government, perceived the obligation of dependence much more feebly, than the inhabitants of the parent isle, who not only saw, but daily felt, the fangs of power. The wide extent and nature of the country contributed to the same effect. The natural seat of freedom is among high mountains, and pathless deserts, such as abound in the wilds of America.

The religion of the colonists also nurtured a love for liberty. They were chiefly protestants, and all protestantism is founded on a strong claim to natural liberty, and the right of private judgement. A majority of them were of that class of men, who, in England, are called Dissenters. Their tenets, being the protestantism of the protestant religion, are hostile to all interference of authority, in matters of opinion, and predispose to a jealousy for civil liberty. They who belonged to the Church of England were for the most part independents, as far as church government and hierarchy, were concerned. They used the liturgy of that church, but were without Bishops, and were strangers to those systems, which make religion an engine of state. That policy, which unites the lowest curate with the greatest metropolitan, and connects both with the sovereign, was unknown among the colonists. Their religion was their own, and neither imposed by authority, nor made subservient to political purposes. Though there was a variety of sects, they all agreed in the communion of liberty, and all reprobated the courtly doctrines of passive obedience, and non-resistance. The same dispositions were fostered by the usual [30] modes of education in the colonies. The study of law was common and fashionable. The infinity of disputes, in a new and free country, made it lucrative, and multiplied its followers. No order of men has, in all ages, been more favourable to liberty, than lawyers. Where they are not won over to the service of government, they are formidable adversaries to it. Professionally taught the rights of human nature, they keenly and quickly perceive every attack made on them. While others judge of bad principles by the actual grievances they occasion, lawyers discover them at a distance, and trace future mischiefs from gilded innovations.

The reading of those colonists who were inclined to books, generally favoured the cause of liberty. Large libraries were uncommon in the New World. Disquisitions on abstruse subjects, and curious researches into antiquity, did not accord with the genius of a people, settled in an uncultivated country, where every surrounding object impelled to action, and little leisure was left for speculation. Their books were generally small in size, and few in number: A great part of them consisted of those fashionable authors, who have defended the cause of liberty. Catos' letters, the Independent Whig, and such productions, were common in one extreme of the colonies, while in the other, histories of the Puritans, kept alive the remembrance of the sufferings of their forefathers, and inspired a warm attachment, both to the civil and the religious rights of human nature.

In the Southern Colonies, slavery nurtured a spirit of liberty, among the free inhabitants. All masters of slaves who enjoy personal liberty will be both proud and jealous of their freedom. It is, in their opinion, not only an enjoyment, but a kind of rank and privilege. In them, the haughtiness of domination, combines with the spirit of liberty. Nothing could more effectually animate the opposition of a planter to the claims of Great-Britain, than a conviction that those claims in their extent, degraded him to a degree of dependence on his fellow subjects, equally humiliating with that which existed between his slaves and himself.

[31] The state of society in the Colonies favoured a spirit of liberty and independence. Their inhabitants were all of one rank. Kings, Nobles and Bishops, were unknown among them. From their first settlement, the English Provinces received impressions favourable to democratic forms of government. Their dependent situation forbad any inordinate ambition among their native sons, and the humility of their society, abstracted as they were from the splendor and amusements of the Old World, held forth few allurements to invite the residence of such from the Mother Country as aspired to hereditary honors. In modern Europe, the remains of the feudal system have occasioned an order of men superior to that of the commonalty, but, as few of that class migrated to the Colonies, they were settled with the yeomanry. Their inhabitants, unaccustomed to that distinction of ranks, which the policy of Europe has established, were strongly impressed with an opinion, that all men are by nature equal. They could not easily be persuaded that their grants of land, or their civil rights, flowed from the munificence of Princes. Many of them had never heard of Magna Charta, and those who knew the circumstances of the remarkable period of English history, when that was obtained, did not rest their claims to liberty and property on the transactions of that important day. They looked up to Heaven as the source of their rights, and claimed, not from the promises of Kings but, from the parent of the universe. The political creed of an American Colonist was short but substantial. He believed that God made all mankind originally equal: That he endowed them with the rights of life, property, and as much liberty as was consistent with the rights of others. That he had bestowed on his vast family of the human race, the earth for their support, and that all government was a political institution between men naturally equal, not for the aggrandizement of one, or a few, but for the general happiness of the whole community. Impressed with sentiments of this kind, they grew up, from their earliest infancy, with that confidence which is well calculated to inspire a love for liberty, and a prepossession in favour of independence.

[32] In consequence of the vast extent of vacant country, every

colonist was, or easily might be, a freeholder. Settled on lands of his own, he was both farmer and landlord—producing all the necessaries of life from his own grounds, he felt himself both free and independent. Each individual might hunt, fish, or fowl, without injury to his neighbours. These immunities which, in old countries, are guarded by the sanction of penal laws, and monopolized by a few, are the common privileges of all, in America. Colonists, growing up in the enjoyment of such rights, felt the restraint of law more feebly than they, who are educated in countries, where long habits have made submission familiar. The mind of man naturally relishes liberty— where from the extent of a new and unsettled country, some abridgements thereof are useless, and others impracticable, the natural desire of freedom is strengthened, and the independent mind revolts at the idea of subjection.

The Colonists were also preserved from the contagion of ministerial influence by their distance from the metropolis. Remote from the seat of power and corruption, they were not over-awed by the one, nor debauched by the other. Few were the means of detaching individuals from the interest of the public. High offices, were neither sufficiently numerous nor lucrative to purchase many adherents, and the most valuable of these were conferred on natives of Britain. Every man occupied that rank only, which his own industry, or that of his near ancestors, had procured him. Each individual being cut off from all means of rising to importance, but by his personal talents, was encouraged to make the most of those with which he was endowed. Prospects of this kind excited emulation, and produced an enterprising laborious set of men, not easily overcome by difficulties, and full of projects for bettering their condition.

The enervating opulence of Europe had not yet reached the colonists. They were destitute of gold and silver, but abounded in the riches of nature. A sameness of circumstances and occupations created a great sense of equality, and disposed them to union in any common cause, [33] from the success of which, they might expect to partake of equal advantages.

The colonies were communities of separate independent individuals, under no general influence, but that of their personal feelings and opinions. They were not led by powerful families, nor by great officers, in church or state. Residing chiefly on lands of their own, and employed in the wholesome labours of the field, they were in a great measure strangers to luxury. Their wants were few, and among the great bulk of the people, for the most part, supplied from their own grounds. Their enjoyments were neither far-fetched, nor dearly purchased, and were so moderate in their kind, as to leave both mind and body unimpaired. Inured from their early years to the toils of a country life, they dwelled in the midst of rural plenty. Unacquainted with ideal wants, they delighted in personal independence. Removed from the pressures of indigence, and the indulgence of affluence, their bodies were strong, and their minds vigorous.

The great bulk of the British colonists were farmers, or planters, who were also proprietors of the soil. The merchants, mechanics and manufacturers, taken collectively, did not amount to one fifteenth of the whole number of inhabitants. While the cultivators of the soil depend on nothing but heaven and their own industry, other classes of men contract more or less of servility, from depending on the caprice of their customers. The excess of the farmers over the collective numbers of all the other inhabitants, gave a cast of independence to the manners of the people, and diffused the exalting sentiments, which have always predominated among those, who are cultivators of their own grounds. These were farther promoted by their moderate circumstances, which deprived them of all superfluity for idleness, or effeminate indulgence.

The provincial constitutions of the English colonies nurtured a spirit of liberty. The King and government of Great-Britain held no patronage in America, which could create a portion of attachment and influence, sufficient to counteract that spirit in popular assemblies, which, when left to itself, illy brooks any authority, that interferes with its own.

[34] The inhabitants of the colonies from the beginning, especially in New-England, enjoyed a government, which was but little short of being independent. They had not only the image, but the substance of the English constitution. They chose most of their magistrates, and paid them all. They had in effect the sole direction of their internal government. The chief mark of their subordination consisted in their making no laws repugnant to the laws of their Mother

Country—their submitting such laws as they made to be repealed by the King, and their obeying such restrictions, as were laid on their trade, by parliament. The latter were often evaded, and with impunity. The other small checks were scarcely felt, and for a long time were in no respects injurious to their interests.

Under these favourable circumstances, colonies in the new world had advanced nearly to the magnitude of a nation, while the greatest part of Europe was almost wholly ignorant of their progress. Some arbitrary proceedings of governors, proprietary partialities, or democratical jealousies, now and then, interrupted the political calm, which generally prevailed among them, but these and other occasional impediments of their prosperity, for the most part, soon subsided. The circumstances of the country afforded but little scope for the intrigues of politicians, or the turbulence of demagogues. The colonists being but remotely affected by the bustlings of the old world, and having but few objects of ambition or contention among themselves, were absorbed in the ordinary cares of domestic life, and for a long time exempted from a great proportion of those evils, which the governed too often experience, from the passions and follies of statesmen. But all this time they were rising higher, and though not sensible of it, growing to a greater degree of political consequence.

One of the first events, which as an evidence of their increasing importance, drew on the colonies a share of public attention, was the taking of Louisbourg from France, while that country was at war 1745 with Great-Britain. This enterprize was projected by Governor Shirley, of Massachusetts, and undertaken by the sole authority of [35] the legislature of that Colony. It was carried by only a single vote to make the attempt, but after the adoption of the measure, there was an immediate union of all parties, and, all were equally zealous in carrying it into execution. The expedition was committed to General Pepperell, and upwards of 5000 men were speedily raised for the service, and put under his command. This force arrived at Canso, on the 4th of April: A British marine force from the West-Indies, commanded by Commodore Warren, which arrived in the same month, acted in concert with these land forces. Their combined operations were carried on with so much judgment, that on the 17th of June the fortress capitulated.

The war in which Louisbourg was taken, was scarcely ended when another began, in which the colonies were distinguished parties. The reduction of that fortress, by colonial troops, must have given both to France and England, enlarged ideas of the value of American territory, and might have given rise to that eagerness for extending the boundaries of their respective colonies, which soon after, by a collision of claims to the same ground, laid the foundation of a bloody war between the two nations. It is neither possible nor necessary to decide on the rights of either to the lands about which this contest began. It is certain that the prospects of convenience and future advantage, had much more influence on both, than the considerations of equity. As the contending powers considered the rights of the native inhabitants of no account, it is not wonderful that they should not agree in settling their own. The war was brought on in the following manner. About the year 1749, a grant of 600,000 acres of land in the neighbourhood of the Ohio, was made out in favour of certain persons in Westminster, London, and Virginia, who had associated under the title of the Ohio company. At this time France was in possession of the country, on both sides of the mouth of the Missisippi, as well as of Canada, and wished to form a communication between these two extremities of her territories in North-America. She was therefore alarmed at the scheme in agitation by the Ohio company [36] in as much as the land granted to them, lay between her Northern and Southern settlements. Remonstrances against British encroachments, as they were called, having been made in vain by the Governor of Canada, the French, at length, seized some

1753

British subjects who were trading among the Twightwees, a nation of Indians near the Ohio, as intruders on the land of his most Christian Majesty, and sent them to a fort on the South side of Lake Erie. The Twightwees, by way of retaliation for capturing British traders, whom they deemed their allies, seized three French traders and sent them to Pennsylvania. The French persisting in their claims to the country on the Ohio, as part of Canada, strengthened themselves by erecting new forts in its vicinity, and at length began to seize and plunder every British trader, found on any part of that river. Repeated complaints of those violences being made to the Governor of Virginia, it was at length determined to send a suitable person to the French commandant near the Ohio, to demand the reason of his hostile proceedings, and to insist on his evacuating a fort he had lately built. Major Washington, being then but little more than 21 years of age, offered his service, which was thankfully accepted. The distance to the French settlement was more than 400 miles, and one half of the rout led through a wilderness, inhabited only by Indians. He nevertheless set out in an uncommonly severe season, attended only by one companion. From Winchester, he proceeded on foot, with his provisions on his back. When he arrived and delivered his message, the French commandant refused to comply, and claimed the country as belonging to the King his master, and declared that he should continue to seize and send as prisoners to Canada, every Englishman that should attempt to trade on the Ohio, or any of its branches. Before Major Washington returned, the Virginians had sent out workmen and materials, to erect a fort at the conflux of the Ohio, and the Monongahela. While they were engaged in this work, the French came upon them—drove them out of the country, and erected a regular fortification on the same spot. These spirited [37] proceedings overset the schemes of the Ohio company, but its members both in England and America, were too powerful to brook the disappointment. It was therefore resolved to instruct the colonies to oppose with arms, the encroachments of the French on the British territories, as these Western lands were called. In obedience to these instructions, Virginia raised three hundred men, put them under the command of Colonel Washington, and sent them on towards the Ohio. An engagement between them and a party of French, took place, in which the latter were defeated. On this Mr. de Villier, the French commandant marched down with 900 men, besides Indians, and attacked the Virginians. Colonel Washington made a brave defence, behind a small unfinished intrenchment, called Fort Necessity; but at length accepted of honorable terms of capitulation.

MAY 28, 1754

From the eagerness discovered by both nations for these lands, it occurred to all, that a rupture between France and England, could not be far distant. It was also evident to the rulers of the latter, that the colonies would be the most convenient centre of operation, for repressing French encroachments. To draw forth their colonial

1754

resources, in an uniform system of operations, then, for the first time, became an object of public attention. To digest a plan for this purpose, a general meeting of the Governors, and most influential members of the Provincial Assemblies, was held at Albany. The commissioners, at this Congress, were unanimously of opinion, that an union of the colonies was necessary, and they proposed a plan to the following effect, "that a grand Council should be formed of members, to be chosen by the Provencial Assemblies, which Council, together with a Governor, to be appointed by the Crown, should be authorised to make general laws, and also to raise money from all the colonies for their common defence.["] The leading members of the Provincial Assemblies, were of opinion, that if this plan was adopted, they could defend themselves from the French, without any assistance from Great-Britain. This plan, when sent to England, was not acceptable to the Ministry, and in lieu thereof, they [38] proposed "that the Governors of all the colonies, attended by one or two members of their respective Councils," which were for the most part of royal appointment, "should from time to time concert measures for the whole colonies—erect forts, and raise troops with a power to draw upon the British treasury in the first instance: but to be ultimately re-imbursed by a tax to be laid on the colonies by act of Parliament." This was as much disrelished by the colonists, as the former plan had been by the British Ministry. The principle of some general power, operating on the whole of the colonies, was still kept in mind, though dropped for the present.

The ministerial plan laid down above, was transmitted to Governor Shirley; and by him communicated to Dr. Franklin, and his opinion thereon requested. That sagacious patriot, sent to the Governor an answer in writing, with remarks upon the proposed plan, in which by his strong reasoning powers, on the first view of the new subject, he anticipated the substance of a controversy, which for twenty years employed the tongues, pens and swords, of both countries.

The policy of repressing the encroachments of the French on the British colonies, was generally approved, both in England and America. It was therefore resolved to take effectual measures for driving them from the Ohio, and also for reducing Niagara, Crown-Point, and the other posts, which they held within the limit claimed by the King of Great-Britain.

To effect the first purpose, General Braddock was sent from Ireland to Virginia, with two regiments, and was there joined by as many more, as amounted, in the whole, to 2200 men. He was a brave man, but destitute of the other qualifications of a great officer. His haughtiness disgusted the Americans, and his severity made him disagreeable to the regular troops. He particularly slighted the country militia, and the Virginia officers. Colonel Washington begged his permission to go before him, and scour the woods with his provincial troops, who were well acquainted with that service, but this was refused. The General with 1400 men pushed on incautiously, till he [39] fell into an ambuscade of French and Indians, by whom he was defeated, and mortally wounded. The regulars, as the British Troops at that time were called, were thrown into confusion, but the Provincials more used to Indian fighting, were not so much disconcerted. They continued in an unbroken body under, Colonel Washington, and by covering the retreat of the regulars, prevented their entirely being cut off.

1755
JUNE 9

glorifies American troops & Washington while making G.B. look bad

Notwithstanding these hostilities, war had not yet been formally declared. Previous to the adoption of that measure, Great-Britain, contrary to the usages of nations, made prisoners of 8000 French sailors. This heavy blow for a long time, crippled the naval operations of France, but at the same time, inspired her with a desire, to retaliate, whenever a proper opportunity should present itself. For two or three years, after Braddock's defeat, the war was carried on against France, without vigor or success, but when Mr. Pitt was placed at the head of the ministry, public affairs assumed a new aspect. Victory, every where, crowned the British arms, and, in a short time, the French were dispossessed, not only of all the British territories, on which they had encroached, but also of Quebec, the capital of their ancient Province, Canada.

1759

In the course of this war, some of the colonies made exertions so far beyond their reasonable quota, as to merit a re-imbursement from the national treasury; but this was not universally the case. In consequence of internal disputes, together with their greater domestic security, the necessary supplies had not been raised in due time, by others, of the Provincial Assemblies. That a British Minister should depend on colony legislatures, for the execution of his plans, did not well accord with the vigorous and decisive genius of Mr. Pitt, but it was not prudent, by any innovation, to irritate the colonies, during a war, in which, from local circumstances, their exertions were peculiarly beneficial. The advantages that would result from an ability, to draw forth the resources of the colonies, by the same authority, which commanded the wealth of the Mother Country, might in these circumstances [40] have suggested the idea of taxing the colonies by authority of the British Parliament. Mr. Pitt is said to have told Mr. Franklin, "that when the war closed, if he should be in the ministry, he would take measures to prevent the colonies from having a power to refuse or delay the supplies that might be wanted for national purposes," but did not mention what those measures should be. As often as money or men were wanted from the colonies, a requisition was made to their legislatures. These were generally and cheerfully complied with. Their exertions with a few exceptions were great, and manifested a serious desire to carry into effect the plans of Great-Britain, for reducing the power of France.

In the prosecution of this war, the advantages which Great-Britain derived from the colonies, were severely felt by her enemies. Upwards of 400 privateers which were fitted out of the ports of the British colonies, successfully cruised on French property. These not only ravaged the West-India islands, belonging to his most Christian Majesty, but made many captures on the coast of France. Besides distressing the French nation by privateering, the colonies furnished 23,800 men, to co-operate with the British regular forces, in North-America. They also sent powerful aids, both in men and provisions, out of their own limits, which facilitated the reduction of Martinique, and of the Havannah. The success of their privateers—the co-operation of their land forces—the convenience of their harbours, and their contiguity to the West-India islands, made the colonies great acquisitions to Britain, and formidable adversaries to France. From their growing importance, the latter had much to fear. Their continued union with Great-Britain, threatened the subversion of the commerce, and American possessions, of France.

After hostilities had raged nearly eight years—a general peace was

1763

concluded, on terms, by which France ceded Canada to Great-Britain. The Spaniards having also taken part in the war, were, at the termination of it, induced to relinquish to the same power, both

East and West-Florida. This peace gave Great-Britain possession [41] of an extent of country equal in dimensions to several of the kingdoms of Europe. The possession of Canada in the North, and of the two Floridas in the South, made her almost sole mistress of the North-American Continent.

This laid a foundation for future greatness, which excited the envy and the fears of Europe. Her navy, her commerce, and her manufactures had greatly increased, when she held but a part of the Continent; and when she was bounded by the formidable powers of France and Spain. Her probable future greatness, when without a rival, and with a growing vent for her manufactures, and increasing employment for her marine, threatened to destroy that balance of power, which European sovereigns have for a long time endeavoured to preserve. Kings are republicans with respect to each other, and behold with democratic jealousy, any one of their order towering above the rest. The aggrandizement of one, tends to excite the combination, or at least the wishes of many, to reduce him to the common level. From motives of this kind, a great part of Europe not long since combined against Venice; and soon after against Louis the XIVth of France. With the same suspicious eye, was the naval superiority of Great-Britain, viewed by her neighbours. They were, in general, disposed to favour any convulsion which promised a diminution of her overgrown power.

The addition to the British empire of new provinces, equal in extent to old kingdoms, not only excited the jealousy of European powers, but occasioned doubts in the minds of enlightened British politicians, whether or not, such immense acquisitions of territory would contribute to the felicity of the parent State. They saw, or thought they saw, the seeds of disunion, planted in the too widely extended empire. Power like all things human, has its limits, and there is a point beyond which the longest and sharpest sword fails of doing execution. To combine in one uniform system of Government, the extensive territory then subjected to the British sway appeared to men of reflection, a work of doubtful practicability: [42] Nor were they mistaken in their conjectures.

The seeds of discord were soon planted, and speedily grew up to the rending of the empire. The high notions of liberty and independence, which were nurtured in the colonies, by their local situation, and the state of society in the new world, were increased by the removal of hostile neighbours. The events of the war, had also given them some experience in military operations, and some confidence in their own ability. Foreseeing their future importance, from the rapid increase of their numbers, and extension of their commerce; and being extremely jealous of their rights, they readily admitted, and with pleasure indulged, ideas and sentiments which were favourable to independence. While combustible materials were daily collecting, in the new world, a spark to kindle the whole was produced in the old. Nor were there wanting those who, from a jealousy of Great-Britain, helped to fan the flame.

The Origin of the disputes between Great-Britain and her Colonies, in the Year 1764, and its progress till 1773.

FROM THE FIRST SETTLEMENT of English America, till the close of the war of 1755, the conduct of Great-Britain towards her colonies, affords an useful lesson to those who are disposed to colonisation. From that era, it is equally worthy of the attention of those who wish for the reduction of great empires to small ones. In the first period, Great-Britain regarded the provinces as instruments of commerce. Without charging herself with the care of their internal police, or seeking a revenue from them; she contented herself with a monopoly of their trade. She treated them as a judicious mother does her dutiful children. They shared in every privilege belonging to her native sons, and but slightly felt the inconveniences of subordination. Small was the catalogue of grievances, with which even democratical jealousy charged the parent state, antecedent to the period before

1750 [43] mentioned. The following appear to have been the chief. An act of the British parliament for prohibiting the cutting down pitch and tar trees, not being within a fence or enclosure, and sundry acts which operated against colonial manufactures. By one of these, it was made illegal after the 24th of June, 1750, to erect in the colonies, any mill or other engine for slitting or rolling of iron, or any plating forge, to work with a tilt-hammer, or any furnace for making steel. By another, hatters were restrained from taking more than two apprentices at a time, or any for less than seven years, and from employing negroes in the business. The colonists were also prohibited from transporting hats, and home manufactured woolens, from one province to another. These regulations were for the most part evaded, but if carried into execution, would have been slightly inconvenient, and only to a few. The articles, the manufacturing of which, were thus prohibited, could be purchased, at a cheaper rate, from England, and the hands who made them, could be as well employed in agriculture.

1763 Though these restrictions were a species of affront, by their implying, that the colonists had not sense enough to discover their own interest, and though they seemed calculated to crush their native talents, and to keep them in a constant state of inferiority, without any hope of arriving at those advantages, to which, by the native riches of their country, they were prompted to aspire, yet if no other grievances had been superadded, to what existed in 1763, these would have been soon forgotten, for their pressure was neither great, nor universal. The good resulting to the colonies, from their connection with Great-Britain, infinitely outweighed the evil.

1764 Till the year 1764, the colonial regulations seemed to have no other object, but the common good of the whole empire. Exceptions, to the contrary, were few, and had no appearance of system. When the approach of the colonies to manhood, made them more capable of resisting impositions, Great-Britain changed the ancient system, under which her colonies had long flourished. When policy would rather have dictated a relaxation of authority, she rose in her demands, and multiplied her restraints.

[44] From the conquest of Canada, in 1759, some have supposed, that France began secretly to lay schemes, for wresting those colonies

from Great-Britain, which she was not able to conquer. Others alledge, that from that period, the colonists, released from all fears of dangerous neighbours, fixed their eyes on independence, and took sundry steps, preparatory to the adoption of the measure. Without recurring to either of these opinions, the known selfishness of human nature is sufficient to account for that demand on the one side, and that refusal on the other, which occasioned the revolution. It was natural for Great-Britain, to wish for an extension of her authority over the colonies, and equally so for them, on their approach to maturity, to be more impatient of subordination, and to resist every innovation, for increasing the degree of their dependence.

The sad story of colonial oppression commenced in the year 1764. Great-Britain, then, adopted new regulations, respecting her colonies, which, after disturbing the ancient harmony of the two countries, for about twelve years, terminated in a dismemberment of the empire.

These consisted in restricting their former commerce, but more   1764 especially in subjecting them to taxation, by the British Parliament. By adhering to the spirit of her navigation act, in the course of a century, the trade of Great-Britain had encreased far beyond the expectation of her most sanguine sons, but by rigidly enforcing the strict letter of the same, in a different situation of public affairs, effects, directly the reverse, were produced.

From the enterprising, commercial spirit of the colonists, the trade of America, after filling all its proper channels to the brim, swelled out on every side, overflowed its proper banks, with a rich redundance. In the cure of evils, which are closely connected with the causes of national prosperity, vulgar precaution ought not to be employed. In severely checking a contraband trade, which was only the overflowing of an extensive fair trade, the remedy was worse then the disease.

For some time before and after the termination of the war of 1755, a considerable intercourse had been carried [45] on between the British and Spanish colonies, consisting of the manufactures of Great Britain, imported by the former, and sold to the latter, by which the British colonies acquired gold and silver, and were enabled to make remittances to the Mother Country. This trade, though it did not clash with the spirit of the British navigation laws, was forbidden by their letter. On account of the advantages, which all parties, and

43

particularly Great-Britain, reaped from this intercourse, it had long been winked at, by persons in power, but at the period beforementioned, some new regulations were adopted, by which it was almost destroyed. This was effected by armed cutters, whose commanders were enjoined to take the usual custom-house oaths, and to act in the capacity of revenue officers. So sudden a stoppage of an accustomed and beneficial commerce, by an unusually rigid execution of old laws, was a serious blow to the Northern colonies. It was their misfortune, that though they stood in need of vast quantities of British manufactures, their country produced very little, that afforded a direct remittance, to pay for them. They were, therefore, under a necessity of seeking elsewhere, a market for their produce, and by a circuitous route, acquiring the means of supporting their credit, with the Mother Country. This they found, by trading with the Spanish and French colonies, in their neighbourhood. From them they acquired gold, silver, and valuable commodities, the ultimate profits of which, centered in Great-Britain. This intercourse gave life to business of every denomination, and established a reciprocal circulation of money and merchandize, to the benefit of all parties concerned. Why a trade, essential to the colonies, and which, so far from being detrimental, was indirectly advantageous to Great-Britain, should be so narrowly watched, and so severely restrained, could not be accounted for by the Americans, without supposing, that the rulers of Great-Britain were jealous of their adventurous commercial spirit, and of their encreasing number of seamen. Their actual sufferings were great, but their apprehensions were greater. Instead of viewing the parent state, as formerly, in the light of an affectionate [46] mother, they conceived her, as beginning to be influenced by the narrow views of an illiberal stepdame.

1764

After the 29th of September, 1764, the trade between the British, and the French, and Spanish colonies, was in some degree legalised, but under circumstances, that brought no relief to the colonists, for it was loaded with such enormous duties, as were equivalent to a prohibition. The preamble to the act, for this purpose, was alarming. "Whereas it is just and necessary, that a revenue be raised in America, for defraying the expences, of defending, protecting, and securing the same, We, the commons, &c. towards raising the same, give, and grant unto your Majesty, the sum of" (here followed a specification of duties upon foreign clayed sugar, indigo, and coffee, of foreign produce, upon all wines, except French, upon all wrought silk, and all calicoes, and upon every gallon of melasses, and syrups, being the produce of a colony, not under the dominion of his Majesty). It was also enacted, that the monies, arising from the importation of these articles, into the colonies, should be paid into the receipt of his Majesty's exchequer, there to be entered separate, and reserved, to be disposed of by Parliament, toward defraying the necessary expences, of defending, protecting, and securing America. Till that act passed, no act avowedly for the purpose of revenue, and with the ordinary title and recital of such, was to be found in the parliamentary statute book. The wording of it made the colonists fear, that the Parliament would go on, in charging them with such taxes, as they pleased, and for the support of such military force, as they should think proper. The act was the more disgusting, because the monies, arising from it, were ordered to be paid in specie, and regulations were adopted, against colonial paper money. To obstruct the avenues of acquiring gold and silver, and at the same time to interdict the use of paper money, appeared to the colonists as a farther evidence, that their interests were either misunderstood, or disregarded. The imposition of duties, for the purpose of raising a revenue, in America, was considered as a dangerous innovation, but the methods adopted, for securing their collection, [47] were resented as arbitrary and unconstitutional. It was enacted by Parliament, that whenever offences should be committed against the acts, which imposed them, the prosecutor might bring his action for the penalty, in the courts of admiralty, by which means the defendant lost the advantage of being tried by a jury, and was subjected to the necessity of having his case decided upon, by a single man, a creature of the crown, whose salary was to be paid out of forfeitures, adjudged by himself; and also according to a course of law, which exempted the prosecutor from the trouble of proving his accusation, and obliged the defendant, either to evince his innocence, or to suffer. By these regulations, the guards, which the constitution had placed round property, and the fences, which the ancestors of both countries had erected, against arbitrary power, were thrown down, as far as they concerned the colonists, charged with violating the laws, for raising a revenue in America.

They who directed public affairs in Great-Britain feared, that if the collection of these duties was enforced, only in the customary way, payment would be often eluded. To obviate that disposition which the colonists discovered to screen one another, in disobeying offensive acts of parliament, regulations were adopted, bearing hard on their constitutional rights. Unwilling as the colonists were to be excluded by the imposition of enormous duties, from an accustomed and beneficial line of business; it is not wonderful that they were disposed to represent these innovations of the Mother Country, in the most unfavourable point of view. The heavy losses to which many individuals were subjected, and the general distress of the mercantile interest, in several of the oldest colonies, soured the minds of many. That the Mother Country should infringe her own constitution, to cramp the commerce of her colonies, was a fruitful subject of declamation: but these murmurings would have evaporated in words, had Great-Britain proceeded to no farther innovations. Instead of this, she adopted the novel idea of raising from the colonies, an efficient revenue, by direct internal taxes, laid by authority of her parliament.

[48] Though all the colonists disrelished, and many, from the pressure of actual sufferings, complained of the British restrictions on their manufactures and commerce, yet a great majority was disposed to submit to both. Most of them acknowledged that the exercise of these powers was incident to the sovereignty of the Mother Country, especially when guarded by an implied contract, that they were to be only used for the common benefit of the empire. It was generally allowed, that as the planting of colonies was not designed to erect an independent government, but to extend an old one, the Parent State had a right to restrain their trade in every way, which conduced to the common emolument.

They for the most part considered the Mother Country as authorised to name ports and nations, to which alone their merchandize should be carried, and with which alone they should trade: but the novel claim of taxing them without their consent, was universally repro-bated, as contrary to their natural, chartered, and constitutional rights. In opposition to it, they not only alledged the general principles of liberty, but ancient usage. During the first 150 years of their existence, they had been left to tax themselves and in their own way. If there were any exceptions to this general rule, they were too inconsiderable to merit notice. In the war of 1755, the events of which were fresh in the recollection of every one, the parliament had in no instance attempted to raise either men or money in the colonies, by its own authority. As the claim of taxation on one side, and the refusal of it on the other, was the very hinge on which the revolution turned, it merits a particular discussion.

Colonies were formerly planted by warlike nations, to keep their enemies in awe, to give vent to a surplus of inhabitants, or to discharge a number of discontented and troublesome citizens. But in modern ages, the spirit of violence, being in some measure sheathed in commerce, colonies have been settled, by the nations of Europe, for the purposes of trade. These were to be attained by their raising, for the Mother Country, such [49] commodities as she did not produce, and supplying themselves from her with such things as they wanted. In subserviency to these views, Great-Britain planted colonies, and made laws, obliging them to carry to her, all their products which she wanted, and all their raw materials which she chose to work up. Besides this restriction, she forbad them to procure manufactures from any other part of the globe, or even the products of European countries, which could rival her, without being first brought to her ports. By a variety of laws, she regulated their trade, in such a manner, as was thought most conducive to their mutual advantage, and her own particular welfare. This principle of commercial monopoly, ran through no less than 29 acts of parliament from 1660, to 1764. In all these acts, the system of commerce was established, as that, from which alone, their contributions to the strength of the empire, were expected. During this whole period, a parliamentary revenue was no part of the object of colonisation. Accordingly, in all the laws which regarded them, the technical words of revenue laws, were avoided. Such have usually a title purporting their being "grants," and the words "give and grant," usually precede their enacting clauses. Although duties were imposed on America, by previous acts of parliament, no one title of "giving an aid to his majesty," or any other of the usual titles to revenue acts, was to be found in any of them. They were intended as regulations of trade, and not as sources of national supplies. Till the year 1764, all stood on commercial regulation, and restraint.

While Great-Britain attended to this first system of colonisation, her American settlements, though exposed in unknown climates, and unexplored wildernesses, grew and flourished, and in the same proportion; the trade and riches of the Mother Country encreased. Some estimate may be made of this increase, from the following statement. The whole export trade of England, including that to the colonies, in the year 1704, amounted to £6,509,000 sterling: but so immensely had the colonies increased, that the exports to them alone [50] in the year 1772, amounted to £6,022,132 sterling, and they were yearly increasing. In the short space of 68 years, the colonies added nearly as much to the export commerce of Great-Britain, as she had grown to by a progressive increase of improvement in 1700 years. And this increase of colonial trade, was not at the expence of the general trade of the kingdom, for that increased in the same time, from six millions, to sixteen millions.

In this auspicious period, the Mother Country contented herself with exercising her supremacy in superintending the general concerns of the colonies, and in harmonising the commercial interest of the whole empire. To this the most of them bowed down with such a filial submission as demonstrated that they, though not subjected to parliamentary taxes, could be kept in due subordination, and in perfect subserviency to the grand views of colonisation.

Immediately after the peace of Paris, 1763, a new scene was opened. The national debt of Great-Britain, then amounted to 148 millions, for which an interest of nearly 5 millions, was annually paid. While the British minister was digesting plans for diminishing this amazing load of debt, he conceived the idea of raising a substantial revenue in the British colonies, from taxes laid by the parliament of the parent state. On the one hand it was urged that the late war originated on account of the colonies—that it was reasonable, more especially as it had terminated in a manner so favourable to their interest, that they should contribute to the defraying of the expences it had occasioned. Thus far both parties were agreed, but Great-Britain contended, that her parliament as the supreme power, was constitutionally vested with an authority to lay them on every part of the empire. This doctrine, plausible in itself, and conformable to the letter of the British constitution, when the whole dominions were represented in one assembly, was reprobated in the colonies, as contrary to the spirit of the same government, when the empire became so far extended, as to have many distinct representative assemblies. The colonists believed that the chief excellence of the [51] British constitution consisted in the right of subjects to grant, or withhold taxes, and in their having a share in enacting the laws, by which they were to be bound.

They conceived, that the superiority of the British constitution, to other forms of government was, not because their supreme council was called Parliament, but because, the people had a share in it, by appointing members, who constituted one of its constituent branches, and without whose concurrence, no law, binding on them, could be enacted. In the Mother Country, it was asserted to be essential to the unity of the empire, that the British Parliament should have a right of taxation, over every part of the royal dominions. In the colonies, it was believed, that taxation and representation were inseparable, and that they could neither be free, nor happy, if their property could be taken from them, without their consent. The common people in America reasoned on this subject, in a summary way: "If a British Parliament," said they, "in which we are unrepresented, and over which we have no control, can take from us any part of our property, by direct taxation, they may take as much as they please, and we have no security for any thing, that remains, but a forbearance on their part, less likely to be exercised in our favour, as they lighten themselves of the burthens of government, in the same proportion, that they impose them on us." They well knew, that communities of mankind, as well as individuals, have a strong propensity to impose on others, when they can do it with impunity, and, especially, when there is a prospect, that the imposition will be attended with advantage to themselves. The Americans, from that jealousy of their liberties, which their local situation nurtured, and which they inherited from their forefathers, viewed the exclusive right of laying taxes on themselves, free from extraneous influence, in the same light, as the British Parliament views its peculiar privilege of raising money, independent of the crown. The parent state appeared to the colonists to stand in the same relation to their local legislatures, as the monarch of Great-Britain, to the British [52] Parliament. His prerogative is limited by that palladium of the people's liberty, the exclusive privilege of granting their own money. While this right rests in the hands of the people, their liberties are secured. In the same manner reasoned the colonists "in order to be stiled freemen, our local assemblies, elected by ourselves, must enjoy the exclusive privilege of imposing taxes upon us." They contended, that men settled in foreign parts to better their condition, and not to submit their liberties—to continue the equals, not to become the slave of their less adventurous fellow-citizens, and that by the novel doctrine of parliamentary power, they were degraded from being the subjects of a King, to the low condition of being subjects of subjects. They argued, that it was essentially involved in the idea of property, that the possessor had such a right therein, that it was a contradiction to suppose any other man, or body of men, possessed a right to take it from him, without his consent. Precedents, in the history of England, justified this mode of reasoning. The love of property strengthened it, and it had a peculiar force on the minds of colonists, 3000 miles removed from the seat of government, and growing up to maturity, in a new world, where, from the extent of country, and the state of society, even the necessary restraints of civil government, were impatiently born. On the other hand, the people of Great-Britain revolted against the claims of the colonists. Educated in habits of submission to parliamentary taxation, they conceived it to be the height of contumacy for their colonists to refuse obedience to the power, which they had been taught to revere. Not adverting to the common interest, which existed between the people of Great-Britain, and their representatives, they believed, that the same right existed, although the same community of interests was wanting. The pride of an opulent, conquering nation, aided this mode of reasoning. "What," said they, "shall we, who have so lately humbled France and Spain, be dictated to by our own colonists? Shall our subjects, educated by our care, and defended by our arms, presume to question the rights of Parliament, to which we are obliged to submit." [53]

Reflections of this kind, congenial to the natural vanity of the human heart, operated so extensively, that the people of Great-Britain spoke of their colonies and of their colonists, as of a kind of possession, annexed to their persons. The love of power, and of property, on the one side of the Atlantic, were opposed by the same powerful passions on the other.

The disposition to tax the colonies, was also strengthened by exaggerated accounts of their wealth. It was said, "that the American planters lived in affluence, and with inconsiderable taxes, while the inhabitants of Great-Britain were born down, by such oppressive burdens, as to make a bare subsistence, a matter of extreme difficulty." The officers who have served in America, during the late war, contributed to this delusion. Their observations were founded on what they had seen in cities, and at a time, when large sums were spent by government, in support of fleets and armies, and when American commodities were in great demand. To treat with attention those, who came to fight for them, and also to gratify their own pride, the colonists had made a parade of their riches, by frequently and sumptuously entertaining the gentlemen of the British army. These, judging from what they saw, without considering the general state of the country, concurred in representing the colonists, as very able to contribute, largely, towards defraying the common expences of the empire.

The charters, which were supposed to contain the principles on which the colonies were founded, became the subject of serious investigation on both sides. One clause was found to run through the whole of them, except that which had been granted to Mr. Penn. This was a declaration, "that the emigrants to America should enjoy the same privileges, as if they had remained, or had been born within the realm;" but such was the subtilty of disputants, that both parties construed this general principle, so as to favour their respective opinions. The American patriots contended, that as English free-holders could not be taxed, but by representatives, in chusing whom they had a vote, neither could the colonists: But [54] it was replied, that if the colonists had remained in England, they must have been bound to pay the taxes, imposed by parliament. It was therefore inferred, that, though taxed by that authority, they lost none of the rights of native Englishmen, residing at home. The partizans of the Mother Country could see nothing in charters, but security against taxes, by royal authority. The Americans, adhering to the spirit more than to the letter, viewed their charters, as a shield, against all taxes, not imposed by representatives of their own choice. This construction they contended to be expressly recognized by the charter of Maryland. In that, King Charles bound, both himself and his successors, not to assent to any bill, subjecting the inhabitants to internal taxation, by external legislation.

The nature and extent of the connection between Great-Britain and America, was a great constitutional question, involving many interests, and the general principles of civil liberty. To decide this, recourse was in vain had to parchment authorities, made at a distant time, when neither the grantor, nor grantees, of American territory, had in contemplation, any thing like the present state of the two countries.

Great and flourishing colonies, daily increasing in numbers, and already grown to the magnitude of a nation, planted at an immense distance, and governed by constitutions, resembling that of the country, from which they sprung, were novelties in the history of the world. To combine colonies, so circumstanced, in one uniform system of government, with the parent state, required a great knowledge of mankind, and an extensive comprehension of things. It was an arduous business, far beyond the grasp of ordinary statesmen, whose minds were narrowed by the formalities of law, or the trammels of office. An original genius, unfettered with precedents, and exalted with just ideas of the rights of human nature, and the obligations of universal benevolence, might have struck out a middle line, which would have secured as much liberty to the colonies, and as great a degree of supremacy to the parent state, as their common good required: But [55] the helm of Great-Britain was not in such hands. The spirit of the British constitution on the one hand, revolted at the idea, that the British parliament should exercise the same unlimited authority over the unrepresented colonies, which it exercised over the inhabitants of Great-Britain. The colonists on the other hand did not claim a total exemption from its authority. They in general allowed the Mother Country a certain undefined prerogative over them, and acquiesced in the right of Parliament, to make many acts, binding them in many subjects of internal policy, and regulating their trade. Where parliamentary supremacy ended, and at what point colonial independency began, was not ascertained. Happy would it have been, had the question never been agitated, but much more so, had it been compromised by an amicable compact, without the horrors of a civil war.

The English colonies were originally established, not for the sake of revenue, but on the principles of a commercial monopoly. While England pursued trade and forgot revenue, her commerce increased at least fourfold. The colonies took off the manufactures of Great-Britain, and paid for them with provisions, or raw materials. They united their arms in war, their commerce and their councils in peace, without nicely investigating the terms on which the connection of the two countries depended.

A perfect calm in the political world is not long to be expected. The reciprocal happiness, both of Great-Britain and of the colonies, was too great to be of long duration. The calamities of the war of 1755, had scarcely ended, when the germ of another war was planted, which soon grew up and produced deadly fruit.

At that time sundry resolutions passed the British parliament, relative to the imposition of a stamp duty in America, which gave a general alarm. By them the right, the equity, the policy, and even the necessity of taxing the colonies was formally avowed. These resolutions being considered as the preface of a system of American revenue, were deemed an introduction of evils of much greater magnitude. They opened a prospect of oppression, [56] boundless in extent, and endless in duration. They were nevertheless not immediately followed by any legislative act. Time, and an invitation, were given to the Americans, to suggest any other mode of taxation, that might be equivalent in its produce to the stamp act: But they objected, not only to the mode, but the principle, and several of their assemblies, though in vain, petitioned against it. An American revenue was in England, a very popular measure. The cry in favour of it was so strong, as to confound and silence the voice of petitions to the contrary. The equity of compelling the Americans to contribute to the common expences of the empire, satisfied many, who, without

1764

enquiring into the policy or justice of taxing their unrepresented fellow subjects, readily assented to the measures adopted by the parliament, for this purpose. The prospect of easing their own burdens, at the expence of the colonists, dazzled the eyes of gentlemen of landed interest, so as to keep out of their view, the probable consequences of the innovation.

The omnipotence of parliament was so familiar a phrase on both sides of the Atlantic, that few in America, and still fewer in Great-Britain, were impressed in the first instance, with any idea of the illegality of taxing the colonists.

The illumination on that subject was gradual. The resolutions in favour of an American stamp act, which passed in March, 1764, met with no opposition. In the course of the year, which intervened between these resolutions, and the passing of a law grounded upon them, the subject was better understood and constitutional objections against the measure, were urged by several, both in Great-Britain and America. This astonished and chagrined the British ministry: But as the principle of taxing America, had been for some time determined upon, they were unwilling to give it up. Impelled by partiality for a long cherished idea, Mr. Grenville brought into the house of commons his long expected bill, for laying a stamp duty in America. By this after passing through the usual forms, it was enacted, that the instruments [57] of writing which are in daily use among a commercial people, should be null and void, unless they were executed on stamped paper or parchment, charged with a duty imposed by the British parliament.

MARCH,
1765

When the bill was brought in, Mr. Charles Townsend concluded a speech in its favour, with words to the following effect, "And now will these Americans, children planted by our care, nourished up by our indulgence, till they are grown to a degree of strength and opulence, and protected by our arms, will they grudge to contribute their mite to relieve us from the heavy weight of that burden which we lie under." To which Colonel Barré replied,

They planted by your care? No, your oppressions planted them in America. They fled from tyranny to a then uncultivated and unhospitable country, where they exposed themselves to almost all the hardships to which human nature is liable; and among others to the cruelty of a savage foe the most subtle, and I will take upon me to say, the most formidable of any people upon the face of God's earth; and yet, actuated by principles of true English liberty, they met all hardships with pleasure compared with those they suffered in their own country, from the hands of those that should have been their friends. They nourished up by your indulgence? They grew by your neglect of them. As soon as you began to care about them, that care was exercised in sending persons to rule them in one department and another, who were perhaps the deputies of deputies to some members of this house, sent to spy out their liberties, to misrepresent their actions and to prey upon them. Men, whose behaviour on many occasions, has caused the blood of those sons of liberty to recoil within them. Men promoted to the highest seats of justice, some who to my knowledge were glad by going to a foreign country, to escape being brought to the bar of a court of justice in their own. They protected by your arms? They have nobly taken up arms in your defence, have exerted a valour amidst their constant and laborious industry, for the defence of a country whose frontier was drenched in blood, while its interior parts yielded all its little savings to your emolument. And believe [58] me, remember I this day told you so, that same spirit of freedom which actuated that people at first will accompany them still: but prudence forbids me to explain myself farther. God knows, I do not at this time speak from any motives of party heat, what I deliver are the genuine sentiments of my heart. However superior to me in general knowledge and experience, the respectable body of this house may be, yet I claim to know more of America than most of you, having seen and been conversant in that country. The people I believe are as truly loyal as any subjects the King has, but a people jealous of their liberties, and who will vindicate them, if ever they should be violated: but the subject is too delicate—I will say no more.

During the debate on the bill, the supporters of it insisted much on the colonies being virtually represented in the same manner as Leeds, Halifax, and some other towns were. A recurrence to this plea was a virtual acknowledgment, that there ought not to be taxation without representation. It was replied, that the connexion between the electors and non-electors of parliament in Great-Britain, was so interwoven, from both being equally liable to pay the same common tax, as to give some security of property to the latter: but with respect to taxes laid by the British parliament, and paid by the Americans, the situation of the parties was reversed. Instead of both parties bearing a proportionable share of the same common burden, what was laid on the one, was exactly so much taken off from the other.

The bill met with no opposition in the house of Lords, and on the 22d of March, it received the royal assent. The night after it passed, Dr. Franklin wrote to Mr. Charles Thomson. "The sun of liberty is set, you must light up the candles of industry and economy." Mr. Thomson answered, "he was apprehensive that other lights would be the consequence," and foretold the opposition that shortly took place. On its being suggested from authority, that the stamp officers would not be sent from Great-Britain: but selected from among the Americans, the colony agents were desired to point out proper persons [59] for the purpose. They generally nominated their friends which affords a presumptive proof, that they supposed the act would have gone down. In this opinion they were far from being singular. That the colonists would be ultimately obliged to submit to the stamp act, was at first commonly believed, both in England and America. The framers of it, in particular, flattered themselves that the confusion which would arise upon the disuse of writings, and the insecurity of property, which would result from using any other than that required by law, would compel the colonies, however reluctant, to use the stamp paper, and consequently to pay the taxes imposed thereon. They therefore boasted that it was a law which would execute itself. By the terms of the stamp act, it was not to take effect till the first day of November, a period of more than seven months after its passing. This give the colonists an opportunity for leisurely canvassing the new subject, and examining it fully on every side. In the first part of this interval, struck with astonishment, they lay in silent consternation, and could not determine what course to pursue. By degrees they recovered their recollection. Virginia led the way in opposition to the stamp act. Mr. Patrick Henry brought into the house of burgesses of that colony, the following resolutions which were substantially adopted.

Resolved, That the first adventurers, settlers of this his Majesty's colony and dominion of Virginia, brought with them and transmitted to

1765

1765

MAY 28, 1765

their posterity, and all other, his Majesty's subjects, since inhabiting in this, his Majesty's said colony, all the liberties, privileges and immunities, that have at any time been held, enjoyed and possessed by the people of Great-Britain.

Resolved, That by two royal charters, granted by King James the first, the colonies aforesaid are declared, and entitled to all liberties, privileges, and immunities of denizens, and natural subjects, to all intents and purposes, as if they had been abiding, and born within the realm of England,

Resolved, That his Majesty's liege people, of this, his ancient colony, have enjoyed the rights of being thus governed [60] by their own assembly, in the article of taxes, and internal police, and that the same 1765 have never been forfeited, or yielded up, but have been constantly recognized by the King and people of Britain.

Resolved, therefore, That the general assembly of this colony, together with his Majesty, or his substitutes, have, in their representative capacity, the only exclusive right and power, to lay taxes and imposts, upon the inhabitants of this colony, and that every attempt to vest such power in any other person or persons, whatsoever, than the general assembly aforesaid, is illegal, unconstitutional, and unjust, and hath a manifest tendency to destroy British, as well as American Liberty.

Resolved, That his Majesty's liege people, the inhabitants of this colony, are not bound to yield obedience to any law, or ordinance whatever, designed to impose any taxation whatever upon them, other, than the laws or ordinances of the general assembly aforesaid.

Resolved, That any person, who shall, by speaking, or writing, assert, or maintain, that any person, or persons, other than the general assembly of this colony, have any right or power, to impose, or lay any taxation on the people here, shall be deemed an enemy to this, his Majesty's colony.

Upon reading these resolutions, the boldness and novelty of them affected one of the members to such a degree, that he cried out, "Treason! Treason!" They were, nevertheless, well received by the people, and immediately forwarded to the other provinces. They circulated extensively, and gave a spring to all the discontented. Till they appeared, most were of opinion, that the act would be quietly adopted. Murmurs, indeed, were common, but they seemed to be such, as would soon die away. The countenance of so respectable a colony, as Virginia, confirmed the wavering, and emboldened the timid. Opposition to the stamp act, from that period, assumed a bolder face. The fire of liberty blazed forth from the press; some well judged publications set the rights of the colonists, in a plain, but strong point of view. The tongues and the pens of the well informed [61] citizens laboured in kindling the latent sparks of patriotism. The flame spread from breast to breast, till the conflagration, became general. In this business, New-England had a principal share. The inhabitants of that part of America, in particular, considered their obligations to the Mother Country for past favours, to be very inconsiderable. They were fully informed, that their forefathers were driven, by persecution, to the woods of America, and had there, without any expence to the parent state, effected a settlement on bare creation. Their resentment, for the invasion of their accustomed right of taxation, was not so much mitigated, by the recollection of late favours, as it was heightened by the tradition of grievous sufferings, to which their ancestors, by the rulers of England, had been subjected. The descendants of the exiled, persecuted, Puritans, of the last century, opposed the stamp act with the same spirit, with which their forefathers were actuated, when they set themselves against the arbitrary impositions of the House of Stuart.

The heavy burdens, which the operation of the stamp-act would have imposed on the colonists, together with the precedent it would establish of future exactions, furnished the American patriots with arguments, calculated as well to move the passions, as to convince the judgments of their fellow colonists. In great warmth they exclaimed, "If the parliament has a right to levy the stamp duties, they may, by the same authority, lay on us imposts, excises, and other taxes, without end, till their rapacity is satisfied, or our abilities are exhausted. We cannot, at future elections, displace these men, who so lavishly grant away our property. Their seats and their power are independent of us, and it will rest with their generosity, where to stop, in transferring the expences of government, from their own, to our shoulders."

It was fortunate for the liberties of America, that News-papers were the subject of a heavy stamp duty. Printers, when uninfluenced by government, have generally arranged themselves on the side of liberty, nor are they less remarkable for attention to the profits of their profession. A stamp duty, which openly invaded the first, [62] and threatened a great diminution of the last, provoked their united zealous opposition. They daily presented to the public, original dissertations, tending to prove, that if the stamp-act was suffered to operate, the liberties of America, were at end, and their property virtually transferred, to their Trans-Atlantic fellow-subjects. The writers among the Americans, seriously alarmed for the fate of their country, came forward, with essays, to prove, that agreeably to the British constitution, taxation and representation were inseparable, that the only constitutional mode of raising money from the colonists, was by acts of their own legislatures, that the Crown possessed no farther power, than that of requisition, and that the parliamentary right of taxation was confined to the Mother Country, and there originated, from the natural right of man, to do what he pleased with his own, transferred by consent from the electors of Great-Britain, to those whom they chose to represent them in Parliament. They also insisted much on the mis-application of public money by the British ministry. Great pains were taken, to inform the colonists, of the large sums, annually bestowed on pensioned favorites, and for the various purposes of bribery. Their passions were inflamed, by high coloured representations of the hardship of being obliged to pay the earnings of their industry, into a British treasury, well known to be a fund for corruption.

The writers on the American side were opposed by arguments, drawn from the unity of the empire. The necessity of one supreme head, the unlimited power of Parliament, and the great numbers in the Mother Country, who, though legally disqualified, from voting at elections, were nevertheless bound to pay the taxes, imposed by the representatives of the nation. To these objections it was replied, that the very idea of subordination of parts, excluded the notion of simple undivided unity. That as England was the head, she could not be the head and the members too—that in all extensive empires, where the dead uniformity of servitude did not prevent, the subordinate parts had many local privileges and immunities—that between these privileges and the supreme [63] common authority, the line was extremely nice; but nevertheless, the supremacy of the head had an ample field of exercise, without arrogating to itself the disposal of the property of the unrepresented subordinate parts. To the assertion, that the power of Parliament was unlimited, the colonists replied, that before it could constitutionally exercise that power, it must be constitutionally formed, and that, therefore, it must at least, in one of its branches, be constituted by the people, over whom it exercised unlimited power. That with respect to Great-Britain, it was so constituted—with respect to America, it was not. They therefore inferred, that its power ought not to be the same over both countries. They argued also, that the delegation of the people was the source of power, in regard to taxation, and as that delegation was wanting in America, they concluded the right of Parliament, to grant away their property, could not exist. That the defective representation in Great-Britain, should be urged as an argument for taxing the Americans, without any representation at all, proved the encroaching nature of power. Instead of convincing the colonists of the propriety of their submission, it demonstrated the wisdom of their resistance; for, said they, "one invasion of natural right is made the justification of another, much more injurious and oppressive."

The advocates for parliamentary taxation laid great stress on the rights, supposed to accrue to Great-Britain, on the score of her having reared up and protected the English settlements, in America, at great expence. It was, on the other hand, contended by the colonists, that in all the wars which were common to both countries, they had taken their full share, but in all their own dangers, in all the difficulties belonging separately to their situation, which did not immediately concern Great-Britain, they were left to themselves, and had to struggle through a hard infancy; and in particular, to defend themselves without any aid from the Parent State, against the numerous savages in their vicinity. That when France had made war upon them, it was not on their own account, but as appendages to Great-Britain. That confining their trade [64] for the exclusive benefit of the Parent State, was an ample compensation for her protection, and a sufficient equivalent for their exemption from parliamentary taxation. That the taxes imposed on the inhabitants of Great-Britain, were incorporated with their manufactures, and ultimately fell on the colonists, who were the consumers.

The advocates for the stamp act, also contended that as the parliament was charged with the defence of the colonies, it ought to

1765

possess the means of defraying the expences incurred thereby. The same argument had been used by King Charles the 1st, in support of ship money; and it was now answered in the same manner, as it was by the patriots of that day. "That the people who were defended or protected, were the first to judge of and to provide the means of defraying the expences incurred on that account." In the mean time, the minds of the Americans underwent a total transformation. Instead of their late peaceable and steady attachment to the British nation, they were dayly advancing to the opposite extreme. A new mode of displaying resentment against the friends of the stamp act, began in Massachusetts, and was followed by the other colonies. A few gentlemen hung out, early in the morning, on the limb of a large tree, towards the enterance of Boston, two effigies, one designed for the stamp master, the other for a jack boot, with a head and horns peeping out at the top. Great numbers both from town and country came to see them. A spirit of enthusiasm was diffused among the spectators. In the evening the whole was cut down and carried in procession by the populace shouting "liberty and property forever, no stamps." They next pulled down a new building, lately erected by Mr. Oliver, the stamp master. They then went to his house, before which they beheaded his effigy, and at the same time broke his windows. Eleven days after similar violences were repeated. The mob attacked the house of Mr. William Story, deputy register of the court of admiralty—broke his windows—forced into his dwelling house, and destroyed the books and files belonging to the said court, and ruined a great part of his furniture. They [65] next proceeded to the house of Benjamin Hallowell, comptroller of the customs, and repeated similar excesses, and drank and destroyed his liquors. They afterwards proceeded to the house of Mr. Hutchinson, and soon demolished it. They carried off his plate, furniture and apparel, and scattered or destroyed manuscripts and other curious and useful papers, which for thirty years he had been collecting. About half a dozen of the meanest of the mob were soon after taken up and committed, but they either broke jail, or otherwise escaped all punishment. The town of Boston condemned the whole proceeding, and for some time, private gentlemen kept watch at night, to prevent further violences.

Similar disturbances broke out in the adjacent colonies, nearly

1765
AUG. 14

about the same time. On the 27th August, the people of New-Port in Rhode-Island, exhibited three effigies intended for Messieurs Howard, Moffatt, and Johnson, in a cart with halters about their necks, and after hanging them on a gallows for some time, cut them down and burnt them, amidst the acclamations of thousands. On the day following, the people collected at the house of Mr. Martin Howard, a lawyer, who had written in defence of the right of Parliament to tax the Americans, and demolished every thing, that belonged to it. They proceeded to Dr. Moffatt's, who, in conversation, had supported the same right, and made a similar devastation of his property.

In Connecticut they exhibited effigies in sundry places, and afterwards committed them to the flames.

In New-York, the stamp master having resigned, the stamp papers were taken into Fort George, by Lieutenant Governor Colden. The people, disliking his political sentiments, broke open his stable, took out his coach, and carried it in triumph, through the principal streets, to the gallows. On one end of this they suspended the effigy of the Lieut. Governor, having in his right hand a stamped bill of lading, and in the other a figure of the devil. After some time, they carried the apparatus to the gate of the fort, and from thence to the bowling green, under the muzzles of the guns, and burned the [66] whole amid the acclamations of many thousands. They went thence to Major James' house, stripped it of every article, and consumed the whole, because he was a friend to the stamp act.

The next evening the mob re-assembled, and insisted upon the Lieutenant Governor delivering the stamped papers into their hands, and threatened, in case of a refusal, to take them by force. After some negotiation, it was agreed that they should be delivered to the corporation, and they were deposited in the city hall. Ten boxes of the same, which came by another conveyance, were burned.

The stamp-act was not less odious to many of the inhabitants of the British West-India islands, than to those on the continent of North America. The people of St. Kitts obliged the stamp officer, and his deputy, to resign. Barbadoes, Canada, and Halifax, submitted to the act.

When the ship, which brought the stamp papers to Philadelphia, first appeared round Gloucester point, all the vessels in the harbour hoisted their colours half mast high. The bells were rung muffled till evening, and every countenance added to the appearance of sincere mourning. A large number of people assembled, and endeavoured to procure the resignation of Mr. Hughes, the stamp distributor. He held out long, but at length found it necessary to comply.

As opportunities offered, the assemblies generally passed resolutions, asserting their exclusive right, to lay taxes on their constituents. The people, in their town meetings, instructed their representatives to oppose the stamp act. As a specimen of these, the instructions given to Thomas Forster, their representative, by the freeholders and other inhabitants of the town of Plymouth, are subjoined. In these the yeomanry of the country spoke the determined language of freemen. After expressing the highest esteem for the British constitution, and setting forth their grievances, they proceeded as follows: OCTOBER, 1765

You, Sir, represent a people, who are not only descended from the first settlers of this country, but inhabit the very spot they first possessed. Here was first laid [67] the foundation of the British empire, in this part of America, which, from a very small beginning, has increased and spread, in a manner very surprising, and almost incredible, especially, when we consider, that all this has been effected, without the aid or assistance of any power on earth; that we have defended, protected and secured ourselves against the invasions and cruelty of savages, and the subtlety and inhumanity of our inveterate and natural enemies, the French; and all this without the appropriation of any tax by stamps, or stamp acts, laid upon our fellow subjects, in any part of the King's dominions, for defraying the expence thereof. This place, Sir, was at first the asylum of liberty, and we hope, will ever be preserved sacred to it, though it was then no more than a barren wilderness, inhabited only by savage men and beasts. To this place our Fathers (whose memories be revered) possessed of the principles of liberty in their purity, disdaining slavery, fled to enjoy those privileges, which they had an undoubted right to, but were deprived of, by the hands of violence and oppression, in their native country. We, Sir, their posterity, the freeholders, and other inhabitants of this town, legally assembled for that purpose, possessed of the same sentiments, and retaining the same ardour for liberty, think it our indispensable duty, on this occasion, to express to you these our sentiments of the stamp-act, and its fatal consequences to this country, and to enjoin upon you, as you regard not only the welfare, but the very being of this people, that you (consistent with our allegiance to the King, and relation to the government of Great Britain) disregarding all proposals for that purpose, exert all your power and influence in opposition to the stamp act, at least till we hear the success of our petitions for relief. We likewise, to avoid disgracing the memories of our ancestors, as well as the reproaches of our own consciences, and the curses of posterity, recommend it to you, to obtain, if possible, in the honorable house of representatives of this province, a full and explicit assertion of our rights, and to have the same entered on their public records, that all generations yet to come, may be convinced, that we have [68] not only a just sense of our rights and liberties, but that we never, with submission to Divine Providence, will be slaves to any power on earth.

The expediency of calling a continental Congress to be composed of deputies from each of the provinces, had early occurred to the people of Massachusetts. The assembly of that province passed a resolution in favour of that measure, and fixed on New-York as the place, and the second Tuesday of October, as the time, for holding the same. Soon after, they sent circular letters to the speakers of the several assemblies, requesting their concurrence. This first advance towards continental union was seconded in South-Carolina, before it had been agreed to by any colony to the southward of New England. The example of this province had a considerable influence in recommending the measure to others, who were divided in their opinions, on the propriety of it.

The assemblies of Virginia, North-Carolina, and Georgia, were prevented, by their governors, from sending a deputation to this Congress. Twenty eight deputies from Massachusetts, Rhode-Island, Connecticut, New-York, New-Jersey, Pennsylvania, Delaware, Maryland, and South-Carolina met at New-York; and after mature deliberation agreed on a declaration of their rights, and on a statement of their grievances. They asserted in strong terms, their exemption from all taxes, not imposed by their own representatives. They also concurred in a petition to the King, and memorial to the House of Lords, and a petition to the House of Commons. The colonies that were prevented from sending their representatives to this Congress, forwarded petitions, similar to those which were adopted by the deputies which attended.

While a variety of legal and illegal methods were adopted to oppose the stamp act, the first of November, on which it was to commence its operation, approached. This in Boston was ushered in by a funeral tolling of bells. Many shops and stores were shut. The effigies of the planners and friends of the stamp act, were carried [69] about the streets in public derision, and then torn in pieces, by the enraged populace. It was remarkable that though a large crowd was assembled, there was not the least violence, or disorder.

At Portsmouth in New-Hampshire, the morning was ushered in, NOV. I with tolling all the bells in town. In the course of the day, notice was given to the friends of liberty, to attend her funeral. A coffin, neatly ornamented inscribed with the word *Liberty* in large letters, was carried to the grave. The funeral procession began from the state house, attended with two unbraced drums. While the inhabitants who followed the coffin were in motion, minute guns were fired, and continued till the corpse arrived at the place of interment. Then an oration in favour of the deceased was pronounced. It was scarcely ended before the corpse was taken up, it having been perceived that some remains of life were left, at which the inscription was immediately altered to "Liberty revived." The bells immediately exchanged their melancholy, for a more joyful sound, and satisfaction appeared in every countenance. The whole was conducted with decency, and without injury or insult, to any man's person or property.

In Maryland, the effigy of the stamp master, on one side of which was written, "Tyranny" on the other "Oppression," and across the breast, "Damn my country I'll get money," was carried through the streets, from the place of confinement, to the whipping post, and from thence to the pillory. After suffering many indignities, it was first hanged and than burnt.

The general aversion to the stamp act, was, by similar methods, in a variety of places, demonstrated. It is remarkable that the proceedings of the populace, on these occasions, were carried on with decorum, and regularity. They were not ebullitions of a thoughtless mob, but for the most part, planned by leading men of character and influence, who were friends to peace and order. These, knowing well that the bulk of mankind, are more led by their senses, than by their reason, conducted the public [70] exhibitions on that principle, with a view of making the stamp act, and its friends, both ridiculous, and odious.

Though the stamp act was to have operated from the first of

November; yet legal proceedings in the courts, were carried on as before. Vessels entered and departed without stamped papers. The printers boldly printed and circulated their news-papers, and found a sufficient number of readers, though they used common paper, in defiance of the act of parliament. In most departments, by common consent, business was carried on, as though no stamp act had existed. This was accompanied by spirited resolutions to risque all consequences, rather than submit to use the paper required by law. While these matters were in agitation, the colonists entered into associations against importing British manufactures, till the stamp act should be repealed. In this manner British liberty was made to operate against British tyranny. Agreeably to the free constitution of Great Britain, the subject was at liberty to buy, or not to buy, as he pleased. By suspending their future purchases on the repeal of the stamp act, the colonists made it the interest of merchants, and manufacturers, to solicit for that repeal. They had usually taken off so great a proportion of British manufactures, that the sudden stoppage of all their orders, amounting, annually, to several millions sterling, threw some thousands in the Mother Country out of employment, and induced them, from a regard to their own interest, to advocate the measures wished for by America. The petitions from the colonies were seconded by petitions from the merchants and manufacturers of Great-Britain. What the former prayed for as a matter of right, and connected with their liberties, the latter also solicited from motives of immediate advantage. In order to remedy the deficiency of British goods, the colonists betook themselves to a variety of necessary domestic manufactures. In a little time, large quantities of course and common clothes were brought to market, and these though dearer, and of a worse quality, were chearfully preferred to similar articles, imported from Britain. That wool might not be wanting, they entered into resolutions [71] to abstain from eating lambs. Foreign elegancies were generally laid aside. The women were as exemplary as the men, in various instances of self denial. With great readiness, they refused every article of decoration for their persons, and of luxury for their tables. These restrictions, which the colonists had voluntarily imposed on themselves, were so well observed, that multitudes of artificers in England, were reduced to great distress, and some of their most flourishing manufactories, were, in a great measure, at a stand. An association was entered into by many of the sons of liberty, the name given to those who were opposed to the stamp act, by which they agreed "to march with the utmost expedition at their own proper costs and expence, with their whole force to the relief of those that should be in danger from the stamp act, or its promoters and abettors, or any thing relative to it, on account of any thing that may have been done, in opposition to its obtaining." This was subscribed by so many in New-York and New-England, that nothing but a repeal could have prevented the immediate commencement of a civil war.

From the decided opposition to the stamp act, which had been by the colonies adopted, it became necessary for Great Britain to enforce, or to repeal it. Both methods of proceeding had supporters. The opposers of a repeal urged arguments, drawn from the dignity of the nation, the danger of giving way to the clamours of the Americans, and the consequences of weakening parliamentary authority over the colonies. On the other hand it was evident, from the determined opposition of the colonies, that it could not be enforced without a civil war, by which, in every event, the nation must be a loser. In the course of these discussions, Dr. Franklin was examined at the bar of the House of Commons, and gave extensive information on the state of American affairs, and the impolicy of the stamp act, which contributed much to remove prejudices, and to produce a disposition that was friendly to a repeal.

Some speakers of great weight, in both houses of parliament, denied their right of taxing the colonies. The [72] most distinguished supporters of this opinion were Lord Camden, in the House of Peers, and Mr. Pitt, in the House of Commons. The former, in strong language, said, "My position is this, I repeat it, I will maintain it to my last hour. Taxation and representation are inseparable. This position is founded on the laws of nature. It is more, it is itself an eternal law of nature. For whatever is a man's own, is absolutely his own. No man has a right to take it from him without his consent. Whoever attempts to do it, attempts an injury, whoever does it, commits a robbery." Mr. Pitt, with an original boldness of expression, justified the colonists, in opposing the stamp-act. "You have no right," said he, "to tax America. I rejoice, that America has resisted. Three millions of our fellow subjects so lost to every sense of virtue, as tamely to give up their liberties, would be fit instruments to make slaves of the rest." He concluded with giving his advice, that the stamp-act be repealed absolutely, totally, and immediately, that the reason for the repeal be assigned, that it was founded on an erroneous principle. "At the same time," said he, "let the sovereign authority of this country, over the colonies, be asserted in as strong terms as can be devised, and be made to extend to every point of legislation whatsoever; that we may bind their trade, confine their manufactures, and exercise every power, except that of taking their money out of their pockets, without their consent." The approbation of this illustrious statesman, whose distinguished abilities had raised Great Britain to the highest pitch of renown, inspired the Americans with additional confidence, in the rectitude of their claims of exemption from parliamentary taxation, and emboldened them to farther opposition, when at a future day, as shall be hereafter related, the project of an American revenue was resumed. After much debating, and two protests in the House of Lords, and passing an act "for securing the dependence of America on Great Britain" the repeal of

MARCH 18 the stamp act was finally carried. This event gave great joy in London. Ships in the river Thames displayed their colours, and houses were illuminated all [73] over the city. It was no sooner known in America, than the colonists rescinded their resolutions, and recommenced their mercantile intercourse with the Mother Country. They presented their homespun clothes to the poor, and imported more largely than ever. The churches resounded with thanksgivings, and their public and private rejoicings knew no bounds. By letters, addresses, and other means, almost all the colonies shewed unequivocal marks of acknowledgment, and gratitude. So sudden a calm recovered after so violent a storm, is without a parallel in history. By the judicious sacrifice of one law, the parliament of Great Britain procured an acquiescence, in all that remained.

There were enlightened patriots, fully impressed with an idea, that the immoderate joy of the colonists was disproportioned to the advantage they had gained.

The stamp act, though repealed, was not repealed on American principles. The preamble assigned as the reason thereof, "That the collecting the several duties and revenues, as by the said act was directed, would be attended with many inconveniencies, and productive of consequences, dangerous to the commercial interests of these kingdoms." Though this reason was a good one in England, it was by no means satisfactory in America. At the same time that the stamp act was repealed, the absolute, unlimited supremacy of parliament was, in words, asserted. The opposers of the repeal contended for this as essential, the friends of that measure acquiesced in it to strengthen their party, and make sure of their object. Many of both sides thought, that the dignity of Great Britain required something of the kind to counterbalance the loss of authority, that might result from her yielding to the clamours of the colonists. The act for this purpose was called the declaratory act, and was in principle more hostile to American rights, than the stamp act; for it annulled those resolutions and acts of the provincial assemblies, in which they had asserted their right to exemption from all taxes, not imposed by their own representatives; and also enacted, "That the parliament [74] had, and of right ought to have, power to bind the colonies, in all cases whatsoever."

The bulk of the Americans, intoxicated with the advantage they had gained, overlooked this statute, which in one comprehensive sentence, not only deprived them of liberty and property, but of every right, incident to humanity. They considered it as a salvo for the honor of parliament, in repealing an act, which had so lately received their sanction, and flattered themselves it would remain a dead letter, and that although the right of taxation was in words retained, it would never be exercised. Unwilling to contend about paper claims of ideal supremacy, they returned to their habits of good humour, with the parent state.

The repeal of the stamp act, in a relative connexion with all its circumstances and consequences, was the first direct step to American independency. The claims of the two countries were not only left undecided, but a foundation was laid for their extending at a future period, to the impossibility of a compromise. Though for the present Great-Britain receded from enforcing her claim of American revenue, a numerous party, adhering to that system, reserved themselves for more favourable circumstances to enforce it; and at the same time the colonists, more enlightened on the subject, and more fully convinced of the rectitude of their claims, were encouraged to oppose it, under whatsoever form it should appear, or under whatsoever disguise it should cover itself.

Elevated with the advantage they had gained, from that day forward, instead of feeling themselves dependent on Great-Britain, they conceived that, in respect to commerce, she was dependent on them. It inspired them with such high ideas of the importance of their trade, that they considered the Mother Country to be brought under greater obligations to them, for purchasing her manufactures, than they were to her for protection and the administration of civil government. The freemen of British America, impressed with the exalting sentiments of patriotism and of liberty, conceived it to be within their power, by future combinations, at any time to [75] convulse, if not to bankrupt the nation, from which they sprung.

Opinions of this kind were strengthened by their local situation, favouring ideas, as extensive as the unexplored continent of which they were inhabitants. While the pride of Britons revolted at the thought of their colonies refusing subjection to that parliament which they obeyed, the Americans with equal haughtiness exclaimed, "shall the petty island of Great-Britain, scarce a speck on the map of the world, controul the free citizens of the great continent of America?"

These high sounding pretensions would have been harmless, or at most, spent themselves in words, had not a ruinous policy, untaught by recent experience, called them into serious action. Though the stamp act was repealed, an American revenue was still a favourite object with many in Great-Britain. The equity and the advantage of taxing the colonists by parliamentary authority were very apparent to their understandings, but the mode of effecting it, without hazarding the public tranquility, was not so obvious. Mr. Charles Townsend, afterwards chancellor of the exchequer, pawned his credit to accomplish what many so earnestly desired. He accordingly brought into parliament a bill for granting duties in the British colonies on glass, paper, painters colours, and tea, which was afterwards enacted into a law. If the small duties imposed on these articles, had preceded the stamp act, they might have passed unobserved: but the late

1767

discussions occasioned by that act, had produced among the colonists, not only an animated conviction of their exemption from parliamentary taxation, but a jealousy of the designs of Great-Britain. The sentiments of the Americans on this subject, bore a great resemblance to those of their British countrymen of the preceding century, in the case of ship money. The amount of that tax was very moderate, little exceeding twenty thousand pounds. It was distributed upon the people with equality, and expended for the honour and advantage of the kingdom, yet all these circumstances could not reconcile the people of England to the imposition. [76] It was entirely arbitrary. "By the same right," said they, "any other tax may be imposed." In like manner the Americans considered these small duties, in the nature of an entering wedge, designed to make way for others, which would be greater and heavier. In a relative connection with late acts of parliament, respecting domestic manufactures and foreign commerce, laws for imposing taxes on British commodities exported to the colonies, formed a complete circle of oppression, from which there was no possibility of escaping. The colonists had been, previously, restrained from manufacturing certain articles, for their own consumption. Other acts confined them to the exclusive use of British merchandize. The addition of duties, put them wholly in the power and discretion of Great-Britain "We are not" said they,

> permitted to import from any nation, other than our own parent state, and have been in some cases by her restrained from manufacturing for ourselves, and she claims a right to do so in every instance which is incompatible with her interest. To these restrictions we have hitherto submitted, but she now rises in her demands, and imposes duties on those commodities, the purchasing of which, elsewhere than at her market, her laws forbid, and the manufacturing of which for our own use, she may any moment she pleases restrain. If her right is valid to lay a small tax, it is equally so to lay a large one, for from the nature of the case, she must be guided exclusively by her own opinions of our ability, and of the propriety of the duties she may impose. Nothing is left for us but to complain, and, pay.

They contended that there was no real difference between the principle of these new duties and the stamp act, they were both designed to raise a revenue in America, and in the same manner. The payment of the duties, imposed by the stamp act, might have been eluded by the total disuse of stamped paper, and so might the payment of these duties, by the total disuse of those articles on which they were laid, but in neither case, without great difficulty. The colonists were therefore reduced to the hard alternative of being obliged totally to disuse articles of the greatest necessity in human [77] life, or to pay a tax without their consent. The fire of opposition, which had been smothered by the repeal of the stamp act, burned afresh against the same principle of taxation, exhibited in its new form. Mr. Dickenson, of Pennsylvania, on this occasion presented to the public a series of letters signed a Farmer, proving the extreme danger which threatened the liberties of America, from their acquiescence in a precedent which might establish the claim of parliamentary taxation. They were written with great animation, and were read with uncommon avidity. Their reasoning was so convincing, that many of the candid and disinterested citizens of Great-Britain, acknowledged that the American opposition to parliamentary taxation was justifiable. The enormous sums which the stamp act would have collected, had thoroughly alarmed the colonists for their property. It was now demonstrated by several writers, especially by the Pennsylvania Farmer, that a small tax, though more specious, was equally dangerous, as it established a precedent which eventually annihilated American property. The declaratory act which at first was the subject of but a few comments, was now dilated upon, as a foundation for every species of oppression; and the small duties, lately imposed, were considered as the beginning of a train of much greater evils.

Had the colonists admitted the propriety of raising a parliamentary revenue among them, the erection of an American board of commissioners for managing it, which was about this time instituted at Boston, would have been a convenience, rather than an injury; but united as they were in sentiments, of the contrariety of that measure to their natural and constitutional rights, they illy brooked the innovation. As it was coeval with the new duties, they considered it as a certain evidence that the project of an extensive American revenue, notwithstanding the repeal of the stamp act, was still in contemplation. A dislike to British taxation naturally produced a dislike to a board which was to be instrumental in that business, and occasioned many insults to its commissioners.

[78] The revenue act of 1767 produced resolves, petitions, addresses, and remonstrances, similar to those, with which the colonists opposed the stamp act. It also gave rise to a second association for suspending farther importations of British manufactures, till these offensive duties should be taken off. Uniformity, in these measures, was promoted by a circular letter from the assembly of Massachusetts to the speakers of the other assemblies. This stated the petitions, and representations, which they had forwarded against the late 1768 duties, and strongly pointed out the great difficulties, that must arise to themselves and their constituents, from the operation of acts of parliament, imposing duties on the unrepresented American colonies, and requesting a reciprocal free communication, on public affairs. Most of the provincial assemblies, as they had opportunities of deliberating on the subject, approved of the proceedings of the Massachusetts assembly, and harmonised with them in the measures, which they had adopted. In resolves, they stated their rights, in firm but decent language, and, in petitions, they prayed for a repeal of the late acts, which they considered as infringements on their liberties.

It is not unreasonable to suppose, that the minister, who planned these duties, hoped, that they would be regarded as regulations of trade. He might also presume, that as they amounted only to an inconsiderable sum, they would not give any alarm. The circular letter of the Massachusetts assembly, which laid the foundation for united petitions against them, gave therefore great offence. Lord Hillsborough, who had lately been appointed Secretary of State, for the American department, wrote letters to the governors of the respective provinces, urging them to exert their influence, to prevent the assemblies from taking any notice of it, and he called on the Massachusetts assembly, to rescind their proceedings on that subject. This measure was both injudicious and irritating. To require a public body to rescind a resolution, for sending a letter, which was already sent, answered, and acted upon, was a bad specimen of the wisdom of the new minister. To call a vote, for sending a circular [79] letter to invite the assemblies of the neighbouring colonies to communicate together in the pursuit of legal measures to obtain a redress of grievances, "a flagitious attempt to disturb the public peace," appeared to the colonists a very injudicious application of harsh epithets to their constitutional right of petitioning. To threaten a new house of Assembly with dissolution, in case of their not agreeing to rescind an act of a former assembly, which was not executory, but executed, clashed no less with the dictates of common sense, than the constitutional rights of British colonists. The proposition for rescinding was negatived, by a majority of 97 to 17. The assembly was immediately dissolved, as had been threatened. This procedure of the new secretary was considered, by the colonists, as an attempt to suppress all communication of sentiments between them, and to prevent their united supplications, from reaching the royal ear. It answered no one valuable purpose, but naturally tended to mischief.

1768
JUNE 10

The bad humour, which from successive irritation already too much prevailed, was about this time wrought up to a high pitch of resentment and violence, on occasion of the seizure of Mr. Hancock's sloop Liberty, for not having entered all the wines she had brought from Madeira. The popularity of her owner, the name of the sloop, and the general aversion to the board of commissioners, and parliamentary taxation, concurred to inflame the minds of the people. They resented the removal of the sloop from the wharf, as implying an apprehension of a rescue. They used every means in their power to interrupt the officers, in the execution of their business; and numbers swore that they would be revenged. Mr. Harrison the collector, Mr. Hallowell the comptroller, and Mr. Irwine the inspector of imports and exports, were so roughly handled, as to bring their lives in danger. The windows of some of their houses were broken, and the boat of the collector was dragged through the town, and burned on the common. Such was the temper and disposition of many of the inhabitants, that the commissioners of the customs thought [80] proper to retire on board the Romney man of war; and afterwards to Castle William. The commissioners, from the first moment of their institution, had been an eye sore to the people of Boston. This, though partly owing to their active zeal in detecting smugglers, principally arose from the association which existed in the minds of the inhabitants, between that board and an American revenue. The declaratory act of 1766, the revenue act of 1767; together with the pomp and expence of this board, so disproportionate to the small income of the present duties, conspired to convince not only the few who were benefited by smuggling, but the great body of enlightened freemen, that farther and greater impositions of parliamentary taxes were intended. In proportion as this opinion gained ground, the inhabitants became more disrespectful to the executive officers of the revenue, and more disposed, in the frenzy of patriotism, to commit outrages on their persons and property. The constant bickering that existed between them and the inhabitants, together with the steady opposition given by the latter, to the discharge of the official duties of the former, induced the commissioners and friends of an American revenue, to solicit the protection of a regular force, to be stationed at Boston. In compliance with their wishes, his Majesty ordered two regiments and some armed vessels to repair thither, for supporting and assisting the officers of the customs in the execution of their duty. This restrained the active exertion of that turbulent spirit, which since the passing of the late revenue laws had revived, but it added to the pre-existing causes thereof.

When it was reported in Boston, that one or more regiments were ordered there, a meeting of the inhabitants was called, and a committee appointed, to request the governor, to issue precepts, for convening a general assembly. He replied, "that he could not comply with their request, till he had received his Majesty's commands for that purpose." This answer being reported, some spirited resolutions were adopted. In particular it was voted, that the select men of SEPT. 13 Boston should write [81] to the select men of other towns, to propose, that a convention be held, of deputies from each, to meet at Faneuil hall, in Boston, on the 22d instant. It was afterwards voted, "That as SEPT. 22 there is apprehension in the minds of many, of an approaching war with France, those inhabitants, who are not provided, be requested to furnish themselves forthwith with arms."

Ninety six towns, and eight districts, agreed to the proposal made by the inhabitants of Boston, and appointed deputies, to attend a convention, but the town of Hatfield refused its concurrence. When the deputies met, they conducted with moderation, disclaimed all legislative authority, advised the people to pay the greatest deference to government, and to wait patiently for a redress of their grievances, from his Majesty's wisdom and moderation. After stating to the world the causes of their meeting, and an account of their proceedings, they dissolved themselves, after a short session, and went home.

Within a day after the convention broke up, the expected regiments arrived, and were peaceably received. Hints had been thrown out by some idle people, that they should not be permitted to come on shore. Preparations were made by the captains of the men of war in the harbour, to fire on the town, in case opposition had been made to their landing, but the crisis for an appeal to arms was not yet arrived. It was hoped by some, that the folly and rage of the Bostonians would have led them to this rash measure, and thereby have afforded an opportunity for giving them some naval and military correction, but both prudence and policy induced them to adopt a more temperate line of conduct.

While the contention was kept alive, by the successive irritations, which have been mentioned, there was, particularly in Massachusetts, a species of warfare carried on between the royal governors, and the provincial assemblies. Each watched the other with all the jealousy, which strong distrust could inspire. The latter regarded the former as instruments of power, wishing to pay their court to the Mother Country, by curbing the spirit of [82] American freedom, and the former kept a strict eye on the latter, lest they might smooth the way to independence, at which they were charged with aiming. Lieut. Governor Hutchinson, of Massachusetts, virtually challenged the assembly to a dispute, on the ground of the controversy between the two countries. This was accepted by the latter, and the subject, discussed with all the subtilty of argument, which the ingenuity of either party could suggest.

The war of words was not confined to the colonies. While the American assemblies passed resolutions, asserting their exclusive right to tax their constituents, the parliament by resolves, asserted their unlimited supremacy in and over the colonies. While the former, in their public acts, disclaimed all views of independence, they were successively represented in parliamentary resolves, royal speeches, and addresses from Lords and commons, as being in a state of disobedience to law and government, and as having proceeded to measures subversive of the constitution, and manifesting a disposition to throw off all subordination to Great Britain.

In February 1769, both houses of parliament went one step beyond all that had preceded. They then concurred in a joint address to his majesty, in which they expressed their satisfaction in the measures his majesty had pursued—gave the strongest assurances, that they would effectually support him in such farther measures as might be found necessary, to maintain the civil magistrates in a due execution of the laws, in Massachusett's Bay, and beseeched him 1769

> to direct the governor to take the most effectual methods of procuring the fullest information, touching all treasons or misprisions of treason, committed within the government, since the 30th day of December, 1767; and to transmit the same together with the names of the persons who were most active in the commission of such offences, to one of the secretaries of state, in order that his majesty might issue a special commission for enquiring of, hearing, and determining, the said offences, within the realm of Great-Britain, pursuant to the provision of the statute of the 35th [83] of King Henry the 8th.

The latter part of this address, which proposed the bringing of delinquents from Massachusetts, to be tried at a tribunal in Great-Britain, for crimes committed in America, underwent many severe animadversions.

It was asserted to be totally inconsistent with the spirit of the constitution, for in England a man charged with a crime, had a right to be tried in the county in which his offence was supposed to have been committed. "Justice is regularly and impartially administered in our courts," said the colonists "and yet by direction of parliament, offenders are to be taken by force, together with all such persons as may be pointed out as witnesses and carried to England, there to be tried in a distant land, by a jury of strangers, and subject to all the disadvantages which result from want of friends, want of witnesses and want of money."

The house of burgesses of Virginia met, soon after official accounts of the joint address of lords and commons on this subject reached

America; and in a few days after their meeting, passed resolutions expressing

> their exclusive right to tax their constituents, and their right to petition their sovereign for redress of grievances, and the lawfulness of procuring the concurrence of the other colonies in praying for the royal interposition, in favour of the violated rights of America: and that all trials for treason, or for any crime whatsoever, committed in that colony, ought to be before his majesty's courts, within the said colony; and that the seizing any person residing in the said colony, suspected of any crime whatsoever, committed therein, and sending such person to places beyond the sea to be tried, was highly derogatory of the rights of British subjects.

The next day lord Botetourt the governour of Virginia, sent for the house of burgesses and addressed them as follows. "Mr. Speaker and gentlemen of the house of burgesses. I have heard of your resolves, and augur ill of their effects. You have made it my duty to dissolve you, and you are dissolved accordingly."

[84] The assembly of North-Carolina adopted resolutions, similar to those of Virginia, for which Tryon their governour dissolved them. The members of the house of burgesses in Virginia, and of the assembly of North-Carolina, after their dissolution, met as private gentlemen, chose their late speakers moderators, and adopted resolutions against importing British goods. The non-importation agreement, was in this manner forwarded by the very measures which were intended to curb the spirit of American freedom, from which it sprung. Meetings of the associators were regularly held in the various provinces. Committees were appointed to examine all vessels arriving from Britain. Censures were freely passed on such as refused to concur in these associations, and their names published in the news-papers as enemies to their country. The regular acts of the provincial assemblies were not so much respected and obeyed as the decrees of these committees, the associations were in general, as well observed as could be expected; but nevertheless there were some collusions. The fear of mobs, of public resentment and contempt, co-operating with patriotism, preponderated over private interest and convenience. One of the importing merchants of Boston, who

hesitated in his compliance with the determination of the inhabitants, was waited upon by a committee of tradesmen, with an axeman and a carpenter at their head, who informed him, "that 1000 men were waiting for his answer, and that if he refused to comply, they could not tell what might be the consequence." He complied, and the news-papers soon after published, that he did it voluntarily.

In Boston, Lieut. Governor Hutchinson endeavoured to promote a counter association, but without effect. The friends of importation objected, that till parliament made provision for the punishment of the confederacies against importation, a counter association would answer no other purpose, than to expose the associators to popular rage.

The Bostonians, about this time, went one step farther. They reshipped goods to Great Britain, instead of [85] storing them as formerly. This was resolved upon in a town meeting, on the infor-mation of an inhabitant, who communicated a letter he had lately received from a member of parliament, in which it was said, "that shipping back ten thousand pounds worth of goods would do more, than storing a hundred thousand." This turned the scale, and procured a majority of votes for reshipping. Not only in this, but in many other instances, the violences of the colonists were fostered by individuals in Great Britain. A number of these were in principle with the Americans, in denying the right of parliament, to tax them, but others were more influenced by a spirit of opposition to the ministerial majority, than by a regard to the constitutional liberties of either country.

The non-importation agreement had now lasted some time, and by degrees had become general. Several of the colonial assemblies had been dissolved, or prorogued, for asserting the rights of their constituents. The royal governours, and other friends to an American revenue, were chagrined. The colonists were irritated. Good men, both in England and America, deplored these untoward events, and beheld with concern an increasing ill humour between those, who were bound by interest and affection, to be friends to each other.

In consequence of the American non-importation agreement, founded in opposition to the duties of 1767, the manufacturers of Great Britain experienced a renewal of the distresses, which followed the adoption of similar resolutions, in the year 1765, the repeal of these duties was therefore solicited by the same influence, which had procured the repeal of the stamp act. The rulers of Great Britain acted without decision. Instead of persevering in their own system of coercion or indeed in any one uniform system of colonial government, they struck out a middle line, embarrassed with the consequences, both of severity and of lenity, and which was without the complete benefits of either. Soon after the spirited address to his

Majesty, last mentioned, had passed both houses of parliament, assurances were given for [86] repealing all the duties, imposed in 1767, excepting that of three-pence per pound on tea.

Anxious on the one hand to establish parliamentary supremacy, and on the other, afraid to stem the torrent of opposition, they conceded enough to weaken the former, and yet not enough to satisfy the latter. Had Great Britain generously repealed the whole, and for ever relinquished all claim to the right, or even the exercise of the right of taxation, the union of the two countries, might have lasted for ages. Had she seriously determined to compel the submission of the colonies, nothing could have been more unfriendly to this design, than her repeated concessions to their reiterated associations. The declaratory act, and the reservation of the duty on tea, left the cause of contention between the two countries, in full force, but the former was only a claim on paper, and the latter might be evaded, by refusing to purchase any tea, on which the parliamentary tax was imposed. The colonists, therefore, conceiving that their commerce might be renewed, without establishing any precedent, injurious to their liberties, relaxed in their associations, in every particular, except tea, and immediately recommenced the importation of all other articles of merchandise. A political calm once more took place. The parent state might now have closed the dispute for ever, and honorably receded, without a formal relinquishment of her claims. Neither the reservation of the duty on tea, by the British parliament, nor the exceptions made by the colonists, of importing no tea, on which a duty was imposed, would, if they had been left to their own operation, have disturbed the returning harmony of the two countries. Without fresh irritation, their wounds might have healed, and not a scar been left behind.

Unfortunately for the friends of union, so paltry a sum as 3 [pence for] so insignificant an article as tea, in consequence of a combination between the British ministry and East-India company, revived the dispute to the rending of the empire.

[87] These two abortive attempts to raise a parliamentary revenue in America, caused a fermentation in the minds of the colonists, and gave birth to many enquiries respecting their natural rights. Reflections and reasonings on this subject produced a high sense of liberty, and a general conviction that there could be no security for their property, if they were to be taxed at the discretion of a British parliament, in which they were unrepresented, and over which they had no controul. A determination not only to oppose this new claim of taxation, but to keep a strict watch, least it might be established in some disguised form, took possession of their minds.

It commonly happens in the discussion of doubtful claims between States, that the ground of the original dispute insensibly changes. When the mind is employed in investigating one subject, others associated with it, naturally present themselves. In the course of enquiries on the subject of parliamentary taxation, the restriction on the trade of the colonists—the necessity that was imposed on them to purchase British and other manufactures, loaded with their full proportion of all taxes paid by those who made or sold them, became more generally known. While American writers were vindicating their country from the charge of contributing nothing to the common expences of the empire, they were led to set off to their credit, the disadvantage of their being confined exclusively to purchase such manufactures in Britain. They instituted calculations by which they demonstrated that the monopoly of their trade, drew from them greater sums for the support of government, than were usually paid by an equal number of their fellow citizens of Great-Britain; and that taxation, superadded to such a monopoly, would leave them in a state of perfect uncompensated slavery. The investigation of these subjects brought matters into view which the friends of union ought to have kept out of sight. These circumstances, together with the extensive population of the Eastern States, and their adventurous spirit of commerce, suggested to some bold spirits that not only British taxation, but British navigation laws were unfriendly to the interests of [88] America. Speculations of this magnitude suited well with the extensive views of some capital merchants, but never would have roused the bulk of the people, had not new matter brought the dispute between the two countries to a point, in which every individual was interested.

On reviewing the conduct of the British ministry, respecting the colonies, much weakness as well as folly appears. For a succession of years there was a steady pursuit of American revenue, but great inconsistence in the projects for obtaining it. In one moment the parliament was for enforcing their laws, the next for repealing them. Doing and undoing, menacing and submitting, straining and relaxing, followed each other, in alternate succession. The object of administration, though twice relinquished as to any present efficiency, was invariably pursued, but without any unity of system.

On the 9th of May, 1769, the King in his speech to parliament, highly applauded their hearty concurrence, in maintaining the execution of the laws, in every part of his dominions. Five days after this speech, lord Hillsborough, secretary of state for the colonies, wrote to lord Botetourt, governor of Virginia:

> I can take upon me to assure you, notwithstanding informations to the contrary, from men, with factious and seditious views, that his Majesty's present administration have at no time entertained a design to propose to parliament, to lay any farther taxes upon America, for the purpose of raising a revenue, and that it is at present their intention to propose the next session of parliament, to take off the duties upon glass, paper, and colours, upon consideration of such duties having been laid contrary to the true principles of commerce.

The governor was also informed, that "his Majesty relied upon his prudence and fidelity, to make such an explanation of his Majesty's measures, as would tend to remove prejudices, and to re-establish mutual confidence and affection between the Mother Country and the colonies." In the exact spirit of his instructions, lord Botetourt addressed the Virginia assembly as follows:

> It may possibly be objected, that as his [89] Majesty's present administration are not immortal, their successors may be inclined to attempt to undo what the present ministers shall have attempted to perform, and to that objection I can give but this answer, that it is my firm opinion, that the plan I have stated to you, will certainly take place,

and that it will never be departed from; and so determined am I forever to abide by it, that I will be content to be declared infamous, if I do not to the last hour of my life, at all times, in all places, and upon all occasions, exert every power, with which I either am, or ever shall be, legally invested, in order to obtain and maintain for the continent of America, that satisfaction, which I have been authorised to promise this day, by the confidential servants of our gracious sovereign, who, to my certain knowledge, rates his honor so high, that he would rather part with his crown, than preserve it by deceit.

These assurances were received with transports of joy by the Virginians. They viewed them as pledging his Majesty for security, that the late design for raising a revenue in America was abandoned, and never more to be resumed. The Assembly of Virginia, in answer to lord Botetourt, expressed themselves thus:

We are sure our most gracious sovereign, under whatever changes may happen in his confidential servants, will remain immutable in the ways of truth and justice, and that he is incapable of deceiving his faithful subjects; and we esteem your lordship's information not only as warranted, but even sanctified by the royal word.

How far these solemn engagements with the Americans were observed, subsequent events will demonstrate. In a perfect reliance on them, most of the colonists returned to their ancient habits of good humour, and flattered themselves that no future parliament would undertake to give, or grant away their property.

From the royal and ministerial assurances given in favour of America, in the year 1769, and the subsequent repeal in 1770, of five sixths of the duties which had been imposed in 1767; together with the consequent renewal of the mercantile intercourse between Great-Britain [90] and the colonies: Many hoped that the contention between the two countries was finally closed. In all the provinces, excepting Massachusetts, appearances seemed to favour that opinion. Many incidents operated there to the prejudice of that harmony, which had begun, elsewhere, to return. The stationing a military force among them, was a fruitful source of uneasiness. The royal army had been brought thither, with the avowed design of enforcing submission to the Mother Country. Speeches from the throne, and addresses

1770

from both houses of parliament, had taught them to look upon the inhabitants as a factious turbulent people, who aimed at throwing off all subordination to Great-Britain. They, on the other hand were accustomed to look upon the soldiery as instruments of tyranny, sent on purpose to dragoon them out of their liberties.

Reciprocal insults soured the tempers, and mutual injuries embittered the passions, of the opposite parties: besides, some fiery spirits who thought it an indignity to have troops quartered among them, were constantly exciting the towns-people to quarrel with the soldiers.

On the second of March, a fray took place near Mr. Gray's ropewalk, between a private soldier of the 29th regiment, and an inhabitant. The former was supported by his comrades, the latter by the rope makers, till several on both sides were involved in the consequences. On the 5th a more dreadful scene was presented. The soldiers, when under arms, were pressed upon, insulted and pelted by a mob armed with clubs, sticks, and snowballs covering stones. They were also dared to fire. In this situation, one of the soldiers who had received a blow, in resentment fired at the supposed aggressor. This was followed by a single discharge from six others. Three of the inhabitants were killed, and five were dangerously wounded. The town was immediately in commotion. Such was the temper, force, and number of the inhabitants, that nothing but an engagement to remove the troops out of the town; together with the advice of moderate men, prevented the townsmen from falling on the soldiers. The killed were buried in one vault, and in a most respectful, [91] manner to express the indignation of the inhabitants at the slaughter of their brethren, by soliders quartered among them, in violation of their civil liberties. Preston the captain who commanded the party, which fired on the inhabitants [was] committed to jail, and afterwards tried. The captain, and six of the men, were acquitted. Two were brought in guilty of man-slaughter. It appeared on the trial, that the soliders were abused, insulted, threatened, and pelted, before they fired. It was also proved, that only seven guns were fired by the eight prisoners. These circumstances induced the jury to make a favourable verdict. The result of the trial reflected great honour on John Adams, and Josiah Quincy, the council for the prisoners, and also on the integrity of the jury, who ventured to give an upright verdict, in defiance of popular opinions.

The events of this tragical night, sunk deep in the minds of the people, and were made subservient to important purposes. The anniversary of it was observed with great solemnity. Eloquent orators, were successively employed to deliver an annual oration, to preserve the rememberance of it fresh in their minds. On these occasions the blessings of liberty—the horrors of slavery—the dangers of a standing army—the rights of the colonies, and a variety of such topics were presented to the public view, under their most pleasing and alarming forms. These annual orations administered fuel to the fire of liberty, and kept it burning, with an incessant flame.

The obstacles to returning harmony, which have already been mentioned, were increased, by making the governor and judges in Massachusetts, independent of the province. Formerly, they had been paid by yearly grants from the assembly, but about this time provision was made for paying their salaries by the crown. This was resented as a dangerous innovation, as an infraction of their charter, and as destroying that balance of power, which is essential to free governments. That the crown should pay the salary of the chief justice, was represented by the assembly, as a species of bribery, tending to bias his judicial determinations. They made it the foundation for [92] impeaching Mr. Justice Oliver, before the governor, but he excepted to their proceedings, as unconstitutional. The assembly, nevertheless, gained two points. They tendered the governor more odious to the inhabitants, and increased the public respect for themselves, as the counterpart of the British house of commons, and as guardians of the rights of the people.

A personal animosity, between Lieut. Governor Hutchinson, and some distinguished patriots, in Massachusetts, contributed to perpetuate a flame of discontent in that province, after it had elsewhere visibly abated. This was worked up, in the year 1773, to a high pitch, by a singular combination of circumstances. Some letters had been written, in the course of the dispute, by governor Hutchinson, lieut. governor Oliver, and others, in Boston, to persons in power and office, in England, which contained a very unfavorable representation of the state of public affairs, and tended to shew the necessity of coercive measures, and of changing the chartered system of government, to secure the obedience of the province. These letters fell into the hands of Dr. Franklin, agent of the province, who transmitted them to Boston. The indignation and animosity, which was excited on the receipt of them, knew no bounds. The house of assembly agreed on a petition and remonstrance to his Majesty, in which they charged their governor and lieut. governor with being betrayers of their trusts, and of the people they governed, and of giving private, partial, and false information. They also declared them enemies to the colonies, and prayed for justice against them, and for their speedy removal from their places. These charges were carried through by a majority of 82 to 12.

JAN. 29, 1774

This petition and remonstrance being transmitted to England, the merits of it were discussed before his Majesty's privy council. After a hearing before that board, in which Dr. Franklin represented the province of Massachusetts, the governor and lieut. governor were acquitted. Mr. Wedderburne, who defended the accused royal servants, in the course of his pleadings, inveighed against Dr. Franklin, in the severest language, as the fomenter of the disputes between the two countries. It [93] was no protection to this venerable sage, that being the agent of Massachusetts, he conceived it his duty to inform his constituents, of letters, written on public affairs, calculated to overturn their chartered constitution. The age, respectability, and high literary character of the subject of Mr. Wedderburne's philippic, turned the attention of the public, on the transaction. The insult offered to one of their public agents, and especially to one, who was both the idol and ornament of his native country, sunk deep in the minds of the Americans. That a faithful servant, whom they loved, and almost adored, should be insulted, for discharging his official duty, rankled in their hearts. Dr. Franklin was also immediately dismissed from the office of deputy postmaster general, which he held under the crown. It was not only by his transmission of these letters, that he had given offence to the British ministry, but by his popular writings, in favor of America. Two pieces of his, in particular, had lately attracted a large share of public attention, and had an extensive influence on both sides of the Atlantic. The one purported to be an edict from the King of Prussia, for taxing the inhabitants of Great-Britain, as descendants of emigrants from his dominions. The other was entitled, "Rules for reducing a great empire to a small one." In both of which he had exposed the claims of the Mother

Country, and the proceedings of the British ministry, with the severity of poignant satire.

For ten years, there had now been but little intermission to the disputes between Great-Britain and her colonies. Their respective claims had never been compromised on middle ground. The calm which followed the repeal of the stamp act, was in a few months disturbed, by the revenue act of the year 1767. The tranquility which followed the repeal of five sixths of that act in the year 1770, was nothing more than a truce. The reservation of the duty on tea, made as an avowed evidence of the claims of Great-Britain to tax her colonies, kept alive the jealousy of the colonists, while at the same time the stationing of a standing army in Massachusetts—the continuance of a board of commissioners in Boston—the constituting the governors and judges of that province [94] independent of the people, were constant sources of irritation. The altercations which, at this period, were common between the royal governors and the provincial assemblies, together with numerous vindications of the claims of America, made the subject familiar to the colonists. The ground of the controversy was canvassed in every company. The more the Americans read, reasoned, and conversed on the subject, the more were they convinced of their right to the exclusive disposal of their property. This was followed by a determination to resist all encroachments on that palladium of British liberty. They were as strongly convinced of their right to refuse and resist parliamentary taxation, as the ruling powers of Great-Britain, of their right to demand and enforce their submission to it.

The claims of the two countries, being thus irreconcileably opposed to each other, the partial calm which followed the concession of parliament in 1770, was liable to disturbance, from every incident. Under such circumstances, nothing less than the most guarded conduct on both sides could prevent a renewal of the controversy. Instead of following those prudential measures which would have kept the ground of the dispute out of sight, an impolitic scheme was concerted, between the British ministry and the East-India company, which placed the claims of Great-Britain and of her colonies in hostile array against each other.

Tea is sent by the East India Company to America,
and is refused, or destroyed, by the Colonists.
Boston port act, &c.

IN THE YEAR 1773, commenced a new era of the American controversy. To understand this in its origin, it is necessary to recur to the
period, when the solitary duty on tea, was excepted from the partial
repeal of the revenue act of 1767. When the duties which had been
laid on glass, paper and painters colours, were taken off, a [95]
respectable minority in parliament contended, that the duty on tea
should also be removed. To this it was replied, "That as the Americans
denied the legality of taxing them, a total repeal would be a virtual
acquiescence in their claims; and that in order to preserve the rights
of the Mother Country, it was necessary to retain the preamble, and
at least one of the taxed articles." It was answered, that a partial
repeal would be a source of endless discontent—that the tax on tea
would not defray the expences of collecting it. The motion in favour

of a total repeal, was thrown out by a great majority. As the parliament thought fit to retain the tax on tea for an evidence of their right of taxation, the Americans in like manner, to be consistent with themselves, in denying that right, discontinued the importation of that commodity. While there was no attempt to introduce tea into the colonies against this declared sense of the inhabitants, these opposing claims were in no danger of collision. In that case the Mother Country might have solaced herself, with her ideal rights, and the colonies, with their favorite opinion of a total exemption from parliamentary taxes, without disturbing the public peace. This mode of compromising the dispute, which seemed at first designed as a salvo for the honor and consistency of both parties, was, by the interference of the East-India Company, in combination with the British ministry, completely overset.

The expected revenue from tea failed, in consequence of the American association to import none, on which a duty was charged. This, though partially violated in some of the colonies, was well observed in others, and particularly in Pennsylvania, where the duty was never paid on more than one chest of that commodity. This proceeded as much from the spirit of gain as of patriotism. The merchants found means of supplying their countrymen with tea, smuggled from countries to which the power of Britain did not extend. They doubtless conceived themselves to be supporting the rights of their country, by refusing to purchase tea from Britain, but they also reflected that if they could bring the same commodity to market, free of duty, their profits would be proportionably greater.

[96] The love of gain was not peculiar to the American merchants. From the diminished exportation to the colonies, the ware-houses of the British East-India company had in them about seventeen millions of pounds of tea, for which a market could not readily be procured. The ministry and East-India company unwilling to lose, the one the expected revenue from the sale of tea in America—the other, their usual commercial profits, agreed on a measure by which they supposed both would be secured.

The East-India company were by law authorized to export their tea free of duties to all places whatsoever. By this regulation, tea, though loaded with an exceptionable duty, would come cheaper to the colonies, than before it had been made a source of revenue: For the duty when taken off it, when exported from Great-Britain, was greater than what was to be paid on its importation into the colonies. Confident of success in finding a market for their tea, thus reduced in its price, and also of collecting a duty on its importation and sale in the colonies, the East-India company freighted several ships, with teas for the different colonies, and appointed agents for the disposal thereof. This measure united several interests in opposition to its execution. The patriotism of the Americans was corroborated by several auxiliary aids, no ways connected with the cause of liberty.

The merchants in England were alarmed at the losses that must accrue to themselves, from the exportations of the East-India company, and from the sales going through the hands of consignees. Letters were written from that country, to colonial patriots, urging that opposition to which they of themselves were prone.

The smugglers who were both numerous and powerful, could not relish a scheme which by underselling them, and taking a profitable branch of business, out of their hands, threatened a diminution of their gains. The colonists were too suspicious of the designs of Great-Britain to be imposed upon.

The cry of endangered liberty once more excited an alarm from New-Hampshire to Georgia. The first opposition [97] to the execution of the scheme adopted by the East-India company began with the American merchants. They saw a profitable branch of their trade likely to be lost, and the benefits of it to be transferred to people in Great-Britain. They felt for the wound that would be inflicted on their country's claim of exemption from parliamentary taxation, but they felt with equal sensibility for the losses they would sustain by the diversion of the streams of commerce, into unusual channels. Though the opposition originated in the selfishness of the merchants, it did not end there. The great body of the people, from principles of the purest patriotism, were brought over to second their wishes. They considered the whole scheme, as calculated to seduce them into an acquiescence with the views of parliament, for raising an American revenue. Much pains were taken to enlighten the colonists on this subject, and to convince them of the eminent hazard to which their liberties were exposed.

CHAPTER III

The provincial patriots insisted largely on the persevering determination of the parent state to establish her claim of taxation, by
compelling the sale of tea in the colonies against the solemn
resolutions and declared sense of the inhabitants, and that at a time
when the commercial intercourse of the two countries was renewed,
and their ancient harmony fast returning. The proposed venders of
the tea were represented as revenue officers, employed in the
collection of an unconstitutional tax, imposed by Great-Britain. The
colonists reasoned with themselves, that as the duty and the price
of the commodity were inseparably blended, if the tea was sold,
every purchaser would pay a tax imposed by the British parliament,
as part of the purchase money. To obviate this evil, and to prevent
the liberties of a great country from being sacrificed by inconsiderate
purchasers, sundry town meetings were held in the capitals of the
different provinces, and combinations were formed to obstruct the
sales of the tea, sent by the East-India company.

[98] The resolutions entered into by the inhabitants of Philadelphia,
on October the 18th 1773, afford a good specimen of the whole—
these were as follows:

1. That the disposal of their own property is the inherent right of
freemen; that there can be no property in that which another can, of
right, take from us without our consent; that the claim of parliament to
tax America, is in other words, a claim of right to levy contributions on
us at pleasure.

2. That the duty imposed by parliament upon tea landed in America,
is a tax on the Americans, or levying contributions on them without
their consent.

3. That the express purpose for which the tax is levied on the
Americans—namely, for the support of government, administration of
justice, and defence of his Majesty's dominions in America, has a direct
tendency to render assemblies useless, and to introduce arbitrary
government and slavery.

4. That a virtuous and steady opposition to this ministerial plan of
governing America, is absolutely necessary to preserve even the shadow
of liberty, and is a duty which every freeman in America owes to his
country, to himself, and to his posterity.

5. That the resolution lately entered into by the East-India company,
to send out their tea to America, subject to the payment of duties on

its being landed here, is an open attempt to enforce this ministerial plan, and a violent attack upon the liberties of America.

6. That it is the duty of every American to oppose this attempt.

7. That whoever shall directly or indirectly, countenance this attempt, or in any wise aid or abet in unloading, receiving, or vending the tea sent, or to be sent out by the East-India company, while it remains subject to the payment of a duty here, is an enemy to his country.

8. That a committee be immediately chosen to wait on those gentlemen, who, it is reported, are appointed by the East-India company, to receive and sell said tea, and request them, from a regard to their own character [99] and the peace and good order of the city and province, immediately to resign their appointment.

As the time approached when the arrival of the tea ships might be soon expected, such measures were adopted as seemed most likely to prevent the landing of their cargoes. The tea consignees, appointed by the East-India company, were in several places compelled to relinquish their appointments, and no others could be found hardy enough to act in their stead. The pilots in the river Delaware, were warned not to conduct any of the tea ships into their harbour. In New-York, popular vengeance was denounced against all who would contribute, in any measure, to forward the views of the East-India company. The captains of the New-York and Philadelphia ships, being apprized of the resolution of the people, and fearing the consequences of landing a commodity, charged with an odious duty, in violation of their declared public sentiments, concluded to return directly to Great-Britain, without making any entry at the custom house.

It was otherwise in Massachusetts. The tea ships designed for the supply of Boston, were consigned to the sons, cousins, and particular friends, of governor Hutchinson. When they were called upon to resign, they answered, "That it was out of their power." The collector refused to give a clearance, unless the vessels were discharged of dutiable articles. The governor refused to give a pass for the vessels, unless properly qualified from the custom-house. The governor likewise requested Admiral Montague to guard the passages out of the harbour, and gave orders to suffer no vessels, coasters excepted, to pass the fortress from the town, without a pass signed by himself.

From a combination of these circumstances, the return of the tea vessels from Boston, was rendered impossible. The inhabitants then, had no option, but to prevent the landing of the tea, or to suffer it to be landed, and depend on the unanimity of the people not to purchase it, or to destroy the tea, or to suffer a deep laid scheme against their sacred liberties to take effect. The first would have required incessant [100] watching by night, as well as by day, for a period of time, the duration of which no one could compute. The second would have been visionary to childishness, by suspending the liberties of a growing country, on the self denial and discretion of every tea drinker in the province. They viewed the tea as the vehicle of an unconstitutional tax, and as inseparably associated with it. To avoid the one, they resolved to destroy the other. About seventeen persons, dressed as Indians, repaired to the tea ships, broke open 342 chests of tea, and without doing any other damage, discharged their contents into the water.

Thus by the inflexibility of the governor, the issue of this business was different, at Boston, from what it was elsewhere. The whole cargoes of tea were returned from New-York and Philadelphia. That which was sent to Charleston was landed and stored, but not offered for sale. Mr. Hutchinson had repeatedly urged government, at home, to be firm and persevering, he could not therefore consistent with his honour depart from a line of conduct, he had so often and so strongly recommended to his superiors. He also believed that the inhabitants would not dare to perfect their engagements, and flattered himself that they would desist, when the critical moment arrived.

Admitting the rectitude of the American claims of exemption, from parliamentary taxation, the destruction of the tea by the Bostonians, was warranted by the great law of self preservation, for it was not possible for them, by any other means, within the compass of probability, to discharge the duty they owed to their country.

The event of this business was very different from what had been expected in England. The colonists acted with so much union and system, that there was not a single chest of any of the cargoes sent out by the East-India, company on this occasion, sold for their benefit.

Intelligence of these proceedings was, on the 7th of March 1774, communicated, in a message from the throne, to both houses of parliament. In this communication the conduct of the colonists was represented as [101] not only obstructing the commerce of Great-Britain, but as subversive of its constitution. The message was accompanied with a number of papers, containing copies and extracts of letters, from the several royal governors and others, from which it appeared that the opposition to the sale of the tea was not peculiar to Massachusetts, but common to all the colonies. These papers were accompanied with accounts setting forth, that nothing short of parliamentary interference was capable of re-establishing order among the turbulent colonists, and that therefore decisive measures should be immediately adopted for securing the dependence of the colonies. If the right of levying taxes on the Americans was vested in the parent state, these inferences were well founded; but if it was not, their conduct in resisting an invasion of their rights was justified, not only by many examples in the history of Britain, but by the spirit of the constitution of that country which they were opposing.

By the destruction of the tea, the people of Boston had incurred the sanction of penal laws. Those in Great-Britain who wished for an opportunity to take vengeance on that town, commonly supposed by them to be the mother of sedition and rebellion, rejoiced that her inhabitants had laid themselves open to castigation.

It was well known that the throwing of the tea into the river, did not originate with the persons who were the immediate instruments of that act of violence. That the whole had been concerted at a public meeting, and was, in a qualified sense, the act of the town. The universal indignation which in Great-Britain was excited against the people of Boston, pointed out to the ministry the suitableness of the present moment for humbling them. Though the ostensible ground of complaint was nothing more than a trespass on private property, committed by private persons, yet it was well known to be part of a long digested plan of resistance to parliamentary taxation. Every measure that might be pursued on the occasion seemed to be big with the fate of the empire. To proceed in the usual forms of law, appeared to the rulers in Great-Britain to be a departure from their [102] dignity. It was urged by the ministry that parliament, and parliament only, was capable of re-establishing tranquility among these turbulent people, and of bringing order out of confusion. To stifle all opposition from the merchants, the public papers were filled with writings which stated the impossibility of carrying on a future trade to America, if this flagrant outrage on commerce should go unpunished.

It was in vain urged by the minority that no good could arise from coercion, unless the minds of the Americans were made easy on the subject of taxation. Equally vain was a motion for a retrospect into the conduct of the ministry, which had provoked their resistance.

The parliament discovered an aversion from looking back to the original ground of the dispute, and confined themselves solely to the late misbehaviour of the Americans, without any enquiry into the provoking causes thereof.

The violence of the Bostonians in destroying an article of commerce, was largely insisted upon, without any indulgence for the jealous spirit of liberty, in the descendants of Englishmen. The connexion between the tea and the unconstitutional duty imposed thereon, was overlooked, and the public mind of Great-Britain solely fixed on the obstruction given to commerce, by the turbulent colonists. The spirit raised against the Americans became as high, and as strong, as their most inveterate enemies could desire. This was not confined to the common people, but took possession of legislators, whose unclouded minds ought to be exalted above the mists of prejudice or partiality. Such, when they consult on public affairs, should be free from the impulses of passion, for it rarely happens that resolutions adopted in anger, are founded in wisdom. The parliament in Great-Britain, transported with indignation against the people of Boston, in a fit of rage resolved to take legislative vengeance, on that devoted town.

Disregarding the forms of her own constitution by which none are to be condemned unheard, or punished without a trial, a bill was finally passed, on the 17th day [103] after it was first moved for, by which the port of Boston was virtually blocked up, for it was legally precluded from the privilege of landing and discharging, or of lading and shipping of goods, wares and merchandise. The minister who proposed this measure, stated in support of it, that the opposition to the authority of parliament, had always originated in that colony, and had always been instigated by the seditious proceedings of the town of Boston: that it was therefore necessary to make an example of that town, which by an unparalleled outrage had violated the freedom of commerce; that Great-Britain would be wanting in the protection she owed to her peaceable subjects, if she did not punish such an insult, in an exemplary manner. He therefore proposed, that the town of Boston should be obliged to pay for the tea which had been destroyed. He was farther of opinion, that making a pecuniary satisfaction for the injury committed, would not alone be sufficient, but that in addition thereto, security must be given in future, that trade may be safely carried on—property protected—laws obeyed— and duties paid. He urged, therefore that it would be proper to take away from Boston the privilege of a port, until his Majesty should be satisfied in these particulars, and publicly declare in council, on a proper certificate, of the good behaviour of the town, that he was so satisfied. Until this should happen he proposed that the custom house officers should be removed to Salem. The minister hoped that this act would execute itself, or at most, that a few frigates would secure its execution. He also hoped, that the prospect of advantage to the town of Salem, from its being made the seat of the custom house, and from the occlusion of the port of Boston, would detach them from the interest of the latter, and dispose them to support a measure, from which they had so much to expect. It was also presumed that the other colonies would leave Boston to suffer the punishment due to her demerits. The abettors of parliamentary supremacy flattered themselves that this decided conduct of Great-Britain would, forever, extinguish all opposition from the refractory colonists to the claims of [104] the Mother Country; and the apparent equity of obliging a delinquent town to make reparation for an injury occasioned by the factious spirit of its inhabitants, silenced many of the friends of America. The consequences resulting from this measure, were the reverse of what were wished for by the first, and dreaded by the last.

By the operation of the Boston port act, the preceding situation of its inhabitants, and that of the East-India company was reversed. The former had more reason to complain of the disproportionate penalty to which they were indiscriminately subjected, than the latter of that outrage on their property, for which punishment had been inflicted. Hitherto the East-India company were the injured party, but from the passing of this act, the balance of injury was on the opposite side. If wrongs received entitled the former to reparation, the latter had a much stronger title on the same ground. For the act of seventeen or eighteen individuals, twice as many thousands were involved in one general calamity.

Both parties viewed the case on a much larger scale than that of municipal law. The people of Boston alledged, in vindication of their conduct, that the tea was a weapon aimed at their liberties, and that the same principles of self preservation which justify the breaking of the assassins sword uplifted for destruction, equally authorised the destruction of that tea which was the vehicle of an unconstitutional tax subversive of their liberties. The parliament of Great-Britain considered the act of the people of Boston, in destroying the tea, as an open defiance of that country. The demerit of the action as an offence against property, was lost, in the supposed superior demerit of treasonable intention to emancipate themselves from a state of colonial dependence. The Americans conceived the case to be intimately connected with their liberties; the inhabitants of Great-Britain with their supremacy, the former considered it as a duty they owed their country, to make a common cause with the people of Boston, the latter thought themselves under equal obligations to support the privileges of parliament.

[105] On the third reading of the Boston port bill, a petition was presented by the lord mayor, in the name of several natives and inhabitants of North America, then residing in London. It was drawn with great force of language, and stated that "the proceedings of parliament against Boston were repugnant to every principle of law and justice, and established a precedent by which no man in America could enjoy a moment's security." The friends of parliamentary supremacy had long regretted the democratic constitutions of the provinces as adverse to their schemes. They saw with concern the steady opposition that was given to their measures by the American legislatures. These constitutions were planned when Great-Britain neither feared nor cared for her colonies. Not suspecting that she was laying the foundation of future states, she granted charters that gave to the people so much of the powers of government as enabled them to make not only a formidable, but a regular, constitutional, opposition, to the country from which they sprung.

Long had her rulers wished for an opportunity to revoke these charters, and to new model these governments. The present moment seemed favourable to this design. The temper of the nation was high, and the resentment against the province of Massachusetts general and violent. The late outrages in Boston furnished a tolerable pretence for the attempt. An act of the British parliament speedily followed the one for shutting up the port of Boston, entitled, an act for the better regulating the government of Massachusetts. The object of this was to alter the charter of the province in the following particulars: The council or second branch of the legislature heretofore elected by the general court, was to be from the first of August 1774, appointed by the crown. The royal governor was also by the same act, invested with the power of appointing and removing all judges of the inferior courts of common pleas—commissioners of oyer and terminer—the attorney general—provost marshal—justices—sheriffs, &c. The town meetings which were sanctioned by the charter, were with a few exceptions [106] expressly forbidden to be held, without the leave of the governor or lieutenant governor in writing, expressing the special business of said meeting, first had and obtained; and with a farther restriction, that no matter should be treated of at these meetings, excepting the election of public officers, and the business expressed in the leave given by the governor or lieutenant governor. Jurymen which had been before elected by the freeholders and inhabitants of the several towns, were to be, by this new act, all summoned and returned, by the sheriffs of the respective counties. The whole executive government was taken out of the hands of the people, and the nomination of all important officers vested in the king or his governor.

This act excited a greater alarm than the port act. The one effected only the metropolis, the other the whole province. The one had the appearance of being merited, as it was well known that an act of violence had been committed by its inhabitants, under the sanction of a town meeting; but the other had no stronger justifying reason than that the proposed alterations were, in the opinion of the parliament, become absolutely necessary, in order to the preservation of the peace and good order of the said province. In support of this bill, the minister who brought it in alledged, that an executive power was wanting in the country. The very people, said he, who commit the riots are the posse comitatus in which the force of the civil power consists. He farther urged the futility of making laws, the execution of which, under the present form of government in Massachusetts, might be so easily evaded, and therefore contended for a necessity to alter the whole frame of their constitution, as far as related to its executive and judicial powers. In opposition it was urged, that the taking away the civil constitution of a whole people, secured by a solemn charter, upon general charges of delinquencies and defects, was a stretch of power of the most arbitrary and dangerous nature.

By the English constitution charters were sacred, and only revokable by a due course of law, and on a conviction [107] of misconduct. They were solemn compacts between the prince and the people, and without the constitutional power of either party. The abettors of the British schemes reasoned in a summary way. Said they,

> the colonies, particularly Massachusetts, by their circular letters; associations and town meetings, have for years past thwarted all the measures of government, and are meditating independency. This turbulent spirit of theirs is fostered by their constitution, which invests them with too much power to be consistent with their state of subordination. Let us therefore lay the axe at the root—new model their charter, and lop off those privileges which they have abused.

When the human mind is agitated with passion it rarely discerns its own interest, and but faintly foresees consequences. Had the parliament stopped short with the Boston port act, the motives to union and to make a common cause with that metropolis, would have been feeble, perhaps ineffectual to have roused the other provinces; but the arbitrary mutilation of the important privileges contained in a solemn charter, without a trial—without a hearing, by the will of parliament, convinced the most moderate that the cause of Massachusetts was the cause of all the provinces.

It readily occurred to those who guided the helm of Great-Britain, that riots would probably take place, in attempting the execution of the acts just mentioned. They also discerned that such was the temper of the people, that trials for murders committed in suppressing riots, if held in Massachusetts, would seldom terminate in favour of the parties, who were engaged on the side of government. To make their system compleat, it was necessary to go one step farther, and to screen their active friends from the apprehended partiality of such trials. It was therefore provided by law, that if any person was indicted for murder, or for any capital offence committed in aiding magistracy, that the governor might send the person so indicted to another colony, or to Great-Britain to be tried. This law was the subject of severe comments. It was considered as an act of indemnity to those who should [108] embrue their hands in the blood of their fellow citizens. It was asked how the relations of a murdered man could effectually prosecute, if they must go three thousand miles to attend that business. It was contended that the act by stopping the usual course of justice, would probably give rise to assassinations and dark revenge among individuals, and encourage all kinds of lawless violence. The charge of partiality was retorted. For said they, "If a party spirit against the authority of Great-Britain would condemn an active officer in Massachusetts as a murderer, the same party spirit for preserving the authority of Great-Britain, would, in that country, acquit a murderer as a spirited performer of his duty.["] The case of captain Preston was also quoted as a proof of the impartial administration of justice in Massachusetts.

The same Natives of America who had petitioned against the Boston port bill, presented a second one against these two bills. With uncommon energy of language, they pointed out many constitutional objections against them, and concluded with fervently beseeching, "that the parliament would not, by passing them, reduce their countrymen to an abject state of misery and humiliation, or drive them to the last resource of despair." The lords of the minority entered also a protest against the passing of each of these bills.

It was fortunate for the people of Boston, and those who wished to promote a combination of the colonies against Great-Britain, that these three several laws passed nearly at the same time. They were presented in quick progression, either in the form of bills or of acts, to the consideration of the inflamed Americans, and produced effects on their minds, infinitely greater than could have been expected from either, especially from the Boston port act alone.

When the fire of indignation, excited by the first, was burning, intelligence of these other acts, operated like fuel, and made it flame

CHAPTER III

out with increasing vehemence. The three laws were considered as
forming a complete system of tyranny, from the operation of which,
there was no chance of making a peaceable escape.

[109] "By the first," said they, "the property of unoffending thousands is arbitrarily taken away, for the act of a few individuals; by
the second our chartered liberties are annihilated; and by the third,
our lives may be destroyed with impunity. Property, liberty, and life,
are all sacrificed on the altar of ministerial vengeance." This mode
of reasoning was not peculiar to Massachusetts. These three acts of
parliament, contrary to the expectation of those who planned them,
became a cement of a firm union among the colonies, from New-
Hampshire to Georgia. They now openly said, "our charters and
other rights and immunities must depend on the pleasure of parliament." They were sensible that they had all concurred, more or less,
in the same line of opposition which had provoked these severe
statutes against Massachusetts; and they believed that vengeance,
though delayed, was not remitted, and that the only favour the least
culpable could expect, was to be the last that would be devoured.
The friends of the colonies contended, that these laws were in direct
contradiction to the letter, and the spirit of the British constitution.
Their opposers could support them on no stronger grounds than
those of political necessity and expedience. They acknowledged them
to be contrary to the established mode of proceeding, but defended
them as tending ultimately to preserve the constitution, from the
meditated independency of the colonies.

Such was the temper of the people in England, that the acts
hitherto passed were popular. A general opinion had gone forth in
the Mother Country, that the people of Massachusetts, by their violent
opposition to government, had drawn on themselves merited correction.

The parliament did not stop here, but proceeded one step farther,
which inflamed their enemies in America, and lost them friends in
Great-Britain. The general clamor in the provinces was, that the
proceedings in the parliament were arbitrary, and unconstitutional.
Before they completed their memorable session in the beginning of
the year 1774, they passed an act respecting the government of
Quebec, which in the opinion of their friends merited these appel-

lations. By this act the government of that [110] province was made to extend southward to the Ohio, and westward to the banks of the Mississippi, and northward, to the boundary of the Hudson's Bay company. The principal objects of the act were to form a legislative council, for all the affairs of the province, except taxation, which council should be appointed by the crown; the office to be held during pleasure, and his Majesty's Roman Catholic subjects to be entitled to a place therein—to establish the French laws, and a trial without jury, in civil cases, and the English laws, with a trial by jury, in criminal—to secure to the Roman Catholic clergy, except the regulars, the legal enjoyment of their estates, and their tythes, from all who were of their own religion. Not only the spirit but the letter of this act were so contrary to the English constitution, that it diminished the popularity of the measures which had been formed against the Americans.

Among the more southern colonists, it was conceived that its evident object was to make the inhabitants of Canada fit instruments, in the hands of power, to reduce them to a state of slavery.

They well remembered the embarrassments occasioned to them in the late war between France and England, by the French inhabitants of Canada—they supposed that the British administration meant, at this time, to use these people in the same line of attack, for their subjugation. As Great-Britain had new modelled the chartered government of Massachusetts, and claimed an authority so to do in every province, the colonists were apprehensive, that in the plenitude of her power, she would impose on each of them, in their turns, a constitution similar to what she had projected, for the province of Canada.

They foresaw, or thought they foresaw, the annihilation of their ancient assemblies, and their whole legislative business transferred to creatures of the crown. The legal parliamentary right to a maintenance conferred on the clergy of the Roman Catholic religion, gave great offence to many in England, but the political consequences expected to result from it, were most dreaded by the colonists.

[111] They viewed the whole act as an evidence that hostilities were intended against them, and that part of it which respected religion, as calculated to make Roman Catholicks subservient to the purposes of military coercion.

CHAPTER III

The session of parliament which passed these memorable acts, had stretched far into summer. As it drew near a close, the most sanguine expectations were indulged, that from the resolution and great unanimity of parliament on all American questions, the submission of the colonies would be immediate, and their future obedience and tranquility effectually secured. The triumphs and congratulations of the friends of the ministry, were unusually great.

In passing the acts which have been just mentioned, dissentients in favour of America, were unusually few. The ministerial majority, believing that the refractory colonists depended chiefly on the countenance of their English abettors, were of opinion, that as soon as they received intelligence of the decrease of their friends, and of the decisive conduct of parliament, they would acquiesce in the will of Great-Britain—the fame and grandeur of the nation was such, that it was never imagined they would seriously dare to contend with so formidable a people. The late triumphs of Great-Britain had made such an impression on her rulers, that they believed the Americans, on seeing the ancient spirit of the nation revive, would not risque a trial of prowess with those fleets and armies, which the combined force of France and Spain, were unable to resist. By an impious confidence in their superior strength, they precipitated the nation into rash measures, from the dire effects of which, the world may learn a useful lesson.

CHAPTER IV

Proceedings of the Colonies in 1774, in consequence of the Boston Port Act, viz.

THE WINTER WHICH FOLLOWED the destruction of the tea in Boston, was an anxious one to those of the [112] colonists who were given to reflection. Many conjectures were formed about the line of conduct, Great-Britain would probably adopt, for the support of her dignity. The fears of the most timid were more than realized by the news of the Boston port bill. This arrived on the 10th of May, and its operation was to commence the first of the next month. Various town meetings were called to deliberate on the state of public affairs. On the 13th of May, the town of Boston passed the following vote.

1774

That it is the opinion of this town, that if the other colonies come into a joint resolution to stop all importation from Great-Britain and the West-Indies, till the act for blocking up this harbour be repealed, the same will prove the salvation of North-America, and her liberties. On the other hand if they continue their exports and imports, there is high reason to fear that fraud, power, and the most odious oppression, will rise triumphant over justice, right, social happiness, and freedom. And moreover that this vote, be transmitted by the moderator, to all our sister colonies, in the name and behalf of this town.

Copies of this vote were transmitted to each of the colonies. The opposition to Great-Britain, had hitherto called forth the pens of the ingenious, and in some instances imposed the self denial of non-importation agreements: but the bulk of the people, had little to do with the dispute. The spirited conduct of the people of Boston, in destroying the tea, and the alarming precedents set by Great-Britain, in consequence thereof, brought subjects into discussion, with which every peasant and day labourer was concerned.

The patriots who had hitherto guided the helm, knew well, that if the other colonies did not support the people of Boston, they must be crushed, and it was equally obvious, that in their coercion a precedent, injurious to liberty, would be established. It was therefore the interest of Boston to draw in the other colonies. It was also the interest of the patriots in all the colonies, to bring over the bulk of the people, to adopt such efficient measures as were likely to extricate the inhabitants of [113] Boston from the unhappy situation in which they were involved. To effect these purposes much prudence as well as patriotism was necessary. The other provinces were but remotely affected by the fate of Massachusetts. They were happy, and had no cause, on their own account, to oppose the government of Great-Britain. That a people so circumstanced, should take part with a distressed neighbour, at the risque of incurring the resentment of the Mother Country, did not accord with the selfish maxims by which states, as well as individuals, are usually governed. The ruled are, for the most part, prone to suffer as long as evils are tolerable, and in general they must feel before they are roused to contend with their oppressors; but the Americans acted on a contrary principle.

They commenced an opposition to Great-Britain, and ultimately engaged in a defensive war, on speculation. They were not so much moved by oppression actually felt, as by a conviction that a foundation was laid, and a precedent about to be established for future oppressions. To convince the bulk of the people, that they had an interest in foregoing a present good, and submitting to a present evil, in order to obtain a future greater good, and to avoid a future greater evil, was the task assigned to the colonial patriots. But it called for the exertion of their utmost abilities. They effected it in a great measure, by means of the press. Pamphlets, essays, addresses and news paper dissertations were daily presented to the public, proving that Massachusetts was suffering in the common cause, and that interest and policy, as well as good neighbourhood, required the united exertions of all the colonies, in support of that much injured province. It was inculcated on the people, that if the ministerial schemes were suffered to take effect in Massachusetts, the other colonies must expect the loss of their charters, and that a new government would be imposed upon them, like that projected for Quebec. The king and parliament held no patronage in America, sufficient to oppose this torrent. The few who ventured to write in their favour found a difficulty in communicating their sentiments to the public. [114] No pensions or preferments awaited their exertions. Neglect and contempt were their usual portion, but popularity, consequence, and fame, were the rewards of those who stepped forward in the cause of liberty. In order to interest the great body of people, the few who were at the helm, disclaimed any thing more decisive, than convening the inhabitants, and taking their sense on what was proper to be done. In the mean time great pains were taken to prepare them for the adoption of vigorous measures.

The words whigs and tories, for want of better, were now introduced, as the distinguishing names of parties. By the former, were meant those who were for making a common cause with Boston, and supporting the colonies in their opposition to the claims of parliament. By the latter those who were at least so far favourers of Great-Britain, that they wished, either that no measures, or only palliative measures, should be adopted in opposition to her schemes.

These parties were so nearly balanced in New-York, that nothing more was agreed to at the first meeting of the inhabitants, than a recommendation to call a Congress.

At Philadelphia the patriots had a delicate part to act. The government of the colony being proprietary, a multitude of officers connected with that interest, had much to fear from convulsions, and nothing to expect from a revolution. A still greater body of people called Quakers, denied the lawfulness of war, and therefore could not adopt such measures for the support of Boston, as naturally tended to produce an event so adverse to their system of religion.

The citizens of Boston, not only sent forward their public letter, to the citizens of Philadelphia; but accompanied it with private communications to individuals of known patriotism and influence, in which they stated the impossibility of their standing alone, against the torrent of ministerial vengeance, and the indispensable necessity, that the leading colony of Pennsylvania, should afford them its support and countenance. The advocates in Philadelphia, for making a common cause [115] with Boston, were fully sensible of the state of parties in Pennsylvania. They saw the dispute with Great-Britain, brought to a crisis, and a new scene opening, which required exertions different from any heretofore made. The success of these they well knew, depended on the wisdom with which they were planned, and the union of the whole people, in carrying them into execution. They saw the propriety of proceeding with the greatest circumspection; and therefore resolved at their first meeting, on nothing more than to call a general meeting of the inhabitants, on the next evening. At this second meeting the patriots had so much moderation and policy, as to urge nothing decisive, contenting themselves with taking the sense of the inhabitants, simply on the propriety of sending an answer to the public letter from Boston. This was universally approved. The letter agreed upon was firm but temperate.

MAY 20

21

They acknowledged the difficulty of offering advice on the present occasion, sympathized with the people of Boston in their distress, and observed that all lenient measures, for their relief, should be first tried. That if the making restitution for the tea destroyed, would put an end to the unhappy controversy, and leave the people of Boston upon their ancient footing of constitutional liberty, it could not admit of a doubt what part they should act. But that it was not the value of the tea, it was the indefeasible right of giving and granting their own money, which was the matter in consideration. That it was the common cause of America; and therefore necessary in their opinion, that a congress of deputies from the several colonies should be convened to devise means for restoring harmony between Great-Britain and the colonies, and preventing matters from coming to extremities. Till this could be brought about, they recommended firmness, prudence, and moderation to the immediate sufferers, assuring them, that the people of Pennsylvania would continue to evince a firm adherence to the cause of American liberty.

In order to awaken the attention of the people, a series of letters was published well calculated to rouse [116] them to a sense of their danger, and point out the fatal consequences of the late acts of parliament. Every newspaper teemed with dissertations in favour of liberty—with debates of the members of parliament, especially with the speeches of the favourers of America, and the protests of the dissenting lords. The latter had a particular effect on the colonists, and were considered by them as irrefragable proofs, that the late acts against Massachusetts were unconstitutional and arbitrary.

The minds of the people being thus prepared, the friends of liberty promoted a petition to the governor, for convening the assembly. This they knew would not be granted, and that the refusal of it, would smooth the way for calling the inhabitants together. The governor having refused to call the assembly, a general meeting of the inhabitants was requested. About 8000 met and adopted sundry spirited resolutions. In these they declared, that the Boston port act was unconstitutional—that it was expedient to convene a continental congress—to appoint a committee for the city and county of Philadelphia, to correspond with their sister colonies and the several counties of Pennsylvania, and to invest that committee with power, to determine on the best mode for collecting the sense of the province, and appointing deputies to attend a general congress. Under the sanction of this last resolve, the committee appointed for that purpose, wrote a circular letter to all the counties of the Province, requesting them to appoint deputies to a general meeting, proposed to be held on the 15th of July, part of this letter was in the following words:

We would not offer such an affront to the well known public spirit of Pennsylvanians, as to question your zeal on the present occasion. Our very existence in the rank of freemen, and the security of all that ought to be dear to us, evidently depends on our conducting this great cause to its proper issue, by firmness, wisdom, and magnanimity. It is with pleasure we assure you, that all the colonies from South-Carolina to New-Hampshire, are animated with one spirit, in the common cause, and consider that as the proper crisis for having our differences with the Mother Country [117] brought to some certain issue, and our liberties fixed upon a permanent foundation, this desirable end can only be accomplished by a free communication of sentiments, and a sincere and fervent regard for the interests of our common country.

The several counties readily complied with the request of the inhabitants of Philadelphia, and appointed deputies, who met at the time appointed, and passed sundry resolves, in which they reprobated the late acts of parliament—expressed their sympathy with Boston, as suffering in the common cause—approved of holding a congress, and declared their willingness to make any sacrifices that might be recommended by a congress, for securing their liberties.

Thus, without tumult, disorder, or divided counsels, the whole province of Pennsylvania was, by prudent management and temperate proceedings, brought into the opposition with its whole weight and influence. This is the more remarkable as it is probable, that if the sentiments of individuals had been separately taken, there would have been a majority against involving themselves in the consequences of taking part with the destroyers of the tea, at Boston.

While these proceedings were carrying on in Pennsylvania, three of the most distinguished patriots of Philadelphia, under color of an excursion of pleasure, made a tour throughout the province, in order to discover the real sentiments of the common people. They were well apprized of the consequences of taking the lead in a dispute which every day became more serious, unless they could depend on being supported by the yeomanry of the country. By freely associating and conversing with many of every class and denomination; they found them unanimous in that fundamental principle of the American controversy, "That the parliament of Great-Britain had no right to tax them." From their general determination on this subject, a favorable prognostic was formed, of a successful opposition to the claims of Great-Britain.

In Virginia the house of burgesses on the 26th of May, 1774, resolved, that the first of June, the day on which [118] the operation of the Boston port bill was to commence, should be set apart by the members as a day of fasting, humiliation and prayer, "devoutly to implore the divine interposition, for averting the heavy calamities which threatened destruction to their civil rights, and the evils of a civil war—to give them one heart and one mind, to oppose by all just and proper means, every injury to American rights." On the publication of this resolution, the royal governor, the Earl of Dunmore dissolved them. The members notwithstanding their dissolution, met in their private capacities, and signed an agreement, in which, among other things, they declared, "that an attack made on one of their sister colonies, to compel submission to arbitrary taxes, was an attack made on all British America, and threatened ruin to the rights of all, unless the united wisdom of the whole be applied."

In South-Carolina the vote of the town of Boston of the 13th of May, being presented to a number of the leading citizens in Charleston, it was unanimously agreed to call a meeting of the inhabitants.

That this might be as general as possible, letters were sent to every parish and district in the province, and the people were invited to attend, either personally, or by their representatives at a general meeting of the inhabitants. A large number assembled, in which were some, from almost every part of the province. The proceedings of the parliament against the province of Massachusetts were distinctly related to this convention. Without one dissenting voice, they passed sundry resolutions, expressive of their rights, and of their sympathy with the people of Boston. They also chose five delegates to represent them in a continental Congress, and invested them "with full powers, and authority, in behalf of them and their constituents, to concert, agree to, and effectually to prosecute such legal measures as in their opinion, and the opinion of the other members, would be most likely to obtain a redress of American grievances."

JULY 18, 1774

The events of this time may be transmitted to posterity, but the agitation of the public mind can never be fully comprehended, but by those who were witnesses of it.

[119] In the counties and towns of the several provinces, as well as in the cities, the people assembled and passed resolutions, expressive of their rights, and of their detestation of the late American

acts of parliament. These had an instantaneous effect on the minds of thousands. Not only the young and impetuous, but the aged and temperate, joined in pronouncing them to be unconstitutional and oppressive. They viewed them as deadly weapons aimed at the vitals of that liberty, which they adored; as rendering abortive the generous pains taken by their forefathers, to procure for them in a new world, the quiet enjoyment of their rights. They were the subjects of their meditation when alone, and of their conversation when in company.

Within little more than a month, after the news of the Boston port bill reached America, it was communicated from state to state, and a flame was kindled, in almost every breast, through the widely extended provinces.

In order to understand the mode by which this flame was spread with such rapidity over so great an extent of country, it is necessary to observe, that the several colonies were divided into counties, and these again subdivided into districts, distinguished by the names of towns, townships, precincts, hundreds or parishes. In New-England the subdivisions which are called towns, were by law, bodies corporate—had their regular meetings, and might be occasionally convened by their proper officers. The advantages derived from these meetings, by uniting the whole body of the people in the measures taken to oppose the stamp act, induced other provinces to follow the example. Accordingly under the association which was formed to oppose the revenue act of 1767, committees were established not only in the capitals of every province, but also in most of the subordinate districts. Great-Britain, without designing it, had by her two preceding attempts at American revenue, taught her colonies not only the advantages, but the means of union. The system of committees, which prevailed in 1765, and also in 1767, was revived in 1774. By them there was a quick transmission of intelligence from the capital towns through [120] the subordinate districts to the whole body of the people, and a union of counsels and measures was effected among widely disseminated inhabitants.

It is perhaps impossible for human wisdom, to contrive any system more subservient to these purposes, than such a reciprocal exchange of intelligence, by committees. From the want of such a communication with each other, and consequently of union among themselves, many states have lost their liberties, and more have been unsuccessful in their attempts to regain them, after they have been lost.

What the eloquence and talents of Demosthenes could not effect among the states of Greece, might have been effected by the simple device of committees of correspondence. The few have been enabled to keep the many in subjection in every age, from the want of union among the latter. Several of the provinces of Spain complained of oppression under Charles the 5th, and in transports of rage took arms against him; but they never consulted or communicated with each other. They resisted separately, and were therefore separately subdued.

The colonists sympathizing with their distressed brethren in Massachusetts, felt themselves called upon, to do something for their relief; but to determine on what was proper to be done, did not so obviously occur. It was a natural idea, that for harmonising their measures, a Congress of deputies from each province should be convened. This early occurred to all, and being agreed to by all, was the means of procuring union and concert among inhabitants, removed several hundred miles from each other. In times less animated, various questions about the place and legality of their meeting, and about the extent of their power, would have produced a great diversity of sentiments; but on this occasion, by the special agency of providence, there was the same universal bent of inclination in the great body of the people. A sense of common danger, extinguished selfish passions. The public attention was fixed on the great cause of liberty. Local attachments and partialities, were sacrificed on the altar of patriotism.

There were not wanting moderate men, who would [121] have been willing to pay for the tea destroyed, if that would have put an end to the controversy, for it was not the value of the tea nor of the tax, but the indefeasible right of giving and granting their money, for which the colonists contended. The act of parliament was so cautiously worded, as to prevent the opening of the port of Boston, even though the East-India company had been reimbursed for all damages, "until it was made [to] appear to his majesty in council, that peace and obedience to the laws were so far restored in the town of Boston, that the trade of Great-Britain might be safely carried on there and his majesty's customs duly collected." The latter part of this limitation, "the due collection of his majesty's customs," was understood to comprehend submission to the late revenue laws. It was therefore inferred, that payment for the tea destroyed, would produce no certain relief, unless they were willing to give operation to the law, for raising a revenue on future importations of that commodity, and also to acquiesce in the late mutilation of their charter. As it was deliberately resolved, never to submit to either the most lukewarm of well informed patriots, possessing the public confidence, neither advised nor wished for the adoption of that measure. A few in Boston, who were known to be in the royal interest, proposed a resolution for that purpose, but they met with no support. Of the many who joined the British in the course of the war, there was scarcely an individual to be found in this early stage of the controversy, who advocated the right of parliamentary taxation. There were doubtless many timid persons, who fearing the power of Britain, would rather have submitted to her encroachments, than risque the vengeance of her arms, but such for the most part suppressed their sentiments. Zeal for liberty, being immediately rewarded with applause, the patriots had every inducement to come forward, and avow their principles; but there was something so unpopular in appearing to be influenced by timidity, interest or excessive caution, when essential interests were attacked, that such persons shunned public notice, and sought the shade of retirement.

[122] In the three first months, which followed the shutting up of the port of Boston, the inhabitants of the colonies in hundreds of small circles, as well as in their provincial assemblies and congresses, expressed their abhorrence of the late proceedings of the British parliament against Massachusetts—their concurrence in the proposed measure of appointing deputies for a general congress, and their willingness to do and suffer whatever should be judged conducive to the establishment of their liberties.

A patriotic flame, created and diffused by the contagion of sympathy, was communicated to so many breasts, and reflected from such a variety of objects, as to become too intense to be resisted.

While the combination of the other colonies to support Boston, was gaining strength, new matter of dissention daily took place in

Massachusetts. The resolution for shutting the port of Boston, was no sooner taken, than it was determined to order a military force to that town. General Gage, the commander in chief of the royal forces in North-America, was also sent thither, in the additional capacity of Governor of Massachusetts. He arrived in Boston on the third day after the inhabitants received the first intelligence of the Boston port bill. Though the people were irritated by that measure, and though their republican jealousy was hurt by the combination of the civil and military character in one person, yet the general was received with all the honours which had been usually paid to his predecessors. Soon after his arrival, two regiments of foot, with a detachment of artillery and some cannon, were landed in Boston. These troops were by degrees re-inforced, with others from Ireland, New-York, Halifax and Quebec.

The governor announced that he had the king's particular command, for holding the general court at Salem, after the first of June. When that eventful day arrived, the act for shutting up the port of Boston commenced its operation. It was devoutly kept at Williamsburgh, as a day of fasting and humiliation. In Philadelphia it was solemnized with every manifestation of public calamity and grief. The inhabitants shut up their houses. After [123] divine service a stillness reigned over the city, which exhibited an appearance of the deepest distress.

In Boston a new scene opened on the inhabitants. Hitherto, that town had been the seat of commerce and of plenty. The immense business carried on therein, afforded a comfortable subsistence to many thousands. The necessary—the useful, and even some of the elegant arts were cultivated among them. The citizens were polite and hospitable. In this happy state they were sentenced on the short notice of twenty one days, to a total deprivation of all means of subsisting. The blow reached every person. The rents of the landholders, either ceased or were greatly diminished. The immense property in stores and wharfs, was rendered comparatively useless. Labourers, artificers and others, employed in the numerous occupations created by an extensive trade, partook in the general calamity. They who depended on a regular income, flowing from previous acquisitions of property, as well as they who with the sweat of their brow, earned their daily subsistence, were equally deprived of the means of support; and the chief difference between them, was that the distresses of the former were rendered more intolerable by the recollection of past enjoyments. All these inconveniencies and hardships, were born with a passive, but inflexible fortitude. Their determination to persist in the same line of conduct, which had been the occasion of their suffering was unabated.

The authors and advisers of the resolution for destroying the tea, were in the town, and still retained their popularity and influence. The execrations of the inhabitants fell not on them, but on the British parliament. Their countrymen acquitted them of all selfish designs, and believed that in their opposition to the measures of Great-Britain, they were actuated by an honest zeal for constitutional liberty. The sufferers in Boston had the consolation of sympathy from the other colonists. Contributions were raised in all quarters for their relief. Letters and addresses came to them from corporate bodies, town meetings and provincial conventions, applauding their conduct, and exhorting them to perseverance.

[124] The people of Marblehead, who by their proximity were likely to reap advantage from the distresses of Boston, generously offered the merchants thereof, the use of their harbour, wharfs, warehouses, and also their personal attendance on the lading or unlading of their goods free of all expence.

The inhabitants of Salem in an address to governor Gage, concluded with these remarkable words,

> By shutting up the port of Boston, some imagine that the course of trade might be turned hither, and to our benefit: But nature in the formation of our harbour, forbid, our becoming rivals in commerce with that convenient mart; and were it otherwise, we must be dead to every idea of justice, lost to all feelings of humanity, could we indulge one thought to seize on wealth, and raise our fortunes on the ruins of our suffering neighbours.

The Massachusetts general court met at Salem, according to adjournment, on the 7th of June. Several of the popular leaders took, in a private way, the sense of the members on what was proper to be done. Finding they were able to carry such measures as the public exigencies required, they prepared resolves and moved for their adoption. But before they went on the latter business, their door was shut.

One member nevertheless contrived means of sending information to governor Gage of what was doing. His secretary was sent off to dissolve the general court, but was refused admission. As he could obtain no entrance, he read the proclamation at the door, and immediately after in council, and thus dissolved the general court. The house while sitting with their doors shut, appointed five of the most respectable inhabitants as their committee, to meet committees from other provinces, that might be convened the first of September at Philadelphia—voted them 75 pounds sterling each, and recommended to the several towns and districts to raise the said sum by equitable proportions. By these means the designs of the governor were disappointed. His situation in every respect was truly disagreeable. It was his duty to forward the execution of laws which were universally execrated. Zeal for [125] his master's service, prompted him to endeavour that they should be carried into full effect, but his progress was retarded by obstacles from every quarter. He had to transact his official business with a people who possessed a high sense of liberty, and were uncommonly ingenious in evading disagreeable acts of parliament. It was a part of his duty to prevent the calling of the town meetings after the first of August, 1774. These meetings were nevertheless held. On his proposing to exert authority for the dispersion of the people, he was told by the select men, that they had not offended against the act of parliament, for that only prohibited the calling of town meetings, and that no such call had been made: A former constitutional meeting before the first of August, having only adjourned themselves from time to time. Other evasions, equally founded on the letter, of even the late obnoxious laws, were practised.

As the summer advanced, the people of Massachusetts received stronger proofs of support from the neighbouring provinces. They were therefore encouraged to farther opposition. The inhabitants of the colonies, at this time, with regard to political opinions, might be divided into three classes; of these, one was for rushing precipitately into extremities. They were for immediately stopping all trade, and could not even brook the delay of waiting till the proposed continental congress should meet. Another party, equally respectable, both as to character, property, and patriotism, was more moderate, but not less firm. These were averse to the adoption of any violent resolutions, till all others were ineffectually tried. They wished that a clear statement of their rights, claims, and grievances, should precede every other measure. A third class disapproved of what was generally going on. A few from principle, and a persuasion that they ought to submit to the Mother Country; some from the love of ease, others from self-interest, but the bulk from fear of the mischievous consequences likely to follow: All these latter classes, for the most part, lay still, while the friends of liberty acted with spirit. If they, or any of them, ventured to oppose popular measures, they [126] were not supported, and therefore declined farther efforts. The resentment of the people was so strong against them, that they sought for peace by remaining quiet. The same indecision that made them willing to submit to Great-Britain, made them apparently acquiesce in popular measures which they disapproved. The spirited part of the community, being on the side of liberty, the patriots had the appearance of unanimity; though many either kept at a distance from public meetings, or voted against their own opinion, to secure themselves from resentment, and promote their present ease and interest.

Under the influence of those who were for the immediate adoption of efficacious measures, an agreement by the name of the solemn league and covenant, was adopted by numbers. The subscribers of this, bound themselves to suspend all commercial intercourse with Great-Britain, until the late obnoxious laws were repealed, and the colony of Massachusetts restored to its chartered rights.

General Gage published a proclamation, in which he stiled this JUNE 29 solemn league and covenant, "An unlawful, hostile, and traiterous combination." And all magistrates were charged, to apprehend and secure for trial, such as should have any agency in publishing or subscribing the same, or any similar covenant. This proclamation had no other effect, than to exercise the pens of the lawyers, in shewing that the association did not come within the description of legal treason, and that therefore the governor's proclamation was not warranted by the principles of the constitution.

The late law, for regulating the government of the provinces, arrived near the beginning of August, and was accompanied with a list of 36 new counsellors, appointed by the crown, and in a mode, variant from that prescribed by the charter. Several of these in the first instance, declined an acceptance of the appointment. Those, who accepted of it, were every where declared to be enemies to their country. The new judges were rendered incapable of proceeding in their official duty. Upon opening the courts, the juries refused to be sworn, or to act in any manner, either under them, or in conformity to the late [127] regulations. In some places, the people assembled, and filled the court-houses and avenues to them in such a manner, that neither the judges, nor their officers could obtain entrance; and upon the sheriff's commanding them, to make way for the court, they answered, "That they knew no court independent of the ancient laws of their country, and to none other would they submit."

AUG. 4

In imitation of his royal master, governor Gage issued a proclamation "for the encouragement of piety and virtue, and for the prevention and punishing vice, prophaneness and immorality." In this proclamation, hypocrisy was inserted as one of the immoralities against which the people were warned. This was considered by the inhabitants, who had often been ridiculed for their strict attention to the forms of religion, to be a studied insult, and as such was more resented than an actual injury. It greatly added to the inflammation which had already taken place in their minds.

The proceedings and apparent dispositions of the people, together with the military preparations which were daily made through the province, induced general Gage to fortify that neck of land which joins Boston to the continent.

He also seized upon the powder which was lodged in the arsenal at Charlestown.

SEPT. 1

This excited a most violent and universal ferment. Several thousands of the people assembled at Cambridge, and it was with difficulty they were restrained from marching directly to Boston, to demand a delivery of the powder, with a resolution in case of refusal to attack the troops.

The people thus assembled, proceeded to lieutenant governor Oliver's house, and to the houses of several of the new counsellors, and obliged them to resign, and to declare that they would no more act under the laws lately enacted. In the confusion of these transactions a rumor went abroad, that the royal fleet and troops were firing upon the town of Boston. This was probably designed by the popular leaders, on purpose to ascertain what aid they might expect from the country in case of extremities. The result exceeded their most sanguine expectations. [128] In less than twenty four hours, there were upwards of 30,000 men in arms, and marching towards the capital. Other risings of the people took place in different parts of the colony, and their violence was such, that in a short time the new counsellors, the commissioners of the customs, and all who had taken an active part in favour of Great-Britain, were obliged to skreen themselves in Boston. The new seat of government at Salem was abandoned, and all the officers connected with the revenue were obliged to consult their safety, by taking up their residence in a place which an act of parliament had proscribed from all trade.

About this time, delegates from every town and district in the county of Suffolk, of which Boston is the county town, had a meeting, at which they prefaced a number of spirited resolutions, containing a detail of the particulars of their intended opposition to the late acts of parliament, with a general declaration, "That no obedience was due from the province to either, or any part of the said acts, but that they should be rejected as the attempts of a wicked administration to enslave America." The resolves of this meeting were sent on to Philadelphia, for the information and opinion of the Congress, which, as shall be hereafter related, had met there about this time.

The people of Massachusetts rightly judged, that from the decision of congress on these resolutions, they would be enabled to determine what support they might expect. Notwithstanding present appearances they feared that the other colonies, who were no more than remotely concerned, would not hazard the consequences of making a common cause with them, should subsequent events make it necessary to repel force by force. The decision of Congress exceeded their expectations. They "most thoroughly approved the wisdom and fortitude with which opposition to wicked ministerial measures had been hitherto conducted in Massachusetts, and recommended to them perseverance in the same firm and temperate conduct as expressed in the resolutions of the delegates from the county of Suffolk." By this approbation and advice, the [129] people of Massachusetts were encouraged to resistance, and the other colonies became bound to support them. The former, more in need of a bridle than a spur, proceeded as they had begun, but with additional confidence.

Governor Gage had issued writs for holding a general assembly at Salem; but subsequent events, and the heat and violence which every where prevailed, made him think it expedient to counteract the writs by a proclamation for suspending the meeting of the members. The legality of a proclamation for that purpose was denied, and in defiance thereof 90 of the newly elected members met at the time and place appointed. They soon after resolved themselves into a provincial congress, and adjourned to Concord, about 20 miles from Charlestown. On their meeting there, they chose Mr. Hancock president, and proceeded to business. One of their first acts was to appoint a committee to wait on the governor, with a remonstrance, in which they apologized for their meeting, from the distressed state of the colony; complained of their grievances, and, after stating their apprehensions, from the hostile preparations on Boston neck, concluded with an earnest request, "That he would desist from the construction of the fortress at the entrance into Boston, and restore that pass to its natural state." The governor found some difficulty in giving them an answer, as they were not, in his opinion, a legal body, but the necessity of the times over-ruled his scruples. He replied, by expressing his indignation at the supposition, "That the lives, liberties or property of any people, except enemies, could be in danger, from English troops." He reminded them, that while they complained of alterations made in their charter, by acts of parliament, they were by their own acts subverting it altogether. He therefore warned them of the rocks they were upon; and to desist from such illegal and unconstitutional proceedings. The governor's admonitions were unavailing. The provincial congress appointed a committee to draw up a plan for the immediate defence of the province. It was resolved to inlist a number of the inhabitants under the name of minute men, who were to be under obligations to turn out at a [130] minute's warning. Jedediah Pribble, Artemas Ward and Seth Pomeroy, were elected general officers to command those minute men and the militia, in case they should be called out to action. A committee of safety, and a committee of supplies were appointed. These consisted of different persons and were intended for different purposes. The first were invested with an authority to assemble the militia when they thought proper, and were to recommend to the committee of supplies the purchase of such articles as the public exigencies required; the last were limited to the small sum of £15,627.15s. sterl. which was all the money at first voted to oppose the power and riches of Great Britain. Under this authority, and with these means, the committees of safety and of supplies, acting in concert, laid in a quantity of stores, partly at Worcester and partly at Concord. The NOV. 23 same congress met again, and soon after resolved to get in readiness twelve thousand men to act on any given emergency; and that a fourth part of the militia should be inlisted as minute men, and receive pay. John Thomas and William Heath were appointed general officers. They also sent persons to New-Hampshire, Rhode-Island and Connecticut, to inform them of the steps they had taken and to request their co-operation in making up an army of 20,000 men. Committees from these several colonies met with a committee from the provincial congress of Massachusetts, and settled their plans. The proper period of commencing opposition to general Gage's troops, was determined to be whenever they marched out with their baggage, ammunition and artillery. The aid of the clergy was called in upon this occasion, and a circular letter was addressed to each of the several ministers in the province, requesting their assistance "in avoiding the dreadful slavery with which they were threatened."

As the winter approached, general Gage ordered barracks for his troops to be erected, but such was the superior influence of the popular leaders, that on their recommendation the workmen desisted from fulfilling the general's wishes, though the money for their labour would have been paid by the crown.

An application to New-York was equally unsuccessful, [131] and it was with difficulty that the troops could be furnished with winter 1774 lodgings. Similar obstructions were thrown in the way of getting winter covering for the soldiery. The merchants of New-York on being applied to, answered, "That they would never supply any article for the benefit of men who were sent as enemies to the country." The inhabitants of Massachusetts encouraged the desertion of the soliders; and acted systematically in preventing their obtaining any other supplies but necessary provisions. The farmers were discouraged from selling them straw, timber, boards and such like articles of convenience. Straw, when purchased for their service, was frequently burnt. Vessels, with bricks intended for their use, were sunk, and carts with wood were overturned, and the king's property by one contrivance or other, was daily destroyed.

A proclamation had been issued by the king, prohibiting the exportation of military stores from Britain, which reached America in the latter end of the year 1774. On receiving intelligence thereof, in Rhode-Island, the people seized upon and removed from the public battery about 40 pieces of cannon; and the assembly passed resolutions for obtaining arms and military stores by every means, and also for raising and arming the inhabitants: soon after 400 men beset

DEC. 14   his majesty's castle at Portsmouth. They sustained a fire from three four-pounders and small arms, but before they could be ready for a second fire, the assailants stormed the fort, and secured and confined the garrison till they broke open the powder house, and took the powder away. The powder being secured, the garrison was released from confinement.

Throughout this whole season, civil government, legislation, judicial proceedings and commercial regulations were in Massachusetts, to all appearance, annihilated. The provincial Congress exercised all the semblance of government which existed. From their coincidence, with the prevailing disposition, of the people, their resolutions had the weight and efficacy of laws. Under the simple stile of recommendation, they organized the militia, made ordinances respecting public monies and such farther regulations [132] as were necessary for

1774   preserving order, and for defending themselves against the British troops.

In this crisis it seemed to be the sense of the inhabitants of Massachusetts to wait events. They dreaded every evil that could flow from resistance, less than the operation of the late acts of parliament, but at the same time were averse to be the aggressors in bringing on a civil war. They chose to submit to a suspension of regular government, in preference to permitting the streams of justice to flow in the channel prescribed by the late acts of parliament, or to conducting them forcibly in the old one, sanctioned by their charter. From the extinction of the old, and the rejection of the new constitution, all regular government was for several months abolished. Some hundred thousands of people, were in a state of nature without legislation, magistrates or executive officers: there was nevertheless a surprising degree of order. Men of the purest morals were among the most active opposers of Great-Britain. While municipal laws ceased to operate, the laws of reason, morality and religion, bound the people to each other as a social band, and preserved as great a degree of a decorum as had at any time prevailed. Even those who were opposed to the proceedings of the populace when they were prudent and moderate, for the most part enjoyed safety both at home and abroad.

Though there were no civil officers, there was an abundance of military ones. These were chosen by the people, but exercised more authority than any who had been honoured with commissions from the governor. The inhabitants in every place devoted themselves to arms. Handling the musket, and training, were the fashionable amusements of the men, while the women by their presence, encouraged them to proceed. The sound of drums and fifes was to be heard in all directions. The young and the old were fired with a martial spirit. On experiment it was found, that to force on the inhabitants, a form of government, to which they were totally averse, was not within the fancied omnipotence of parliament.

During these transactions in Massachusetts effectual [133] measures had been taken by the colonies for convening a continental   1774 Congress, though there was no one entitled to lead in this business, yet in consequence of the general impulse on the public mind, from a sense of common danger, not only the measure itself, but the time and place of meeting, were with surprising unanimity agreed upon. The colonies though formerly agitated with local prejudices, jealousies and aversions, were led to assemble together in a general diet, and to feel their weight and importance in a common union. Within four months from the day on which the first intelligence of the Boston port bill reached America, the deputies of eleven provinces had convened in Philadelphia, and in four days more, by the arrival of delegates from North-Carolina, there was a complete representation of twelve colonies, containing three millions of people, disseminated over 260,000 square miles of territory. Some of the delegates were appointed by the constitutional assemblies[;] in other provinces, where they were embarrassed by royal governors, the appointments were made in voluntary meetings of the people. Perhaps there never was a body of delegates more faithful to the interest of their constituents than the Congress of 1774. The public voice elevated none to a seat in that august assembly, but such as in addition to considerable abilities, possessed that ascendancy over the minds of their fellow citizens, which can neither be acquired by birth nor purchased by wealth. The instructions given to these deputies were various, but in general they contained strong professions of loyalty, and of constitutional dependence on the Mother Country: the framers of them acknowledged the prerogatives of the crown, and disclaimed every wish of separation from the Parent State. On the other hand, they were firm in declaring that they were entitled to all the rights of British born subjects, and that the late acts respecting Massachusetts were unconstitutional and oppressive.

They particularly stated their grievances, and for the most part concurred in authorising their deputies to concert and agree to such measures in behalf of their constituents [134], as in their joint opinion would be most likely to obtain a redress of American grievances, ascertain American rights, on constitutional principles, and establish union and harmony between Great-Britain and the colonies. Of the various instructions, on this occasion, those which were drawn up by a convention of delegates, from every county in the province of Pennsylvania, and presented by them in a body to the constitutional assembly, were the most precise and determinate. By these it appears, that the Pennsylvanians were disposed to submit to the acts of navigation, as they then stood, and also to settle a certain annual revenue on his majesty, his heirs and successors, subject to the control of parliament, and to satisfy all damages done to the East-India company, provided their grievances were redressed, and an amicable compact was settled, which, by establishing American rights in the manner of a new Magna Charta, would have precluded future disputes.

Of the whole number of deputies, which formed the Continental Congress, of 1774, one half were lawyers. Gentlemen of that profession had acquired the confidence of the inhabitants by their exertions in the common cause. The previous measures in the respective provinces had been planned and carried into effect, more by lawyers than by any other order of men. Professionally taught the rights of the people, they were among the foremost to decry every attack made on their liberties. Bred in the habits of public speaking, they made a distinguished figure in the meetings of the people, and were particularly able to explain to them the tendency of the late acts of parliament. Exerting their abilities and influence in the cause of their country, they were rewarded with its confidence.

On the meeting of Congress, they chose Peyton Randolph their president, and Charles Thomson their secretary. They agreed as one of the rules of their doing business, that no entry should be made on their journals of any propositions discussed before them, to which they did not finally assent.

This august body, to which all the colonies looked up [135] for wisdom and direction, had scarcely convened, when a dispute arose 1774 about the mode of conducting business, which alarmed the friends of union. It was contended by some, that the votes of the small provinces should not count as much as those of the larger ones. This was argued with some warmth and invidious comparisons were made between the extensive dominion of Virginia, and the small colonies of Delaware and Rhode-Island. The impossibility of fixing the comparative weight of each province, from the want of proper materials, induced Congress to resolve, that each should have one equal vote. The mode of conducting business being settled, two committees were appointed. One, to state the rights of the colonies, the several instances in which these rights had been violated, and the means most proper to be pursued for obtaining a restoration of them; the other, to examine and report the several statutes which affected the trade and manufactures of the colonies. The first committee were farther instructed to confine themselves to the consideration of such rights as had been infringed since the year 1763.

Congress soon after their meeting, agreed upon a declaration of their rights, by which it was among other things declared, that the inhabitants of the English colonies in North-America, by the immutable laws of nature, the principles of the English constitution, and the several charters or compacts, were entitled to life, liberty and property; and that they had never ceded to any sovereign power whatever, a right to dispose of either, without their consent. That their ancestors, who first settled the colonies were entitled to all the rights, liberties and immunities of free and natural born subjects within the realm of England, and that by their migrating to America, they by no means forfeited, surrendered or lost any of those rights; that the foundation of English liberty, and of all free government was, a right in the people to participate in their legislative council, and that as the English colonists were not, and could not be properly represented in the British parliament, they were entitled to a free and exclusive power of legislation in their [136] several provincial legislatures, in all cases of taxation and internal polity, subject only to the negative of their sovereign. They then run the line, between the supremacy of parliament, and the independency of the colonial legislatures by provisoes and restrictions, expressed in the following words.

1774

> But from the necessity of the case, and a regard to the mutual interests of both countries, we cheerfully consent to the operation of such acts of the British parliament, as are *bona fide*, restrained to the regulation of our external commerce, for the purpose of securing the commercial advantages of the whole empire to the Mother Country, and the commercial benefits of its respective members, excluding every idea of taxation, internal and external for raising a revenue on the subjects in America without their consent.

This was the very hinge of the controversy. The absolute unlimited supremacy of the British parliament, both in legislation and taxation, was contended for on one side; while on the other, no farther authority was conceded than such a limited legislation, with regard to external commerce, as would combine the interest of the whole empire. In government, as well as in religion, there are mysteries from the close investigation of which little advantage can be expected.

From the unity of the empire it was necessary, that some acts should extend over the whole. From the local situation of the colonies it was equally reasonable that their legislatures should at least in some matters be independent. Where the supremacy of the first ended and the independency of the last began, was to the best informed a puzzling question. Happy would it have been for both countries, had the discussion of this doubtful point never been attempted.

Congress also resolved, that the colonists were entitled to the common law of England, and more especially to the privilege of being tried by their peers of the vicinage. That they were entitled to the benefit of such of the English statutes as existed at the time of their colonization, and which they had found to be applicable to their local circumstances, and also to the immunities and privileges granted and confirmed to them by royal charters or secured [137] by provincial laws. That they had a right peaceably to assemble, consider of their grievances, and petition the king; that the keeping a standing army in the colonies, without the consent of the legislature of the colony where the army was kept, was against law. That it was indispensibly necessary to good government, and rendered essential by the English constitution, that the constituent branches of the legislature be independent of each other, and that therefore, the exercise of legislative power, in several colonies by a council, appointed during pleasure by the crown, was unconstitutional, dangerous and destructive to the freedom of American legislation. All of these liberties, Congress in behalf of themselves and their constituents, claimed, demanded and insisted upon as their indubitable rights, which could not be legally taken from them, altered or abridged by any power whatever, without their consent. Congress then resolved, that sundry acts, which had been passed in the reign of George the Third, were infringements and violations of the rights of the colonists, and that the repeal of them was essentially necessary, in order to restore harmony between Great-Britain and the colonies. The acts complained of, were as follow: The several acts of 4 George III. ch. 15 and ch. 34; 5 Geo. III. ch. 25; 6 Geo. III. ch. 52; 7 Geo. III. ch. 41 and ch. 46; 8 Geo. III. ch. 22 which imposed duties for the purpose of raising a revenue in America, extended the power of the admiralty courts beyond their ancient limits, deprived the American subject of trial by jury, authorized the judges certificate to indemnify the prosecutor from damages, that he might otherwise be liable to requiring oppressive security from a claimant of ships and goods seized before he was allowed to defend his property.

Also 12 Geo. III. ch. 24 entitled, "An act for the better securing his majesty's dock yards, magazines, ships, ammunition and stores," which declares a new offence in America, and deprives the American subject of a constitutional trial by jury of the vicinage, by authorizing the trial of any person charged with the committing any offence described in the said act out of the realm, to be indicted [138] and tried for the same in any shire or county within the realm.

1774

Also the three acts passed in the last session of parliament for stopping the port and blocking up the harbour of Boston, for altering the charter and government of Massachusetts Bay, and that which is entitled, "An act for the better administration of justice, &c."

Also the act passed in the same session, for establishing the Roman Catholic religion in the province of Quebec, abolishing the equitable system of English laws, and erecting a tyranny there to the great danger (from so total a dissimilarity of religion, law and government) of the neighbouring British colonies, by the assistance of whose blood and treasure the said country had been conquered from France.

Also the act passed in the same session, for the better providing suitable quarters for officers and soldiers in his majesty's service in North-America.

Also that the keeping a standing army in several of these colonies in time of peace, without the consent of the legislature of that colony in which such army was kept, was against law.

Congress declared, that they could not submit to these grievous acts and measures. In hopes that their fellow subjects in Great-Britain would restore the colonies to that state in which both countries found happiness and prosperity, they resolved for the present only to pursue the following peaceable measures: 1st, To enter into a non-importation, non-consumption and non-exportation agreement or association; 2d, To prepare an address to the people of Great-Britain, and a memorial to the inhabitants of British America; and 3dly, to prepare a loyal address to his majesty.

By the association they bound themselves and their constituents, from and after the 1st day of December next, not to import into British America, from Great-Britain or Ireland, any goods, wares or merchandize, whatsoever; not to purchase any slave, imported after the said first day of December; not to purchase or use any tea, imported on account of the East-India company, or [139] any on which a duty hath been or shall be paid; and from and after the first day of the next ensuing March, neither to purchase or use any East-India tea whatever. That they would not after the tenth day of the next September, if their grievances were not previously redressed, export any commodity whatsoever, to Great-Britain, Ireland or the West-Indies, except rice to Europe. That the merchants should, as soon as possible, write to their correspondents in Great-Britain and Ireland, not to ship any goods to them on any pretence whatever; and if any merchant there, should ship any goods for America, in order to contravene the non-importation agreement, they would not afterwards have any commercial connexion with such merchant; that such as were owners of vessels, should give positive orders to their captains and masters, not to receive on board their vessels, any goods prohibited by the said non-importation agreement; that they would use their endeavours to improve the breed of sheep and increase their numbers to the greatest extent; that they would encourage frugality, oeconomy and industry, and promote agriculture, arts and American manufactures; that they would discountenance and discourage every species of extravagance and dissipation, and that on the death of relations or friends, they would wear no other mourning than a small piece of black crape or ribbon; that such as were venders of goods, should not take any advantage of the scarcity so as to raise their prices; that if any person should import goods after the first day of December, and before the first day of February, then next ensuing, the same ought to be immediately reshipped or delivered up to a committee to be stored or sold: in the last case, all the clear profits to be applied towards the relief of the inhabitants of Boston; and that if any goods should be imported after the first day of February, then next ensuing, they should be sent back without breaking any of the packages; that committees be chosen in every county, city and town, to observe the conduct of all persons touching the association, and to publish in gazettes, the names of the violaters of it, as foes to the rights of British America; that the committees of correspondence [140] in the respective colonies frequently inspect the entries of their custom houses, and inform each other from time to time of the true state thereof; that all manufactures of America should be sold at reasonable prices; and no advantages be taken of a future scarcity of goods; and lastly, that they would have no dealings or intercourse whatever, with any province or colony of North-America, which should not accede to, or should violate the aforesaid associations.

These several resolutions, they bound themselves and their constituents, by the sacred ties of virtue, honour and love of their country, to observe till their grievances were redressed.

In their address to the people of Great-Britain they complimented them for having at every hazard maintained their independence, and transmitted the rights of man and the blessings of liberty to their posterity, and requested them not to be surprised, that they who were descended from the same common ancestors, should refuse to surrender their rights, liberties and constitution. They proceeded to state their rights and their grievances, and to vindicate themselves from the charges of being seditious, impatient of government and desirous of independency. They summed up their wishes in the following words, "Place us in the same situation that we were, at the close of the last war, and our former harmony will be restored."

In the memorial of Congress to the inhabitants of the British colonies, they recapitulated the proceedings of Great-Britain against them, since the year 1763, in order to impress them with a belief, that a deliberate system was formed for abridging their liberties. They then proceeded to state the measures they had adopted to counteract this system, and gave the reasons which induced them to adopt the same. They encouraged them to submit to the inconveniencies of non-importation and non-exportation by desiring them "to weigh in the opposite balance the endless miseries, they and their descendants must endure from an established arbitrary power." They concluded with informing them "that the schemes agitated against the colonies, had been so conducted as to render it prudent [141] to extend their views to mournful events, and to be in all respects prepared for every contingency."

In the petition of Congress to the king, they begged leave to lay their grievances before the throne. After a particular enumeration of these, they observed that they wholly arose from a destructive system of colony administration, adopted since the conclusion of the last

1774

war. They assured his majesty that they had made such provision for defraying the charges of the administration of justice, and the support of civil government, as had been judged just and suitable to their respective circumstances, and that for the defence, protection and security of the colonies, their militia would be fully sufficient in time of peace, and in case of war they were ready and willing, when constitutionally required, to exert their most strenuous efforts in granting supplies and raising forces. They said, "we ask but for peace, liberty and safety. We wish not a diminution of the prerogative, nor do we solicit the grant of any new right in our favour. Your royal authority over us, and our connexion with Great-Britain, we shall always carefully and zealously endeavour to support and maintain." They then solicited for a redress of their grievances, which they had enumerated, and appealing to that Being, who searches thoroughly the hearts of his creatures, they solemnly professed, "that their counsels had been influenced by no other motives, than a dread of impending destruction." They concluded with imploring his majesty, "for the honor of Almighty God, for his own glory, for the interests of his family, for the safety of his kingdoms and dominions, that as the loving father of his whole people, connected by the same bonds of law, loyalty, faith and blood, though dwelling in various countries, he would not suffer the transcendent relation formed by these ties, to be farther violated by uncertain expectation of effects, that if attained never could compensate for the calamities through which they must be gained."

The Congress also addressed the French inhabitants of Canada. In this they stated the right they had on becoming English subjects, to the benefits of the English [142] constitution. They explained what these rights were, and pointed out the difference between the constitution imposed on them by act of parliament, and that to which as British subjects they were entitled. They introduced their countryman Montesquieu, as reprobating their parliamentary constitution, and exhorting them to join their fellow colonists in support of their common rights. They earnestly invited them to join with the other colonies in one social compact, formed on the generous principles of equal liberty, and to this end recommended, that they would chuse delegates to represent them in Congress.

1774

All these addresses were written with uncommon ability. Coming from the heart, they were calculated to move it. Inspired by a love of liberty, and roused by a sense of common danger, the patriots of that day spoke, wrote and acted, with an animation unknown in times of public tranquility; but it was not so much on the probable effect of these addresses, that Congress founded their hopes of obtaining a redress of their grievances, as on the consequences which they expected from the operation of their non-importation, and non-exportation agreement. The success that had followed the adoption of a measure similar to the former, in two preceding instances, had encouraged the colonists to expect much from a repetition of it. They indulged, in extravagant opinions of the importance of their trade to Great-Britain. The measure of a non-exportation of their commodities was a new expedient, and from that, even more was expected than from the non-importation agreement. They supposed that it would produce such extensive distress among the merchants and manufacturers of Great-Britain, and especially among the inhabitants of the British West-India islands, as would induce their general co-operation in procuring a redress of American grievances. Events proved that young nations, like young people, are prone to over rate their own importance.

OCTOBER 26   Congress having finished all this important business, in less than eight weeks, dissolved themselves, after giving their opinion, "that another Congress should be held on the 10th of May next ensuing at Philadelphia, unless [143] the redress of their grievances should be 1774   previously obtained," and recommended "to all the colonies to chuse deputies as soon as possible, to be ready to attend at that time and place, should events make their meeting necessary."

On the publication of the proceedings of Congress, the people obtained that information which they desired. Zealous to do something for their country, they patiently waited for the decision of that body, to whose direction they had resigned themselves. Their determinations were no sooner known, than they were cheerfully obeyed. Though their power was only advisory, yet their recommendations were more generally and more effectually carried into execution, than the laws of the best regulated states. Every individual felt his liberties endangered, and was impressed with an idea, that his safety consisted in union. A common interest in warding off a common danger, proved a powerful incentive to the most implicit submission; provincial congresses and subordinate, committees were every where instituted. The resolutions of the Continental Congress, were sanctioned with the universal approbation of these new representative bodies, and institutions were formed under their direction to carry them into effect.

The regular constitutional assemblies also gave their assent to the measures recommended. The assembly of New-York, was the only legislature which withheld its approbation. Their metropolis had long been head quarters of the British army in the colonies, and many of their best families were connected with people of influence in Great-Britain. The unequal distribution of their land, fostered an aristocratic spirit. From the operation of these and other causes, the party for royal government, was both more numerous and respectable in New-York, than in any of the other colonies.

The assembly of Pennsylvania, though composed of a majority of Quakers, or of those who were friendly to their interests, was the first legal body of representatives that ratified unanimously the acts of the general Congress. They not only voted their approbation of what that [144] body had done, but appointed members to represent them in the new Congress, proposed to be held on the 10th day of May next ensuing, and took sundry steps to put the province in a posture of defence. 1774

To relieve the distresses of the people of Boston, liberal collections were made throughout the colonies, and forwarded for the supply of their immediate necessities. Domestic manufactures were encouraged, that the wants of the inhabitants from the non-importation agreement might be diminished, and the greatest zeal was discovered by a large majority of the people, to comply with the determinations of these new made representative bodies. In this manner, while the forms of the old government subsisted, a new and independent authority was virtually established. It was so universally the sense of the people, that the public good required a compliance with the recommendations of Congress, that any man who discovered an anxiety about the continuance of trade and business, was considered as a selfish individual, preferring private interest to the good of his country. Under the influence of these principles, the intemperate zeal of the populace, transported them frequently so far beyond the limits of moderation, as to apply singular punishments to particular persons, who contravened the general sense of the community.

The British ministry were not less disappointed than mortified at this unexpected combination of the colonies. They had flattered themselves with a belief, that the malcontents in Boston were a small party headed by a few factious men, and that the majority of the inhabitants would arrange themselves on the side of government, as soon as they found Great-Britain determined to support her authority, and should even Massachusetts take part with its offending capital, they could not believe that the other colonies would make a common cause in supporting so intemperate a colony: but should even that expectation fail, they conceived that their association must be founded on principles so adverse to the interests and feelings of individuals, that it could not be of long duration. They were encouraged in these ill founded opinions by [145] the recollection that the colonies were frequently quarrelling about boundaries, clashing in interest, differing in policy, manners, customs, forms of government and religion, and under the influence of a variety of local prejudices, jealousies and aversions. They also remembered the obstacles which prevented the colonies from acting together, in the execution of schemes, planned for their own defence, in the late war against the French and Indians. The failure of the expected co-operation of the colonies in one uniform system at that time, was not only urged by the British ministry, as a reason for parliamentary control over the whole, but flattered them with a delusive hope, that they never could be brought to combine their counsels and their arms. Perhaps the colonists apprehended more danger from British encroachments on their liberties, than from French encroachment on Indian territories, in their neighbourhood: or more probably the time to part being come, the Governor of the Universe, by a secret influence on their minds, disposed them to union. From whatever cause it proceeded, it is certain, that a disposition to do, to suffer, and to accommodate, spread from breast to breast, and from colony to colony, beyond the reach of human calculation. It seemed as though one mind inspired the whole. The merchants put far behind them the gains of trade,

1774

and cheerfully submitted to a total stoppage of business, in obedience to the recommendations of men, invested with no legislative powers. The cultivators of the soil, with great unanimity assented to the determination, that the hard earned produce of their farms, should remain unshipped, although in case of a free exportation, many would have been eager to have purchased it from them, at advanced prices. The sons and daughters of ease, renounced imported conveniencies, and voluntarily engaged to eat, drink, and wear, only such articles as their country afforded. These sacrifices were made, not from the pressure of present distress, but on the generous principle of sympathy, with an invaded sister colony, and the prudent policy of guarding against a precedent which might, in a future day, operate against their liberties.

[146] This season of universal distress, exhibited a striking proof, 1774 how practicable it is for mankind to sacrifice ease, pleasure, and interest, when the mind is strongly excited by its passions. In the midst of their sufferings, cheerfulness appeared in the face of all the people. They counted every thing cheap in comparison with liberty, and readily gave up whatever tended to endanger it. A noble strain of generosity and mutual support was generally excited. A great and powerful diffusion of public spirit took place. The animation of the times, raised the actors in these scenes above themselves, and excited them to deeds of self denial, which the interested prudence of calmer seasons can scarcely credit.

CHAPTER V

Transactions in Great-Britain, in consequence of the proceedings of Congress, in 1774.

SOME TIME BEFORE THE PROCEEDINGS of Congress reached England, it was justly apprehended that a non-importation agreement would be one of the measures they would adopt. The ministry apprehending that this event, by distressing the trading and manufacturing towns, might influence votes against the court, in the election of a new parliament, which was of course to come on in the succeeding year, suddenly dissolved the parliament, and immediately ordered a new one to be chosen. It was their design to have the whole business of elections over, before the inconveniences of a non-importation agreement could be felt. The nation was thus surprised into an election without knowing that the late American acts, had driven the colonies into a firm combination, to support, and make a common cause, with the people of Massachusetts. A new parliament was returned, which met in thirty-four days after the proceedings of Congress were first published in Philadelphia, and before they were known in Great-Britain. This, for the most part consisted, either of the former members, or of those who held similar sentiments.

1774

[147] On the 30th of November, the king in his speech to his new parliament informed them,

> that a most daring spirit of resistance and disobedience to the laws, unhappily prevailed in the province of Massachusetts, and had broke forth in fresh violences of a very criminal nature, and that these proceedings had been countenanced and encouraged in his other colonies, and unwarrantable attempts had been made to obstruct the commerce of his kingdoms by unlawful combinations, and that he had taken such measures, and given such orders as he judged most proper and effectual, for carrying into execution the laws which were passed in the last session of the late parliament, relative to the province of Massachusetts.

An address which was proposed in the house of commons in answer to this speech, produced a warm debate. The minister was reminded of the great effects he had predicted from the late American acts. "They were to humble that whole continent, without further trouble, and the punishment of Boston, was to strike so universal a panic on all the colonies, that it would be totally abandoned, and instead of obtaining relief, a dread of the same fate would awe the other provinces to a most respectful submission." An address re-echoing the royal speech, was nevertheless carried by a great majority. A similar address was carried, after a spirited debate, in the upper house, but the lords Richmond, Portland, Rockingham, Stamford, Stanhope, Torrington, Ponsonby, Wycombe and Camden, entered a protest against it, which concluded with these remarkable words.

> Whatever may be the mischievous designs, or the inconsiderate temerity which leads others to this desperate course, we wish to be known as persons who have disapproved of measures so injurious in their past effects, and future tendency, and who are not in haste, without enquiry or information, to commit ourselves in declarations, which may precipitate our country into all the calamities of a civil war.

Soon after the meeting of the new parliament, the proceedings of the Congress reached Great-Britain. The first impression made by them, was in favour of [148] America. Administration seemed to be staggered, and their opposers triumphed, in the eventual truth of their prediction, that an universal confederacy to resist Great-Britain, would be the consequence of the late American acts. The secretary of state, after a days perusal, during which a council was held, said that the petition of Congress to the King, was a decent and proper one. He also cheerfully undertook to present it, and afterwards reported, that his majesty was pleased very graciously to receive it, and to promise to lay it before his two houses of parliament. From these favourable circumstances, the sanguine friends of America, concluded that it was intended to make the petition, the foundation of a change of measures, but these hopes were of short duration.

The warmer partisans of administration, placed so much confidence in the efficacy of the measures, they had lately taken to bring the Americans to obedience, that they regarded the boldest resolutions of Congress, as the idle clamors of an unruly multitude, which proper exertions on the part of Great-Britain would speedily silence. So much had been asserted and contradicted by both parties, that the bulk of the people could form no certain opinion, on the subject.

The parliament adjourned for the christmas holidays, without coming to any decision on American affairs. As soon as they met in January, a number of papers, containing information, were laid before them. These were mostly letters from governors, and other servants of his majesty, which detailed the opposition of the colonists, in language calculated to give a bad impression of their past conduct, and an alarming one of their future intentions.

It was a circumstance unfavourable to the lovers of peace, that the rulers of Great-Britain received almost the whole of their American intelligence from those, who had an interest in deceiving them. Governors, judges, revenue-officers, and other royal servants, being both appointed and paid by Great-Britain, fancied that zeal for the interest of that country, would be the most likely way to ensure their farther promotion. They were therefore, [149] in their official dispatches, to government, often tempted to abuse the colonists, with a view of magnifying their own watchfulness and recommending themselves to Great-Britain. The plain, simple language of truth, was not acceptable to courtly ears. Ministers received and caressed those, and those only, whose representations coincided with their own views and wishes. They who contended that by the spirit of the English constitution British subjects, residing on one side of the Atlantic, were entitled to equal privileges with those who resided on the other, were unnoticed, while the abettors of ministerial measures were heard with attention.

In this hour of national infatuation lord Chatham, after a long retirement, resumed his seat in the house of lords, and exerted his unrivalled eloquence, in sundry attempts to dissuade his countrymen from attempting to subdue the Americans by force of arms. The native dignity of his superior genius, and the recollection of his important services, entitled him to distinguished notice. His language, voice, and gesture, were calculated to force conviction on his hearers. Though venerable for his age, he spoke with the fire of youth. He introduced himself with some general observations on the importance of the American quarrel. He enlarged on the dangerous events that were coming on the nation, in consequence of the present dispute. He arraigned the conduct of ministers with great severity, and reprobated their whole system of American politics, and moved that an humble address, be presented to his majesty, most humbly to advise and beseech him to dispatch orders to general Gage, to remove his majesty's forces from the town of Boston. His lordship supported this motion in a pathetic animated speech, but it was rejected by a great majority. From this and other circumstances it soon became evident, that the Americans could expect no more favour from the new parliament, than they had experienced from the late one. A majority in both houses was against them, and resolved to compel them to obedience; but a respectable minority in their favour was strongly seconded by petitions from the merchants and manufacturers, [150] throughout the kingdom, and particularly by those of London and Bristol. As these were well apprised of the consequences that must follow from a prosecution of coercive measures, and deeply interested in the event, they made uncommon exertions to prevent their adoption. They circumstantially pointed out the various evils that would result from them, and faithfully warned their countrymen of the danger, to which their commercial interests were exposed.

When the petition from the merchants of London was read in the house of commons, it was moved to refer it to the committee appointed to take into consideration the American papers; but it was moved by way of amendment on the ministerial side, that it should be referred to a separate committee, to meet on the 27th, the day succeeding that appointed for the consideration of American papers. This, though a dishonorable evasion, was carried by a majority of more than two to one.

A similar fate attended the petitions from Bristol, Glasgow, Norwich, Liverpool, Manchester, Birmingham, Woolverhampton, Dudley, and some other places. These on their being presented, were in like manner consigned to what the opposition humorously termed, the committee of oblivion.

About the same time a petition was offered from Mr. Bollan, Dr. Franklin, and Mr. Lee, stating that they were authorized by Congress to present their petition to the king, which his majesty had referred to that house, and that they were enabled to throw great light on the subject, and praying to be heard at the bar, in support of the said petition. The friends of the ministry alledged, that as Congress was not a legal body, nothing could be received from them. It was in vain replied, that the Congress, however illegal as to other purposes, was sufficiently legal for presenting a petition, and that as it was signed by the individual members of Congress, it might be received as a petition from individuals. That the signers of it were persons of great influence in America, and it was the right of all subjects to have their petitions heard.

1775

[151] In the course of the debate on Lord Chatham's motion for addressing his majesty to withdraw his troops from Boston, it had been observed by some lords in administration, that it was common and easy to censure their measures, but those who did so, proposed nothing better. Lord Chatham answered, that he should not be one of those idle censurers, that he had thought long and closely upon

FEB. 1st

the subject, and purposed soon to lay before their lordships the result of his meditations, in a plan for healing the differences between Great-Britain and the colonies, and for restoring peace to the empire. When he had matured his plan, he introduced it into the house, in the form of a bill for settling the troubles in America. In this he proposed that the colonists should make a full acknowledgement of the supremacy of the legislature, and the superintending power of the British parliament. The bill did not absolutely decide on the right of taxation, but partly as a matter of grace, and partly as a compromise, declared and enacted, "that no tollage tax, or other charge, should be levied in America, except by common consent in their provincial assemblies." It asserted the right of the king to send a legal army to any part of his dominions at all times, but declared, "that no military force could ever be lawfully employed to violate or destroy the just rights of the people." It also legalised the holding a Congress in the ensuing May for the double purpose "of recognising the supreme legislative authority, and superintending power of parliament over the colonies, and for making a free grant to the king, his heirs and successors, of a certain and perpetual revenue, subject to the disposition of parliament, and applicable to the alleviation of the national debt." On these conditions the bill proposed, "to restrain the powers of the admiralty courts to their ancient limits, and suspended for a limited time, those acts which had been complained of by Congress." It proposed to place the judges in America on the same footing, as to the holding of their salaries and offices, with those in England, and secured to the colonies all the privileges, franchises, and immunities, granted by their several charters and constitutions. His lordship introduced this [152] plan with a speech, in which he explained and supported every part of it. When he sat down, lord Dartmouth rose and said, "it contained matter of such magnitude as to require consideration, and therefore hoped, that the noble Earl did not expect their lordships to decide upon it by an immediate vote, but would be willing it should lie on the table for consideration." Lord Chatham answered, "that he expected no more," but lord Sandwich rose, and in a petulant speech opposed its being received at all, and gave his opinion, "that it ought immediately to be rejected with the contempt it deserved. That he could not believe it to be the production of any British peer—that it appeared to him rather the work of some American," and turning his face towards Dr. Franklin, who was leaning on the bar, said, "he fancied he had in his eye the person who drew it up, one of the bitterest and most mischievous enemies this country had ever known." This turned the eyes of many lords on the insulted American, who, with that self

1775

command, which is peculiar to great minds, kept his countenance unmoved. Several other lords of the administration gave their sentiments also, for rejecting lord Chatham's conciliatory bill, urging that it not only gave a sanction to the traiterous proceedings of the Congress already held, but legalised their future meeting. They enlarged on the rebellious temper and hostile disposition of the Americans, and said, "that, though the duty on tea was the pretence, the restrictions on their commerce, and the hopes of throwing them off, were the real motives of their disobedience, and that to concede now, would be to give up the point forever."

The Dukes of Richmond and Manchester, lord Camden, lord Lyttleton and others, were for receiving lord Chatham's conciliatory bill—some from approbation of its principles, but others only from a regard to the character and dignity of the house.

Lord Dartmouth who, from indecision rarely had any will or judgment of his own, and who with dispositions for the best measures, could be easily prevailed upon to join in support of the worst, finding the opposition from [153] his coadjutors in administration unexpectedly strong, turned round and gave his voice with them for immediately rejecting the plan; lord Chatham, in reply to lord Sandwich, declared,

> the bill proposed by him to be entirely his own, but he made no scruple to declare, that if he were the first minister of the country, and had the care of settling this momentous business, he should not be ashamed of publicly calling to his assistance a person so perfectly acquainted with the whole of the American affairs as the gentleman alluded to, and so injuriously reflected upon [(]Dr. Franklin). One whom all Europe held in high estimation for his knowledge and wisdom, and ranked with her Boyles and her Newtons—who was an honour, not only to the English nation, but to human nature.

The plan proposed by lord Chatham was rejected, by a majority of 64 to 32, and without being admitted to lie on the table. That a bill on so important a subject, offered by one of the first men of the age, and who, as prime minister of the nation, had but a few years before taken up Great-Britain when in the lowest despondency, and conducted her to victory and glory, through a war with two of the most powerful kingdoms of Europe, should be rejected without any consideration, or even a second reading, was not only a breach of decency, but a departure from that propriety of conduct which should mark the proceedings of a branch of the national legislature. It could not but strike every thinking American, that such legislators, influenced by passion, prejudice, and party spirit, many of whom were totally ignorant of the subject, and who would not give themselves an opportunity by a second reading, or farther consideration, to inform themselves better, were very unfit to exercise unlimited supremacy over three millions of virtuous, sensible people, inhabiting the other side of the globe.

On the day after the rejection of lord Chatham's bill, a petition was presented to the house of commons, from the planters of the sugar colonies residing in Great-Britain, and the merchants of London trading to the colonies. In this they stated, that the British property in [154] the West-India islands amounted to upwards of 30 millions, 1775 and that a further property of many millions was employed in the commerce created by the said islands, and that the profits and produce of these immense capitals which ultimately centered in Great-Britain, would be deranged and endangered by the continuance of the American troubles. The petitioners were on the 16th of the next month admitted to a hearing, when Mr. Glover, as their agent, ably demonstrated the folly and danger of persevering in the contest, but without any effect. The immediate coercion of the colonies was resolved upon, and the ministry would not suffer themselves to be diverted from its execution. They were confident of success, if they could once bring the controversy to the decision of arms. They expected more from conquest than they could promise themselves by negotiation or compromise. The free constitutions of the colonies and their rapid progress in population, were beheld with a jealous eye, as the natural means of independence. They conceived the most effectual method of retaining them long, would be to reduce them soon. They hoped to be able to extinguish remonstrance and debate by such a speedy and decisive conquest, as would give them an opportunity to new model the colonial constitutions, on such principles as would have prevented future altercations on the subject of their chartered rights. Every representation that tended to retard or obstruct the coercion of the colonies, was therefore considered as tending only to prolong the controversy. Confident of victory, and believing that nothing short of it would restore the peace of the empire, the ministry turned a deaf ear to all petitions and representations. They even presumed that the petitioners, when they found Great-Britain determined on war, would assist in carrying it on with vigour, in order to expedite the settlement of the dispute. They took it for granted, that when the petitioning towns were convinced that a renewal of the commercial intercourse between the two countries would be sooner obtained by going on, than turning back, that the same interest which led them at first to petition, would lead them afterwards to support coercive [155] measures, as the most effectual and shortest way of securing commerce from all future interruptions.

The determination of ministers to persevere was also forwarded by hopes of the defection of New-York from her sister colonies. They flattered themselves, that when one link of the continental chain gave way, it would be easy to make an impression on the disjointed extremities.

Every attempt to close the breach which had been opened by the former parliament, having failed, and the ministry having made up their minds on the mode of proceeding with the colonists, their proposed plan was briefly unfolded. This was to send a greater force to America, and to bring in a temporary act to put a stop to all the foreign trade of the New England colonies, till they should make proper submissions and acknowledgments. An address to his majesty was at the same time moved for, to "beseech him to take the most effectual measures, to enforce due obedience to the laws and authority of the supreme legislature."

Truly critical was that moment to the union of the empire. A new parliament might, without the charge of inconsistency, have repealed acts, passed by a former one, which had been found inconvenient on experiment; but pride and passion, under the specious names of national dignity and zeal for the supremacy of parliament, induced the adoption of measures, for immediately compelling the submission of the colonies.

The repeal of a few acts of parliament would, at this time, have satisfied America. Though she had been extending her claims, yet she was still willing that Great-Britain should monopolize her trade, and that the parliament should regulate it for the common benefit of the empire; nor was she disposed to abridge his majesty of any of his usual prerogatives. This authority was sufficient for the Mother Country to retain the colonists in a profitable state of subordination, and yet not so much as to be inconsistent with their claims, or the security of their most important interests. Britain viewed the matter in a different light. To recede at this time, would be to acknowledge, that the ministry had hitherto been in the [156] wrong, a concession rarely made by private persons, but more rarely still by men in public stations. The leading members in parliament, not distinguishing the opposition of freemen to unconstitutional innovations, from the turbulence of licentious mobs breaking over the bounds of law and constitution, supposed that to redress grievances, was to renounce sovereignty. This inference, in some degree, resulted from the broad basis which they had assigned to the claims of the Mother Country. If, as was contended, on the part of Great-Britain, they had a right to bind the colonies in all cases whatsoever, and the power of parliament over them was absolute and unlimited, they were precluded from rescinding any act of theirs, however oppressive, when demanded as a matter of right. They were too highly impressed with ideas of their unlimited authority to repeal any of their laws, on the principle, that they had not a constitutional power to enact them, and too unwise to adopt the same measure on the ground of political expediency. Unfortunately for both countries, two opinions were generally believed, neither of which was perhaps true in its utmost extent, and one of which was most assuredly false. The ministry and parliament of England proceeded on the idea, that the claims of the colonists amounted to absolute independence, and that a fixed resolution to renounce the sovereignty of Great-Britain was concealed, under the specious pretext of a redress of grievances. The Americans on the other hand, were equally confident that the Mother Country not only harboured designs unfriendly to their interests, but seriously intended to introduce arbitrary government. Jealousies of each other were reciprocally indulged to the destruction of all confidence, and to the final dismemberment of the empire.

In discussing the measures proposed by the minister for the coercion of the colonies, the whole ground of the American contro-

1775

versy was traversed. The comparative merits of concession and coercion were placed in every point of view. Some of the minority in both houses of parliament, pointed out the dangers that would attend a war with America—the likelihood of the interference of [157] other powers—the probability of losing, and the impossibility of gaining any thing more than was already possessed. On the other hand, the friends of the ministry asserted that the Americans had been long aiming at independence—that they were magnifying pretended grievances to cover a premeditated revolt—that it was the business and duty of Englishmen, at every hazard to prevent its completion, and to bring them back to a remembrance that their present greatness was owing to the Mother Country; and that even their existence had been purchased at an immense expence of British blood and treasure. They acknowledged the danger to be great, but said "it must be encountered; that every day's delay increased the evil, and that it would be base and cowardly to shift off for the present an unavoidable contest, which must fall with accumulated weight on the heads of their posterity." The danger of foreign interference was denied, and it was contended that an appearance of vigorous measures, with a farther reinforcement of troops at Boston, would be sufficient to quell the disturbances; and it was urged, that the friends of government were both strong and numerous, and only waited for proper support, and favourable circumstances, to declare themselves.

After long and warm debates, and one or two protests, the ministerial plans were carried by great majorities. In consequence thereof, on the 9th of February, 1775, a joint address, from both lords and commons, was presented to his majesty, in which

> they returned thanks for the communication of the papers relative to the state of the British colonies in America, and gave it as their opinion, that a rebellion actually existed in the province of Massachusetts, and beseeched his majesty that he would take the most effectual measures to enforce due obedience to the laws and authority of the supreme legislature, and begged in the most solemn manner to assure his majesty that it was their fixed resolution, at the hazard of their lives and properties, to stand by his majesty against all rebellious attempts, in the maintenance of the just rights of his majesty, and the two houses of parliament.

CHAPTER V

[158] The lords, Richmond, Craven, Archer, Abergaveny, Rockingham, Wycombe, Courtenay, Torrington, Ponsonby, Cholmonde-
ley, Abingdon, Rutland, Camden, Effingham, Stanhope, Scarborough,
Fitzwilliam and Tankerville, protested against this address,

> as founded on no proper parliamentary information, being introduced
> by refusing to suffer the presentation of petitions against it (though it
> be the undoubted right of the subject to present the same)—as following
> the rejection of every mode of conciliation—as holding out no substantial
> offer of redress of grievances, and as promising support to those ministers
> who had inflamed America, and grossly misconducted the affairs of
> Great-Britain.

By the address, against which this protest was entered, the
parliament of Great-Britain passed the Rubicon. In former periods,
it might be alledged that the claims of the colonies were undefined,
and that their unanimous resolution to defend them was unknown;
but after a free representation from twelve provinces had stated their
rights, and pledged themselves to each other to support them, and
their determinations were known, a resolution that a rebellion
actually existed, and that at the hazard of their lives and properties,
they would stand by his majesty against all rebellious attempts, was
a virtual declaration of war. Both parties were now bound in
consequence of their own acts, to submit their controversy to the
decision of arms. Issue was joined by the approbation Congress had
given to the Suffolk resolves, and by this subsequent joint address
of both houses of parliament to his majesty. It is probable that
neither party, in the beginning, intended to go thus far, but by the
inscrutable operations of providence, each was permitted to adopt
such measures as not only rent the empire, but involved them both,
with their own consent, in all the calamities of a long and bloody
war. The answer from the throne to the joint address of parliament,
contained assurances of taking the most speedy and effectual measures for enforcing due obedience to the laws, and authority of the
supreme legislature. This answer was accompanied with a message
to the commons, in [159] which they were informed that some
augmentation to the forces by sea and land would be necessary. An
augmentation of 4383 men to the land forces, and of 2000 seamen,
to be employed for the ensuing year, was accordingly asked for, and

carried without difficulty. By the first it was stated, that the force at Boston would be ten thousand men, a number supposed to be sufficient for enforcing the laws. Other schemes, in addition to a military force, were thought advisable for promoting the projected coercion of the colonies. With this view a punishment was proposed, so universal in its operation, that it was expected the inhabitants of the New-England colonies, to obtain a riddance of its heavy pressure, would interest themselves in procuring a general submission to parliament. Lord North moved for leave to bring in a bill to restrain the trade and commerce of the provinces of Massachusetts Bay, and New-Hampshire, the colonies of Connecticut and Rhode-Island, and Providence Plantations in North-America, to Great-Britain, Ireland, and the British islands in the West-Indies, and to prohibit such provinces and colonies from carrying on any fishery on the banks of Newfoundland, or other places therein to be mentioned, under certain conditions, and for a limited time. The motion for this bill was supported, by declaring that as the Americans had refused to trade with the Mother Country, they ought not to be permitted to trade with any other. It was known that the New-England colonies carried on a circuitous trade and fishing, on the banks of Newfoundland, to a great extent. To cut them off from this resource, they were legislatively forbidden to fish, or to carry on foreign trade. It was presumed that the wants of a large body of people, deprived of employment, would create a clamor in favour of reconciliation.

The British ministry expected to excite the same temper in the unemployed New-England men, that Congress meant to raise by the non-importation agreement, among the British merchants and manufacturers. The motion for this bill brought into view, the whole of the American controversy. The opposers of it said, that its cruelty [160] exceeded the examples of hostile rigour with avowed enemies; for that in the most dangerous wars, the fishing craft was universally spared—they desired the proposer of the bill to recollect, that he had often spoken of the multitude of friends he had in those provinces, and that now he confounded the innocent with the guilty—friends with enemies, and involved his own partizans in one common ruin with his opposers. They alledged farther, that the bill would operate against the people of Great-Britain, as the people of New England were in debt to them, and had no other means of paying that debt, but through the fishery, and the circuitous trade dependent on it. It was observed, that the fishermen being cut off from employment must turn soldiers, and that therefore while they were provoking the Americans to resistance by one set of acts, they were furnishing them with the means of recruiting an army by another. The favourers of the bill denied the charge of severity, alledging that the colonists could not complain of any distress the bill might bring on them, as they not only deserved it, but had set the example, that they had entered into lawful combinations to ruin the merchants and manufacturers of Great-Britain. It was said, that if any foreign power had offered a similar insult or injury, the whole nation would have demanded satisfaction. They contended that it was a bill of humanity and mercy; for, said they, the colonists have incurred all the penalties of rebellion, and are liable to the severest military execution. Instead of inflicting the extent of what they deserved, the bill only proposes to bring them to their senses, by restricting their trade. They urged farther that the measure was necessary, for said they, "the Americans have frequently imposed on us, by threatening to withdraw their trade, hoping through mercantile influence to bend the legislature to their demands—that this was the third time they had thrown the commerce of Great-Britain into a state of confusion. That both colonies and commerce were better lost than preserved on such terms.["] They added farther, that they must either relinquish their connexion with America, or fix it on such a basis as would prevent [161] a return of these evils. They admitted the bill to be coercive,   1775 but said, "That the coercion which put the speediest end to the dispute, was eventually the most merciful."

In the progress of the bill, a petition from the merchants and traders of London, who were interested in the American commerce, was presented against it. They were heard by their agent, Mr. David Barclay, and a variety of witnesses were examined before the house. In the course of their evidence it appeared that in the year 1764, the four provinces of New-England employed in their several fisheries no less than 45,880 ton of shipping, and 6002 men; and that the produce of their fisheries that year, in foreign markets, amounted to 322,220£. 16s. sterling. It also appeared that the fisheries had very much increased since that time—that all the materials used in them, except salt, and the timber of which the vessels were built, were purchased from Great-Britain; and that the net proceeds of the whole were remitted thither. All this information was disregarded. After much opposition in both houses, and a protest in the house of lords, the bill was, by a great majority, finally ratified. So intent was the ministry and parliament on the coercion of the colonists, that every other interest was sacrificed to its accomplishment. They conceived the question between the two countries to be simply whether they should abandon their claims, and at once give up all the advantages arising from sovereignty and commerce, or resort to violent measures for their security.

Since the year 1769, when a secretary of state officially disclaimed all views of an American revenue, little mention had been made of that subject, but the decided majority which voted with the ministry on this occasion, emboldened lord North once more to present it to the view of his countrymen; he therefore brought into parliament a scheme which had the double recommendation of holding forth the semblance of conciliation, and the prospect of an easement of British taxes, by a productive revenue from the colonies. This was a resolution which passed on the 20th of February.

[162] Resolved, That when the governor, council, and assembly, or general court, of any of his majesty's provinces or colonies in America, shall propose to make provision according to the condition, circumstances, and situations of such province or colony, for contributing their proportion for the common defence, (such proportion to be raised under the authority of the general court or general assembly of such province or colony, and disposable by parliament) and shall engage to make provision also for the support of the civil government, and the administration of justice in such province or colony, it will be proper, if such proposal shall be approved by his majesty and the two houses of parliament, and for so long as such provision shall be made accordingly, to forbear, in respect of such province or colony, to levy any duty, tax, or assessment, except only such duties as it may be expedient to continue to levy or to impose for the regulation of commerce, the net produce of the duties last mentioned, to be carried to the account of such province or colony respectively.

This was introduced by the minister in a long speech, in which he asserted that it would be an infallible touch stone to try the Americans; "if" said he, "their opposition is only founded on the principles which they pretend, they must agree with this proposition, but if they have designs in contemplation different from those they avow, their refusal will convict them of duplicity." The oppositions to the minister's motion originated among those who had supported him in previous questions. They objected to the proposal that in effect it was an acknowledgment of something grievous in the idea of taxing America by parliament, and that it was therefore a departure from their own principles. They contended that it was improper to make concessions to rebels with arms in their hands, or to enter into any measures for a settlement with the Americans, in which they did not, as a preliminary, acknowledge the supremacy of parliament. The minister was likely to be deserted by some of his partizans, till others explained the consistency of the scheme with their former declarations. [163] It was asked, "what shall parliament lose by acceding to this resolution? Not the right of taxing America, for this is most expressly reserved. Not the profitable exercise of this right, for it proposed to enforce the only essential part of taxation, by compelling the Americans to raise not only what they, but what we, think reasonable. We are not going to war for trifles and a vain point of honor, but for substantial revenue." The minister farther declared, that he did not expect his proposition to be generally relished by the Americans. But said he, if it does no good in the colonies, it will do good here, it will unite the people of England, by holding out to them a distinct object of revenue. He added farther, as it tends to unite England, it is likely to disunite America, for if only one province accepts the offer, their confederacy, which only makes them formidable, will be broken.

1775

The opposers of ministry attacked the proposition with the combined force of wit and argument. They animadverted on the inconsistency of holding forth the same resolution as a measure of concession, and as an assertion of authority. They remarked that hitherto it had been constantly denied that they had any contest about an American revenue—that the whole had been a dispute about obedience to trade-laws, and the general legislative authority of parliament, but now ministers suddenly changed their language, and proposed to interest the nation—console the manufacturers and animate the soldiery, by persuading them that it is not a contest for empty honour, but for the acquisition of a substantial revenue. It was said that the Americans would be as effectually taxed, without their consent, by being compelled to pay a gross sum, as by an aggregate of small duties to the same amount. That this scheme of taxation exceeded in oppression any that the rapacity of mankind had hitherto devised. In other cases a specific sum was demanded, and the people might reasonably presume that the remainder was their own; but here they were wholly in the dark as to the extent of the demand.

1775   This proposition, however for conciliation, though illy [164] relished by many of the friends of ministry, was carried on a division of 274 to 88. On its transmission to the colonies, it did not produce the effects of disunion expected from it. It was unanimously rejected. The reason for this cannot be expressed better than in the act of Congress on that subject, which after a recital of the said conciliatory motion, proceeded in the following words,

> The Congress took the said resolution into consideration, and are thereupon of opinion,
>
> That the colonies of America are entitled to the sole and exclusive privilege of giving and granting their own money. That this involves a right of deliberating whether they will make any gift, for what purposes it shall be made, and what shall be its amount; and that it is a high breach of this privilege for any body of men, extraneous to their Constitutions, to prescribe the purposes for which money shall be levied on them, to take to themselves the authority of judging of their conditions, circumstances, and situations, and of determining the amount of the contribution to be levied.
>
> That as the colonies possess a right of appropriating their gifts, so are they entitled at all times to enquire into their application, to see that they be not wasted among the venal and corrupt for the purpose of undermining the civil rights of the givers, nor yet be diverted to the support of standing armies, inconsistent with their freedom and subversive of their quiet. To propose therefore, as this resolution does, that the monies given by the colonies shall be subject to the disposal of parliament alone, is to propose that they shall relinquish this right of

enquiry, and put it in the power of others to render their gifts ruinous, in proportion as they are liberal.

That this privilege of giving, or of withholding our monies, is an important barrier against the undue exertion of prerogative, which, if left altogether without controul, may be exercised to our great oppression; and all history shews how efficacious is its intercession for redress of grievances, and re-establishment of rights, and how improvident it would be to part with so powerful a mediator.

We are of opinion that the proposition contained in [165] this resolution is unreasonable and insidious: Unreasonable, because, if we declare we accede to it, we declare without reservation, we will purchase the favour of parliament, not knowing at the same time at what price they will please to estimate their favour; it is insidious, because, individual colonies, having bid and bidden again, till they find the avidity of the seller too great for all their powers to satisfy, are then to return into opposition, divided from their sister colonies whom the minister will have previously detached by a grant of easier terms, or by an artful procrastination of a definitive answer.

That the suspension of the exercise of their pretended power of taxation being expressly made commensurate with the continuance of our gifts, these must be perpetual to make that so. Whereas no experience has shewn that a gift of perpetual revenue secures a perpetual return of duty or of kind disposition. On the contrary, the parliament itself, wisely attentive to this observation, are in the established practice of granting their supplies from year to year only.

Desirous, and determined as we are to consider, in the most dispassionate view, every seeming advance towards a reconciliation made by the British parliament, let our brethren of Britain reflect what would have been the sacrifice to men of free spirits had even fair terms been proffered, as these insidious proposals were, with circumstances of insult and defiance. A proposition to give our money, accompanied with large fleets and armies, seems addressed to our fears rather than to our freedom. With what patience would Britons have received articles of treaty from any power on earth when born on the point of a bayonet by military Plenipotentiaries?

We think the attempt unnecessary to raise upon us by force or by threats our proportional contributions to the common defence, when all know, and themselves acknowledge, we have fully contributed, whenever called upon to do so in the character of freemen.

We are of opinion it is not just that the colonies should be required

1775

to oblige themselves to other contributions, while Great-Britain possesses a Monopoly of their trade. [166] This of itself lays them under heavy contribution. To demand, therefore, additional aids in the form of a tax, is to demand the double of their equal proportion, if we are to contribute equally with the other parts of the empire, let us equally with them, enjoy free commerce with the whole world. But while the restrictions on our trade shut to us the resources of wealth, is it just we should bear all other burthens, equally with those to whom every resource is open?

We conceive that the British parliament has no right to intermeddle with our provisions for the support of civil government, or administration of justice. The provisions we have made are such as please ourselves, and are agreeable to our own circumstances: They answer the substantial purposes of government and of justice, and other purposes than these should not be answered. We do not mean that our people shall be burthened with oppressive taxes, to provide sinecures for the idle or the wicked, under colour of providing for a civil list. While parliament pursue their plan of civil government within their own jurisdiction, we also hope to pursue ours without molestation.

We are of opinion the proposition is altogether unsatisfactory; because it imports only a suspension of the mode, not a renunciation of the pretended right to tax us: Because too it does not propose to repeal the several acts of parliament, passed for the purposes of restraining the trade, and altering the form of government of one of our colonies; extending the boundaries and changing the government of Quebec; enlarging the jurisdiction of the courts of admiralty and vice-admiralty; taking from us the rights of a trial by jury of the vicinage, in cases affecting both life and property; transporting us into other countries to be tried for criminal offences; exempting by mock-trial the murderers of colonists from punishment; and quartering soldiers on us in times of profound peace. Nor do they renounce the power of suspending our own legislatures, and for legislating for us themselves, in all cases whatsoever. On the contrary, to shew they mean no discontinuance of injury, they pass acts, at the very [167] time of holding out this proposition, for restraining the commerce and fisheries of the provinces of New-England, and for interdicting the trade of other colonies with all foreign nations, and with each other. This proves unequivocally they mean not to relinquish the exercise of indiscriminate legislation over us.

Upon the whole, this proposition seems to have been held up to the world, to deceive it into a belief that there was nothing in dispute between us but the mode of levying taxes; and that the parliament having now been so good as to give up this, the colonies are unreasonable if not perfectly satisfied: whereas, in truth, our adversaries still claim a right of demanding *ad libitum*, and of taxing us themselves to the full amount of their demand, if we do comply with it. This leaves us without any thing we can call property. But, what is of more importance, and what in this proposal they keep out of sight, as if no such point was now in contest between us, they claim a right to alter our charters and establish laws, and leave us without any security for our lives or liberties. The proposition seems also to have been calculated more particularly to lull into fatal security, our well affected fellow subjects on the other side of the water, till time should be given for the operation of those arms, which a British minister pronounced would instantaneously reduce the "cowardly" sons of America to unreserved submission. But when the world reflects, how inadequate to justice are these vaunted terms; when it attends to the rapid and bold succession of injuries, which, during a course of eleven years, have been aimed at these colonies; when it reviews the pacific and respectful expostulations, which, during that whole time, were the sole arms we opposed to them; when it observes that our complaints were either not heard at all, or were answered with new and accumulated injuries; when it recollects that the minister himself on an early occasion declared, "that he would never treat with America, till he had brought her to his feet," and that an avowed partisan of ministry has more lately denounced against us the dreadful sentence "*delenda est Carthago*," that this was done [168] in presence of a British senate, and being unreproved by them, must be taken to be their own sentiment, (especially as the purpose has already in part been carried into execution, by their treatment of Boston and burning of Charlestown); when it considers the great Armaments with which they have invaded us, and the circumstances of cruelty with which these have commenced and prosecuted hostilities; when these things, we say, are laid together and attentively considered, can the world be deceived into an opinion that we are unreasonable, or can it hesitate to believe with us, that nothing but our own exertions may defeat the ministerial sentence of death or abject submission.

1775

Other plans for conciliation with the colonies, founded on principles very different from those which were the basis of lord North's conciliatory motion, were brought forward in the house of commons, but without receiving its approbation. The most remarkable of these was proposed by Mr. Edmund Burke, in a speech which for strength of argument, extent of information, and sublimity of language, would bear a comparison with the most finished performance that ancient or modern times have produced. In his introduction to this admirable speech, he examined and explained the natural and accidental circumstances of the colonies, with respect to situation, resources, number, population, commerce, fisheries and agriculture, and from those considerations shewed their importance. He then enquired into their unconquerable spirit of freedom; and he traced it to its original sources; from these circumstances he inferred the line of policy which should be pursued with regard to America—he shewed that all proper plans of government must be adapted to the feelings, established habits, and received opinions of the people. On these principles he reprobated all plans of governing the colonies by force; and proposed as the ground work of his plan, that the colonists should be admitted to an interest in the constitution. He then went into an historical detail of the manner in which British privileges had been extended to Ireland, Wales, and the counties palatine of Chester and Durham—the [169] state of confusion previously to that event—and the happy consequences which followed it. He contended that a communication to the members of an interest in the constitution, was the great ruling principle of British government. He therefore proposed to go back to the old policy for governing the colonies. He was for a parliamentary acknowledgment of the legal competency of the colony assemblies for the support of their government in peace, and for public aids in time of war—and of the futility of parliamentary taxation as a method of supply. He stated that much had been given in the old way of colonial grant, that from the year 1748 to 1763, the journals of the house of commons repeatedly acknowledged that the colonies not only gave, but gave to satiety; and that from the time in which parliamentary imposition had superceded the free gifts of the provinces, there was much discontent, but little revenue. He therefore moved six resolutions affirmatory of these facts, and grounded on them resolutions for repealing the acts complained of by the Americans, trusting to the liberality of their future voluntary contributions. This plan of conciliation, which promised immediate peace to the whole empire, and a lasting obedience of the colonies, though recommended by the charms of the most persuasive eloquence, and supported by the most convincing arguments, was by a great majority rejected.

Mr. D. Hartley, not discouraged by the negative which had been given to Mr. Burke's scheme, came forward with another for the same purpose. This proposed that a letter of requisition should be sent to the colonies by a secretary of state, on a motion from the house for a contribution to the expences of the whole empire. He meant to leave to the provincial assemblies the right to judge of the expedience of the grant—its amount and application. In confidence that the colonies would give freely when called on in this constitutional way, he moved to suspend the acts complained of by the Americans. This was also rejected. Another plan which shall be more particularly explained was digested in private by Dr. Franklin, on the part of the Americans, and Dr. Fothergill and David [170] Barclay on behalf of the British ministry. There appeared a disposition to concede something considerable on both sides, but the whole came to nothing, in consequence of an inflexible determination to refuse a repeal of the act of parliament for altering the chartered government of Massachusetts; Dr. Franklin agreed, that the tea destroyed should be paid for—the British ministers, that the Boston port act should be repealed, but the latter contended, "that the late Massachusetts acts being real amendments of their constitution, must for that reason be continued as well as to be a standing example of the power of parliament." On the other hand it was declared by Dr. Franklin, "that while the parliament claimed and exercised a power of internal legislation for the colonies, and of altering American constitutions at pleasure, there could be no agreement, as that would render the Americans unsafe in every privilege they enjoyed, and would leave them nothing in which they could be secure."

This obstinate adherence to support parliament in a power of altering the laws and charters of the provinces, particularly to enforce their late laws for new modelling the chartered constitution of Massachusetts, was the fatal rock by dashing on which the empire broke in twain; for every other point, in dispute between the two countries, seemed in a fair way for an amicable compromise.

MARCH 27

1775

The fishery bill was speedily followed by another, for restraining the trade and commerce of the colonies and provinces of New-Jersey, Pennsylvania, Maryland, Virginia and South-Carolina: The reasons assigned for this were the same with those offered for the other. These provinces had adopted the continental association. The British minister thought it proper, that as they had voluntarily interdicted themselves from trade with Great-Britain, Ireland, and the West-Indies, they should be restrained from it with all other parts of the world. He contended that the inhabitants of the colonies might render this act a dead letter, by relinquishing their own resolutions, as then they would meet with no restraint in carrying on trade in its ancient legal channel. It is remarkable, that three of the associated colonies, viz. New-York, [171] Delaware and North-Carolina, were omitted in this restraining bill. Whatever might be the view of the British ministry for this discrimination, it was considered in the colonies as calculated to promote disunion among them. It is certain, that the colonies which were exempted from its operation, might have reaped a golden harvest from the exemption in their favour, had they been disposed to avail themselves of it. But such was the temper of the times, that a renunciation of immediate advantage in favour of the public was fashionable. The selfish passions which in seasons of peace are too often the cause of quarrels, were hushed by the pressure of common danger. The exempted colonies spurned the proffered favour, and submitted to the restraints imposed on their less favoured neighbours, so as to be equal sharers of their fate. The indulgence granted to New-York, in being kept out of this restraining bill, was considered by some as a premium for her superior loyalty. Her assembly had refused to approve the proceedings of the Congress, and had, in some other instances, discovered less warmth than the neighbouring legislatures. Much was expected from her moderation. At the very time the British parliament was framing the restraining acts just mentioned, the constitutional assembly of New-York petitioned the British parliament for a redress of their grievances. Great stress had been laid on the circumstance that Congress was not a legal assembly, and the want of constitutional sanction had been assigned as a reason for the neglect with which their petition had been treated. Much praise had been lavished on the colony of New-

1775

York for its moderation, and occasion had been taken, from their refusing to approve the proceedings of the Congress to represent the resolutions and claims of that body to be more the ebullitions of incendiaries, than the sober sentiments of the temperate citizens. It was both unexpected and confounding to those who supported these opinions, that the representation and remonstrance of the very loyal assembly of New-York stated, "that an exemption from internal taxation, and the exclusive right of providing for their own civil government, and the administration of justice in [172] the colony, were esteemed by them as their undoubted and unalienable rights."

1775

A motion being made in the house of commons for bringing up this representation and remonstrance of the assembly of New-York, it was amended on the suggestion of lord North, by adding, "in which the assembly claim to themselves rights derogatory to, and inconsistent with the legislative authority of parliament, as declared by the declaratory act." The question, so amended, being put, it passed in the negative. The fate of this representation extinguished the hopes of those moderate persons, both in the parent state and the colonies, who flattered themselves that the disputes subsisting between the two countries might be accommodated by the mediation of the constitutional assemblies. Two conclusions were drawn from this transaction, both of which were unfriendly to a reconciliation. The decided language with which the loyal assembly of New-York claimed exemption from parliamentary taxation, proved to the people of Great-Britain that the colonists, however they might differ in modes of opposition, or in degrees of warmth, were nevertheless, united in that fundamental principle. The rejection of their representation proved that nothing more was to be expected from proceeding in the constitutional channel of the legal assemblies, than from the new system of a continental Congress. Solid revenue and unlimited supremacy were the objects of Great-Britain, and exemption from parliamentary taxation that of the most moderate of the colonies. So wide were the claims of the two countries from each other, that to reconcile them on any middle ground seemed to be impossible.

Some special transactions of Dr. Franklin in London,
in behalf of America.

[173] WHILE THE BREACH BETWEEN Great-Britain and the colonies was daily increasing, the enlightened and liberal, who loved peace, and the extension of human happiness, saw with regret the approaching horrors of a civil war, and wished to avert them. With these views Dr. Fothergill, Mr. David Barclay and Dr. Franklin, held sundry conferences in London on American affairs. The two former were English gentlemen of most amiable characters, and highly esteemed by the British ministry. The last was by birth an American, but a citizen of the world, who loved and was beloved by all good men. He was also agent for several of the colonies. At one of their conferences held at the house of Dr. Fothergill on the 4th December, 1774, before the proceedings of Congress had reached England—a paper drawn up by the last, at the request of the two first, was submitted to their

joint consideration, which with a few additions proposed and agreed to by common consent was as follows.

Hints for conversation upon the subjects of terms, that might probably produce a durable union between Britain and the colonies.

1st. The tea destroyed to be paid for.

2d. The tea duty act to be repealed, and all the duties that have been received upon it to be repaid into the treasuries of the several provinces from which they have been collected.

3d. The acts of navigation to be all re-enacted in the colonies.

4th. A naval officer to be appointed by the crown to see that these acts are observed.

5th. All the acts restraining manufactories in the colonies to be reconsidered.

6th. All duties arising on the acts for regulating trade with the colonies to be for the public use of the respective colonies and paid into their treasuries.

[174] The collectors and custom house officers to be appointed by each governor and not sent from England. 1775

7th. In consideration of the Americans maintaining their own peace establishment, and the monopoly Britain is to have of their commerce, no requisition is to be made from them in time of peace.

8th. No troops to enter and quarter in any colony, but with the consent of its legislature.

9th. In time of war on requisition by the king with consent of parliament, every colony shall raise money by the following rules in proportion, viz. If Britain on account of the war, raises three shillings in the pound to its land tax, then the colonies to add to their last general provincial peace tax, a sum equal to one fourth part thereof, and if Britain on the same account pays four shillings in the pound, then the colonies to add to their last peace tax, a sum equal to the half thereof, which additional tax is to be granted to his majesty, and to be employed in raising and paying men for land or sea service, and furnishing provisions, transports, or for such other purposes as the king shall require and direct, and though no colony may contribute less, each may add as much by voluntary grant as it shall think proper.

10th. Castle William to be restored to the province of Massachusetts

Bay, and no fortress to be built by the crown in any province, but with the consent of its legislature.

11th. The late Massachusetts and Quebec acts to be repealed, and a free government granted to Canada.

12th. All judges to be appointed during good behavior, with equally permanent salaries to be paid out of the province revenues by appointment of the assemblies, or if the judges are to be appointed during the pleasure of the crown, let the salaries be during the pleasure of the assemblies as heretofore.

13th. Governors to be supported by the assemblies of each province.

14th. If Britain will give up her monopoly of the American commerce, then the aid abovementioned to be given in time of peace, as well as in time of war.

1775

[175] 15th. The extension of the act of Henry the 8th, concerning treasons to the colonies to be formally disowned by parliament.

16th. The American admiralty courts to be reduced to the same powers they have in England, and the acts establishing them to be re-enacted in America.

17th. All power of internal legislation in the colonies to be disclaimed by parliament.

On reading this paper a second time, Dr. Franklin gave his reasons at length for each article. Some of his reasons were as follows.

On the first article he observed, that when the tea was destroyed at Boston, Great-Britain had a right to reparation, and would certainly have had it on demand, as was the case when injuries were done by mobs in the time of the stamp act, or she might have a right to return an equal injury if she rather chose to do that; but Great-Britain could not have a right both to reparation and to return an equal injury, much less had she a right to return the injury ten or twenty fold, as she had done by blocking up the port of Boston. All which extra injury ought to be repaired by Great-Britain. That therefore if paying for the tea was agreed to, as an article fit to be proposed, it was merely from a desire of peace, and in compliance with the opinions of Dr. Fothergill and David Barclay, expressed at their first meeting; that this was indispensible, that the dignity of Great-Britain required it, and that if this was agreed to, every thing else would be easy.

On the second, it was observed that the tea duty act should be repealed as having never answered any good purpose, as having been the cause of the present mischief, and never likely to be executed. That the act being considered as unconstitutional by the Americans, and what parliament had no right to enact they must consider all the money extorted by it as so much wrongfully taken, and of which therefore restitution ought to be made, and the rather as it would furnish a fund out of which the tea destroyed would be best defrayed.

On the third and fourth articles it was observed, that the Americans were frequently charged with views of abolishing [176] the navigation act, but that in truth those parts of it, which were of most importance to Britain, as tending to increase its naval strength, were as acceptable to the colonists as they could be to the inhabitants of the Parent State, since they wished to employ their own ships in preference to those of foreigners, and they had no desire to see foreign ships enter their ports. That it would prevent disputes if they were re-enacted in the colonies, as that would demonstrate their consent to them, and then if all the duties arising on them were to be collected by officers appointed and paid in the respective governments, and the produce paid into their treasuries, the acts would be better and more faithfully executed, and at much less expence, and a great source of misunderstanding between the two countries removed—that the extension of the admiralty jurisdiction so much complained of would then no longer be necessary.

In support of the 7th article it was observed, that if every distinct part of the king's dominions supported its own government in time of peace, it was all that could justly be required of it. That all the other confederated colonies had done so from their beginning, that their taxes for that purpose were very considerable, that new countries had many expences which old ones were free from, the work being done to their land by their ancestors, such as making roads and bridges, erecting churches, courthouses, forts, quays and other public buildings, founding schools and places of education, hospitals and almshouses—that the voluntary subscriptions and legal taxes for such purposes taken together amounted to more than was paid by equal estates in Great-Britain; that it would be best not to take money from the Americans as a contribution to its public expence

1775

in time of peace, first for that just so much less would be got from them in commerce, and secondly, that coming into the hands of British ministers accustomed to prodigality of public money, it would be squandered and dissipated without answering any general good purposes. That on the whole it would be best for both countries, that no aids should be asked from the colonies in time of peace, [177] that it would then be their interest to grant bountifully, and exert themselves, in time of war, the sooner to put an end to it.

In support of the 8th article, it was said, that if the king could bring into any one part of his dominions troops raised in any other part of them, without the consent of the legislature of the part to which they were brought, he might bring armies raised in America to England without the consent of parliament.

The 9th article was drawn in compliance with an idea of Dr. Fothergill, that the British government would probably not be satisfied with the promise of voluntary grants in time of war from the American assemblies, of which the quantity must be uncertain, that therefore it would be best to proportion them in some way to the shilling in the pound raised in England.

In support of the 10th article, was urged the injustice of seizing that fortress which had been built at an immense charge by the province, for the defence of their port against national enemies, and turning it into a citadel for awing the town, restraining their trade, blocking up their port, and depriving them of their privileges. That a great deal had been said of their injustice in destroying the tea, but here was a much greater injustice uncompensated, that castle having cost the province £300,000.

In support of the 11th article, it was said, that as the Americans had assisted in the conquest of Canada, at a great expence of blood and treasure, they had some right to be considered in the settlement of it; that the establishing an arbitrary government on the bank of their settlements would be dangerous to them all. That as to amending the Massachusetts government, though it might be shewn that every one of these pretended amendments were real mischiefs, yet, that as charters were compacts between two parties, the king and the people, no alteration could be made in them even for the better, but by the consent of both parties; that the parliamentary claim and exercise of power to alter American charters, had rendered all their constitutions uncertain and set them [178] quite afloat. That by this claim of altering laws and charters at will they deprived the colonists of all rights and privileges whatever, but what they should hold at their pleasure. That this was a situation they could not be in and must risque life and every thing rather than submit to it.

The 12th article was explained by stating the former situation of the judges in most of the colonies, viz. that they were appointed by the crown and paid by the assemblies, that the appointment being during the pleasure of the crown, the salary had been during the pleasure of the assembly; that when it was urged against the assemblies that their making judges dependent on them for their salaries, was aiming at an undue influence over the courts of justice, the assemblies usually replied, that making them dependent on the crown for continuance in their places was also retaining an undue influence over those courts, and that one undue influence was a proper balance for another; but that whenever the crown would consent to the appointment of judges only during good behaviour, the assemblies would at the same time grant their salaries to be permanent during their continuance in office; that instead of agreeing to this equitable offer the crown now claimed to make the judges in the colonies dependant on its favour for place, as well as salary, and both to be continued at its pleasure. This the colonies must oppose as inequitable, as putting both the weights into one of the scales of justice.

In favour of the 13th it was urged that the governors sent to the colonies were often men of no estate or principle, who came merely to make fortunes, and had no natural regard for the country they were to govern. That to make them quite independent of the people, was to make them careless of their conduct, and giving a loose to their rapacious and oppressive dispositions. That the dependance of the governors on the people for their salaries could never operate to the prejudice of the king's service, or to the disadvantage of Britain, since each governor was bound by a particular set of instructions which he had given surety to observe, and all the laws he assented [179] to were subject to be repealed by the crown. That the payment of the salaries by the people was more satisfactory to them, and was productive of a good understanding between governors and governed,

1775

1775

and that therefore the innovations lately made at Boston and New-York, should be laid aside.

The 14th article was expunged on the representation of Dr. Fothergill and David Barclay, that the monopoly of the American commerce would never be given up, and that the proposing of it would only give offence, without answering any good purpose.

The 15th article was readily agreed to.

The 16th was thought to be of little consequence, if the duties were given to the colony treasuries.

The 17th it was thought could hardly be obtained, but it was supported by Dr. Franklin, alleging that without it, any compact made with the Americans, might be evaded by acts of the British parliament, restraining the intermediate proceedings, which were necessary for carrying it into effect.

This paper of hints was communicated to lord Dartmouth by Dr. Fothergill, who also stated the arguments which in conversation had been offered in support of them. When objections were made to them, as being humiliating to Great-Britain Dr. Fothergill replied "that she had been unjust, and ought to bear the consequences, and alter her conduct—that the pill might be bitter, but it would be salutary and must be swallowed; that sooner or later these or similar measures must be followed, or the empire would be divided and ruined."

These hints were handed about amongst ministers, and conferences were held on them. The result was on the 4th of February 1775 communicated to Dr. Franklin, in the presence of Dr. Fothergill and David Barclay, which as far as concerned the leading articles, was as follows:

1. The first article was approved.

2. The second agreed to so far as related to the tea act, but repayment of the duties that had been collected, was refused.

3. The third not approved, as it implied a deficiency of power in the parliament that made the acts. [180]

4. The fourth approved.

5. The fifth agreed to, but with a reserve that no change prejudicial to Britain was to be expected.

6. The sixth agreed to, so far as related to the appropriation of the

duties, but the appointment of the officers and of their salaries to remain as at present.

7. The seventh relating to aids in time of war, agreed to.

8. The eighth relating to troops, was inadmissible.

9. The ninth could be agreed to with this difference, that no proportion should be observed with regard to preceding taxes, but each colony should give at pleasure.

10. The tenth agreed to as to the restitution of Castle William, but the restriction on the crown in building fortresses refused.

11. The eleventh refused absolutely, except as to the Boston port bill which would be repealed, and the Quebec act might be so far amended, as to reduce that province to its ancient limits. The other MASSACHUSETTS ACTS BEING REAL AMENDMENTS OF THEIR CONSTITUTION, MUST FOR THAT REASON BE CONTINUED, AS WELL AS TO BE A STANDING EXAMPLE OF THE POWER OF PARLIAMENT.

12. The twelfth agreed to, that the judges should be appointed during good behaviour, on the assemblies providing permanent salaries, such as the Crown should approve of.

13. The thirteenth agreed to, provided the assemblies make provision, as in the preceding article.

15. The fifteenth agreed to.

16. The sixteenth agreed to, supposing the duties paid to the colony treasuries.

17. The seventeenth inadmissible.

At this interview the conversation was shortened by Dr. Franklin's observing, that while the parliament claimed and exercised a power of internal legislation for the colonies, and of altering American constitutions, at pleasure, there could be no agreement, as that would render the Americans unsafe in every privilege they enjoyed, [181] and would leave them nothing, in which they could be secure. It being hinted how necessary an agreement was for America, since it was so easy for Britain to burn all her seaport towns, Dr. Franklin replied, 1775

that the chief part of his little property consisted of houses in such towns, that they might make bonfires of them whenever they pleased. That the fear of losing them would never alter his resolution of resisting to the last extremity, that claim of parliament, and that it behoved Great-Britain to take care what mischief she did to America, for that sooner or later she would certainly be obliged to make good all damages with interest.

On the 16th of February, 1775, the three beforementioned gentle-men met, when a paper was produced by David Barclay entitled, "A plan which it is believed would produce a permanent union between Great-Britain and her colonies.["] This, in the first article, proposed a repeal of the tea act, on payment being made for the tea destroyed. Dr. Franklin agreed to the first part, but contended that all the other Massachusetts acts should also be repealed, but this was deemed inadmissible. Dr. Franklin declared that the people of Massachusetts would suffer all the hazards and mischiefs of war, rather than admit the alteration of their charters and laws, by parliament. He was for securing the unity of the empire, by recognising the sanctity of charters, and by leaving the provinces to govern themselves, in their internal concerns, but the British ministry could not brook the idea of relinquishing their claim to internal legislation for the colonies, and especially to alter and amend their charters. The first was for communicating the vital principles of liberty to the provinces, but the latter though disposed to redress a few of their existing grievances, would by no means consent to a repeal of the late act of parliament, for altering the chartered government of Massachusetts, and least of all to renounce all claim to future amendments of charters, or of internal legislation for the colonies.

1775
Dr. Franklin laboured hard to prevent the breach from becoming irreparable, and candidly stated the outlines [182] of a compact which he supposed would procure a durable union of the two countries, but his well meant endeavours proved abortive, and in the mean time he was abused as the fomenter of those disturbances which he was anxiously endeavouring to prevent. That the ministry might have some opening to proceed upon, and some salvo for their personal honor, he was disposed to engage, that pecuniary compen-sation should be made for the tea destroyed, but he would not give up essential liberty, for the purpose of procuring temporary safety. Finding the ministry bent on war, unless the colonists would consent

to hold their rights, liberties and charters at the discretion of a British parliament, and well knowing that his countrymen would hazard every thing, rather than consent to terms so degrading as well as inconsistent with the spirit of the British constitution, he quitted Great-Britain in March 1775, and returned to Philadelphia. Dr. Fothergill, his worthy coadjutor in the great business of peace, wrote to him on the evening before he left London. "That whatever specious pretences were offered, they were all hollow, and that to get a larger field on which to fatten a herd of worthless parasites, was all that was intended." With this conviction founded on personal observations, as well as the testimony of his esteemed friend, who in the course of his daily visits among the great, in the practice of his profession, had an opportunity of knowing their undisguised sentiments, Dr. Franklin joined his countrymen, and exerted his great abilities in conducting them through a war he had in vain laboured to prevent.

Consequences in America, resulting from the
preceding transactions of Parliament; and of the
commencement of Hostilities.

THE YEAR 1774 TERMINATED IN AMERICA, with an expectation
that a few months would bring them a redress of their grievances;
but the probability of that event [183] daily diminished. The colonists
had indulged themselves in an expectation that the people of Great-
Britain, from a consideration of the dangers and difficulties of a war
with their colonies, would in their election have preferred those who
were friends to peace and a reconciliation; but when they were
convinced of the fallacy of these hopes, they turned their attention
to the means of self defence. It had been the resolution of many
never to submit to the operation of the late acts of parliament. Their
number daily increased, and in the same proportion that Great-
Britain determined to enforce, did they determine to oppose. Intelligence of the rejection of lord Chatham's bill, of the address of both

1775

houses of parliament to the king of the 9th of February, and of the fishery bill, all arrived among the colonists, about the same time, and diminished what remained of their first hopes of a speedy accommodation. The fishery bill excited a variety of emotions. The obvious tendency of it was to starve thousands. The severity of it did not strike an Englishman, for he viewed it as a merited correction for great provincial offences; but it appeared in the blackest colours to an American, who felt no consciousness of guilt, and who fancied that heaven approved his zeal in defence of liberty. It alienated the affections of the colonists, and produced in the breasts of thousands, a hatred of Great-Britain.

The penal acts of parliament in 1774, were all levelled against Massachusetts, but the fishery bill extended to New-Hampshire, Connecticut and Rhode-Island. The reasons assigned for this by lord North were, that they had aided and abetted their offending neighbors, and were so near to them that the intentions of parliament would be frustrated, unless they were in like manner comprehended in the proposed restraints. The extension of this penal statute to three additional provinces, operated powerfully in favour of union, and convinced the most moderate, of the increasing necessity for all the provinces to make a common cause of their opposition. Whatever might be the designs of parliament, their acts had a natural tendency to enlarge the demands of the Americans, [184] and to cement their confederacy, by firm principles of union. At first they only claimed exemption from internal taxation, but by the combination of the East-India company and the British ministry, an external tax was made to answer all the purposes of a direct internal tax. They therefore in consistence with their own principles, were constrained to deny the right of taxing in any form for a supply. Nothing could more contribute to make the colonists deny the parliamentary claim of internal legislation, than the manner in which it was exercised, in depriving them of their charters, and passing an act relative to trials, which promised indemnity to murderers. This convinced them that an opposition to so injurious a claim was essentially necessary to their security. But they still admitted the power of parliament to bind their trade. This was conceded by Congress but a few months before an act passed that they should have no foreign trade, nor be

1775

allowed to fish on their own coasts. The British ministry by their successive acts, impelled the colonists to believe, that while the Mother Country retained any authority over them, that authority would, in some shape or other, be exerted so as to answer all the purposes of a power to tax. While Great-Britain stretched that portion of controling supremacy which the colonists were disposed to allow her, to such an extent as covered oppression equally grievous with that which they would not allow, the way was fast opening for a total renunciation of her sovereignty. The coercive measures adopted by the Parent State, produced a disposition in the colonies to extend their claims, and the extension of their claims produced an increasing disposition in Great-Britain to coerce them still more. The jealousy of liberty on one side, and the desire of supremacy on the other, were reciprocally cause and effect; and urged both parties, the one to rise in their demands, and the other to enforce submission. In the contest between Great-Britain and her colonies, there had been a fatal progression from small to greater grounds of dissention. The trifling tax of 3d per pound on tea, roused the jealous inhabitants of Boston to throw 340 chests of it into the ocean. [185] This provoked the British parliament to shut up their port, and to new model their charter. Statutes so unconstitutional and alarming, excited a combination in twelve of the colonies, to stop all trade with Great-Britain, Ireland, and the West-Indies. Their combination gave birth to the restraining acts of parliament, by which nine of the colonies were interdicted all other trade but that from which they had voluntarily excluded themselves; and four of these nine were farther devoted to famine, by being forbidden to fish on their coasts. Each new resolution on the one side, and new act on the other, reciprocally gave birth to something from the opposite party, that was more irritating or oppressive, than what had preceded.

The beginning of strife between the Parent State and her colonies, was like the letting out of waters. From inconsiderable causes love was changed into suspicion that gradually ripened into ill will, and soon ended in hostility. Prudence, policy, and reciprocal interest, urged the expediency of concession; but pride, false honour, and misconceived dignity, drew in an opposite direction. Undecided claims and doubtful rights, which under the influence of wisdom and

1775

humility might have been easily compromised, imperceptibly widened into an irreconcileable breach. Hatred at length took the place of kind affections, and the calamities of war were substituted, in lieu of the benefits of commerce.

From the year 1768, in which a military force had been stationed in Boston, there was a constant succession of insulting words, looks, and gestures. The inhabitants were exasperated against the soldiers, and they against the inhabitants. The former looked on the latter as the instruments of tyranny, and the latter on the former as seditious rioters, or fraudulent smugglers. In this irritable state, every incident however trifling, made a sensible impression. The citizens apprehended constant danger from an armed force, in whose power they were; the soldiers on the other hand, considered themselves as in the midst of enemies, and exposed to attacks from within and from without. In proportion [186] as the breach between Great-Britain 1775 and her colonies widened, the distrust and animosity between the people and the army increased. From the latter end of 1774, hostile appearances daily threatened that the flames of war would be kindled from the collision of such inflammable materials. Whatsoever was done by either party by way of precaution, for the purposes of self defence, was construed by the other as preparatory to an intended attack. Each disclaimed all intentions of commencing hostilities, but reciprocally manifested suspicion of the others sincerity. As far as was practicable without an open rupture, the plans of the one were respectively thwarted by the other. From every appearance it became daily more evident that arms must ultimately decide the contest. To suffer an army that was soon expected to be an enemy, quietly to fortify themselves, when the inhabitants were both able and willing to cut them off, appeared to some warm spirits the height of folly; but the prudence and moderation of others, and especially the advice and recommendation of Congress, restrained their impetuosity. It was a fortunate circumstance for the colonies that the royal army was posted in New-England. The people of that northern country have their passions more under the command of reason and interest, than in the southern latitudes, where a warmer sun excites a greater degree of irascibility. One rash offensive action against the royal forces at this early period, though successful, might have done great mischief to the cause of America. It would have lost them European friends, and weakened the disposition of the other colonies to assist them. The patient and the politic New-England men, fully sensible of their situation, submitted to many insults, and bridled their resentment. In civil wars or revolutions it is a matter of much consequence who strikes the first blow. The compassion of the world is in favour of the attacked, and the displeasure of good men on those who are the first to imbrue their hands in human blood. For the space of nine months after the arrival of general Gage, the behaviour of the people of Boston is particularly worthy of imitation, by those who wish to [187] overturn established governments. They conducted their opposition with exquisite address. They avoided every kind of outrage and violence, preserved peace and good order among themselves, successfully engaged the other colonies to make a common cause with them, and counteracted general Gage so effectually as to prevent his doing any thing for his royal master, while by patience and moderation they skreened themselves from censure. Though resolved to bear as long as prudence and policy dictated, they were all the time preparing for the last extremity. They were furnishing themselves with arms and ammunition, and training their militia.

Provisions were also collected and stored in different places, particularly at Concord, about 20 miles from Boston. General Gage, though zealous for his royal master's interest, discovered a prevailing desire after a peaceable accommodation. He wished to prevent hostilities by depriving the inhabitants of the means necessary for carrying them on. With this view he determined to destroy the stores which he knew were collected for the support of a provincial army. Wishing to accomplish this without bloodshed, he took every precaution to effect it by surprise, and without alarming the country. At eleven o'clock at night 800 grenadiers and light infantry, the flower of the royal army, embarked at the Common, landed at Phipps's farm, and marched for Concord, under the command of lieutenant colonel Smith. Neither the secrecy with which this expedition was planned—the privacy with which the troops marched out, nor an order that no one inhabitant should leave Boston, were sufficient to prevent intelligence from being sent to the country militia, of what

1775

APRIL 18

was going on. About two in the morning 130 of the Lexington militia had assembled to oppose them, but the air being chilly and intelligence respecting the regulars uncertain, they were dismissed, with orders to appear again at beat of drum. They collected a second time to the number of 70, between 4 and 5 o'clock in the morning, and the British regulars soon after made their appearance. Major Pitcairn, who led the advanced corps, rode up to them and called out, "Disperse you [188] rebels, throw down your arms and disperse." They still continued in a body, on which he advanced nearer—discharged his pistol—and ordered his soldiers to fire. This was done with a huzza. A dispersion of the militia was the consequence, but the firing of the regulars was nevertheless continued. Individuals finding they were fired upon, though dispersing, returned the fire. Three or four of the militia were killed on the green. A few more were shot after they had begun to disperse. The royal detachment proceeded on to Concord, and executed their commission. They disabled two 24 pounders—threw 500 lb. of ball into rivers and wells, and broke in pieces about 60 barrels of flour. Mr. John Butterick of Concord, major of a minute regiment, not knowing what had passed at Lexington, ordered his men not to give the first fire, that they might not be the aggressors. Upon his approaching near the regulars, they fired, and killed captain Isaac Davis, and one private of the provincial minute men. The fire was returned, and a skirmish ensued. The king's troops having done their business, began their retreat towards Boston. This was conducted with expedition, for the adjacent inhabitants had assembled in arms, and began to attack them in every direction. In their return to Lexington they were exceedingly annoyed, both by those who pressed on their rear, and others who pouring in from all sides, fired from behind stone walls, and such like coverts, which supplied the place of lines and redoubts. At Lexington the regulars were joined by a detachment of 900 men, under lord Piercy, which had been sent out by general Gage to support lieutenant colonel Smith. This reinforcement having two pieces of cannon awed the provincials, and kept them at a greater distance, but they continued a constant, though irregular and scattering fire, which did great execution. The close firing from behind the walls by good marksmen, put the regular troops in no small

19th

1775

confusion, but they nevertheless kept up a brisk retreating fire on the militia and minute men. A little after sunset the regulars reached Bunkers-hill, worn down with excessive fatigue, having marched that day between thirty and forty miles. On [189] the next day they crossed Charlestown ferry, and returned to Boston.

1775

There never were more than 400 provincials engaged at one time, and often not so many. As some tired and gave out, others came up and took their places. There was scarcely any discipline observed among them. Officers and privates fired when they were ready, and saw a royal uniform without waiting for the word of command. Their knowledge of the country enabled them to gain opportunities by crossing fields and fences, and to act as flanking parties against the king's troops who kept to the main road.

The regulars had 65 killed, 180 wounded, and 28 made prisoners. Of the provincials 50 were killed, and 38 wounded and missing.

As arms were to decide the controversy, it was fortunate for the Americans that the first blood was drawn in New-England. The inhabitants of that country are so connected with each other by descent, manners, religion, politics, and a general equality, that the killing of a single individual interested the whole, and made them consider it as a common cause. The blood of those who were killed at Lexington and Concord proved the firm cement of an extensive union.

APRIL 22

To prevent the people within Boston from co-operating with their countrymen without in case of an assault which was now daily expected, General Gage agreed with a committee of the town, that upon the inhabitants lodging their arms in Faneuil-hall or any other convenient place, under the care of the selectmen, all such inhabitants as were inclined, might depart from the town, with their families and effects. In five days after the ratification of this agreement, the inhabitants had lodged 1778 fire arms, 634 pistols, 273 bayonets and 38 blunderbusses. The agreement was well observed in the beginning, but after a short time obstructions were thrown in the way of its final completion, on the plea that persons who went from Boston to bring in the goods of those who chose to continue within the town, were not properly treated. Congress remonstrated on the infraction of [190] the agreement, but without effect. The general, on a farther consideration of the consequences of moving the whigs out of Boston, evaded it in a manner not consistent with good faith. He was in some measure compelled to adopt this dishonourable measure, from the clamor of the tories, who alleged that none but enemies to the British government were disposed to remove, and that when they were all safe with their families and effects, the town would be set on fire. To prevent the provincials from obtaining supplies which they much wanted, a quibble was made on the meaning of the word effects, which was construed by the general as not including merchandize. By this construction, unwarranted by every rule of genuine interpretation, many who quitted the town were deprived of their usual resources for a support. Passports were not universally refused, but were given out very slowly, and the business was so conducted that families were divided—wives were separated from their husbands, children from their parents, and the aged and infirm from their relations and friends. The general discovered a disinclination to part with the women and children, thinking that, on their account, the provincials would be restrained from making an assault on the town. The select-men gave repeated assurances that the inhabitants had delivered up their arms, but as a cover for violating the agreement, general Gage issued a proclamation, in which he asserted that he had full proof to the contrary. A few might have secreted some favourite arms, but nearly all the training arms were delivered up. On this flimsy pretence the general sacrificed his honour, to policy and the clamors of the tories. Contrary to good faith he detained many, though fairly entitled by agreement to go out, and when he admitted the departure of others he would not allow them to remove their families and effects.

The provincial congress of Massachusetts, which was in session at the time of the Lexington battle, dispatched an account of it to Great-Britain, accompanied with many depositions, to prove that the British troops were the aggressors. They also made an address to the inhabitants [191] of Great-Britain, in which, after complaining of their sufferings, they say, "these have not yet detached us from our royal sovereign; we profess to be his loyal and dutiful subjects, and though hardly dealt with, as we have been, are still ready with our lives and fortunes, to defend his person, crown, and dignity. Never-

1775

theless, to the persecution and tyranny of his evil ministry, we will not tamely submit. Appealing to heaven for the justice of our cause, we determine to die or be free." From the commencement of hostilities, the dispute between Great-Britain and the colonies took a new direction.

Intelligence that the British troops had marched out of Boston into the country on some hostile purpose, being forwarded by expresses from one committee to another, great bodies of the militia, not only from Massachusetts but the adjacent colonies, grasped their arms and marched to oppose them. The colonies were in such a state of irritability, that the least shock in any part was, by a powerful and sympathetic affection, instantaneously felt throughout the whole. The Americans who fell were revered by their countrymen, as martyrs who had died in the cause of liberty. Resentment against the British burned more strongly than ever. Martial rage took possession of the breasts of thousands. Combinations were formed and associations subscribed, binding the inhabitants to one another by the sacred ties of honour, religion, and love of country, to do whatever their public bodies directed for the preservation of their liberties. Hitherto the Americans had no regular army. From principles of policy they cautiously avoided that measure, least they might subject themselves to the charge of being aggressors. All their military regulations were carried on by their militia, and under the old established laws of the land. For the defence of the colonies, the inhabitants had been, from their early years, enrolled in companies, and taught the use of arms. The laws for this purpose had never been better observed than for some months previous to the Lexington battle. These military arrangements, which had been previously adopted for defending the colonies from hostile French and Indians, [192] were on this occasion turned against the troops of the Parent State. Forts, magazines, and arsenals, by the constitution of the country, were in the keeping of his majesty. Immediately after the Lexington battle, these were for the most part taken possession of throughout the colonies, by parties of the provincial militia. Ticonderoga, in which was a small royal garrison, was surprised and taken by adventurers from different states. Public money which had been collected in consequence of previous grants, was also seized for common services. Before the

1775

commencement of hostilities these measures would have been condemned by the moderate even among the Americans, but that event
justified a bolder line of opposition than had been adopted. Sundry
citizens having been put to death by British troops, self preservation
dictated measures which, if adopted under other circumstances,
would have disunited the colonists. One of the most important of
this kind was the raising an army. Men of warm tempers, whose
courage exceeded their prudence, had for months urged the necessity
of raising troops; but they were restrained by the more moderate,
who wished that the colonies might avoid extremities, or at least
that they might not lead in bringing them on. The provincial congress
of Massachusetts being in session at the time the battle of Lexington
was fought, voted that "an army of 30,000 men be immediately raised,
that 13,600 be of their own province, and that a letter and delegate
be sent to the several colonies of New-Hampshire, Connecticut and
Rhode Island." In consequence of this vote, the business of recruiting
was begun, and in a short time a provincial army was paraded in the
vicinity of Boston, which though far below what had been voted by
the provincial congress, was much superior in numbers to the royal
army. The command of this force was given to general Ward.

Had the British troops confined themselves to Boston, as before
the 18th of April, the assembling an American army, though only for
the purpose of observation and defence, would have appeared in the
nature of a challenge, and would have made many less willing to
support [193] the people of Massachusetts, but after the British had   1775
commenced hostilities the same measure was adopted without subjecting the authors of it to censure, and without giving offence or
hazarding the union. The Lexington battle not only furnished the
Americans with a justifying apology for raising an army, but inspired
them with ideas of their own prowess. Amidst the most animated
declarations of sacrificing fortune, and risquing life itself for the
security of American rights, a secret sigh would frequently escape
from the breasts of her most determined friends, for fear that they
could not stand before the bravery and discipline of British troops.
Hoary sages would shake their heads and say, "Your cause is good
and I wish you success, but I fear that your undisciplined valour
must be overcome, in the unequal contest. After a few thousands of

you have fallen, the provinces must ultimately bow to that power which has so repeatedly humbled France and Spain." So confident were the British of their superiority in arms, that they seemed desirous that the contest might be brought to a military decision. Some of the distinguished speakers in parliament had publicly asserted that the natives of America had nothing of the soldier in them, and that they were in no respect qualified to face a British army. European philosophers had published theories, setting forth that not only vegetables and beasts, but that even men degenerated in the western hemisphere. Departing from the spirit of true philosophy, they overlooked the state of society in a new world, and charged a comparative inferiority, on every production that was American. The colonists themselves had imbibed opinions from their forefathers, that no people on earth were equal to those with whom they were about to contend. Impressed with high ideas of British superiority, and dissident of themselves, their best informed citizens, though willing to run all risques, feared the consequence of an appeal to arms. The success that attended their first military enterprize, in some degree banished these suggestions. Perhaps in no subsequent battle did the Americans appear to greater advantage than in their first essay at Lexington. It is almost without parallel [194] in military history, for the yeomanry of the country to come forward in a single disjointed manner, without order, and for the most part without officers, and by an irregular fire to put to flight troops equal in discipline to any in the world. In opposition to the bold assertions of some, and the desponding fears of others, experience proved that Americans might effectually resist British troops. The dissident grew bold in their country's cause, and indulged in chearful hopes that heaven would finally crown their labours with success.

1775

Soon after the Lexington battle, and in consequence of that event, not only the arms, ammunition, forts and fortifications in the colonies were secured for the use of the provincials, but regular forces were raised, and money struck for their support. These military arrangements were not confined to the New-England states, but were general throughout the colonies. The determination of the king and parliament to enforce submission to their acts, and the news of the Lexington battle, came to the distant provinces nearly about the

same time. It was supposed by many that the latter was in consequence of the former, and that general Gage had recent orders to
proceed immediately to subdue the refractory colonists.

From a variety of circumstances the Americans had good reason
to conclude that hostilities would soon be carried on vigorously in
Massachusetts, and also to apprehend that, sooner or later, each
province would be the theatre of war. "The more speedily therefore
said they, we are prepared for that event, the better chance we have
for defending ourselves." Previous to this period, or rather to the
19th of April 1775, the dispute had been carried on by the pen, or at
most by associations and legislative acts; but from this time forward
it was conducted by the sword. The crisis was arrived when the
colonies had no alternative, but either to submit to the mercy, or to
resist the power of Great-Britain. An unconquerable love of liberty
could not brook the idea of submission, while reason more temperate
in her decisions, suggested to the people their insufficiency to make
effectual opposition. They were fully apprized of the power [195] of
Britain—they knew that her fleets covered the ocean, and that her
flag had waved in triumph through the four quarters of the globe;
but the animated language of the time was, "It is better to die
freemen, than to live slaves." Though the justice of their cause, and
the inspiration of liberty gave, in the opinion of disinterested judges
a superiority to the writings of Americans, yet in the latter mode of
conducting their opposition, the candid among themselves acknowledged an inferiority. Their form of government was deficient in that
decision, dispatch, and coercion, which are necessary to military
operations.

Europeans, from their being generally unacquainted with fire arms
are less easily taught the use of them than Americans, who are from
their youth familiar with these instruments of war; yet on other
accounts they are more susceptible of military habits. The proportion
of necessitous men in the new world is small to that in the old.

To procure subsistence is a powerful motive with an European to
enlist, and the prospect of losing it makes him afraid to neglect his
duty; but these incitements to the punctual discharge of military
services, are wanting in America. In old countries the distinction of
ranks and the submission of inferiors to superiors, generally takes

1775

place, but in the new world an extreme sense of liberty and equality indisposes to that implicit obedience which is the soul of an army. The same causes which nurtured a spirit of independence in the colonies, were hostile to their military arrangements. It was not only from the different state of society in the two countries, but from a variety of local causes, that the Americans were not able to contend in arms, on equal terms, with their Parent State. From the first settlement of the British colonies, agriculture and commerce, but especially the former, had been the favourite pursuits of their inhabitants. War was a business abhorrent from their usual habits of life. They had never engaged in it from their own motion, nor in any other mode than as appendages to British troops, and under British establishments. By these means the military spirit of the colonies had no opportunity of expanding itself. At the commencement of hostilities, the British [196] troops possessed a knowledge of the science and discipline of war, which could be acquired only by a long series of application, and substantial establishments. Their equipments, their artillery, and every other part of their apparatus for war approached perfection. To these important circumstances was added a high national spirit of pride, which had been greatly augmented by their successes in their last contest with France and Spain. On the other hand the Americans were undisciplined, without experienced officers, and without the shadow of military establishments. In the wars which had been previously carried on, in or near the colonies, the provincials had been, by their respective legislatures, frequently added to the British troops, but the pride of the latter would not consider the former, who were without uniformity of dress, or the pertness of military airs, to be their equals. The provincial troops were therefore for the most part, assigned to services which, though laborious, were not honourable.

The ignorance of British generals commanding in the woods of America, sometimes involved them in difficulties from which they had been more than once relieved by the superior local knowledge of the colonial troops. These services were soon forgotten, and the moment the troops who performed them could be spared, they were disbanded. Such like obstacles had hitherto depressed military talents in America, but they were now overcome by the ardor of the people.

In the year 1775, a martial spirit pervaded all ranks of men in the colonies. They believed their liberties to be in danger, and were generally disposed to risque their lives for their establishment. Their ignorance of the military art, prevented their weighing the chances of war with that exactness of calculation which, if indulged, might have damped their hopes. They conceived that there was little more to do than fight manfully for their country. They consoled themselves with the idea, that though their first attempt might be unsuccessful; their numbers would admit of a repetition of the experiment, till the invaders were finally exterminated. Not considering [197] that in modern war the longest purse decides oftener than the longest sword, they feared not the wealth of Britain. They both expected and wished that the whole dispute would be speedily settled in a few decisive engagements. Elevated with the love of liberty, and buoyed above the fear of consequences, by an ardent military enthusiasm, unabated by calculations about the extent, duration, or probable issue of the war, the people of America seconded the voice of their rulers, in an appeal to heaven for the vindication of their rights. At the time the colonies adopted these spirited resolutions, they possessed not a single ship of war, nor so much as an armed vessel of any kind. It had often been suggested that their seaport towns lay at the mercy of the navy of Great-Britain; this was both known and believed, but disregarded. The love of property was absorbed in the love of liberty. The animated votaries of the equal rights of human nature, consoled themselves with the idea that though their whole sea coast should be laid in ashes, they could retire to the western wilderness, and enjoy the luxury of being free; on this occasion it was observed in Congress by Christopher Gadsden, one of the South-Carolina delegates, "Our houses being constructed of brick, stone, and wood, though destroyed may be rebuilt, but liberty once gone is lost forever."

The sober discretion of the present age will more readily censure than admire, but can more easily admire than imitate the fervid zeal of the patriots of 1775, who in idea sacrificed property in the cause of liberty, with the ease that they now sacrifice almost every other consideration for the acquisition of property.

The revenues of Britain were immense, and her people were

habituated to the payment of large sums in every form which contributions to government have assumed; but the American colonies possess neither money nor funds, nor were their people accustomed to taxes equal to the exigences of war. The contest having begun about taxation, to have raised money by taxes for carrying it on, would have been impolitic. The temper of the times precluded the necessity of attempting the dangerous [198] expedient, for such was the enthusiasm of the day, that the colonists gave up both their personal services and their property to the public, on the vague promises that they should at a future time be reimbursed. Without enquiring into the solidity of funds, or the precise period of payment, the resources of the country were commanded on general assurances, that all expences of the war should ultimately be equalised. The Parent State abounded with experienced statesmen and officers, but the dependent form of government exercised in the colonies, precluded their citizens from gaining that practical knowledge which is acquired from being at the head of public departments. There were very few in the colonies who understood the business of providing for an army, and still fewer who had experience and knowledge to direct its operations. The disposition of the finances of the country, and the most effectual mode of drawing forth its resources, were subjects with which scarce any of the inhabitants were acquainted. Arms and ammunition were almost wholly deficient; and though the country abounded with the materials of which they are manufactured, yet there was neither time nor artists enough to supply an army with the means of defence. The country was destitute both of fortifications and engineers. Amidst so many discouragements there were some flattering circumstances. The war could not be carried on by Great-Britain, but to a great disadvantage, and at an immense expence. It was easy for ministers at St. James's to plan campaigns, but hard was the fate of the officer from whom the execution of them in the woods of America was expected. The country was so extensive, and abounded so much with defiles; that by evacuating and retreating, the Americans though they could not conquer, yet might save themselves from being conquered. The authors of the acts of parliament for restraining the trade of the colonies, were most excellent recruiting officers for the Congress. They imposed a necessity on thousands to become soldiers. All other business being suspended, the whole resources of the country were applied in supporting an army. Though [199] the colonists were without discipline, they possessed native valour. Though they had neither gold nor silver, they possessed a mine in the enthusiasm of their people. Paper for upwards of two years produced to them more solid advantages than Spain derived from her superabounding precious metals. Though they had no ships to protect their trade or their towns, they had simplicity enough to live without the former, and enthusiasm enough to risque the latter, rather than submit to the power of Britain. They believed their cause to be just, and that heaven approved their exertions in defence of their rights. Zeal originating from such motives, supplied the place of discipline, and inspired a confidence and military ardor which overleaped all difficulties.

Resistance being resolved upon by Americans—the pulpit—the press—the bench and the bar, severally laboured to unite and encourage them. The clergy of New-England were a numerous, learned and respectable body, who had a great ascendancy over the minds of their hearers. They connected religion and patriotism, and in their sermons and prayers, represented the cause of America as the cause of heaven. The synod of New-York and Philadelphia, also sent forth a pastoral letter, which was publicly read in their churches. This earnestly recommended such sentiments and conduct as were suitable to their situation. Writers and printers followed in the rear of the preachers, and next to them had the greatest hand in animating their countrymen. Gentlemen of the bench and of the bar denied the charge of rebellion, and justified the resistance of the colonists. A destinction founded on law, between the king and his ministry, was introduced. The former, it was contended, could do no wrong. The crime of treason was charged on the latter, for using the royal name to varnish their own unconstitutional measures. The phrase of a ministerial war became common, and was used as a medium for reconciling resistance with allegiance.

Coeval with the resolutions for organizing an army, was one appointing the 20th day of July, 1775, a day of public humiliation, fasting and prayer to Almighty God, [200] ["]to bless their rightful sovereign king George, and to inspire him with wisdom to discern

1775

and pursue the true interest of his subjects; and that the British nation might be influenced to regard the things that belonged to her peace, before they were hid from her eyes—that the colonies might be ever under the care and protection of a kind providence, and be prospered in all their interests—that America might soon behold a gracious interposition of heaven, for the redress of her many grievances; the restoration of her invaded rights, a reconciliation with the Parent State, on terms constitutional and honourable to both." The forces which had been collected in Massachusetts, were stationed in convenient places for guarding the country from farther excursions of the regulars from Boston. Breast works were also erected in different places for the same purpose. While both parties were attempting to carry off stock from the several islands with which the bay of Boston is agreeably diversified, sundry skirmishes took place. These were of real service to the Americans. They habituated them to danger, and perhaps much of the courage of old soldiers, is derived from an experimental conviction, that the chance of escaping unhurt from engagements is much greater than young recruits suppose.

About the latter end of May a great part of the reinforcements ordered from Great-Britain, arrived at Boston. Three British generals, Howe, Burgoyne and Clinton, whose behaviour in the preceding war had gained them great reputation, also arrived about the same time. General Gage, thus reinforced, prepared for acting with more decision, but before he proceeded to extremities he conceived it due to ancient forms to issue a proclamation, holding forth to the inhabitants the alternative of peace or war. He therefore offered pardon in the king's name to all who should forthwith lay down their arms, and return to their respective occupations and peaceable duties, excepting only from the benefit of that pardon "Samuel Adams, and John Hancock, whose offences were said to be of too flagitious a nature to admit of any other consideration than that of condign punishment." He also [201] proclaimed that not only the persons above named and excepted, but also their adherents, associates, and correspondents, should be deemed guilty of treason and rebellion, and treated accordingly. By this proclamation it was also declared "that as the courts of judicature were shut, martial law should take place, till a due course of justice should be re-established." It was supposed that

MAY 25

JUNE 12

1775

this proclamation was a prelude to hostilities, and preparations were accordingly made by the Americans. A considerable height, by the name of Bunkers-hill, just at the entrance of the peninsula of Charlestown, was so situated as to make the possession of it a matter of great consequence, to either of the contending parties. Orders JUNE 16 were therefore issued by the provincial commanders that a detachment of a thousand men should intrench upon this height. By some mistake Breed's-hill, high and large like the other, but situated nearer Boston, was marked out for the intrenchments, instead of Bunkershill. The provincials proceeded to Breed's-hill and worked with so much diligence, that between midnight and the dawn of the morning, they had thrown up a small redoubt about 8 rods square. They kept such a profound silence that they were not heard by the British, on board their vessels, though very near. These having derived their first information of what was going on from the sight of the work near completion, began an incessant firing upon them. The provincials bore this with firmness, and though they were only young soldiers continued to labour till they had thrown up a small breastwork, extending from the east side of the redoubt to the bottom of the hill. As this eminence overlooked Boston general Gage thought it necessary to drive the provincials from it. About noon therefore he detached major general Howe and brig. general Pigot, with the flower of his army, consisting of four battalions, ten companies of the grenadiers JUNE 17 and ten of light infantry, with a proportion of field artillery, to effect this business. These troops landed at Moreton's point, and formed after landing, but remained in that position till they were reinforced by a second detachment of light infantry and grenadier companies, a battalion of land forces and a battalion of marines, [202] making in the whole nearly 3000 men. While the troops who first landed 1775 were waiting for this reinforcement, the provincials for their farther security, pulled up some adjoining post and rail fences, and set them down in two parallel lines at a small distance from each other, and filled the space between with hay, which having been lately mowed, remained on the adjacent ground.

The king's troops formed in two lines, and advanced slowly, to give their artillery time to demolish the American works. While the British were advancing to the attack, they received orders to burn Charlestown. This was not done because they were fired upon from the houses in that town, but from the military policy of depriving enemies of a cover in their approaches. In a short time this ancient town, consisting of about 500 buildings, chiefly of wood, was in one great blaze. The lofty steeple of the meeting house formed a pyramid of fire above the rest, and struck the astonished eyes of numerous beholders with a magnificent but awful spectacle. In Boston the heights of every kind were covered with the citizens, and such of the king's troops as were not on duty. The hills around the adjacent country which afforded a safe and distinct view, were occupied by the inhabitants of the country.

Thousands, both within and without Boston, were anxious spectators of the bloody scene. The honour of British troops beat high in the breasts of many, while others with a keener sensibility, felt for the liberties of a great and growing country. The British moved on but slowly, which gave the provincials a better opportunity for taking aim. The latter in general reserved themselves till their adversaries were within ten or twelve rods, but then began a furious discharge of small arms. The stream of the American fire was so incessant, and did so great execution that the king's troops retreated in disorder and precipitation. Their officers rallied them and pushed them forward with their swords, but they returned to the attack with great reluctance. The Americans again reserved their fire till their adversaries were near, and then put them a second time to flight. General Howe and the officers redoubled their exertions, and were again [203] successful, though the soldiers discovered a great aversion to going on. By this time the powder of the Americans began so far to fail that they were not able to keep up the same brisk fire as before. The British also brought some cannon to bear which raked the inside of the breast work from end to end. The fire from the ships, batteries, and field artillery was redoubled—the soldiers in the rear were goaded on by their officers. The redoubt was attacked on three sides at once. Under these circumstances a retreat from it was ordered, but the provincials delayed, and made resistance with their discharged muskets as if they had been clubs, so long that the king's troops who easily mounted the works had half filled the redoubt before it was given up to them.

While these operations were going on at the breast work and redoubt, the British light infantry were attempting to force the left point of the former, that they might take the American line in flank. Though they exhibited the most undaunted courage, they met with an opposition which called for its greatest exertions. The provincials here, in like manner, reserved their fire till their adversaries were near, and then poured it upon the light infantry, with such an incessant stream, and in so true a direction as mowed down their ranks. The engagement was kept up on both sides with great resolution. The persevering exertions of the king's troops could not compel the Americans to retreat, till they observed that their main body had left the hill. This, when begun, exposed them to new danger, for it could not be effected but by marching over Charlestown neck, every part of which was raked by the shot of the Glasgow man of war, and of two floating batteries. The incessant fire kept up across this neck prevented any considerable reinforcement from joining their countrymen who were engaged; but the few who fell on their retreat, over the same ground proved, that the apprehensions of those provincial officers who declined passing over to succour their companions, were without any solid foundation.

The number of Americans engaged, amounted only to 1500. It was apprehended that the conquerors would [204] push the advantage they had gained, and march immediately to American head quarters 1775 at Cambridge, but they advanced no farther than Bunker's-hill. There they threw up works for their own security. The provincials did the same on Prospect-hill in front of them. Both were guarding against an attack, and both were in a bad condition to receive one. The loss of the peninsula depressed the spirits of the Americans, and their great loss of men produced the same effect on the British. There have been few battles in modern wars, in which all circumstances considered, there was a greater destruction of men than in this short engagement. The loss of the British, as acknowledged by general Gage, amounted to 1054. Nineteen commissioned officers were killed, and 70 more were wounded. The battle of Quebec in 1759, which gave Great-Britain the province of Canada, was not so destructive to British officers as this affair of a slight intrenchment, the work only of a few hours. That the officers suffered so much, must be imputed to their being aimed at. None of the provincials in this engagement were riflemen, but they were all good marksmen. The whole of their previous military knowledge had been derived, from hunting, and the ordinary amusements of sportsmen. The dexterity which by long habit they had acquired in hitting beasts, birds, and marks, was fatally applied to the destruction of British officers. From their fall much confusion was expected. They were therefore particularly singled out. Most of those who were near the person of general Howe were either killed or wounded, but the general, though he greatly exposed himself, was unhurt. The light infantry and grenadiers lost three-fourths of their men. Of one company not more than five, and of another, not more than fourteen escaped. The unexpected resistance of the Americans was such as wiped away the reproaches of cowardice, which had been cast on them by their enemies in Britain. The spirited conduct of the British officers merited and obtained great applause, but the provincials were justly entitled to a large portion of the same, for having made the utmost exertions of their adversaries necessary to dislodge them [205] from lines, which were the work only of a single night.

1775

The Americans lost five pieces of cannon. Their killed amounted to 139. Their wounded and missing to 314. Thirty of the former fell into the hands of the conquerors. They particularly regretted the death of general Warren. To the purest patriotism and most undaunted bravery, he added the virtues of domestic life, the eloquence of an accomplished orator, and the wisdom of an able statesman. Nothing but a regard to the liberty of his country induced him to oppose the measures of government. He aimed not at a separation from, but a coalition with the Mother Country. He took an active part in defence of his country, not that he might be applauded and rewarded for a patriotic spirit, but because he was, in the best sense of the word, a real patriot. Having no interested or personal views to answer the friends of liberty, confided in his integrity. The soundness of his judgment, and his abilities as a public speaker, enabled him to make a distinguished figure in public councils, but his intrepidity and active zeal, induced his countrymen to place him in the military line. Within four days after he was appointed a major general, he fell a noble sacrifice to a cause which he had espoused from the purest principles. Like Hambden he lived and like Hambden he died, universally beloved and universally regretted. His many virtues were celebrated in an elegant eulogium written by Dr. Rush, in language equal to the illustrious subject. The burning of Charlestown, though a place of great trade did not discourage the provincials. It excited resentment and execration, but not any disposition to submit. Such was the high toned state of the public mind, and so great the indifference for property when put in competition with liberty, that military conflagrations, though they distressed and impoverished, had no tendency to subdue the colonists. They might answer in the old world, but were not calculated for the new, where the war was undertaken, not for a change of masters, but for securing essential rights. The action at Breed's-hill, or Bunker's-hill, as it has been commonly called, produced many and very important [206] consequences. It taught the British so much respect for Americans 1775 intrenched behind works, that their subsequent operations were retarded with a caution that wasted away a whole campaign, to very little purpose. It added to the confidence the Americans began to have in their own abilities, but inferences, very injurious to the future interests of America, were drawn from the good conduct of the new troops on that memorable day. It inspired some of the leading members of Congress, with such high ideas of what might be done by militia, or men engaged for a short term of enlistment, that it was long before they assented to the establishment of a permanent army. Not distinguishing the continued exertions of an army through a series of years, from the gallant efforts of the yeomanry of the country, led directly to action, they were slow in admitting the necessity of permanent troops. They conceived the country might be defended by the occasional exertions of her sons, without the expence and danger of an army engaged for the war. In the progress of hostilities, as will appear in the sequel, the militia lost much of their first ardor, while leading men in the councils of America, trusting to its continuance, neglected the proper time of recruiting for a series of years. From the want of perseverance in the militia, and the want of a disciplined standing army, the cause for which arms were at first taken up, was more than once brought to the brink of destruction.

The second Congress meets and organises a regular Continental Army—makes sundry public addresses, and petitions the King, &c. Transactions in Massachusetts.

1775   IT HAS ALREADY BEEN MENTIONED, that Congress previous to its dissolution, on the 26th of October, 1774, recommended to the colonies, to chuse members for another to meet on the tenth of May 1775, unless the redress of their grievances was previously obtained. A circular letter had been addressed by lord Dartmouth, to the [207] several colonial governors, requesting their interference to prevent the meeting of this second Congress: but ministerial requisitions had lost their influence, delegates were elected not only for the twelve colonies that were before represented, but also for the parish of St. John's in Georgia, and in July following, for the whole province. The time of the meeting of this second Congress was fixed at so distant a day, that an opportunity might be afforded for obtaining information of the plans adopted by the British parliament in the winter of 1774, 1775. Had these been favourable, the delegates would either not have met, or dispersed after a short session, but as the resolution was then fixed to compel the submission of the colonies, and hostilities had already commenced, the meeting of Congress on the tenth of May, which was at first eventual, became fixed. MAY 10

On their meeting, they chose Peyton Randolph for their President, and Charles Thomson for their secretary. On the next day Mr. Hancock laid before them a variety of depositions, proving that the king's troops were the aggressors in the late battle at Lexington, together with sundry papers relative to the great events which had lately taken place in Massachusetts: Whereupon Congress resolved itself into a committee of the whole, to take into consideration the state of America. They proceeded in the same line of moderation and firmness, which marked the acts of their predecessors in the past year.

The city and county of New-York having applied to Congress for advice, how they should conduct themselves with regard to the troops expected to land there, they were advised "to act on the MAY 15 defensive so long as might be consistent with their safety—to permit the troops to remain in the barracks, so long as they behaved peaceably, but not to suffer fortifications to be erected, or any steps to be taken for cutting off the communication between the town and country." Congress also resolved, "That exportation to all parts of MAY 17 British America, which had not adopted their association, should immediately cease;" and that, "no provision of any kind, or other necessaries be furnished to the British fisheries on the American [208] coasts." And 1775

that no bill of exchange, draught, or order, of any officer in the British JUNE 2 army or navy, their agents or contractors, be received or negociated, or any money supplied them, by any person in America—that no provisions or necessaries of any kind, be furnished or supplied, to or for the use of the British army or navy, in the colony of Massachusetts Bay—that no vessel employed in transporting British troops to America, or from one part of North-America to another, or warlike stores or provisions for said troops, be freighted or furnished with provisions or any necessaries.

These resolutions may be considered as the counterpart of the British acts for restraining the commerce, and prohibiting the fisheries of the colonies. They were calculated to bring distress on the British islands in the West-Indies, whose chief dependence for subsistance, was on the importation of provision from the American continent. They also occasioned new difficulties in the support of the British army and fisheries. The colonists were so much indebted to Great-Britain, that government bills for the most part found among them a ready market. A war in the colonies was therefore made subservient to commerce, by increasing the sources of remittance. This enabled the Mother Country, in a great degree, to supply her troops without shipping money out of the kingdom. From the operation of these resolutions, advantages of this nature were not only cut off, but the supply of the British army rendered both precarious and expensive. In consequence of the interdiction of the American fisheries, great profits were expected by British adventurers in that line. Such frequently found it most convenient to obtain supplies in America for carrying on their fisheries; but as Great-Britain had deprived the colonists of all benefits from that quarter, they now in their turn, interdicted all supplies from being furnished to British fishermen. To obviate this unexpected embarrassment, several of the vessels employed in this business, were obliged to return home, to bring out provisions for their associates. These restrictive resolutions, were not so much the effect of resentment as of policy. The colonists conceived, that [209] by distressing the British commerce, they would encrease the number of those who would interest themselves in their behalf.

1775

The new Congress had convened but a few days when their venerable president Peyton Randolph, was under a necessity of returning home. On his departure John Hancock was unanimously chosen his successor. The objects of deliberation presented to this new Congress were, if possible, more important than those which in the preceding year, had engaged the attention of their predecessors. The colonists had now experienced the inefficacy of those measures, from which relief had been formerly obtained. They found a new parliament disposed to run all risques in inforcing their submission. They also understood that administration was united against them, and its members firmly established in their places. Hostilities were commenced. Reinforcements had arrived, and more were daily expected. Added to this, they had information that their adversaries had taken measures to secure the friendship and co-operation of the Indians; and also of the Canadians.

The coercion of the colonies being resolved upon, and their conquest supposed to be inevitable, the British ministry judged that it would be for the interest of both countries to proceed in that vigorous course, which bid fairest for the speediest attainment of their object. They hoped by pressing the colonists on all quarters, to intimidate opposition, and ultimately to lessen the effusion of human blood.

In this awful crisis Congress had but a choice of difficulties. The New-England states had already organized an army and blockaded general Gage. To desert them would have been contrary to plighted faith and to sound policy. To support them would make the war general, and involve all the provinces in one general promiscuous state of hostility. The resolution of the people in favour of the latter was fixed, and only wanted public sanction for its operation. Congress therefore resolved, "that for the express purpose of defending and securing the colonies, and preserving them in safety, against [210] all attempts to carry the late acts of a parliament into execution, by force of arms, they be immediately put in a state of defence; but as they wished for a restoration of the harmony formerly subsisting between the Mother Country and the colonies, to the promotion of this most desirable reconciliation, an humble and dutiful petition be presented to his majesty." To resist and to petition were coeval resolutions. As freemen they could not tamely submit, but as loyal subjects, wishing for peace as far as was compatible with their rights, they once more, in the character of petitioners, humbly stated their grievances to the common father of the empire. To dissuade the Canadians from co-operating with the British, they again addressed them, representing the pernicious tendency of the Quebec act, and apologizing for their taking Ticonderoga and Crown-Point, as measures which were dictated by the great law of self preservation. About the same time Congress took measures for warding off the danger that threatened their frontier inhabitants from Indians. Commissioners to treat with them were appointed, and a supply of goods for their use was ordered. A talk was also prepared by Congress, and

MAY 26

1775

transmitted to them, in which the controversy between Great-Britain and her colonies was explained, in a familiar Indian style. They were told that they had no concern in the family quarrel, and were urged by the ties of ancient friendship and a common birth place, to remain at home, keep their hatchet buried deep, and to join neither side.

The novel situation of Massachusetts made it necessary for the ruling powers of that province to ask the advice of Congress on a very interesting subject, "The taking up and exercising the powers of civil government." For many months they had been kept together in tolerable peace and order by the force of ancient habits, under the simple style of recommendation and advice from popular bodies, invested with no legislative authority. But as war now raged in their borders, and a numerous army was actually raised, some more efficient form of government became necessary. At this early day it neither [211] comported with the wishes nor the designs of the colonists to erect forms of government independent of Great-Britain, Congress therefore recommended only such regulations as were immediately necessary, and these were conformed as near as possible to the spirit and substance of the charter, and were only to last till a governor of his majesty's appointment would consent to govern the colony according to its charter.

On the same principles of necessity, another assumption of new powers became unavoidable. The great intercourse that daily took place throughout the colonies, pointed out the propriety of establishing a general post-office. This was accordingly done, and Dr. Franklin, who had by royal authority been dismissed from a similar employment about three years before, was appointed by his country, the head of the new department.

While Congress was making arrangements for their proposed continental army, it was thought expedient once more to address the inhabitants of Great-Britain, and to publish to the world a declaration setting forth their reasons for taking up arms—to address the speaker and gentlemen of the assembly of Jamaica, and the inhabitants of Ireland, and also to prefer a second humble petition to the king. In their address to the inhabitants of Great-Britain, they again vindicated themselves from the charge of aiming at independency, professed their willingness to submit to the several acts of trade and navigation which were passed before the year 1763, recapitulated their reasons for rejecting lord North's conciliatory motion—stated the hardships they suffered from the operations of the royal army in Boston, and insinuated the danger the inhabitants of Britain would be in of losing their freedom, in case their American brethren were subdued.

In their declaration, setting forth the causes and necessity of their taking up arms, they enumerated the injuries they had received, and the methods taken by the British ministry to compel their submission, and then said, "We are reduced to the alternative of choosing an unconditional submission to the tyranny of irritated ministers, or [212] resistance by force. The latter is our choice. We have counted the cost of this contest, and find nothing so dreadful as voluntary slavery." They asserted "that foreign assistance was undoubtedly attainable." This was not founded on any private information, but was an opinion derived from their knowledge of the principles of policy, by which states usually regulate their conduct towards each other.

In their address to the speaker and gentlemen of the assembly of Jamaica, they dilated on the arbitrary systems of the British ministry, and informed them that in order to obtain a redress of their grievances, they had appealed to the justice, humanity, and interest of Great-Britain. They stated, that to make their schemes of non-importation and non-exportation produce the desired effects, they were obliged to extend them to the islands. "From that necessity, and from that alone, said they, our conduct has proceeded." They concluded with saying, "the peculiar situation of your island forbids your assistance, but we have your good wishes—from the good wishes of the friends of liberty and mankind we shall always derive consolation."

In their address to the people of Ireland they recapitulated their grievances, stated their humble petitions, and the neglect with which they had been treated. "In defence of our persons and properties under actual violations, said they, we have taken up arms. When that violence shall be removed, and hostilities cease on the part of the aggressors, they shall cease on our part also."

These several addresses were executed in a masterly manner, and were well calculated to make friends to the colonies. But their petition

1775

to the king, which was drawn up at the same time, produced more solid advantages in favour of the American cause, than any other of their productions. This was in a great measure carried through Congress by Mr. Dickinson. Several members, judging from the violence with which parliament proceeded against the colonies, were of opinion that farther petitions were nugatory; but this worthy citizen, a friend to both countries, and devoted to a reconciliation on [213] constitutional principles, urged the expediency and policy of trying once more the effect of an humble, decent, and firm petition, to the common head of the empire. The high opinion that was conceived of his patriotism and abilities, induced the members to assent to the measure, though they generally conceived it to be labour lost. The petition agreed upon was the work of Mr. Dickinson's pen. In this, among other things, it was stated,

1775

JULY 8

> that notwithstanding their sufferings, they had retained too high a regard for the kingdom from which they derived their origin, to request such a reconciliation as might in any manner be inconsistent with her dignity and welfare. Attached to his majesty's person, family, and government, with all the devotion that principle and affection can inspire, connected with Great-Britain by the strongest ties that can unite society, and deploring every event that tended in any degree to weaken them, they not only most fervently desired the former harmony between her and the colonies to be restored, but that a concord might be established between them, upon so firm a basis as to perpetuate its blessings, uninterrupted by any future dissentions, to succeeding generations, in both countries. They therefore beseeched that his majesty would be pleased to direct some mode by which the united applications of his faithful colonists to the throne, in pursuance of their common councils, might be improved into a happy and permanent reconciliation.

By this last clause Congress meant that the Mother Country should propose a plan for establishing by compact, something like Magna Charta for the colonies. They did not aim at a total exemption from the controul of parliament, nor were they unwilling to contribute in their own way, to the expences of government; but they feared the horrors of war less than submission to unlimited parliamentary supremacy. They wished for an amicable compact, in which doubtful, undefined points, should be ascertained so as to secure that proportion of authority and liberty which would be for the general good of the whole empire. They fancied themselves in the condition of the barons at Runnymede; but with this difference, that in [214] addition to opposing the king, they had also to oppose the parliament. This difference was more nominal than real, for in the latter case the king and parliament stood precisely in the same relation to the people of America, which subsisted in the former between the king and people of England. In both, popular leaders were contending with the sovereign for the privileges of subjects. This well meant petition was presented on September 1st, 1775, by Mr. Penn and Mr. Lee, and on the 4th lord Dartmouth informed them, "that to it no answer would be given." This slight contributed not a little to the union and perseverance of the colonists. When pressed by the calamities of war, a doubt would sometimes arise in the minds of scrupulous persons, that they had been too hasty in their opposition to their protecting Parent State. To such it was usual to present the second petition of Congress to the king, observing thereon, that all the blood and all the guilt of the war, must be charged on British, and not on American counsels. Though the colonists were accused in a speech from the throne, as meaning only, "to amuse by vague expressions of attachment to the Parent State, and the strongest protestations of loyalty to their king, while they were preparing for a general revolt, and that their rebellious war was manifestly carried on for the purpose of establishing an independent empire." Yet at that time, and for months after, a redress of grievances was their ultimate aim. Conscious of this intention, and assenting in the sincerity of their souls to the submissive language of their petition, they illy brooked the contempt with which their joint supplication was treated, and still worse, that they should be charged from the throne with studied duplicity. Nothing contributes more to the success of revolutions than moderation. Intemperate zealots overshoot themselves, and soon spend their force, while the calm and dispassionate persevere to the end. The bulk of the people in civil commotions are influenced to a choice of sides, by the general complexion of the measures adopted by the respective parties. When these appear to be dictated by justice and prudence, and to be [215] uninfluenced by passion, ambition or avarice, they are disposed to favour them. Such was the effect of this second petition, through a long and trying war, in which

1775

OCT. 26

men of serious reflection were often called upon to examine the rectitude of their conduct.

Though the refusal of an answer to this renewed application of Congress to the king, was censured by numbers in Great-Britain, as well as in the colonies, yet the partisans of ministry varnished the measure as proper and expedient. They contended that the petition, as it contained no offers of submission, was unavailing, as a ground work of negociation. Nothing was farther from the thoughts of Congress than such concessions as were expected in Great-Britain. They conceived themselves to be more sinned against than sinning. They claimed a redress of grievances as a matter of right, but were persuaded that concessions for this purpose were acts of justice and not of humiliation, and therefore could not be disgraceful to those by whom they were made. To prevent future altercations they wished for an amicable compact to ascertain the extent of parliamentary supremacy. The Mother Country wished for absolute submission to her authority, the colonists for a repeal of every act that imposed taxes, or that interfered in their internal legislation. The ministry of England being determined not to repeal these acts, and the Congress equally determined not to submit to them, the claims of the two countries were so wide of each other as to afford no reasonable ground to expect a compromise. It was therefore concluded, that any notice taken of the petition would only afford an opportunity for the colonies to prepare themselves for the last extremity.

A military opposition to the armies of Great-Britain being resolved upon by the colonies, it became an object of consequence to fix on a proper person to conduct that opposition. Many of the colonists had titles of high rank in the militia, and several had seen something of real service, in the late war between France and England; but there was no individual of such superior military experience as to entitle him to a decided pre-eminence, or even [216] to qualify him, on that ground, to contend on equal terms with the British masters of the art of war. In elevating one man, by the free voice of an invaded country, to the command of thousands of his equal fellow citizens, no consideration was regarded but the interest of the community. To bind the uninvaded provinces more closely to the common cause, policy directed the views of Congress to the south.

1775

Among the southern colonies Virginia, for numbers, wealth, and influence, stood pre-eminent. To attach so respectable a colony to the aid of Massachusetts, by selecting a commander in chief from that quarter, was not less warranted by the great military genius of one of her distinguished citizens, than dictated by sound policy. George Washington was, by an unanimous vote appointed, com- JUNE 15 mander in chief of all the forces raised, or to be raised, for the defence of the colonies. It was a fortunate circumstance attending his election, that it was accompanied with no competition, and followed by no envy. That same general impulse on the public mind, which led the colonists to agree in many other particulars, pointed to as the most proper person for presiding over the military arrangements of America. Not only Congress but the inhabitants in the east and the west, in the north and, the south, as well before as at the time of embodying a continental army were in a great degree unanimous in his favour. An attempt to draw the character of this truly great man would look like flattery. Posterity will doubtless do it justice. His actions, especially now, while fresh in remembrance, are his amplest panegyric. Suffice it, in his life time, only to particularise those qualities, which being more common, may be mentioned without offending the delicate sensibility of the most modest of men.

General Washington was born on the 11th of February 1732. His education was such as favoured the production of a solid mind and a vigorous body. Mountain air, abundant exercise in the open country—the wholesome toils of the chace, and the delightful scenes of rural life, expanded his limbs to an unusual but graceful [217] and well proportioned size. His youth was spent in the acquisition of 1775 useful knowledge, and in pursuits, tending to the improvement of his fortune, or the benefit of his country. Fitted more for active, than for speculative life, he devoted the greater proportion of his time to the latter, but this was amply compensated by his being frequently in such situations, as called forth the powers of his mind, and strengthened them by repeated exercise. Early in life, in obedience to his country's call, he entered the military line, and began his career of fame in opposing that power in concert with whose troops, he acquired his last and most distinguished honours. He was with general Braddock in 1755, when that unfortunate officer from an excess of bravery, chose rather to sacrifice his army than retreat from an unseen foe. The remains of that unfortunate corpse were brought off the field of battle chiefly by the address and good conduct of colonel Washington. After the peace of Paris 1763, he retired to his estate, and with great industry and success pursued the arts of peaceful life. When the proceedings of the British parliament alarmed the colonists with apprehensions that a blow was levelled at their liberties, he again came forward into public view, and was appointed a delegate to the Congress, which met in September 1774. Possessed of a large proportion of common sense directed by a sound judgment, he was better fitted for the exalted station to which he was called, than many others who to a greater brilliancy of parts frequently add the eccentricity of original genius. Engaged in the busy scenes of life, he knew human nature, and the most proper method of accomplishing proposed objects. His passions were subdued and kept in subjection to reason. His soul superior to party spirit, to prejudice and illiberal views, moved according to the impulses it received from an honest heart, a good understanding, common sense, and a sound judgment. He was habituated to view things on every side, to consider them in all relations, and to trace the possible and probable consequences of proposed measures. Much addicted to close thinking, his mind was constantly employed. By frequent exercise, [218] his understanding and judgment expanded so as to be able to discern truth, and to know what was proper to be done in the most difficult conjunctures.

1775

Soon after general Washington was appointed commander in chief of the American army. Four major generals, one adjutant general, with the rank of a brigadier, and eight brigadiers general were appointed in subordination to him which were as follows.

1st. Major General	Artemas Ward
2d.	Charles Lee
3d.	Philip Schuyler
4th.	Israel Putnam
Adjutant General	Horatio Gates

The 8 Brigadiers were

1st.	Seth Pomeroy
2d.	Richard Montgomery
3d.	David Wooster
4th.	William Heath
5th.	Joseph Spencer
6th.	John Thomas
7th.	John Sullivan
8th.	Nathaniel Greene

General Washington replied to the president of Congress, announcing his appointment in the following words.

Mr. President,

Though I am truly sensible of the high honour done me in this appointment, yet, I feel great distress from a consciousness, that my abilities and military experience may not be equal to the extensive and important trust: however as the Congress desire it, I will enter upon the momentous duty, and exert every power I possess in their service, and for support of the glorious cause. I beg they will accept my most cordial thanks for this distinguished testimony of their approbation.

But, lest some unlucky event should happen unfavourable to my reputation, I beg it may be remembered by every gentleman in the room, that I this day declare with the utmost sincerity, I do not think myself equal to the command I am honoured with.

[219] As to pay sir, I beg leave to assure the Congress, that as no pecuniary consideration could have tempted me to accept this arduous employment, at the expence of my domestic ease and happiness, I do not wish to make any profit from it. I will keep an exact account of my expences. Those I doubt not they will discharge, and that is all I desire.

A special commission was drawn up and presented to him, and at the same time an unanimous resolution was adopted by Congress, "That they would maintain and assist him, and adhere to him with their lives and fortunes in the cause of American liberty." Instructions were also given him for his government, by which after reciting various particulars he was directed, "to destroy or make prisoners of all persons who now are, or who hereafter shall appear in arms

1775

against the good people of the colonies:" but the whole was summed up in authorising him "to order and dispose of the army under his command as might be most advantageous for obtaining the end for which it had been raised, making it his special care in discharge of the great trust committed to him, that the liberties of America received no detriment." About the same time twelve companies of

JUNE
14–22

riflemen were ordered to be raised in Pennsylvania, Maryland and Virginia. The men to the amount of 1430 were procured and forwarded with great expedition. They had to march from 4 to 700 miles, and yet the whole business was compleated and they joined the American army at Cambridge, in less than two months from the day on which the first resolution for raising them was agreed to.

JUNE 22

Coeval with the resolution for raising an army, was another for emitting a sum not exceeding two millions of Spanish milled dollars in bills of credit for the defence of America, and the colonies were pledged for the redemption of them. This sum was increased from time to time by farther emissions. The colonies having neither money nor revenues at their command, were forced to adopt this expedient, the only one which was in their power for supporting an army. No

1775

one delegate [220] opposed the measure. So great had been the credit of the former emissions of paper in the greater part of the colonies, that very few at that time foresaw or apprehended the consequences of unfunded paper emissions, but had all the consequences which resulted from this measure in the course of the war been forseen, it must notwithstanding have been adopted, for it was a less evil, that there should be a general wreck of property, than that the essential rights and liberties of a growing country should be lost. A happy ignorance of future events combined with the ardor of the times, prevented many reflections on this subject, and gave credit and circulation to these bills of credit.

General Washington soon after his appointment to the command of the American army set out for the camp at Cambridge. On his way thither, he received an address from the provincial congress of New-York, in which they expressed their joy at his appointment. They also said, "we have the fullest assurances that whenever this important contest shall be decided by that fondest wish of each American soul, an accommodation with our Mother Country, you will chearfully resign the important deposit committed into your hands, and re-assume the character of our worthiest citizen.["] The general after declaring his gratitude for the regard shewn him, added,

> Be assured that every exertion of my worthy colleagues and myself, will be extended to the re-establishment of peace and harmony between the Mother Country and these colonies. As to the fatal but necessary operations of war, when we assumed the soldier, we did not lay aside the citizen, and we shall most sincerely rejoice with you in that happy hour, when the re-establishment of American liberty, on the most firm and solid foundations shall enable us to return to our private stations, in the bosom of a free, peaceful, and happy country.

The general on his way to camp was treated with the highest honours in every place through which he passed. Large detachments of volunteers composed of private gentlemen turned out to escort him. A committee from the Massachusetts Congress received him about 100 miles [221] from Boston, and conducted him to the army. He was soon after addressed by the Congress of that colony in the most affectionate manner, in his answer he said,   1775

> Gentlemen, your kind congratulations on my appointment and arrival, demand my warmest ackowledgements, and will ever be retained in grateful remembrance. In exchanging the enjoyments of domestic life for the duties of my present honourable but arduous station, I only emulate the virtue and public spirit of the whole province of Massachusetts, which, with a firmness and patriotism without example, has sacrificed all the comforts of social and political life, in support of the rights of mankind and the welfare of our common country. My highest ambition is to be the happy instrument of vindicating these rights, and to see this devoted province again restored to peace, liberty and safety.

When general Washington arrived at Cambridge, he was received with the joyful acclamations of the American army. At the head of his troops he published a declaration, previously drawn up by Congress, in the nature of a manifesto, setting forth the reasons for taking up arms. In this, after enumerating various grievances of the   JULY 3 colonies, and vindicating them from a premeditated design of establishing independent states, it was added,

> In our own native land, in defence of the freedom which is our birthright, and which we ever enjoyed till the late violation of it—for the protection of our property, acquired solely by the industry of our forefathers and ourselves, against violence actually offered, we have taken up arms, we shall lay them down when hostilities shall cease on the part of the aggressors, and all danger of their being renewed shall be removed, and not before.

When general Washington joined the American army, he found the British intrenched on Bunker's-hill, having also three floating batteries in Mystic river, and a twenty gun ship below the ferry, between Boston and Charlestown. They had also a battery on Copse's hill, and were strongly fortified on the neck. The Americans were intrenched at Winter-hill, Prospect-hill, and Roxbury, communicating with one another by small posts, [222] over a distance of ten miles. There were also parties stationed in several towns along the sea coast. They had neither engineers to plan suitable works, nor sufficient tools for their erection.

In the American camp was collected a large body of men, but without those conveniencies which ancient establishments have introduced for the comfort of regular armies. Instead of tents, sails now rendered useless by the obstructions of commerce, were applied for their covering; but even of them, there was not a sufficiency. The American soldiers having joined the camp in all that variety of clothing which they used in their daily labour, were without uniformity of dress. To abolish provincial distinctions, the hunting shirt was introduced. They were also without those heads of departments in the line of commissaries or quarter masters, which are necessary for the regular and economical supply of armies. The troops from Connecticut had proper officers appointed to procure them supplies, but they who came from the other colonies were not so well furnished. Individuals brought to camp their own provisions on their own horses. In some parts committees of supplies were appointed, who purchased necessaries at public expence, sent them on to camp, and distributed them to such as were in want, without any regularity or

1775

system; the country afforded provisions, and nothing more was wanting to supply the army than proper systems for their collection and distribution. Other articles, though equally necessary, were almost wholly deficient, and could not be procured but with difficulty. On the 4th of August the whole stock of powder in the American camp, and in the public magazines of the four New-England provinces, would make but little more than nine rounds a man. The continental army remained in this destitute condition for a fortnight or more. This was generally known among themselves, and was also communicated to the British, by a deserter, but they suspecting a plot would not believe it. A supply of a few tons was sent on to them from the committee of Elizabeth-town, but this was done privately, lest the adjacent inhabitants, who were equally destitute [223] should stop it for their own use. The public rulers in Massachusetts issued a 1775 recommendation to the inhabitants, not to fire a gun at beast, bird or mark, in order that they might husband their little stock for the more necessary purpose of shooting men. A supply of several thousand pounds weight of powder, was soon after obtained from Africa in exchange for New-England rum. This was managed with so much address, that every ounce for sale in the British forts on the African coasts, was purchased up and brought off for the use of the Americans.

Embarrassments from various quarters occurred in the formation of a continental army. The appointment of general officers made by Congress, was not satisfactory. Enterprising leaders had come forward with their followers on the commencement of hostilities, without scrupulous attention to rank. When these were all blended together, it was impossible to assign to every officer the station which his services merited, or his vanity demanded. Materials for a good army were collected. The husbandmen who flew to arms were active, zealous, and of unquestionable courage, but to introduce discipline and subordination, among free men who were habituated to think for themselves, was an arduous labour.

The want of system and of union, under proper heads, pervaded every department. From the circumstance that the persons employed in providing necessaries for the army were unconnected with each other, much waste and unnecessary delays were occasioned. The troops of the different colonies came into service under variant establishments—some were enlisted with the express condition of choosing their officers. The rations promised by the local legislatures varied both as to quantity, quality and price. To form one uniform mass of these discordant materials, and to subject the licentiousness of independent freemen to the controul of military discipline, was a delicate and difficult business.

The continental army put under the command of general Washington, amounted to about 14,500 men. These had been so judiciously stationed round Boston, as [224] to confine the British to the town, and to exclude them from the forage and provisions which the adjacent country and islands in Boston-bay afforded. This force was thrown into three grand divisions. General Ward commanded the right wing at Roxbury. General Lee the left at Prospect-hill, and the centre was commanded by general Washington. In arranging the army, the military skill of adjutant-general Gates was of great service. Method and punctuality were introduced. The officers and privates were taught to know their respective places, and to have the mechanism and movements as well as the name of an army.

When some effectual pains had been taken to discipline the army, it was found that the term for which enlistments had taken place, was on the point of expiring. The troops from Connecticut and Rhode-Island were only engaged till the 1st day of December 1775, and no part of the army longer than the first day of January 1776. Such mistaken apprehensions respecting the future conduct of Great-Britain prevailed, that many thought the assumption of a determined spirit of resistance would lead to a redress of all their grievances.

OCT. 10   Towards the close of the year, general Gage sailed for England, and the command devolved on general Howe.

NOV.   The Massachusetts assembly and continental Congress both resolved, to fit out armed vessels to cruise on the American coast, for the purpose of interrupting warlike stores and supplies designed for the use of the British army. The object was at first limited, but as the prospect of accommodation vanished, it was extended to all British property afloat on the high seas. The Americans were diffident of their ability to do any thing on water in opposition to the greatest naval power in the world, but from a combination of circumstances, their first attempts were successful.

NOV. 29   The Lee privateer, captain Manly, took the brig Nancy, an ordnance ship from Woolwich, containing a large brass mortar, several pieces of brass cannon, a large quantity of arms and ammunition, with all manner of tools, [225] utensils and machines, necessary for camps and artillery. Had Congress sent an order for supplies, they could not have made out a list of articles more suitable to their situation, than what was thus providentially thrown into their hands.

In about 9 days after three ships, with various stores for the British army, and a brig from Antigua with rum, were taken by capt. Manly. Before five days more had elapsed, several other store ships were captured. By these means the distresses of the British troops, in Boston, were increased, and supplies for the continental army were procured. Naval captures, being unexpected, were matter of triumph to the Americans, and of surprize to the British. The latter scarcely believed that the former would oppose them by land with a regular army, but never suspected that a people, so unfurnished as they were with many things necessary for arming vessels, would presume to attempt any thing on water. A spirit of enterprize, invigorated by patriotic zeal, prompted the hardy New Englandmen to undertake the hazardous business, and their success encouraged them to proceed. Before the close of the year, Congress determined to build 5 vessels of 32 guns, 5 of 28, and 3 of 24. While the Americans were fitting out armed vessels, and before they had made any captures, an event took place which would have disposed a less determined people to desist from provoking the vengeance of the British navy. This was the burning of Falmouth in the northern parts of Massachusetts. Captain Mowat, in the Canceaux of sixteen guns, destroyed 139 houses and 278 stores, and other buildings in that town.

This spread an alarm on the coast, but produced no disposition to submit, many moved from the sea ports with their families and effects, but no solicitations were preferred for the obtaining of British protection.

In a few days after the burning of Falmouth, the old south meeting house in Boston, was taken into possession by the British, and destined for a riding school, and the service of the light dragoons. These proceedings produced, in the minds of the colonists, a more determined spirit of resistance, and a more general aversion to Great-Britain.

1775

DEC. 8

DEC. 13

OCT. 18

Ticonderoga taken, and Canada invaded.

[226] IT EARLY OCCURRED TO MANY, that if the sword decided the controversy between Great-Britain and her colonies, the possession of Ticonderoga would be essential to the security of the latter. Situated on a promontary, formed at the junction of the waters of lake George and lake Champlain, it is the key of all communication between New-York and Canada. Messrs. Deane, Wooster, Parsons, Stevens, and others of Connecticut, planned a scheme for obtaining possession of this valuable post. Having procured a loan of 1800 dollars of public money, and provided a sufficient quantity of powder and ball, they set off for Bennington, to obtain the co-operation of colonel Allen of that place. Two hundred and seventy men, mostly of that brave and hardy people, who are called green mountain boys, were speedily collected at Castleton, which was fixed on as the place

of rendezvous. At this place colonel Arnold, who, though attended only with a servant, was prosecuting the same object, unexpectedly joined them. He had been early chosen a captain of a volunteer company, by the inhabitants of New-Haven, among whom he resided. As soon as he recieved news of the Lexington battle, he marched off with his company for the vicinity of Boston, and arrived there, though 150 miles distant, in a few days. Immediately after his arrival he waited on the Massachusetts committee of safety, and informed them, that there were at Ticonderoga many pieces of cannon and a great quantity of valuable stores, and that the fort was in a ruinous condition, and garrisoned only by about 40 men. They appointed him a colonel, and commissioned him to raise 400 men, and to take Ticonderoga. The leaders of the party which had previously rendez-voused at Castleton, admitted colonel Arnold to join them, and it was agreed that colonel Allen should be the commander in chief of the expedition, and that colonel Arnold should be his assistant. They proceeded without delay, and arrived in the night at lake Champlain, opposite to Ticonderoga. [227] Allen and Arnold crossed over with 83 men, and landed near the garrison. They contended who should go in first, but it was at last agreed that they should both go in together. They advanced abreast, and entered the fort at the dawning of day. A sentry snapped his piece at one of them, and then retreated through the covered way to the parade. The Americans followed and immediately drew up. The commander surprised in his bed, was called upon to surrender the fort. He asked, by what authority? Colonel Allen replied, "I demand it in the name of the great Jehovah, and the Continental Congress." No resistance was made, and the fort with its valuable stores, and forty-eight prisoners, fell into the hands of the Americans. The boats had been sent back for the remainder of the men, but the business was done before they got over. Colonel Seth Warner was sent off with a party to take possession of Crown-point, where a serjeant and 12 men performed garrison duty. This was speedily effected. The next object, calling for the attention of the Americans, was to obtain the command of lake Champlain, but to accomplish this, it was necessary for them to get possession of a sloop of war, lying at St. John's, at the northern extremity of the lake. With the view of capturing this sloop it was agreed to man and

1775

MAY 9

MAY 10

arm a schooner lying at South Bay, and that Arnold should command her, and that Allen should command some batteaux on the same expedition. A favourable wind carried the schooner a-head of the batteaux, and colonel Arnold got immediate possession of the sloop by surprise. The wind again favouring him, he returned with his prize to Ticonderoga, and rejoined colonel Allen. The latter soon went home, and the former with a number of men agreed to remain there in garrison. In this rapid manner the possession of Ticonderoga, and the command of lake Champlain was obtained, without any loss, by a few determined men. Intelligence of these events was in a few days communicated to Congress, which met for the first time, at 10 o'clock of the same day, in the morning of which, Ticonderoga was taken. They rejoiced in the spirit of enterprise, displayed by their

1775

[228] countrymen, but feared the charge of being aggressors, or of doing any thing to widen the breach between Great-Britain and the colonies; for an accommodation was at that time, nearly their unanimous wish. They therefore recommended to the committees of the cities and counties of New-York and Albany, to cause the cannon and stores to be removed from Ticonderoga to the south end of lake George, and to take an exact inventory of them, "in order that they might be safely returned when the restoration of the former harmony between Great-Britain and the colonies, so ardently wished for by the latter, should render it prudent and consistent with the overruling law of self-preservation."

Colonel Arnold having begun his military career with a series of successes, was urged by his native impetuosity to project more extensive operations. He wrote a letter to Congress, strongly urging

JUNE 13

an expedition into Canada, and offering with 2000 men to reduce the whole province. In his ardent zeal to oppose Great-Britain, he had advised the adoption of offensive war, even before Congress had organised an army or appointed a single military officer. His importunity was at last successful, as shall hereafter be related, but not till two months had elapsed, subsequent to his first proposition of conducting an expedition against Canada. Such was the increasing fervor of the public mind in 1775, that what, in the early part of the year, was deemed violent and dangerous, was in its progress pronounced both moderate and expedient.

Sir Guy Carleton, the king's governor in Canada no sooner heard that the Americans had surprised Ticonderoga and Crown-point, and obtained the command of lake Champlain, than he planned a scheme for their recovery. Having only a few regular troops under his command, he endeavoured to induce the Canadians and Indians to co-operate with him, but they both declined. He established martial law that he might compel the inhabitants to take arms. They declared themselves ready to defend the province, but refused to march out of it, or to commence hostilities on their neighbors. Colonel Johnston had, on the same occasion, repeated conferences with the [229] Indians, and endeavoured to influence them to take up the hatchet, but they steadily refused. In order to gain their co-operation he invited them to feast on a Bostonian, and to drink his blood. This, in the Indian style, meant no more than to partake of a roasted ox and a pipe of wine, at a public entertainment, which was given on design to influence them to co-operate with the British troops. The colonial patriots, affected to understand it in its literal sense. It furnished, in their mode of explication, a convenient handle for operating on the passions of the people.

These exertions in Canada, which were principally made with a view to recover Ticonderoga, Crown-point, and the command of lake Champlain, induced Congress to believe that a formidable invasion of their northwestern frontier was intended, from that quarter. The evident tendency of the Quebec act favoured this opinion. Believing it to be the fixed purpose of the British ministry to attack the united colonies on that side, they conceived that they would be inexcusable if they neglected the proper means for warding off so terrible a blow. They were also sensible that the only practicable plan to effect this purpose, was to make a vigorous attack upon Canada, while it was unable to resist the unexpected impression. Their success at Ticonderoga and Crown-point, had already paved the way for this bold enterprize, and had broken down the fences which guarded the entrance into that province. On the other hand, they were sensible that by taking this step, they changed at once the whole nature of the war. From defensive it became offensive, and subjected them to the imputation of being the aggressors. They were well aware that several who had espoused their cause in Britain, would probably be

1775

offended at this measure, and charge them with heightening the mischiefs occasioned by the dispute. They knew that the principles of resistance, as far as they had hitherto acted upon them, were abetted by a considerable party even in Great-Britain; and that to forfeit their good opinion, might be of great disservice. Considerations of this kind made them weigh well the important step before [230] they ventured upon it. They on the other hand reflected that the eloquence of the minority in parliament, and the petitions and remonstrances of the merchants in Great-Britain, had produced no solid advantages in their favour; and that they had no chance of relief, but from the smiles of heaven on their own endeavors. The danger was pressing. War was not only inevitable, but already begun. To wait till they were attacked by a formidable force at their backs, in the very instant when their utmost exertions would be requisite, perhaps insufficient, to protect their cities and sea coast against an invasion from Britain, would be the summit of folly. The laws of war and of nations justified the forestalling of an enemy. The colonists argued that to prevent known hostile intentions, was a matter of self defence; they were also sensible they had already gone such lengths as could only be vindicated by arms; and that if a certain degree of success did not attend their resistance, they would be at the mercy of an irritated government, and their moderation in the single instance of Canada, would be an unavailing plea for indulgence. They were also encouraged to proceed, by certain information that the French inhabitants of Canada, except the noblesse and the clergy, were as much discontended with their present system of government as even the British settlers. It seemed therefore probable, that they would consider the provincials, rather as friends than as enemies. The invasion of that province was therefore determined upon, if found practicable, and not disagreeable to the Canadians.

Congress had committed the management of their military arrangements, in this northern department, to general Schuyler and general Montgomery. While the former remained at Albany, to attend an Indian treaty, the latter was sent forward to Ticonderoga, with a body of troops from New-York and New-England. Soon after reaching Ticonderoga, he made a movement down Lake Champlain. General Schuyler overtook him at Cape le Motte; from thence they moved on to Isle aux Noix. About this time general Schuyler addressed the inhabitants informing them, "that the only views of [231] Congress were to restore to them those rights which every subject of the British empire, of whatever religious sentiments he may be, is entitled to; and that in the execution of these truths he had received the most positive orders to cherish every Canadian, and every friend to the cause of liberty, and sacredly to guard their property." The Americans, about 1000 in number, effected a landing at St. John's, which being the first British post in Canada, lies only 115 miles to the northward of Ticonderoga. The British piquets were driven into the fort. The environs were then reconnoitered, and the fortifications were found to be much stronger than had been suspected. This induced the calling of a council of war, which recommended a retreat to Isle aux Noix, twelve miles south of St. John's, to throw a boom across the channel, and to erect works for its defence. Soon after this event, an extreme bad state of health induced general Schuyler to retire to Ticonderoga, and the command devolved on general Montgomery.

1775

SEP. 10

This enterprising officer in a few days returned to the vicinity of St. John's, and opened a battery against it. Ammunition was so scarce, that the siege could not be carried on with any prospect of speedy success. The general detached a small body of troops, to attempt the reduction of fort Chamblee, only six miles distant. Success attended this enterprize. By its surrender six tons of gun powder were obtained, which enabled the general to prosecute the siege of St. John's with vigor. The garrison, though straitened for provisions, persevered in defending themselves with unabating fortitude. While general Montgomery was prosecuting this siege, the governor of the province collected, at Montreal, about 800 men chiefly militia and Indians. He endeavoured to cross the river St. Lawrence, with this force, and to land at Lonqueil, intending to proceed thence to attack the besiegers, but colonel Warner with 300 green mountain boys, and a four pounder, prevented the execution of the design. The governor's party was suffered to come near the shore, but was then fired upon with such effect as to make them retire after sustaining great loss.

[232] An account of this affair being communicated to the garrison

in St. John's, major Preston, the commanding officer surrendered, on receiving honorable terms of capitulation. By these it was agreed, that the garrison should march out with the honors of war, that the officers and privates should ground their arms on the plain—the officers keep their side arms and their fire arms, be reserved for them, and that the people of the garrison should retain their effects. About 500 regulars and 100 Canadians became prisoners to the provincials. They also acquired 39 pieces of cannon, seven mortars, and two howitzers, and about 800 stand of arms. Among the cannon were many brass field pieces, an article of which the Americans were nearly destitute.

While the siege of St. John's was pending, colonel Allen, who was returning with about 80 men from a tour on which he had been sent by his general, was captured by the British near Montreal, loaded with irons, and in that condition sent to England. Major Brown proposed that colonel Allen should return to Lonqueil, procure canoes, and cross the river St. Lawrence, a little to the north of Montreal, while he with a force of about 200 men crossed a little to the south of it. The former crossed in the night, but the latter by some means failed on his part. Colonel Allen found himself the next morning unsupported, and exposed to immediate danger, but nevertheless concluded on maintaining his ground. General Carleton, knowing his weakness, marched out against him with a superior force. The colonel defended himself with his wonted bravery, but being deserted by several of his party, and having lost fifteen of his men, he was compelled to surrender with the remainder amounting to 38.

After the reduction of St. John's, general Montgomery proceeded towards Montreal. The few British forces there, unable to stand their ground, repaired for safety on board the shipping in hopes of escaping down the river, but they were prevented by colonel Easton, who was stationed at the point of Sorel river, with a number of continental troops, some cannon, and an armed gondola. [233] General Prescot, who was on board with several officers, and about 120 privates, having no chance of escape, submitted to be prisoners on terms of capitulation. Eleven sail of vessels, with all their contents, consisting of ammunition, provision, and intrenching tools, became the property

1775

of the provincials. Governor Carleton, was about this time conveyed in a boat with muffled paddles, by a secret way to the Three Rivers, and from thence to Quebec in a few days.

When Montreal was evacuated by the troops, the inhabitants applied to general Montgomery for capitulation. He informed them, that as they were defenceless, they could not expect such a concession, but he engaged upon his honour to maintain the individuals and religious communities of the city, in the peaceable enjoyment of their property, and the free exercise of their religion. In all his transactions, he spoke, wrote, and acted, with dignity and propriety, and in particular treated the inhabitants with liberality and politeness.

Montreal which at this time surrendered to the provincials carried on an extensive trade, and contained many of those articles, which from the operation of the resolutions of Congress, could not be imported into any of the united colonies. From these stores the American soldiers, who had hitherto suffered from the want of suitable clothing, obtained a plentiful supply.

General Montgomery, after leaving some troops in Montreal, and sending detachments into different parts of the province to encourage the Canadians, and to forward provisions, advanced towards the capital. His little army arrived with expedition before Quebec. Success had hitherto crowned every attempt of general Montgomery, but notwithstanding, his situation was very embarrassing. Much to be pitied is the officer, who having been bred to arms, in the strict discipline of regular armies, is afterwards called to command men who carry with them the spirit of freedom into the field. The greater part of the Americans, officers as well as soldiers, having never seen any service, were ignorant of their duty, and but feebly impressed with the military ideas of union, subordination [234] and discipline. 1775 The army was continental in name and pay, but in no other respect. Not only the troops of different colonies conceived themselves independent of each other, but in some instances the different regiments of the same colony, were backward to submit to the orders of officers in a higher grade of another line. They were also soon tired of a military life. Novelty and the first impulse of passion had led them to camp; but the approaching cold season, together with the fatigues and dangers incident to war, induced a general wish to relinquish the service. Though by the terms of their enlistment, they were to be discharged in a few weeks, they could not brook an absence from their homes for that short space of time. The ideas of liberty and independence, which roused the colonists to oppose the claims of Great-Britain, operated against that implicit obedience which is necessary to a well regulated army.

Even in European states, where long habits have established submission to superiors as a primary duty of the common people, the difficulty of governing recruits, when first led to the field from civil occupations, is great; but to exercise discipline over freemen, accustomed to act only from the impulse of their own minds, required not only a knowledge of human nature, but an accommodating spirit, and a degree of patience which is rarely found among officers of regular armies. The troops under the immediate command of general Montgomery, were from their usual habits, averse to the ideas of subordination, and had suddenly passed from domestic ease, to the numberless wants and distresses which are incident to marches through strange and desert countries. Every difficulty was increased by the short term for which they were enlisted. To secure the affections of the Canadians, it was necessary for the American general to restrain the appetites, and control the licentiousness of his soldiery, while the appearance of military harshness was dangerous, lest their good will might be forfeited. In this choice of difficulties, the genius of Montgomery surmounted many obstacles. During his short but 1775 glorious [235] career, he conducted with so much prudence, as to make it doubtful whether we ought to admire most the goodness of the man, or the address of the general.

About the same time that Canada was invaded, in the usual route from New-York, a considerable detachment from the American army at Cambridge, was conducted into that royal province by a new and unexpected passage. Colonel Arnold, who successfully conducted this bold undertaking, thereby acquired the name of the American SEP. 13 Hannibal. He was detached with a thousand men, from Cambridge to penetrate into Canada, by ascending the river Kennebeck, and descending by the Chaundiere to the river St. Lawrence. Great were the difficulties these troops had to encounter in marching by an unexplored route, 300 miles through an uninhabited country. In ascending the Kennebeck, they were constantly obliged to work upwards against an impetuous current. They were often compelled by cataracts or other impediments, to land and to haul their batteaux up rapid streams, and over falls of rivers. Nor was their march by land more eligible than this passage by water. They had deep swamps, thick woods, difficult mountains, and craggy precipices alternatively to encounter. At some places they had to cut their way for miles together through forests so embarrassed, that their progress was only four or five miles a day. The constant fatigue caused many men to fall sick. One third of the number which set out, were from want of necessaries obliged to return; the others proceeded with unabated fortitude and constancy. Provisions grew at length so scarce, that some of the men ate their dogs, cartouch boxes, breeches and shoes. When they were an hundred miles from any habitation or prospect of a supply their whole store was divided, which yielded four pints of flour for each man. After they had baked and eaten their last morsel, they had thirty miles to travel before they could expect any farther supply. The men bore up under these complicated distresses with the greatest fortitude. They gloried in the hope of completing a march which would rival the fame of similar expeditions undertaken by the heroes of antiquity. [236] Having spent thirty one days in traversing a hideous wilderness, without ever seeing any thing human, they at length reached the inhabited parts of Canada. They were there well received, and supplied with every thing necessary for their comfort. The Canadians were struck with amazement when they saw this armed force emerging from the wilderness. It had never entered their conceptions that it was possible for human beings to traverse such immense wilds. The most pointed instructions had been given to this corps, to conciliate the affections of the Canadians. It was particularly enjoined upon them, if the son of lord Chatham, then an officer in one of the British regiments in that province, should fall into their hands, to treat him with all possible attention, in return for the great exertions of his father in behalf of American liberty. A manifesto subscribed by general Washington, which had been sent from Cambridge with this detachment, was circulated among the inhabitants of Canada. In this they were invited to arrange themselves under the standard of general liberty; and they were informed that

1775

the American army was sent into the province, not to plunder but to protect them.

While general Montgomery lay at Montreal, colonel Arnold arrived at Point Levy, opposite to Quebec. Such was the consternation of the garrison and inhabitants at his unexpected appearance, that had not the river intervened, an immediate attack in the first surprize and confusion, might have been successful. The bold enterprise of one American army marching through the wilderness, at a time when success was crowning every undertaking of another invading in a different direction, struck terror into the breasts of those Canadians who were unfriendly to the designs of Congress. The embarrassments of the garrison were increased by the absence of sir Guy Carleton. That gallant officer, on hearing of Montgomery's invasion, prepared to oppose him in the extremes of the province. While he was collecting a force to attack invaders in one direction, a different corps, emerging out of the depths of an unexplored wilderness, suddenly appeared from another. In a few days after colonel Arnold [237] had arrived at Point Levy, he crossed the river St. Lawrence, but his chance of succeeding by a coup de main was in that short space greatly diminished. The critical moment was past. The panic occasioned by his first appearance had abated, and solid preparations for the defence of the town were adopted. The inhabitants, both English and Canadians as soon as danger pressed, united for their common defence. Alarmed for their property, they were, at their own request, embodied for its security. The sailors were taken from the shipping in the harbour, and put to the batteries on shore. As colonel Arnold had no artillery, after parading some days on the heights near Quebec, he drew off his troops, intending nothing more until the arrival of Montgomery, than to cut off supplies from entering the garrison.

So favourable were the prospects of the united colonies at this period, that general Montgomery set on foot a regiment of Canadians, to be in the pay of Congress. James Livingston, a native of New York, who had long resided in Canada, was appointed to the command thereof, and several recruits were engaged for the term of twelve months. The inhabitants on both sides of the river St. Laurence, were very friendly. Expresses in the employ of the Americans, went without molestation, backwards and forwards, between Montreal and

NOV. 8

1775

Quebec. Many individuals performed signal services in favour of the invading army. Among a considerable number Mr. Price stands conspicuous, who advanced 5000£. in specie, for their use.

Various causes had contributed to attach the inhabitants of Canada, especially those of the inferior classes, to the interest of Congress, and to alienate their affections from the government of Great-Britain. The contest was for liberty, and there is something in that sound, captivating to the mind of man in a state of original simplicity. It was for the colonies, and Canada was also a colony. The objects of the war were therefore supposed to be for their common advantage. The form of government lately imposed on them by act of parliament, was far from being so free as the constitutions of the other [238] colonies, and was in many respects particularly oppressive. The common people had no representative share in enacting the laws by which they were to be governed, and were subjected to the arbitrary will of persons, over whom they had no constitutional control. Distinctions so degrading were not unobserved by the native Canadians, but were more obvious to those who had known the privileges enjoyed in the neighbouring provinces. Several individuals educated in New-England and New-York, with the high ideas of liberty inspired by their free constitutions, had in the interval between the peace of Paris 1763, and the commencement of the American war, migrated into Canada. Such, sensibly felt the difference between the governments they had left, and the arbitrary constitution imposed on them, and both from principle and affection, earnestly persuaded the Canadians to make a common cause with the United Colonies.

Though motives of this kind induced the peasantry of the country to espouse the interest of Congress, yet sundry individuals, and some whole orders of men, threw the weight of their influence into the opposite scale. The legal privileges which the Roman Catholic clergy enjoyed, made them averse to a change, lest they should be endangered by a more intimate connection with their protestant neighbours. They used their influence in the next world, as an engine to operate on the movements of the present. They refused absolution to such of their flocks as abetted the Americans. This interdiction of the joys of heaven, by those who were supposed to hold the keys of it, operated powerfully on the opinions and practices of the superstitious multitude. The seigneurs had also immunities unknown in the other colonies. Such is the fondness for power in every human breast, that revolutions are rarely favoured by any order of men who have reason to apprehend that their future situation will, in case of a change, be less pre-eminent than before. The sagacious general Montgomery, no less a man of the world than an officer, discovered great address in accommodating himself to these clashing interests. Though he knew the part the popish clergy had acted in opposition [239] to

him, yet he conducted towards them as if totally ignorant of the matter; and treated them and their religion with great respect and attention. As far as he was authorised to promise, he engaged that their ecclesiastical property should be secured, and the free exercise of their religion continued. To all he held forth the flattering idea of calling a convention of representatives, freely chosen, to institute by its own will, such a form of government as they approved. While the great mind of this illustrious man, was meditating schemes of liberty and happiness, a military force was collecting and training to oppose him, which in a short time put a period to his valuable life.

At the time the Americans were before Montreal, general Carleton, as has been related, escaped through their hands, and got safe to Quebec. His presence was itself a garrison. The confidence reposed in his talents, inspired the men under his command to make the most determined resistance. Soon after his arrival he issued a proclamation, setting forth, "That all persons liable to do militia duty, and residing in Quebec, who refused to arm in conjunction with the royal army, should in four days quit Quebec with their families, and withdraw themselves from the limits of the district by the first of December, on pain of being treated afterwards as spies or rebels." All who were unwilling to co-operate with the British army, being thus disposed of, the remaining inhabitants, though unused to arms, became in a little time so far acquainted with them as to be very useful in defending the town. They supported fatigues and submitted to command with a patience and chearfulness, that could not be exceeded by men familiarized to the hardships and subordination of a military life.

General Montgomery having effected at Point aux Trembles, a junction with colonel Arnold, commenced the siege of Quebec. Upon his arrival before the town, he wrote a letter to the British governor, recommending an immediate surrender, to prevent the dreadful consequences of a storm. Though the flag which conveyed this letter was fired upon, and all communication refused, [240] general Montgomery found other means to convey a letter of the same tenor into the garrison, but the inflexible firmness of the governor could not be moved either by threats or dangers. The Americans soon after commenced a bombardment with five small mortars, but with very little effect. In a few days general Montgomery opened a six gun battery, at the distance of seven hundred yards from the walls, but his metal was too light to make any impression.

1775

The news of general Montgomery's success in Canada had filled the colonies with expectations, that the conquest of Quebec would soon add fresh lustre to his already brilliant fame. He knew well the consequences of popular disappointment, and was besides of opinion that unless something decisive was immediately done, the benefit of his previous acquisitions would in a great degree be lost to the American cause. On both accounts, he was strongly impelled to make every exertion for satisfying the expectations and promoting the interest of a people, who had honoured him with so great a share of their confidence. The government of Great-Britain, in the extensive province of Canada, was at that time reduced to the single town of Quebec. The astonished world saw peaceable colonists suddenly transformed into soldiers, and these marching through unexplored wildernesses, and extending themselves by conquests, in the first moment after they had assumed the profession of arms. Towards the end of the year, the tide of fortune began to turn. Dissentions broke out between colonel Arnold and some of his officers, threatening the annihilation of discipline. The continental currency had no circulation in Canada, and all the hard money furnished for the expedition, was nearly expended. Difficulties of every kind were daily increasing. The extremities of fatigue were constantly to be encountered. The American general had not a sufficient number of men to make the proper reliefs in the daily labours they underwent; and that inconsiderable number, worn down with toil, was constantly exposed to the severities of a Canada winter. The period for which a great part of his men had enlisted, being on the point of expiration, [241] he apprehended that they who were entitled to it, would insist on their discharge. On the other hand, he saw no prospect of staggering the resolution of the garrison. They were well supplied with every thing necessary for their defence, and were daily acquiring additional firmness. The extremity of winter was fast approaching. From these combined circumstances, general Montgomery was impressed with a conviction, that the siege should either be raised, or brought to a summary termination. To storm the place was the only feasible method of effecting the latter purpose. But this was an undertaking, in which success was but barely possible. Great minds are seldom exact calculators of danger. Nor do they minutely attend to the difficulties which obstruct the attainment of their objects. Fortune, in contempt of the pride of man, has ever had an influence in the success or failure of military enterprises. Some of the greatest atchievements, of that kind, have owed their success to a noble contempt of common forms.

The upper part of Quebec was surrounded with very strong works, and the access from the lower town was excessively difficult, from its almost perpendicular steepness. General Montgomery, from a native intrepidity, and an ardent thirst for glory, overlooked all these dangers, and resolved at once either to carry the place or perish in the attempt. Trusting much to his good fortune—confiding in the bravery of his troops, and their readiness to follow whithersoever he should lead; and depending somewhat on the extensiveness of the works, he determined to attempt the town by escalade.

The garrison of Quebec at this time consisted of about 1520 men, of which 800 were militia, and 450 were seamen, belonging to the king's frigates, or merchant ships in the harbour. The rest were marines, regulars, or colonel Maclean's new raised emigrants. The American army consisted of about 800 men. Some had been left at Montreal, and near a third of Arnold's detachment, as has been related, had returned to Cambridge.

General Montgomery having divided this little force into four detachments, ordered two feints to be made [242] against the upper town, one by colonel Livingston, at the head of the Canadians against St. John's gate; and the other by major Brown, against cape Diamond, reserving to himself and colonel Arnold the two principal attacks, against the lower town. At five o'clock in the morning general Montgomery advanced against the lower town. He passed the first barrier, and was just opening to attack the second, when he was DEC. 31 killed, together with his aid de camp, captain John M'Pherson, captain Cheesman, and some others. This so dispirited the men that colonel Campbell, on whom the command devolved, thought proper to draw them off. In the mean time colonel Arnold, at the head of about 350 men, passed through St. Roques, and approached near a two gun battery, without being discovered. This he attacked, and though it was well defended, carried it, but with considerable loss. In this attack colonel Arnold received a wound, which made it necessary to carry him off the field of battle. His party nevertheless continued the assault, and pushing on, made themselves masters of a second barrier. These brave men sustained the force of the whole garrison for three hours, but finding themselves hemmed in, and without hopes either of success, relief or retreat, they yielded to numbers, and the advantageous situation of their adversaries. The loss of the Americans in killed and wounded, was about 100, and 300 were taken prisoners. Among the slain were captain Kendricks, lieutenant Humphries, and lieutenant Cooper. The behaviour of the provincial troops was such as might have silenced those who had reproached them for being deficient in courage. The most experienced veterans could not have exceeded the firmness they displayed in their last attack. The issue of this assault relieved the garrison of Quebec from all apprehensions for its safety. The provincials were so much weakened, as to be scarcely equal to their own defence. However, colonel Arnold had the boldness to encamp within three miles of the town, and had the address, even with his reduced numbers, to impede the conveyance of refreshments and provisions into the garrison. His situation was extremely difficult. He was [243] at an immense distance from those parts where effectual assistance 1775 could be expected. On his first entrance into the province, he had experienced much kind treatment from the inhabitants. The Canadians, besides being fickle in their resolutions, are apt to be biassed by success. Their disposition to aid the Americans, became therefore daily more precarious. It was even difficult to keep the provincial troops from returning to their respective homes. Their sufferings were great. While their adversaries were comfortably housed in Quebec, they were exposed in the open air to the extreme rigour of the season. The severity of a Canada winter was far beyond any thing with which they were acquainted. The snow lay above four feet deep on a level.

This deliverance of Quebec may be considered as a proof how much may be done by one man for the preservation of a country. It also proves that soldiers may in a short time be formed out of the mass of citizens.

The conflict being over, the ill will which had subsisted, during the siege, between the royal and provincial troops gave way to sentiments of humanity. The Americans, who surrendered, were treated with kindness. Ample provisions were made for their wounded, and no unnecessary severity shewn to any. Few men have ever fallen in battle, so much regretted by both sides, as general Montgomery. His many amiable qualities had procured him an uncommon share of private affection, and his great abilities an equal proportion of public esteem. Being a sincere lover of liberty, he had engaged in the American cause from principle, and quitted the enjoyment of an easy fortune, and the highest domestic felicity, to take an active share in the fatigues and dangers of a war, instituted for the defence of the community of which he was an adopted member. His well known character was almost equally esteemed by the friends and foes of the side which he had espoused. In America he was celebrated as a martyr to the liberties of mankind; in Great-Britain as a misguided good man, sacrificing to what he supposed to be the rights of his country. His name was mentioned in parliament with singular respect.

1775 Some of the most [244] powerful speakers in that illustrious assembly, displayed their eloquence in sounding his praise and lamenting his fate. Those in particular who had been his fellow soldiers in the late war, expatiated on his many virtues. The minister himself acknowledged his worth, while he reprobated the cause for which he fell. He concluded an involuntary panegyric, by saying, "Curse on his virtues, they have undone his country."

Though the invasion of Canada was finally unsuccessful, yet the advantages which the Americans gained in the months of September and October, gave fresh spirits to their army and people. The boldness of the enterprise, might have taught Great-Britain the folly of persisting in the design of subjugating America. But instead of preserving the union, and restoring the peace of the empire by repealing a few of her laws, she from mistaken dignity, resolved on a more vigorous prosecution of the war.

Transactions in Virginia, the Carolinas, Georgia, and
the general state of Public Affairs in the Colonies.

IT HAS ALREADY BEEN MENTIONED, that the colonists from the
rising of Congress in October 1774, and particularly after the Lexington battle, were attentive to the training their militia, and making
the necessary preparations for their defence.

The effects of their arrangements, for this purpose, varied with
circumstances.

Where there were no royal troops, and where ordinary prudence
was observed, the public peace was undisturbed. In other cases, the
intemperate zeal of governors, and the imprudent warmth of the
people, anticipated the calamities of war before its proper time.
Virginia, though there was not a single British soldier within its
limits, was, by the indiscretion of its governor, lord Dunmore,
involved, for several months, in difficulties, but little short of those

to which the inhabitants of Massachusetts were [245] subjected. His lordship was but illy fitted to be at the helm in this tempestuous season. His passions predominated over his understanding, and precipitated him into measures injurious both to the people whom he governed, and to the interest of his royal master. The Virginians from the earliest stages of the controversy, had been in the foremost line of opposition to the claims of Great-Britain, but at the same time treated lord Dunmore with the attention that was due to his station. In common with the other provinces they had taken effectual measures to prepare their militia for the purposes of defence.

1775

While they were pursuing this object, his lordship engaged a party belonging to a royal vessel in James' river, to convey some public powder from a magazine in Williamsburg on board their ship. The value or quantity of the powder was inconsiderable, but the circumstances attending its removal begat suspicions that lord Dunmore meant to deprive the inhabitants of the means of defence. They were therefore alarmed, and assembled with arms to demand its restitution. By the interposition of the mayor and corporation of Williamsburg, extremities were prevented. Reports were soon after spread that a second attempt to rob the magazine was intended. The inhabitants again took arms, and instituted nightly patroles, with a determined resolution to protect it. The governor was irritated at these commotions, and in the warmth of his temper threatened to set up the royal standard—enfranchise the negroes, and arm them against their masters. This irritated, but did not intimidate. Several public meetings were held in the different counties, in all of which the removal of the powder from the magazine, and the governor's threats, were severely condemned. Some of the gentlemen of Hanover and the neighbouring counties assembled in arms, under the conduct of Mr. Patrick Henry, and marched towards Williamsburg, with an avowed design to obtain restitution of the powder, and to take measures for securing the public treasury. This ended in a negociation, by which it was agreed that payment for the powder, by [246] the receiver general of the colony, should be accepted in lieu of restitution; and that upon the engagement of the inhabitants of Williamsburg to guard both the treasury and the magazine, the armed parties should return to their habitations.

APR. 20

The alarm of this affair induced lord Dunmore to send his lady and family on board the Fowey man of war in James' river. About the same time his lordship, with the assistance of a detachment of marines, fortified his palace and surrounded it with artillery. He soon after issued a proclamation, in which Mr. Henry and his associates were charged with rebellious practices, and the present commotions were attributed to a desire in the people of changing the established form of government. Several meetings were held in the neighbouring counties, in which the conduct of Mr. Henry and of his associates was applauded, and resolutions were adopted, that at every risque he and they should be indemnified. About this time copies of some letters from governor Dunmore to the minister of the American department were made public. These in the opinion of the Virginians contained unfair and unjust representations of facts, and also of their temper and disposition. Many severe things were said on both sides, and fame as usual, magnified or misrepresented whatever was said or done. One distrust begat another. Every thing tended to produce a spirit of discontent, and the fever of the public mind daily increased.

In this state of disorder the governor convened the general assembly. The leading motive for this unexpected measure, was to procure their approbation and acceptance of the terms of the conciliatory motion agreed to in parliament, on the 20th of the preceding February. His lordship introduced this to their consideration, in a long and plausible speech. In a few days they presented their address in answer, in which, among other grounds of rejection they stated that, "the proposed plan only changed the form of oppression, without lessening its burthen;" but they referred the papers for a final determination, to Congress. For themselves they declared,

1775

[247] We have exhausted every mode of application which our invention could suggest, as proper and promising. We have decently remonstrated with parliament. They have added new injuries to the old. We have wearied our king with supplications; he has not deigned to answer us. We have appealed to the native honour and justice of the British nation. Their efforts in our favour have been hitherto ineffectual.

The assembly, among their first acts, appointed a committee to enquire into the causes of the late disturbances, and particularly to examine the state of the magazine. They found most of the remaining powder buried; the muskets deprived of their locks, and spring guns planted in the magazine. These discoveries irritated the people, and occasioned intemperate expressions of resentment. Lord Dunmore MAY 8 quitted the palace privately, and retired on board the Fowey man of war, which then lay near York-town. He left a message for the house of burgesses, acquainting them

that he thought it prudent to retire to a place of safety, having reason to believe that he was in constant danger of falling a sacrifice to popular fury; he nevertheless, hoped they would proceed in the great business before them; and he engaged to render the communication between him and the house as easy and as safe as possible. He assured them that he would attend as heretofore, to the duties of his office, and that he was well disposed to restore that harmony which had been unhappily interrupted.

This message produced a joint address from the council and house of burgesses, in which they represented his lordship's fears to be groundless, and declared their willingness to concur in any measure he would propose for the security of himself and family; and concluded by intreating his return to the palace. Lord Dunmore in a reply, justified his apprehensions of danger from the threats which had been repeatedly thrown out. He charged the house of burgesses with countenancing the violent proceedings of the people, and with a design to usurp the executive power, and subvert the constitution. This produced a reply fraught with recrimination and defensive [248] arguments. Every incident afforded fresh room for altercation. There 1775 was a continued intercourse by addresses, messages and answers, between the house of burgesses and the Fowey, but little of the public business was completed. His lordship was still acknowledged as the lawful governor of the province, but did not think proper to set his foot on shore, in the country over which his functions were to be exercised.

At length, when the necessary bills were ready for ratification, the council and burgesses jointly intreated the governor's presence, to give his assent to them and finish the session. After several messages and answers, lord Dunmore peremptorily refused to meet the assembly at the capital, their usual place of deliberation; but said he would be ready to receive them on the next Monday, at his present residence on board the Fowey, for the purpose of giving his assent to such bills as he should approve of. Upon receiving this answer, the house of burgesses passed resolutions in which they declared, that the message requiring them to attend the governor on board a ship of war, was a high breach of their rights and privileges—that they had reason to fear a dangerous attack was meditated against the colony, and it was therefore their opinion, that they should prepare for the preservation of their rights and liberties. After strongly professing loyalty to the king, and amity to the Mother Country, they broke up their session.

JULY 18   The royal government in Virginia, from that day ceased. Soon after, a convention of delegates was appointed, to supply the place of the assembly. As these had an unlimited confidence reposed in them, they became at once possessed of undefined discretionary powers, both legislative and executive. They exercised this authority for the security of their constituents. They raised and embodied an armed force, and took other measures for putting the colony in a state of defence. They published a justification of their conduct, and set forth the necessity of the measures they had adopted. They concluded with professions of loyalty, and declared that though they were determined at every hazard, to maintain their rights and privileges,

1775   [249] it was also their fixed resolution to disband such forces as were raised for the defence of the colony, whenever their dangers were removed. The headstrong passions of lord Dunmore precipitated him into farther follies. With the aid of the loyalists, run away negroes, and some frigates that were on the station, he established a marine force. By degrees, he equipped and armed a number of vessels of different kinds and sizes, in one of which he constantly resided, except when he went on shore in a hostile manner. This force was calculated only for depredation, and never became equal to any essential service. Obnoxious persons were seized and taken on board. Negroes were carried off—plantations ravaged—and houses burnt. These proceedings occasioned the sending of some detachments of the new raised provincial forces to protect the coasts. This produced a predatory war, from which neither honour nor benefit could be acquired, and in which every necessary from on shore was purchased at the risque of blood. The forces under his lordship attempted to burn Hampton; but the crews of the royal vessels employed in that business, though they had begun to cannonade it, were so annoyed by riflemen from on shore, that they were obliged to quit their station. In a few days after this repulse, a proclamation was issued by the governor, dated on board the ship William, off Norfolk, declaring, that as the civil law was at present insufficient to punish treason and traitors, martial law should take place and be executed throughout the colony; and requiring all persons capable of bearing arms, to repair to his majesty's standard, or to be considered as traitors. He also declared all indented servants, negroes and others, appertaining to rebels, who were able and willing to bear arms, and who joined his majesty's forces, to be free.

Among the circumstances which induced the rulers of Great-Britain to count on an easy conquest of America, the great number of slaves had a considerable weight. On the sea coast of five of the most southern provinces, the number of slaves exceeded that of freemen. It was supposed that the proffer of freedom would detach them [250] from their master's interest, and bind them by strong ties to support the royal standard. Perhaps, under favourable circumstances, these expectations would in some degree have been realised; but lord Dunmore's indiscretion deprived his royal master of this resource. Six months had elapsed since his lordship first threatened its adoption. The negroes had in a great measure ceased to believe, and the inhabitants to fear. It excited less surprize, and produced less effect, than if it had been more immediate and unexpected. The country was now in a tolerable state of defence, and the force for protecting the negroes, in case they had closed with his lordship's offer, was far short of what would have been necessary for their security. The injury done the royal cause by the bare proposal of the scheme, far outweighed any advantage that resulted from it. The colonists were struck with horror, and filled with detestation of a government which was exercised in loosening the bands of society, and destroying domestic security. The union and vigor which was given to their opposition, was great, while the additional force, acquired by his lordship, was inconsiderable. It nevertheless produced some effect in Norfolk and the adjoining country, where his lordship was joined by several hundreds, both whites and blacks. The governor having once more got footing on the main, amused himself with hopes of acquiring the glory of reducing one part of the province by means of the other. The provincials had now an object against which they might direct their arms. An expedition was therefore concerted against the force which had taken post at Norfolk. To protect his adherents lord Dunmore constructed a fort at the great bridge, on the Norfolk side, and furnished it with artillery. The provincials also fortified themselves near to the same place, with a narrow causeway in their front. In this state both parties continued quiet for some days. The royalists commenced an attack. Captain Fordyce, at the head of about 60 British grenadiers, passed the causeway, and boldly marched up to the provincial entrenchments with fixed bayonets. They were exposed without cover to the fire of the provincials [251] in front, and enfiladed by another part of their works. The brave captain and several of his men fell. The lieutenant, with others, were taken, and all who survived were wounded. The slaves in this engagement were more prejudicial to their British employers than to the provincials. Captain Fordyce was interred by the victors, with military honors. The English prisoners were treated with kindness, but the Americans who had joined the king's standard, experienced the resentment of their countrymen.

The royal forces, on the ensuing night, evacuated their post at the great bridge, and lord Dunmore shortly after abandoned Norfolk, and retired with his people on board his ships. Many of the tories, a name which was given to those who adhered to the royal interest, sought the same asylum, for themselves and moveable effects. The provincials took possession of Norfolk, and the fleet, with its new incumberances, moved to a greater distance. The people on board, cut off from all peaceable intercourse with the shore, were distressed for provisions and necessaries of every kind. This occasioned sundry unimportant contests between the provincial forces and the armed ships and boats. At length, on the arrival of the Liverpool man of war from England, a flag was sent on shore to put the question, whether they would supply his majesty's ships with provisions. An answer was returned in the negative. It was then determined to

destroy the town. This was carried into effect, and Norfolk was
reduced to ashes. The whole loss was estimated at 300,000£. sterling.
The provincials, to deprive the ships of every resource of supply,
destroyed the houses and plantations that were near the water, and
obliged the people to move their cattle, provisions, and effects, farther
into the country. Lord Dunmore, with his fleet, continued for several
months on the coast and in the rivers of Virginia. His unhappy
followers suffered a complication of distresses. The scarcity of water
and provisions, the closeness and filth of the small vessels, produced
diseases which were fatal to many, especially to the negroes. Though
his whole force was trifling when compared with [252] the resources
of Virginia, yet the want of suitable armed vessels made its expulsion
impracticable. The experience of that day evinced the inadequacy
of land forces for the defence of a maritime country; and the extensive
mischief which may be done, by even an inconsiderable marine,
when unopposed in its own way. The want of a navy was both seen
and felt. Some arrangements to procure one, were therefore made.
Either the expectation of an attack from this quarter, or the sufferings
of the crews on board, induced his lordship in the summer 1776 to
burn the least valuable of his vessels, and to send the remainder,
amounting to 30 or 40 sail, to Florida, Bermuda, and the West-Indies.
The hopes which lord Dunmore had entertained of subduing Virginia
by the cooperation of the negroes, terminated with this movement.
The unhappy Africans who had engaged in it, are said to have almost
universally perished.

While these transactions were carrying on, another scheme, in
which lord Dunmore was a party, in like manner miscarried. It was
in contemplation to raise a considerable force at the back of the
colonies, particularly in Virginia and the Carolinas. One Connelly, a
native of Pennsylvania, was the framer of the design. He had gained
the approbation of lord Dunmore, and had been sent by him to
general Gage at Boston, and from him he received a commission to
act as colonel commandant. It was intended that the British garrisons
at Detroit, and some other remote posts, with their artillery and
ammunition, should be subservient to this design. Connelly also
hoped for the aid of the Canadians and Indians. He was authorised
to grant commissions, and to have the supreme direction of the new

forces. As soon as they were in readiness he was to penetrate through Virginia, and to meet lord Dunmore near Alexandria, on the river Potowmac. Connelly was taken up on suspicion, by one of the committees in Maryland, while on his way to the scene of action. The papers found in his possession betrayed the whole. Among these was a general sketch of the plan, and a letter from lord Dunmore to one of the Indian chiefs. He was imprisoned, [253] and the papers published. So many fortunate escapes induced a belief among serious Americans, that their cause was favoured by heaven. The various projects which were devised and put in operation against them, pointed out the increasing necessity of union, while the havock made on their coasts—the proffer of freedom to their slaves, and the encouragement proposed to Indians for making war on their frontier inhabitants, quickened their resentment against Great-Britain.

North-Carolina was more fortunate than Virginia. The governors of both were perhaps equally zealous for the royal interest, and the people of both equally attached to the cause of America, but the former escaped with a smaller portion of public calamity. Several regulations were at this time adopted by most of the provinces. Councils of safety, committees, and conventions, were common substitutes for regular government. Similar plans for raising, arming and supporting troops, and for training the militia, were from north to south generally adopted. In like manner royal governors throughout the provinces, were exerting themselves in attaching the people to the schemes of Great-Britain. Governor Martin, of North-Carolina, was particularly zealous in this business. He fortified and armed his palace at Newbern, that it might answer the double purpose of a garrison and magazine. While he was thus employed, such commotions were excited among the people, that he thought it expedient to retire on board a sloop of war in Cape Fear river. The people on examining, found powder and various military stores which had been buried in his garden and yard. Governor Martin, though he had abandoned his usual place of residence, continued his exertions for reducing North-Carolina to obedience. He particularly addressed himself to the regulators and Highland emigrants. The former had acquired this name from their attempting to regulate the administration of justice in the remote settlements, in a summary manner subversive of the public peace. They had suffered the consequences of opposing royal government, and from obvious principles of human nature, were disposed to [254] support the authority whose power to punish they had recently experienced. The Highland emigrants had been but a short time in America, and were yet more under the influence of European ideas than those which their new situation was calculated to inspire. Governor Martin sent commissions among these people for raising and commanding regiments; and he granted one to Mr. M'Donald to act as their general. He also sent them a proclamation commanding all persons, on their allegiance, to repair to the royal standard. This was erected by general M'Donald, about the middle of February. Upon the first intelligence of their assembling brigadier general Moore, with some provincial troops and militia, and some pieces of cannon, marched to oppose them. He took possession of Rock fish bridge and threw up some works. He had not been there many days when M'Donald approached, and sent a letter to Moore, enclosing the governor's proclamation, and advising him and his party to join the king's standard; and adding, that in case of refusal they must be treated as enemies. To this Moore replied, that he and his officers considered themselves as engaged in a cause the most glorious and honourable in the world, the defence of mankind; and in his turn offered, that if M'Donald's party laid down their arms they should be received as friends, but, otherwise they must expect consequences similar to those which they threatened. Soon after this, general M'Donald with his adherents pushed on to join governor Martin, but colonels Lillington and Caswell, with about 1000 militia men, took possession of Moore's creek bridge, which lay in their way, and raised a small breast work to secure themselves.

On the next morning the Highland emigrants attacked the militia posted at the bridge, but M'Cleod, the second in command, and some more of their officers being killed at the first onset, they fled with precipitation. General M'Donald was taken prisoner, and the whole of his party broken and dispersed. This overthrow produced consequences very injurious to the British interest. A royal fleet and army was expected on the coast. A [255] junction formed between them and the Highland emigrants in the interior country, might have made a sensible impression on the province. From an eagerness to do

1776

1776
FEB. 27

something, the insurgents prematurely took arms, and being crushed before the arrival of proper support, their spirits were so entirely broken, that no future effort could be expected from them.

While the war raged only in Massachusetts, each province conducted as under the expectation of being next attacked. Georgia, though a majority of its inhabitants were at first against the measures, yet about the middle of this year, joined the other colonies. Having not concurred in the petitions from Congress to the king, they petitioned by themselves, and stated their rights and grievances, in firm and decided language. They also adopted the continental association, and sent on their deputies to Congress.

In South-Carolina there was an eagerness to be prepared for defence, which was not surpassed in any of the provinces. Regiments were raised—forts were built—the militia trained, and every necessary preparation made for that purpose. Lord William Campbell, the royal governor, endeavoured to form a party for the support of government, and was in some degree successful. Distrusting his personal safety on shore, about the middle of September, he took up his residence on board an armed vessel, then in the harbour.

The royal government still existed in name and form; but the real power which the people obeyed, was exercised by a provincial congress, a council of safety, and subordinate committees. To conciliate the friendship of the Indians, the popular leaders sent a small supply of powder into their country. They who were opposed to Congress embodied, and robbed the waggons which were employed in its transportation. To inflame the minds of their adherents, they propagated a report that the powder was intended to be given to the Indians, for the purpose of massacreing the friends of royal government. The inhabitants took arms, some to support royal government, but others to support the American measures. The royalists [256] acted feebly and were easily overpowered. They were disheartened by the superior numbers that opposed them. They every where gave way and were obliged either to fly or feign submission. Solicitations had been made about this time for royal forces to awe the southern provinces, but without effect till the proper season was over. One scheme for this purpose was frustrated by a singular device. Private intelligence had been received of an express being sent from Sir

1776

James Wright, governor of Georgia, to general Gage. By him the necessity of ordering a part of the royal army to the southward was fully stated. The express was waylaid, and compelled by two gentlemen to deliver his letters. One to general Gage was kept back, and another one forwarded in its room. The seal and hand writing were so exactly imitated that the deception was not suspected. The forged letter was received and acted upon. It stated such a degree of peace and tranquility as induced an opinion that there was no necessity of sending royal troops to the southward. While these states were thus left to themselves, they had time and opportunity to prepare for extremities, and in the mean time the friends of royal government were severally crushed. A series of disasters followed the royal cause in the year 1775. General Gage's army was cooped up in Boston, and rendered useless. In the southern states, where a small force would have made an impression, the royal governors were unsupported. Much was done to irritate the colonists and to cement their union, but very little, either in the way of conquest or concession, to subdue their spirits or conciliate their affections.

In this year the people of America generally took their side. Every art was made use of by the popular leaders to attach the inhabitants to their royal cause; nor were the votaries of the royal interest inactive. But little impression was made by the latter, except among the uninformed. The great mass of the wealth, learning, and influence, in all the southern colonies, and in most of the northern, was in favour of the American cause. Some aged persons were exceptions to the contrary. Attached to ancient habits, and enjoying the fruits of their industry, [257] they were slow in approving new measures subversive of the former, and endangering the latter. A few who had basked in the sunshine of court favour, were restrained by honour, principle and interest, from forsaking the fountain of their enjoyments. Some feared the power of Britain, and others doubted the perseverance of America; but a great majority resolved to hazard every thing in preference to a tame submission. In the beginning of the year, the colonists were farmers, merchants and mechanics; but in its close they had assumed the profession of soldiers. So sudden a transformation of so numerous, and so dispersed a people, is without a parallel.

1776

This year was also remarkable for the general termination of royal government. This was effected without any violence to its executive officers. The new system was not so much forcibly imposed or designedly adopted, as introduced through necessity, and the imperceptible agency of a common danger, operating uniformly on the mind of the public. The royal governors, for the most part, voluntarily abdicated their governments, and retired on board ships of war. They assigned for reason, that they apprehended personal danger, but this, in every instance, was unfounded. Perhaps these representatives of royalty thought, that as they were constitutionally necessary to the administration of justice, the horrors of anarchy would deter the people from prosecuting their opposition. If they acted from this principle, they were mistaken. Their withdrawing from the exercise of their official duties, both furnished an apology, and induced a necessity, for organising a system of government independent of royal authority. By encouraging opposition to the popular measures, they involved their friends in great distress. The unsuccessful insurrections which they fomented, being improperly timed, and unsupported, were easily overthrown, and actually strengthened the popular government, which they meant to destroy.

Transactions in Massachusetts, and Evacuation of Boston.

[258] AS THE YEAR 1775 DREW NEAR TO A CLOSE, the friends of   1776
Congress were embarrassed with a new difficulty. Their army was
temporary, and only engaged to serve out the year. The object for
which they had taken up arms was not yet obtained. Every reason
which had previously induced the provinces to embody a military
force still existed, and with increasing weight. It was therefore resolved
to form a new army. The same flattering hopes were indulged, that
an army for the ensuing year would answer every purpose. A
committee of Congress, consisting of Dr. Franklin, Mr. Lynch, and
Mr. Harrison, repaired to head quarters at Cambridge, and there in
conjunction with general Washington made arrangements for organising an army for the year 1776. It was presumed that the spirit
which had hitherto operated on the yeomanry of the country, would

induce most of the same individuals to engage for another twelve-month, but on experiment it was found that much of their military ardor had already evaporated. The first impulse of passion, and the novelty of the scene, had brought many to the field, who had great objections against continuing in the military line. They found, that to be soldiers required sacrifices of which, when they assumed that character, they had no idea. So unacquainted were the bulk of the people with the mode of carrying on modern war, that many of them flew to arms with the delusive expectation of settling the whole dispute by a few decisive and immediate engagements. Experience soon taught them to risque life in open fighting, was but a part of the soldier's duty. Several of the inferior officers retired—the men frequently refused to enlist, unless they were allowed to chuse their officers. Others would not engage unless they were indulged with furloughs. Fifty would apply together for leave of absence; indulgence threatened less ruinous consequences than a refusal would probably have produced. On the whole enlistments went on slowly. Though the recruits [259] for the new army had not arrived, yet the Connecticut troops, whose time expired on the first of December, could not be persuaded to continue in service. On their way home several of them were stopped by the country people and compelled to return. When every thing seemed to be exposed, by the departure of so great a part of the late army, the militia was called on for a temporary aid. A new difficulty obstructed, as well the recruiting of the army, as the coming in of the militia. Sundry persons infected with the small pox, were sent out of Boston and landed at Point Shirley. Such was the dread of that disease, that the British army scarcely excited equal terror. So many difficulties retarded the recruiting service, that on the last day of the year 1775, the whole American army amounted to no more than 9650 men. Of the remarkable events with which this important year was replete, it was not the least, that within musket shot of twenty British regiments, one army was disbanded and another enlisted.

All this time the British troops at Boston were suffering the inconvenience of a blockade. From the 19th of April they were cut off from those refreshments which their situation required. Their supplies from Britain did not reach the coast for a long time after they were expected. Several were taken by the American cruisers, and others were lost at sea. This was in particular the fate of many of their coal ships. The want of fuel was peculiarly felt in a climate where the winter is both severe and tedious. They relieved themselves in part from their sufferings on this account, by the timber of houses which they pulled down and burnt. Vessels were dispatched to the West-Indies to procure provisions; but the islands were so straitened, that they could afford but little assistance. Armed ships and transports were ordered to Georgia with an intent to procure rice, but the people of that province, with the aid of a party from South-Carolina, so effectually opposed them, that of eleven vessels, only two got off safe with their cargoes. It was not till the stock of the garrison was nearly exhausted that the transports from England entered the port of [260] Boston, and relieved the distresses of the garrison. 1776

While the troops within the lines were apprehensive of suffering from want of provisions, the troops without were equally uneasy for want of employment. Used to labour and motion on their farms, they but illy relished the inactivity and confinement of a camp life. Fiery spirits declaimed in favour of an assault. They preferred a bold spirit of enterprize, to that passive fortitude which bears up under present evils, while it waits for favourable junctures. To be in readiness for an attempt of this kind, a council of war recommended to call in 7280 militia men, from New-Hampshire or Connecticut. This number JANUARY added to the regular army before Boston, would have made an 17–18 operating force of about 17,000 men.

The provincials laboured under great inconveniencies from the want of arms and ammunition. Very early in the contest, the king of Great-Britain, by proclamation, forbad the exportation of warlike forces to the colonies. Great exertions had been made to manufacture salt petre and gun powder, but the supply was slow and inadequate. A secret committee of Congress had been appointed, with ample powers to lay in a stock of this necessary article. Some swift sailing vessels had been dispatched to the coast of Africa to purchase what could be procured in that distant region. A party from Charleston forcibly took about 17000 lbs. of powder from a vessel near the bar of St. Augustine. Some time after, commodore Hopkins stripped Providence, one of the Bahama islands of a quantity of artillery and stores; but the whole, procured from all these quarters, was far short of a sufficiency. In order to supply the new army before Boston with the necessary means of defence, an application was made to Massachusetts for arms, but on examination it was found that their public stores afforded only 200. Orders were issued to purchase firelocks from private persons, but few had any to sell, and fewer would part with them. In the month of February, there were 2000 of the American infantry, who were destitute of arms. Powder was equally scarce, and yet daily applications were made for dividends

1776

of the small quantity [261] which was on hand, for the defence of various parts threatened with invasion. The eastern colonies presented an unusual sight. A powerful enemy safely intrenched in their first city, while a fleet was ready to transport them to any part of the coast. A numerous body of husbandmen was resolutely bent on opposition, but without the necessary arms and ammunition for self defence. The eyes of all were fixed on general Washington, and from him it was unreasonably expected that he would by a bold exertion, free the town of Boston from the British troops. The dangerous situation of public affairs led him to conceal the real scarcity of arms and ammunition, and with that magnanimity which is characteristical of great minds, to suffer his character to be assailed, rather than vindicate himself by exposing his many wants. There were not wanting persons, who judging from the superior numbers of men in the American army, boldly asserted, that if the commander in chief was not desirous of prolonging his importance at the head of an army, he might by a vigorous exertion gain possession of Boston. Such suggestions were reported and believed by several, while they were uncontradicted by the general, who chose to risque his fame, rather than expose his army and his country.

Agreeably to the request of the council of war, about 7000 of the militia had rendezvoused in February. General Washington stated to his officers that the troops in camp, together with the reinforcements which had been called for, and were daily coming in, would amount nearly to 17,000 men—that he had not powder sufficient for a bombardment, and asked their advice whether, as reinforcements might be daily expected to the enemy, it would not be prudent before that event took place, to make an assault on the British lines. The proposition was negatived; but it was recommended to take possession of Dorchester heights. To conceal this design, and to divert the attention of the garrison, a bombardment of the town from other directions commenced, and was carried on for three days with as much briskness as a deficient stock of powder would admit. In this first essay, [262] three of the mortars were broken, either from a defect in their construction, or more probably from ignorance of the proper mode of using them.

1776

The night of the 4th of March was fixed upon for taking possession of Dorchester heights. A covering party of about 800 men led the way. These were followed by the carts with the intrenching tools, and 1200 of a working party, commanded by general Thomas. In the rear there were more than 200 carts, loaded with fascines, and hay in bundles. While the cannon were playing in other parts, the greatest silence was kept by this working party. The active zeal of the industrious provincials completed lines of defence by the morning, which astonished the garrison. The difference between Dorchester heights on the evening of the 4th, and the morning of the 5th, seemed to realise the tales of romance. The admiral informed general Howe, that if the Americans kept possession of these heights, he would not be able to keep one of his majesty's ships in the harbour. It was therefore determined in a council of war, to attempt to dislodge them. An engagement was hourly expected. It was intended by general Washington, in that case, to force his way into Boston with 4000 men, who were to have embarked at the mouth of Cambridge river. The militia had come forward with great alertness, each bringing three days provision, in expectation of an immediate assault. The men were in high spirits, and impatiently waiting for the appeal.

They were reminded that it was the 5th of March, and were called upon to avenge the death of their countrymen killed on that day. The many eminences in and near Boston, which overlooked the ground on which it was expected that the contending parties would engage, were crouded with numerous spectators. But general Howe did not intend to attack till the next day. In order to be ready for it, the transports went down in the evening towards the castle. In the night a most violent storm, and towards morning a heavy flood of rain, came on. A carnage was thus providentially prevented, that would probably have equalled, if not exceeded, the fatal [263] 17th of June, at Bunker's-hill. In this situation it was agreed by the British, in a council of war, to evacuate the town as soon as possible.

In a few days after, a flag came out of Boston, with a paper signed by four select men, informing, "that they had applied to general Robertson, who, on application to general Howe, was authorised to assure them, that he had no intention of burning the town, unless the troops under his command were molested, during their embarkation, or at their departure, by the armed force without." When this paper was presented to general Washington, he replied, "that as it was an unauthenticated paper, and without an address, and not obligatory on general Howe, he could take no notice of it;" but at the same time intimated his good wishes for the security of the town.

A proclamation was issued by general Howe, ordering all woollen and linen goods to be delivered to Crean Brush, Esq. Shops were opened and stripped of their goods. A licentious plundering took place. Much was carried off, and more was wantonly destroyed. These irregularities were forbidden in orders, and the guilty threatened with death, but nevertheless every mischief which disappointed malice could suggest, was committed.

The British amounting to more than 7000 men, evacuated Boston, leaving their barracks standing, and also a number of pieces of cannon spiked, four large iron sea mortars, and stores, to the value of £ 30, 000. They demolished the castle, and knocked off the trunnions of the cannon. Various incidents caused a delay of nine days after the evacuation, before they left Nantasket road.

This embarkation was attended with many circumstances of distress and embarrassment. On the departure of the royal army from Boston, a great number of the inhabitants attached to their sovereign, and afraid of public resentment, chose to abandon their country. From the great multitude about to depart, there was no possibility of procuring purchasers for their furniture, neither was there a sufficiency of vessels for its convenient transportation. Mutual jealousy subsisted between the [264] army and navy; each charging the other as the cause of some part of their common distress. The army was full of discontent. Reinforcements though long promised, had not arrived. Both officers and soldiers thought themselves neglected.

Five months had elapsed since they had received any advice of their destination. Wants and inconveniencies increased their ill humour. Their intended voyage to Halifax subjected them to great dangers. The coast at all times hazardous, was eminently so at that tempestuous equinoctial season. They had reason to fear they would be blown off to the West-Indies, and without a sufficient stock of provisions. They were also going to a barren country. To add to their difficulties, this dangerous voyage when completed, was directly so much out of their way. Their business lay to the southward, and they were going northward. Under all these difficulties, and with all these gloomy prospects, the fleet steered for Halifax. Contrary to appearances, the voyage thither was both short and prosperous. They remained there for some time, waiting for reinforcements and instructions from England. When the royal fleet and army departed from Boston, several ships were left behind for the protection of vessels coming from England, but the American privateers were so alert that they nevertheless made many prizes. Some of the vessels which they captured, were laden with arms and warlike stores. Some transports, with troops on board, were also taken. These had run into the harbour, not knowing that the place was evacuated. The boats employed in the embarkation of the British troops, had scarcely completed their business when general Washington, with his army, marched into Boston. He was received with marks of approbation more flattering than the pomps of a triumph. The inhabitants released from the severities of a garrison life, and from the various indignities to which they were subjected, hailed him as their deliverer. Reciprocal congratulations between those who had been confined within the British lines, and those [who] were excluded from entering them, were exchanged with an ardor which cannot be discribed. General Washington [265] was honoured by Congress with a vote of thanks. 1776 They also ordered a medal to be struck, with suitable devices to perpetuate the rememberance of the great event. The Massachusetts council and house of representatives complimented him in a joint address, in which they expressed their good wishes in the following words, "May you still go on approved by heaven—revered by all good men, and dreaded by those tyrants, who claim their fellow men as their property." His answer was modest and proper.

The evacuation of Boston had been previously determined upon by the British ministry, from principles of political expedience. Being resolved to carry on the war for purposes affecting all the colonies, they conceived a central position to be preferable to Boston. Reasoning of this kind had induced the adoption of the measure, but the American works on Roxbury expedited its execution. The abandonment of their friends, and the withdrawing their forces from Boston, was the first act of a tragedy in which evacuations and retreats were the scenes which most frequently occurred, and the epilogue of which was a total evacuation of the United States.

CHAPTER XI

Transactions in Canada.

THE TIDE OF GOOD FORTUNE which in the autumn of 1775 flowed in upon general Montgomery, induced Congress to reinforce the army under his command. Chamblee, St. Johns, and Montreal having surrendered to the Americans, a fair prospect opened of expelling the British from Canada, and of annexing that province to the united colonies. While they were in imagination anticipating these events, the army in which they confided was defeated, and the general whom they adored was killed. The intelligence transmitted from general Montgomery, previous to his assault on Quebec, encouraged Congress to resolve that nine battalions should be kept up and maintained in Canada. The repulse of their army, [266] though discouraging, did not extinguish the ardor of the Americans. It was no sooner known, at headquarters in Cambridge, than general Washington convened a

JAN. 8, 1776

council of war by which it was resolved, "That as no troops could be spared from Cambridge, the colonies of Massachusetts, Connecticut and New-Hampshire, should be requested to raise three regiments and forward them to Canada.["] Congress also resolved to forward the reinforcements previously voted, and to raise four battalions in New-York, for the defence of that colony, and to garrison Crown-Point, and the several posts to the southward of that fortress. That the army might be supplied with blankets for this winter expedition, a committee was appointed to procure from householders, such as could be spared from their families. To obtain a supply of hard money for the use of the army in Canada, proper persons were employed to exchange paper money for specie. Such was the enthusiasm of the times that many thousand Mexican dollars were freely exchanged at par, by individuals for the paper bills of Congress. It was also resolved, to raise a corps of artillery for this service, and to take into the pay of the colonies one thousand Canadians, in addition to colonel Livingston's regiment. Moses Hazen, a native of Massachusetts, who had resided many years in Canada, was appointed to the command of this new corps.

JAN. 24

Congress addressed a letter to the Canadians in which they observed, "Such is the lot of human nature, that the best of causes are subject to vicissitudes; but generous souls, enlightened and warmed with the fire of liberty, become more resolute as difficulties increase.["] They stated to them, "that eight battalions were raising to proceed to their province, and that if more force was necessary it should be sent." They requested them to seize with eagerness the favourable opportunity then offered to co-operate in the present glorious enterprise, and they advised them to establish associations in their different parishes—to elect deputies for forming a provincial assembly, and for representing them in Congress.

1776

The cause of the Americans had received such powerful aid from many patriotic publications in their gazettes, [267] and from the fervent exhortations of popular preachers, connecting the cause of liberty with the animating principles of religion, that it was determined to employ these two powerful instruments of revolutions—printing and preaching, to operate on the minds of the Canadians. A complete apparatus for printing, together with a printer and a clergyman, were therefore sent into Canada.

Congress also appointed Dr. Franklin, Mr. Chase and Mr. Carrol, the two first of whom were members of their body, and the last a respectable gentleman of the Roman catholic persuasion to proceed to Canada with the view of gaining over the people of that colony to the cause of America, and authorised them to promise on behalf of the united colonies, that Canada should be received into their association on equal terms, and also that the inhabitants thereof should enjoy the free exercise of their religion, and the peaceable possession of all their ecclesiastical property.

The desire of effecting something decisive in Canada before the approaching spring, would permit relief to ascend the river St. Lawrence, added to the enthusiasm of the day, encountered difficulties which, in less animated times, would be reckoned unsurmountable. Arthur St. Clair who was appointed colonel of one of the Pennsylvania regiments received his recruiting orders on the 10th of January, and notwithstanding the shortness of the period, his regiment was not only raised, but six companies of it had, in this extreme cold season, completed their march from Pennsylvania to Canada, a distance of several hundred miles, and on the eleventh of April following, joined the American army before Quebec.

Though Congress and the states made great exertions to support the war in Canada, yet from the fall of Montgomery their interest in that colony daily declined. The reduction of Quebec was an object to which their resources were inadequate. Their unsuccessful assault on Quebec made an impression both on the Canadians and Indians unfavorable to their views. A woman infected with the small-pox had either been sent out, or voluntarily came out of Quebec, and by mixing with the American soldiers [268] propagated that scourge of the new world to the great diminution of the effective force of their army. The soldiers inoculated themselves, though their officers issued positive orders to the contrary. By the first of May so many new troops had arrived that the American army, in name, amounted to 3000, but from the prevalence of the small-pox there were only 900 fit for duty. The increasing number of invalids retarded their military operations, and discouraged their friends, while the opposite party was buoyed up with the expectation that the advancing season would soon bring them relief. To these causes of the declining interest of Congress, it must be added that the affections of the Canadians were

1776

alienated. They had many and well founded complaints against the American soldiers. Unrestrained by the terror of civil law and refusing obedience to a military code, the hope of impunity and the love of plunder, led many of the invading army to practices not less disgraceful to themselves, than injurious to the cause in which they had taken arms. Not only the common soldiers but the officers of the American army deviated, in their intercourse with the Canadians, from the maxims of sound policy. Several of them having been lately taken from obscure life were giddy with their exaltation. Far from home they were unawed by those checks which commonly restrain the ferocity of man.

The reduction of Chamblee, St. Johns', and Montreal, together with the exposed situation of Quebec, being known in England, measures were without delay adopted by the British ministry to introduce into Canada, as soon as possible, a force sufficient for the double purpose of recovering what they had lost, and of prosecuting offensive operations from that quarter against the revolted colonies. MAY 5 The van of this force made good its passage, very early in the spring, through the ice up the river St. Lawrence. The expectation of their coming had for some time damped the hopes of the besiegers, and had induced them to think of a retreat. The day before the first of the British reinforcements arrived, that measure was resolved upon by a council of war, and arrangements were made for carrying it into execution.

1776 [269] Governor Carleton was too great a proficient in the art of war, to delay seizing the advantages which the consternation of the besiegers, and the arrival of a reinforcement, afforded. A small detachment of soldiers and marines from the ships which had just ascended the river St. Lawrence, being landed and joined to the garrison in Quebec, he marched out at their head to attack the Americans. On his approach, he found every thing in confusion. The late besiegers abandoning their artillery and military stores, had in great precipitation retreated. In this manner at the expiration of five months, the mixed siege and blockade of Quebec was raised. The fortitude and perseverance of the garrison reflected honour on both officers and privates.

The reputation acquired by general Carleton in his military character, for bravely and judiciously defending the province committed to his care, was exceeded by the superior applause, merited from his exercise of the virtues of humanity and generosity. Among the numerous sick in the American hospitals, several incapable of being moved were left behind. The victorious general proved himself worthy of success by his treatment of these unfortunate men, he not only fed and cloathed them, but permitted them when recovered to return home, apprehending that fear might make some conceal themselves in the woods, rather than by applying for relief, make themselves known, he removed their doubts by a proclamation, in which he engaged, "that as soon as their health was restored, they should have free liberty of returning to the respective provinces." This humane line of conduct was more injurious to the view of the leaders in the American councils, than the severity practised by other British commanders. The truly politic, as well as humane general Carleton, dismissed these prisoners after liberally supplying their wants with a recommendation, "to go home, mind their farms, and keep themselves and their neighbours from all participation in the unhappy war." MAY 10

The small force which arrived at Quebec early in May, was followed by several British regiments; together with [270] the Brunswic troops in such a rapid succession, that in a few weeks the whole was estimated at 13,000 men. 1776

The Americans retreated forty five miles before they stopped. After a short halt, they proceeded to the Sorel, at which place they threw up some slight works for their safety. They were there joined by some battalions coming to reinforce them. About this time general Thomas, the commander in chief in Canada was seized with the small pox and died, having forbidden his men to inoculate, he conformed to his rule, and refused to avail himself of that precaution. On his death, the command devolved at first on general Arnold, and afterwards on general Sullivan. It soon became evident, that the Americans must abandon the whole province of Canada.

From a desire to do something which might counterbalance in the minds of the Canadians, the unfavourable impression which this farther retreat would communicate, General Thomson projected an attack on the British post at the Three Rivers. This lies about half way between Quebec and Montreal, and is so called from the vicinity of one of the branches of a large river, whose waters are discharged through three mouths into the St. Lawrence. With this view a detachment of six hundred men was put under the command of colonel St. Clair. At their head he advanced to the village of Nicolette. When every thing was ready for the enterprise, intelligence was received that six transports escorted by two frigates from Quebec, had arrived and brought a large addition to the late force at the Three Rivers. This caused some new movements, and a delay till more troops could be brought forward. General Thomson then came on with a reinforcement and took the command of the whole. It was determined to make the proposed attack in four different places at the same time. One division commanded by colonel Wayne was to gain the eastern extremity of the town. One commanded by colonel Maxwell was to enter from the northward about the center, and the other two divisions commanded by colonels Sinclair and Irvine were to enter from the westward. The whole [271] having embarked at midnight, landed at the Point du Lac, about three hours before day. At some distance from this point, there are two ways of approaching Three Rivers, one by a road that leads along the banks of the St. Lawrence, the other by a road almost parallel, but at a considerable distance. It had been determined to advance on the last. Intelligence was brought to general Thomson, soon after his landing that a party of 3 or 400 men were posted at three miles distance. The troops were instantly put in motion to dislodge them. The intelligence proved to be false but it had carried the detachment, some distance beyond the point, where the roads separated. To have returned, would have consumed time that could not be spared as the day was fast approaching. It was therefore resolved to proceed in a diagonal direction towards the road they had left. After being much retarded by very difficult grounds, they arrived at a morass which seemed impassable. Here the day broke, when they were six miles from the object. General Thomson suspecting the fidelity of his guides, put them under arrest—reversed the order of his march, and again reached the road by the river. He had advanced but a small distance before he was fired upon by two armed vessels. All expectation of succeeding by surprise, was now at an end. It was therefore instantly determined to make an open attack. The sun was rising. The drums were ordered to beat, and the troops moved on with the greatest alacrity. Having advanced three miles farther, the ships of war began to fire on them. The American officer who led the advance, struck into a road on the left, which also led to the town, and was covered from the fire of the ships. This last road was circuitous and led through a vast tract of woodland at that season almost impassable. He nevertheless entered the wood, and the rest of the detachment followed. After incredible labour, and wading a rivulet breast deep, they gained the open country north of the village. A party of the British were soon discovered about a mile to the left of the Americans, and between them and the town. Colonel Wayne, ardent for action immediately attacked them. The onset was gallant [272] and vigorous, but the contest was unequal. The Americans were soon repulsed and forced to retreat. In the beginning of the action general Thomson left the main body of his corps to join that which was engaged. The woods were so thick, that it was difficult for any person in motion, after losing sight of an object to recover it. The general therefore never found his way back. The situation of colonel St. Clair, the next in command became embarrassing. In his opinion a retreat was necessary, but not knowing the precise situation of his superior officer, and every moment expecting his return, he declined giving orders for that purpose. At last when the British were discovered on the river road, advancing in a direction to gain the rear of the Americans, colonel St. Clair in the absence of gen. Thomson, ordered a retreat. This was made by treading back their steps through the same dismal swamp by which they had advanced. The British marched directly for the point du Lac with the expectation of securing the American batteaux. On their approach major Wood, in whose care they had been left, retired with them to the Sorel. At the point du Lac, the British halted and took a very advantageous position. As soon as it was discovered that the Americans had retired, a party of the British pursued them. When the former arrived near the place of their embarkation, they found a large party of their enemies posted in their front, at the same time that another was only three quarters of a mile in their rear. Here was a new and trying dilemma, and but little time left for consideration. There was an immediate necessity,

1776

either to lay down their arms or attempt by a sudden March to turn the party in front and get into the country beyond it. The last was thought practicable. Colonel St. Clair having some knowledge of the country from his having served in it in the preceding war, gave them a route by the Acadian village where the river de Loups is fordable. They had not advanced far when colonel St. Clair found himself unable to proceed from a wound, occasioned by a root which had penetrated through his shoe. His men offered to carry him, but this generous proposal was declined. [273] He and two or three officers, who having been worn down with fatigue, remained behind with him, found an asylum under cover of a large tree which had been blown up by the roots. They had not been long in this situation when they heard a firing from the British in almost all directions. They nevertheless lay still, and in the night stole off from the midst of surrounding foes. They were now pressed with the importunate cravings of hunger, for they were entering on the third day without food. After wandering for some time, they accidentally found some peasants, who entertained them with great hospitality. In a few days they joined the army at Sorel, and had the satisfaction to find that the greatest part of the detachment had arrived safe before them. In their way through the country, although they might in almost every step of it have been made prisoners, and had reason to fear that the inhabitants from the prospect of reward, would have been tempted to take them, yet they met with neither injury nor insult. General Thomson was not so fortunate. After having lost the troops and falling in with colonel Irwine, and some other officers, they wandered the whole night in thick swamps, without being able to find their way out. Failing in their attempts to gain the river, they had taken refuge in a house, and were there made prisoners.

The British forces having arrived, and a considerable body of them having rendezvoused at the Three Rivers, a serious pursuit of the American army commenced. Had Sir Guy Carleton taken no pains to cut off their retreat, and at once attacked their post, or rather their fortified camp at Sorel, it would probably have fallen into his hands; but either the bold, though unsuccessful attack, at the Three rivers had taught him to respect them, or he wished to reduce them without bloodshed. In the pursuit he made three divisions of his army, and arranged them so as to embrace the whole American encampment, and to command it in every part. The retreat was delayed so long that the Americans evacuated Sorel, only about two hours before one division of the British made its appearance.

[274] While the Americans were retreating, they were daily assailed by the remonstrances of the inhabitants of Canada, who had either joined or befriended them. Great numbers of Canadians had taken a decided part in their favour, rendered them essential services, and thereby incurred the heavy penalties annexed to the crime of supporting rebellion. These, though Congress had assured them but a few months before "that they would never abandon them to the fury of their common enemies" were from the necessity of the case left exposed to the resentment of their provincial rulers. Several of them with tears in their eyes, expostulated with the retreating army, and bewailing their hard fate prayed for support. The only relief the Americans could offer was an assurance of continued protection, if they retreated with them, but this was a hard alternative to men who had wives, children and immoveable effects. They generally concluded, that it was the least of two evils to cast themselves on the mercy of that government, against which they had offended.

The distresses of the retreating army were great. The British were close on their rear and threatening them with destruction. The unfurnished state of the colonies in point of ordnance, imposed a necessity of preserving their cannon. The men were obliged to drag their loaded batteaus up the rapids by mere strength, and when they were to the middle in water. The retreating army was also incumbered with great numbers labouring under the small-pox, and other diseases. Two regiments, at one time, had not a single man in health. Another had only six, and a fourth only forty, and two more were in nearly the same condition.

To retreat in face of an enemy is at all times hazardous; but on this occasion it was attended with an unusual proportion of embarrassments. General Sullivan, who conducted the retreat, nevertheless acted with so much judgment and propriety, that the baggage and public stores were saved, and the numerous sick brought off. The American army reached Crown-Point on the first of July, and at that place made their first stand.

[275] A short time before the Americans evacuated the province of Canada, General Arnold convened the merchants of Montreal, and proposed to them to furnish a quantity of specified articles, for the use of the army in the service of Congress. While they were deliberating on the subject, he placed centinels at their shop doors, and made such arrangements, that what was at first only a request, operated as a command. A great quantity of goods were taken on pretence that they were wanted for the use of the American army, but in their number were many articles only serviceable to women, and to persons in civil life. His nephew soon after opened a store in Albany, and publicly disposed of goods which had been procured at Montreal.

The possession of Canada so eminently favoured the plans of defence adopted by Congress, that the province was evacuated with great reluctance. The Americans were not only mortified at the disappointment of their favourite scheme, of annexing it as a fourteenth link in the chain of their confederacy, but apprehended the most serious consequences from the ascending of the British power in that quarter. Anxious to preserve a footing there, they had persevered for a long time in stemming the tide of unfavourable events.

General Gates was about this time appointed to command in Canada, but on coming to the knowledge of the late events in that province, he concluded to stop short within the limits of New-York. The scene was henceforth reversed. Instead of meditating the recommencement of offensive operations, that army which had lately excited so much terror in Canada, was called upon to be prepared for repelling an invasion threatened from that province.

The attention of the Americans being exclusively fixed on plans of defence, their general officers commanding in the northern department, were convened to deliberate on the place and means most suitable for that purpose. To form a judgment on this subject, a recollection of the events of the late war, between France and England, was of advantage. The same ground was to be fought over, [276] and the same posts to be again contended for. On the confines of Lake George and Lake Champlain two inland seas, which stretch almost from the sources of Hudson's river to the St. Lawrence, are situated the famous posts of Ticonderoga and Crown-Point. These are of primary necessity to any power which contends for the possession of the adjacent country, for they afford the most convenient stand either for its annoyance or defence. In the opinion of some American officers, Crown-Point to which the army on the evacuation of Canada had retreated, was the most proper place for erecting works of defence, but it was otherwise determined, by the council convened, on this occasion. It was also by their advice resolved, to move lower down, and to make the principal work on the strong ground east of Ticonderoga, and especially by every means to endeavour to maintain a naval superiority in Lake Champlain. In conformity to these resolutions general Gates with about 12,000 men, which collected in the course of the summer, was fixed in command of Ticonderoga, and a fleet was constructed at Skenesborough. This was carried on with so much rapidity, that in a short time there were afloat, in Lake Champlain, one sloop, three schooners, and six gondolas, carrying in the whole 58 guns, 86 swivels, and 440 men. Six other vessels were also nearly ready for launching at the same time. The fleet was put under the command of general Arnold, and he was instructed by general Gates, to proceed beyond Crown-Point, down Lake Champlain, to the Split Rock; but most peremptorily restrained from advancing any farther, as security against an apprehended invasion was the ultimate end of the armament.

AUGUST 22

The expulsion of the American invaders from Canada, was but a part of the British designs in that quarter. They urged the pursuit no farther than St. John's, but indulged the hope of being soon in a condition for passing the lakes, and penetrating through the country to Albany, so as to form a communication with New-York. The objects they had in view were great, and the obstacles in the way of their accomplishment equally so. [277] Before they could advance with any prospect of success, a fleet superior to that of the Americans on the lakes, was to be constructed. The materials of some large vessels were, for this purpose, brought from England, but their transportation, and the labour necessary to put them together required both time and patience. The spirit of the British commanders rose in proportion to the difficulties which were to be encountered. Nevertheless it was so late as the month of October, before their

1776

fleet was prepared to face the American naval force, on Lake Champlain. The former consisted of the ship Inflexible, mounting 18 twelve pounders, which was so expeditiously constructed, that she sailed from St. John's 28 days after laying her keel. One schooner mounting 14 and another 12 six pounders. A flat bottomed radeau carrying six 24 and six 12 pounders, besides howitzers, and a gondola with seven nine pounders. There were also twenty smaller vessels with brass field pieces, from 9 to 24 pounders, or with howitzers. Some long boats were furnished in the same manner. An equal number of large boats acted as tenders. Besides these vessels of war, there was a vast number destined for the transportation of the army, its stores, artillery, baggage and provisions. The whole was put under the command of captain Pringle. The naval force of the Americans, from the deficiency of means, was far short of what was brought against them. Their principal armed vessel was a schooner, which mounted only 12 six and four pounders, and their whole fleet in addition to this, consisted of only fifteen vessels of inferior force.

No one step could be taken towards accomplishing the designs of the British, on the northern frontiers of New-York, till they had the command of Lake Champlain. With this view their fleet proceeded up the lake, and engaged the Americans. The wind was so unfavourable to the British, that their ship Inflexible, and some other vessel of force, could not be brought to action. This lessened the inequality between the contending fleets so much, that the principal damage sustained by the Americans, was the loss of a schooner and gondola. At the [278] approach of night the action was discontinued. The vanquished took the advantage, which the darkness afforded to make their escape. This was effected by general Arnold, with great judgment and ability. By the next morning the whole fleet under his command was out of sight. The British pursued with all the sail they could croud. The wind having become more favourable, they overtook the Americans, and brought them to action near Crown-Point. A smart engagement ensued and was well supported on both sides for about two hours. Some of the American vessels which were most ahead escaped to Ticonderoga. Two gallies and five gondolas remained and resisted an unequal force, with a spirit approaching to desperation. One of the gallies struck and was taken. General Arnold, though he

OCT. 11

1776

OCT. 13

knew that to escape was impossible, and to resist unavailing, yet instead of surrendering, determined that his people should not become prisoners, nor his vessels a re-inforcement to the British. This spirited resolution was executed with a judgment, equal to the boldness, with which it had been adopted. He ran the Congress galley, on board of which he was, together with the five gondolas on shore, in such a position, as enabled him to land his men and blow up the vessels. In the execution of this perilous enterprise, he paid a romantic attention to a point of honour. He did not quit his own galley till she was in flames, lest the British should board her, and strike his flag. The result of this action, though unfavourable to the Americans, raised the reputation of general Arnold, higher than ever. In addition to the fame of a brave soldier, he acquired that of an able sea officer.

The American naval force being nearly destroyed, the British had undisputed possession of Lake Champlain. On this event a few continental troops which had been at Crown-Point, retired to their main body at Ticonderoga. General Carleton took possession of the ground from which they had retreated, and was there soon joined by his army. He sent out several reconnoitering parties, and at one time pushed forward a strong detachment on both sides of the lake, which approached near [279] to Ticonderoga. Some British vessels appeared at the same time, within cannon shot of the American works, at that place. It is probable he had it in contemplation, if circumstances favoured to reduce the post, and that the apparent strength of the works, restrained him from making the attempt, and induced his return to Canada. 1776

Such was the termination of the northern campaign in 1776. Though after the surrender of Montreal evacuations, defeats, and retreats, had almost uninterruptedly been the portion of the Americans, yet with respect to the great object of defence on the one side, and of conquest on the other, a whole campaign was gained to them, and lost to their adversaries.

The British had cleared Canada of its invaders, and destroyed the American fleet on the lakes, yet from impediments thrown in their way, they failed in their ulterior designs. The delays contrived by general Gates, retarded the British for so great a part of the summer, that by the time they had reached Ticonderoga, their retreat on account of the approaching winter, became immediately necessary. On the part of the Americans, some men, and a few armed vessels were lost, but time was gained, their army saved, and the frontier of the adjacent states secured from a projected invasion. On the part of the British, the object of a campaign, in which 13,000 men were employed, and near a million of money expended, was rendered in a great measure abortive.

The Proceedings of Parliament, against the Colonies,
1775–6. Operations in South-Carolina, New-York,
and New-Jersey.

THE OPERATIONS CARRIED ON AGAINST the united colonies, in
the year 1775, were adapted to cases of criminal combination among
subjects not in arms. The military arrangements for that year, were
therefore made on the idea of a trifling addition to a peace establishment. [280] It was either not known, that a majority of the Americans
had determined to resist the power of Great-Britain, rather than
submit to the late coercive laws, or it was not believed that they had
spirit sufficient to act in conformity to that determination. The
propensity in human nature, to believe that to be true, which is
wished to be so, had deceived the royal servants in America, and
the British ministry in England, so far as to induce their general
belief, that a determined spirit on the part of government, and a few
thousand troops to support that determination, would easily compose
the troubles in America. Their military operations in the year 1775,
were therefore calculated on the small scale of strengthening the

1776

civil power, and not on the large one of resisting an organised army. Though it had been declared by parliament in February, 1775, that a rebellion existed in Massachusetts, yet it was not believed that the colonists would dare to abet their opposition by an armed force. The resistance made by the militia at Lexington, the consequent military arrangements adopted, first by Massachusetts, and afterwards by Congress, together with the defence of Bunker's-hill, all conspired to prove that the Americans were far from being contemptible adversaries. The nation finding itself, by a fatal progression of the unhappy dispute, involved in a civil war, was roused to recollection. Though several corporate bodies, and sundry distinguished individuals in Great-Britain, were opposed to coercive measures, yet there was a majority for proceeding. The pride of the nation was interested in humbling the colonists, who had dared to resist the power which had lately triumphed over the combined force of France and Spain. The prospect of freeing their own estates from a part of the heavy taxes charged thereon, induced numbers of the landed gentlemen in Great-Britain to support the same measures. They conceived the coercion of the colonies to be the most direct mode of securing their contribution towards sinking the national debt. Influenced by these opinions, such not only justified the adoption of rigorous measures, but chearfully consented to present additional taxes with the same spirit [281] which induces litigants in private life to advance money for forwarding a lawsuit, from the termination of which great profits are expected. Lord North, the prime minister of England, finding himself supported by so many powerful interests, was encouraged to proceed. He had already subdued a powerful party in the city of London, and triumphed over the East-India company. The submission of the colonies was only wanting to complete the glory of his administration. Previous success emboldened him to attempt the arduous business. He flattered himself that the accomplishment of it would, not only restore peace to the empire, but give a brilliancy to his name, far exceeding that of any of his predecessors.

1775

Such was the temper of a great part of the nation, and such the ambitious views of its prime minister, when the parliament was convened, on the 24th of October 1775. In the speech from the throne great complaints were made of the leaders in the colonies, who were said by their misrepresentatives to have infused into the minds of the deluded multitude opinions, repugnant to their constitutional subordination, and afterwards to have proceeded to the commencement of hostilities, and the usurpation of the whole powers of government. His majesty also charged his subjects in America with "meaning only to amuse by vague expressions of attachment to the Parent State, while they were preparing for a general revolt." And he farther asserted "that the rebellious war now levied by them was become more general, and manifestly carried on for the purpose of establishing an independent empire, and that it was become the art of wisdom, and in its effects, of clemency to put a speedy end to these disorders, by the most decisive exertions."

Information was also given, that "the most friendly offers of foreign assistance had been received, and that his majesty's electoral troops were sent to the garrison of Gibraltar and Port Mahon, in order that a large number of the established forces of the kingdom might be applied to the maintenance of its authority." The severity of these assertions was mitigated by a declaration, "that when the unhappy and deluded multitude against [282] whom this force should be directed, would become sensible of their error, his majesty would be ready to receive the misled with tenderness and mercy," "and that to prevent inconveniences, he should give authority to certain persons on the spot, to grant general or particular pardons and indemnities to such as should be disposed to return to their allegiance." The sentiments expressed in this speech and the heavy charges therein laid against the colonists, were re-echoed in addresses to the king from both houses of parliament, but not without a spirited protest in the house of lords. In this, nineteen dissenting members asserted the American war to be "unjust and impolitic in its principles, and fatal in its consequences." They also declared, that they could not consent to an address, "which might deceive his majesty and the public into a belief of the confidence of their house in the present ministers, who had disgraced parliament, deceived the nation—lost the colonies, and involved them in a civil war against their clearest interests, and upon the most unjustifiable grounds wantonly spilling the blood of thousands of their fellow subjects."

The sanction of parliament being obtained for a vigorous prosecution of the American war, estimates for the public service, were agreed to on the idea of operating against the colonies as an hostile

1775

armed foreign power. To this end it was voted to employ 28,000 seamen, and 55,900 land forces, and the sanction of authority was not long after given to measures for engaging foreign mercenaries. No ministry had in any preceding war exerted themselves more to prosecute military operations against alien enemies, than the present to make the ensuing campaign decisive of the dispute between the Mother Country and the colonies. One legislative act was still wanting

to give full efficacy to the intended prosecution of hostilities. This was brought into parliament in a bill interdicting all trade and intercourse with the thirteen united colonies. By it all property of Americans, whether of ships or goods, on the high seas, or in harbour, was declared "to be forfeited to the captors, being the officers and crews of his majesty's ships of war." It farther enacted [283] "that the masters, crews and other persons found on board captured American vessels, should be entered on board his majesty's vessels of war, and there considered to be in his majesty's service to all intents and purposes, as if they had entered of their own accord." This bill also authorised the crown to appoint commissioners, who over and above granting pardons to individuals were empowered to "enquire into general and particular grievances, and to determine whether any colony or part of a colony was returned to that state of obedience, which might entitle it to be received within the king's peace and protection." In that case upon a declaration from the commissioners "the restrictions of the proposed law were to cease."

It was said in favour of this bill,

> that as the Americans were already in a state of war, it became necessary that hostilities should be carried on against them, as was usual against alien enemies. That the more vigorously and extensively military operations were prosecuted, the sooner would peace and order be restored. That as the commissioners went out with the sword in one hand, and terms of conciliation in the other, it was in the power of the colonists to prevent the infliction of any real or apparent severities, in the proposed statute.

In opposition to it, it was said, "that treating the Americans as a foreign nation, was chalking out the way for their independence."

One member observed, that as the indiscriminate rapine of property authorised by the bill, would oblige the colonists to coalesce as one man, its title ought to be "A bill for carrying more effectually into execution the resolves of Congress." The clause for vesting the property of the seizures in the captors, was reprobated as tending to extinguish in the breasts of seamen the principles of patriotism—of national pride and glory, and to substitute in their room habits of cruelty, of piracy and robbery. But of all parts of this bill none was so severely condemned as that clause by which persons taken on board the American vessels, were indiscriminately compelled to serve as common sailors in British ships of war. This was said to be "a refinement of [284] tyranny worse than death." It was also said, 1776 "That no man could be despoiled of his goods as a foreign enemy, and at the same time obliged to serve as a citizen, and that compelling captives to bear arms against their families, kindred, friends and country—and after being plundered themselves to become accomplices in plundering their brethren, was unexampled, except among pirates, the outlaws and enemies of human society." To all these high charges the ministry replied, "that the measure was an act of grace and favour, for" said they, "the crews of American vessels, instead of being put to death, the legal punishment of their demerits, as traitors and rebels, are by this law to be rated on the king's books, and treated as if they were on the same footing with a great body of his most useful and faithful subjects." It was also said, "that their pay and emoluments in the service of their lawful sovereign would be a compensation for all scruples that might arise from the supposed violation of their principles."

In the progress of the debates on this bill, lord Mansfield declared, "that the questions of original right and wrong were no longer to be considered—that they were engaged in a war, and must use their utmost efforts to obtain the ends proposed by it, that they must either fight or be pursued, and that the justice of the cause must give way to their present situation." Perhaps no speech in or out of parliament operated more extensively on the irritated minds of the colonists than this one.

The great abilities and profound legal knowledge of lord Mansfield were both known and admired in America. That this illustrious oracle of law should declare from the seat of legislation, that the justice of the cause was no longer to be regarded, excited the astonishment, and cemented the union of the colonists. "Great-Britain, said they, has commenced war against us for maintaining our constitutional liberties, and her lawgivers now declare they must proceed without any retrospect to the merits of the original ground of dispute. Our peace and happiness must be sacrificed to British honour and consistency, in their continuing to prosecute [285] an unjust invasion of our rights." A number of lords, as usual, entered a spirited protest against the bill, but it was carried by a great majority in both houses of parliament, and soon after received the royal assent.

DEC. 21, 1775

This law arrived in the colonies in March 1776. The effects resulting from it were such as had been predicted by its opposers. It not only united the colonies in resisting Great-Britain, but produced a favourable opinion of independence in the minds of thousands, who previously reprobated that measure. It was considered from New-Hampshire to Georgia, as a legal discharge from allegiance to their native sovereign. What was wanting to produce a decided majority of the party for breaking off all connexion with Great-Britain, was speedily obtained from the irritation excited by the hiring of foreign troops to fight against the colonists. This measure was nearly coincident with the ratification of the prohibitory law just mentioned, and intelligence of both arrived in the colonies about the same time.

The treaties which had been lately concluded with the Landgrave of Hesse Cassel, the duke of Brunswic, and the hereditary prince of Hesse Cassel for hiring their troops to the king of Great-Britain, to be employed in the American service being laid before the house of commons, a motion was made thereon for referring them to the committee of supply. This occasioned a very interesting debate on the propriety of employing foreign troops against the Americans. The measure was supported on the necessity of prosecuting the war, and the impracticability of raising a sufficient number of domestic levies. It was also urged "that foreign troops inspired with the military maxims, and ideas of implicit submission, would be less apt to be biassed by that false lenity, which native soldiers might indulge, at the expence of national interest." It was said,

FEB. 29, 1776

Are we to sit still and suffer an unprovoked rebellion to terminate in the formation of an independent hostile empire? Are we to suffer our colonies, the object of the great national expence, and of two bloody wars to be lost forever to us, and given away to strangers from a scruple of [286] employing foreign troops to preserve our just rights, over colonies for which we have paid so dear a purchase? As the Americans by refusing the obedience and taxes of subjects, deny themselves to be a part of the British empire, and make themselves foreigners, they cannot complain that foreigners are employed against them.

1775

On the other side the measure was severely condemned. The necessity of the war was denied, and the nation was represented as disgraced by applying to the petty princes of Germany, for succours against her own rebellious subjects. The tendency of the example to induce the Americans to form alliances with foreign powers, was strongly urged. It was said,

hitherto the colonists have ventured to commit themselves singly in this arduous contest, without having recourse to foreign aid, but it is not to be doubted, that in future they will think themselves fully justified both by our example, and the laws of self preservation, to engage foreigners to assist them in opposing those mercenaries, whom we are about to transport for their destruction. Nor is it doubtful that in case of their application, European powers of a rank far superior to that of those petty princes, to whom we have so abjectly sued for aid, will consider themselves to be equally entitled to interfere in the quarrel between us and our colonies.

The supposition of the Americans receiving aid from France or Spain, was on this and several other occasions ridiculed, on the idea that these powers would not dare to set to their own colonies the dangerous example of encouraging those of Great-Britain, in opposing their sovereign. It was also supposed, that they would be influenced by considerations of future danger to their American possessions, from the establishment of an independent empire in their vicinity. In this session of parliament between the 26th of October, 1775, and the 23d, of May 1776, the ultimate plan for reducing the colonies was completely fixed. The Americans were declared out of the royal protection, and 16,000 foreign mercenaries, employed by national authority, to effect their subjugation. These measures [287] induced Congress in the following summer to declare themselves independent, and to seek for foreign aid: Events which shall be hereafter more fully explained.

Parliamentary sanction for carrying on the war against the colonists, as against alien enemies being obtained, it became necessary to fix on a commander of the royal forces to be employed on this occasion. This as a matter of right was, in the first instance, offered to general Oglethorpe, as being the first on the list of general officers. To the surprise of the minister that respectable veteran, readily accepted the command, on condition of his being properly supported. A numerous well appointed army and a powerful fleet were promised him, to which he replied, "I will undertake the business without a man or a ship of war, provided you will authorise me to assure the colonists on my arrival among them, that you will do them justice." He added farther, "I know the people of America well, and am satisfied, that his majesty has not in any part of his dominions, more obedient, or more loyal subjects. You may secure their obedience by doing them justice, but you will never subdue them by force of arms." These opinions so favourable to the Americans, proved general Oglethorpe to be an improper person for the purpose intended by the British ministry. He was therefore passed over, and the command given to Sir William Howe.

It was resolved to open the campaign, with such a powerful force as "would look down all opposition, and effectuate submission without bloodshed," and to direct its operations to the accomplishment of three objects. The first was the relief of Quebec, and the recovery of Canada, which also included a subsequent invasion of the north-western frontiers of the adjacent provinces. The second was a strong impression on some of the southern colonies. The third and principal, was to take possession of New-York, with a force sufficiently powerful to keep possession of Hudson's-River, and form a line of communication with the royal army in Canada, or to over-run the adjacent country.

The partial success of the first part of this plan, has been in the preceding chapter explained. The execution [288] of the second part was committed to general Clinton, and Sir Peter Parker. The former with a small force having called at New-York, and also visited in Virginia lord Dunmore, the late royal governor of that colony, and finding that nothing could be done at either place, proceeded to Cape-Fear-River. At that place he issued a proclamation from on board the Pallas transport, offering free pardon to all such as should lay down their arms, excepting Cornelius Hasnett, and Robert Howe, but the recent defeat of the regulators and Highlanders, restrained even their friends from paying any attention to this act of grace.

At Cape-Fear a junction was formed between Sir Henry Clinton, and Sir Peter Parker, the latter of whom had sailed with his squadron directly from Europe. They concluded to attempt the reduction of Charleston as being, of all places within the line of their instructions, the object at which they could strike with the greatest prospect of advantage. They had 2,800 land forces, which they hoped, with the co-operation of their shipping, would be fully sufficient.

For some months past every exertion had been made to put the colony of South-Carolina, and especially its capital Charleston, in a respectable posture of defence. In subserviency to this view, works had been erected on Sullivan's island, which is situated so near the channel leading up to the town, as to be a convenient post for annoying vessels approaching it.

Sir Peter Parker attacked the fort on that island, with two fifty gun JULY 28 ships, the Bristol and Experiment, four frigates, the Active, Acteon, Solebay and Syron, each of 28 guns. The Sphynx of 20 guns, the Friendship armed vessel of 22 guns, Ranger sloop, and Thunder bomb, each of 8 guns. On the fort were mounted 26 cannon, 26, 18 and 9 pounders. The attack commenced between ten and eleven in the forenoon, and was continued for upwards of ten hours. The garrison consisting of 375 regulars and a few militia, under the command of colonel Moultrie, made a most gallant defence. They fired deliberately, for the most part took [289] aim and seldom missed their object. The ships were torn almost to pieces, and the killed 1776 and wounded on board exceeded 200 men. The loss of the garrison was only ten men killed, and 22 wounded. The fort being built of palmetto, was little damaged. The shot which struck it were ineffectually buried in its soft wood. General Clinton had some time before the engagement, landed with a number of troops on Long-Island, and it was expected that he would have co-operated with Sir Peter Parker, by crossing over the narrow passage, which divides the two islands, and attacking the fort in its unfinished rear; but the extreme danger to which he must unavoidably have exposed his men, induced him to decline the perilous attempt. Colonel Thomson with 7 or 800 men was stationed at the east end of Sullivan's island, to oppose their crossing. No serious attempt was made to land either from the fleet, or the detachment commanded by Sir Henry Clinton. The firing ceased in the evening, and soon after the ships slipped their cables. Before morning they had retired about two miles from the island. Within a few days more the troops re-embarked and the whole sailed from New-York. The thanks of Congress were given to general Lee, who had been sent on by Congress to take the command in Carolina, and also to colonels Moultrie and Thomson, for their good conduct on this memorable day. In compliment to the commanding officer the fort from that time was called Fort Moultrie.

During the engagement the inhabitants stood with arms in their hands at their respective posts, prepared to receive the enemy wherever they might land. Impressed with high ideas of British power and bravery, they were apprehensive that the fort would be either silenced or passed, and that they should be called to immediate action. They were cantoned in the various landing places near Charleston, and their resolution was fixed to meet the invaders at the water's edge, and dispute every inch of ground, trusting the event to heaven.

By the repulse of this armament the southern states obtained a respite from the calamities of war for two years and a half. The defeat the British met with at Charleston, [290] seemed in some measure to counterbalance the unfavourable impression made, by their subsequent successes, to the northward. Throughout the whole summer, and till the close of the year, Congress had little else than the victory on Sullivan's island, to console them under the various evacuations, retreats, and defeats, to which, as shall hereafter be related, their armies were obliged to submit in every other part of the union. The event of the expedition contributed greatly to establish the cause which it was intended to overset. In opposition to the bold assertions of some, and the desponding fears of others, experience

1776

proved that America might effectually resist a British fleet and army. Those, who from interested motives had abetted the royal government, ashamed of their opposition to the struggles of an infant people for their dearest rights, retired into obscurity.

The effects of this victory, in animating the Americans, were much greater than could be warranted, by the circumstances of the action. As it was the first attack made by the British navy, its unsuccessful issue inspired a confidence which a more exact knowledge of military calculations would have corrected. The circumstance of its happening in the early part of the war, and in one of the weaker provinces, were happily instrumental in dispelling the gloom which overshadowed the minds of many of the colonists, on hearing of the powerful fleets and numerous armies which were coming against them.

The command of the force which was designed to operate against New-York in this campaign, was given to admiral lord Howe, and his brother Sir William, officers who, as well from their personal characters, as the known bravery of their family, stood high in the confidence of the British nation. To this service was allotted a very powerful army, consisting of about 30,000 men. This force was far superior to any thing that America had heretofore seen. The troops were amply provided with artillery, military stores, and warlike materials of every kind, and were supported by a numerous fleet. The admiral and general, in addition to their military powers, were appointed commissioners for restoring peace to the colonies.

[291] General Howe having in vain waited two months at Halifax for his brother, and the expected re-inforcements from England, impatient of farther delays, sailed from that harbour, with the force which he had previously commanded in Boston, and directing his course towards New-York, arrived in the latter end of June, off Sandy-Hook. Admiral lord Howe, with part of the re-inforcement from England, arrived at Halifax, soon after his brother's departure. Without dropping anchor he followed, and soon after joined him near Staten-Island. The British general, on his approach, found every part of New-York island, and the most exposed parts of Long-Island fortified and well defended by artillery. About fifty British transports anchored near Staten-Island, which had not been so much the object of attention. The inhabitants thereof, either from fear, policy, or

1776

JUN. 10

JUN. 12

affection, expressed great joy on the arrival of the royal forces. General Howe was there met by Tryon, late governor of the province, and by several of the loyalists, who had taken refuge with him in an armed vessel. He was also joined by about sixty persons from New-Jersey, and 200 of the inhabitants of Staten-Island were embodied, as a royal militia. From these appearances, great hopes were indulged that as soon as the army was in a condition to penetrate into the country, and protect the loyalists, such numbers would flock to their standard as would facilitate the attainment of the objects of the campaign.

On the fourth day after the British transports appeared off Sandy-Hook. Congress, though fully informed of the numbers and appointment of the force about to be employed against the colonies, ratified their famous declaration of independence. This was publicly read to the American army, and received by them with unfeigned acclamations of joy. Though it was well known, that Great-Britain had employed a force of 55,000 men, to war upon the new-formed states, and that the continental army was not near equal to half that number, and only engaged for a few months, and that Congress was without any assurance of foreign aid, yet both the American [292] officers and privates gave every evidence of their hearty approbation of the decree which severed the colonies from Great-Britain, and submitted to the decision of the sword, whether they should be free states, or conquered provinces. Now, said they, "we know the ground on which we stand. Now we are a nation. No more shall the opprobrious term of rebel, with any appearance of justice, be applied to us. Should the fortune of war throw us into the hands of our enemies, we may expect the treatment of prisoners, and not the punishment of rebels. The prize for which we contend is of such magnitude that we may freely risque our lives to obtain it."

It had early occurred to general Washington, that the possession of New-York, would be with the British a favourite object. Its central situation and contiguity to the ocean, enabled them to carry with facility the war to any part of the sea coast. The possession of it was rendered still more valuable by the ease with which it could be maintained. Surrounded on all sides by water, it was defensible by a small number of British ships, against adversaries whose whole

1776

navy consisted only of a few frigates. Hudson's river, being navigable for ships of the largest size to a great distance, afforded an opportunity of severing the eastern from the more southern states, and of preventing almost any communication between them.

From these well known advantages, it was presumed by the Americans, that the British would make great exertions to effect the reduction of New-York. General Lee, while the British were yet in possession of the capital of Massachusetts had been detached from Cambridge, to put Long-Island and New-York into a posture of defence. As the departure of the British from Boston became more certain, the probability of their instantly going to New-York, increased the necessity of collecting a force for its safety. It had been therefore agreed in a council of war, that five regiments, together with a rifle battalion should march without delay to New-York, and that the states of New-York and New-Jersey should be requested to furnish the former two thousand, and the [293] latter one thousand men for its immediate defence. General Washington soon followed, and early in April fixed his head quarters in that city. A new distribution of the American army took place. Part was left in Massachusetts. Between two and three thousand were ordered to Canada: But the greater part rendezvoused at New-York.

Experience had taught the Americans the difficulty of attacking an army, after it had effected a lodgment. They therefore made strenuous exertions to prevent the British from enjoying the advantages in New-York, which had resulted from their having been permitted to land and fortify themselves in Boston. The sudden commencement of hostilities in Massachusetts, together with the previous undisturbed landing of the royal army, allowed no time for deliberating on a system of war. A change of circumstances indicated the propriety of fixing on a plan for conducting the defence of the new formed states. On this occasion general Washington, after much thought, determined on a war of posts. This mode of conducting military operations gave confidence to the Americans, and besides, it both retarded and alarmed their adversaries. The soldiers in the American army were new levies, and had not yet learned to stand uncovered, before the instruments of death. Habituating them to the sound of fire arms, while they were sheltered from danger, was one step towards inspiring them with a portion of mechanical courage. The British remembered Bunker's-hill, and had no small reverence for even slight fortifications, when defended by freemen. From views of this kind, works were erected in and about New-York, on Long-Island, and the heights of Haerlem. These, besides batteries, were field redoubts, formed of earth with a parapet and ditch. The former were sometimes fraised, and the latter palisadoed, but they were in no instance formed to sustain a siege. Slight as they were, the campaign was nearly wasted away before they were so far reduced, as to permit the royal army to penetrate into the country.

1776

[294] The war having taken a more important turn than in the preceding year had been foreseen, Congress at the opening of the campaign, found themselves distitute of a force sufficient for their defence. They therefore in June determined on a plan to reinforce their continental army by bringing into the field, a new species of troops, that would be more permanent than the common militia, and yet more easily raised than regulars. With this view they instituted a flying camp, to consist of an intermediate corps, between regular soldiers and militia. Ten thousand men were called for from the

JUNE 3

states of Pennsylvania, Maryland, and Delaware, to be in constant service to the first day of the ensuing December. Congress at the same time called for 13,800 of the common militia from Massachusetts, Connecticut, New-York, and New-Jersey. The men for forming the flying camp were generally procured, but there were great deficiences of the militia, and many of those who obeyed their country's call, so far as to turn out, manifested a reluctance to submit to the necessary discipline of camps.

The difficulty of providing the troops with arms while before Boston, was exceeded by the superior difficulty of supplying them, in their new position. By the returns of the garrison at fort Montgomery, in the Highlands in April, it appeared that there were 208 privates, and only forty one guns fit for use. In the garrison at fort Constitution, there were 136 men, and only 68 guns fit for use. Flints were also much wanted. Lead would have been equally deficient, had not a supply for the musquetry been obtained by stripping dwelling houses.

The uncertainty of the place, where the British would commence their operations, added much to the imbarrassment of general Washington. Not only each colony, but each seaport town, supposed itself to be the object of the British, and was ardent in its supplications, to the commander in chief for his puculiar attention. The people of Massachusetts were strongly impressed with an idea, that the evacuation of Boston was only a feint, and that the British army would soon return. They were for that reason very desirous, that the continental troops should not be withdrawn [295] from their state. The inhabitants of Rhode-Island urged in a long petition, that their maritime situation exposed them to uncommon danger, while their great exertions in fitting out armed vessels, had deprived them of many of their citizens. They therefore prayed for a body of continental soldiers, to be stationed for their constant and peculiar defence. So various were the applications for troops, so numerous the calls for arms, that a decided conduct became necessary to prevent the feeble American force, and the deficient stock of public arms from being divided and subdivided, so as to be unequal to the proper defence of any one place.

1776

In this crisis of particular danger, the people of New-York acted with spirit. Though they knew they were to receive the first impression of the British army, yet their convention resolved, "that all persons residing within the state of New-York, and claiming protection from its laws, owed it allegiance, and that any person owing it allegiance and levying war against the state, or being an adherent to the king of Great-Britain, should be deemed guilty of treason and suffer death." They also resolved ["]that one fourth of the militia of West-Chester, Dutchess and Orange counties, should be forthwith drawn out for the defence of the liberties, property, wives and children, of the good people of the state, to be continued in service till the last day of December," and, "that as the inhabitants of King's county, had determined not to oppose the enemy, a committee should be appointed to enquire into the authenticity of these reports, and to disarm and secure the disaffected. To remove or destroy the stock of grain, and if necessary to lay the whole country waste."

The two royal commissioners, admiral and general Howe, thought proper, before they commenced their military operations, to try what might be done in their civil capacity, towards effecting a re-union between Great-Britain and the colonies. It was one of the first acts of lord Howe, to send on shore a circular letter to several of the royal governors in America, informing them of the late act of parliament, "for restoring peace to the colonies, [296] and granting pardon to such as should deserve mercy," and desiring them to publish a declaration which accompanied the same. In this he informed the colonists of the power with which his brother and he were intrusted "of granting general or particular pardons to all those who though they had deviated from their allegiance, were willing to return to their duty," and of declaring "any colony, province, county or town, port, district or place to be at the peace of his majesty." Congress, impressed with a belief, that the proposals of the commissioners, instead of disuniting the people, would have a contrary effect, ordered them to be speedily published in the several American news-papers. Had a redress of grievances been at this late hour offered, though the honour of the states was involved in supporting their late declaration of independence, yet the love of peace, and the bias of great numbers to their Parent State, would in all probability have made a powerful party for rescinding the act of separation, and for re-uniting with Great-Britain. But when it appeared that the power of the royal commissioners was little more than to grant pardons, Congress appealed to the good sense of the people, for the necessity of adhering to the act of independence. The resolution for publishing the circular letter, and the declaration of the royal commissioners, assigned as a reason thereof,

that the good people of the United States may be informed of what nature are the commissioners, and what the terms, with expectation of which the insidious court of Great-Britain had endeavoured to amuse and disarm them, and that the few who still remain suspended by a hope, founded either in the justice or moderation of their late king, may now at length be convinced that the valour alone of their country is to save its liberties.

About the same time flags were sent ashore by lord Howe, with a letter directed to George Washington, Esq. which he refused to receive as not being addressed to him with the title due to his rank. In his letter to Congress on this subject, he wrote as follows, "I would not on any occasion sacrifice essentials to punctilio, but in this instance I deemed it a duty to my country and appointment, to insist [297] on that respect, which in any other than a public view, I would willingly have waved." Congress applauded his conduct in a public resolution, and at the same time directed ["]that no letter or message should be received on any occasion whatever, from the enemy, by the commander in chief, or others the commanders of the American army, but such as were directed to them in the characters they severally sustained."

Some time after, adjutant general Patterson was sent to New-York, by general Howe, with a letter addressed to George Washington, &c. &c. &c. On an interview the adjutant general, after expressing his high esteem for the person and character of the American general, and declaring, that it was not intended to derogate from the respect due to his rank, expressed his hopes, that the *et ceteras* would remove the impediments to their correspondence. General Washington replied, "That a letter directed to any person in a public character, should have some description of it, otherwise it would appear a mere private letter. That it was true the *et ceteras* implied every thing, but they also implied any thing, and that he should therefore decline the receiving any letter directed to him as a private person, when it related to his public station.["] A long conference ensued, in which the adjutant general observed, that "the commissioners were armed with great powers, and would be very happy in effecting an accommodation." He received for answer, "that from what appeared, their powers were only to grant pardon, that they who had committed no fault, wanted no pardon." Soon after this interview, a letter from Howe, respecting prisoners, which was properly addressed to Washington was received.

While the British, by their manifestoes and declarations, were endeavouring to separate those who preferred a reconciliation with Great-Britain from those who were the friends of independence, Congress, by a similar policy, was attempting to detach the foreigners, who had come with the royal troops from the service of his Britannic majesty. Before hostilities had commenced, the following resolution was adopted and circulated among those [298] on whom it was intended to operate.

1776

Resolved, that these states will receive all such foreigners who shall leave the armies of his Britannic majesty in America, and shall chuse to become members of any of these states, and they shall be protected in the free exercise of their respective religions, and be invested with the rights, privileges and immunities of natives, as established by the laws of these states, and moreover, that this congress will provide for every such person, fifty acres of unappropriated lands in some of these states, to be held by him and his heirs, as absolute property.

The numbers which were prepared to oppose the British, when they should disembark, made them for some time cautious of proceeding to their projected land operations, but the superiority of their navy enabled them to go by water, whithersoever they pleased.

A British forty gun ship, with some smaller vessels, sailed up North-River, without receiving any damage of consequence, though fired upon from the batteries of New-York, Paules-Hook, Red-Bank, and Governor's Island. An attempt was made, not long after, with two fire ships, to destroy the British vessels in the North-River, but without effecting any thing more than the burning of a tender. They were also attacked with row gallies, but to little purpose. After some time the Phoenix and Rose men of war, came down the river, and joined the fleet. Every effort of the Americans from their batteries on land, as well as their exertions on the water, proved ineffectual. The British ships passed with less loss than was generally expected, but nevertheless the damage they received was such as deterred them from frequently repeating the experiment. In two or three instances they ascended the North-River, and in one or two the East-River, but those which sailed up the former, speedily returned, and by their return, a free communication was opened through the upper part of the state.

The American army in and near New-York amounted to 17,225 men. These were mostly new troops, and were divided in many small and unconnected posts, some of which were fifteen miles removed from others. The [299] British force before New-York was increasing by frequent successive arrivals from Halifax, South-Carolina, Florida, the West-Indies and Europe. But so many unforeseen delays had taken place, that the month of August was far advanced, before they were in a condition to open the campaign.

When all things were ready, the British commanders resolved to make their first attempt on Long-Island. This was preferred to New-York, as it abounded with those supplies which their forces required.

The British landed without opposition, between two small towns, Utrecht and Gravesend. The American works protected a small peninsula having Wallabout-Bay to the left, and stretching over to Red-Hook on the right, and the East-River being in their rear. General Sullivan, with a strong force, was encamped within these works at Brooklyne. From the east-side of the narrows runs a ridge of hills covered with thick wood, about five or six miles in length, which terminates near Jamaica. There were three passes through these hills, one near the narrows, a second on the Flatbush road, and a third on the Bedford road, and they are all defensible. These were the only roads which could be passed from the southside of the hills to the American lines, except a road which led round the easterly end of the hills to Jamaica. The Americans had 800 men on each of these roads, and colonel Miles was placed with his battalion of riflemen, to guard the road from the south of the hills to Jamaica, and to watch the motions of the British.

General de Heister, with his Hessians, took post at Flatbush, in the evening. In the following night the greater part of the British army, commanded by general Clinton, marched to gain the road leading round the easterly end of the hills to Jamaica, and to turn the left of the Americans. He arrived about two hours before day, within half a mile of this road. One of his parties fell in with a patrol of American officers, and took them all prisoners, which prevented the early transmission of intelligence. Upon the first appearance of day general Clinton advanced, and took possession of the heights over [300] which the road passed. General Grant, with the left wing, advanced along the coast by the west road, near the narrows; but this was intended chiefly as a feint.

The guard which was stationed at this road, fled without making any resistance. A few of them were afterwards rallied, and lord Stirling advanced with 1500 men, and took possession of a hill, about two miles from the American camp, and in front of general Grant.

An attack was made very early in the morning by the Hessians from Flatbush, under general de Heister, and by general Grant on

AUGUST 26

1776

AUG. 27

the coast, and was well supported for a considerable time by both sides. The Americans who opposed general de Heister were first informed of the approach of general Clinton, who had come round on their left. They immediately began to retreat to their camp, but were intercepted by the right wing under general Clinton, who got into the rear of their left, and attacked them with his light infantry and dragoons, while returning to their lines. They were driven back till they were met by the Hessians. They were thus alternately chased and intercepted, between general de Heister and general Clinton. Some of their regiments nevertheless found their way to the camp. The Americans under lord Stirling, consisting of colonel Miles' two battalions, colonel Atlee's, colonel Smallwood's, and colonel Hatche's, regiments, who were engaged with general Grant, fought with great resolution for about six hours. They were uninformed of the movements made by general Clinton, till some of the troops under his command, had traversed the whole extent of country in their rear. Their retreat was thus intercepted, but several notwithstanding, broke through and got into the woods. Many threw themselves into the marsh, some were drowned, and others perished in the mud, but a considerable number escaped by this way to their lines.

The king's troops displayed great valour throughout the whole day. The variety of the ground occasioned a succession of small engagements, pursuits and slaughter, which lasted for many hours. British discipline in every instance, triumphed over the native valour of raw 1776 troops, [301] who had never been in action, and whose officers were unacquainted with the stratagems of war.

The loss of the British and Hessians was about 450. The killed, wounded and prisoners of the Americans, including those who were drowned or perished in the woods or mud, considerably exceeded a thousand. Among the prisoners of the latter were two of their general officers, Sullivan and lord Stirling. Three Colonels, 4 lieutenant colonels, 3 majors, 18 captains, 43 lieutenants, and 11 ensigns. Smallwood's regiment, the officers of which were young men of the best families in the state of Maryland, sustained a loss of 259 men. The British after their victory were so impetuous, that it was with difficulty, they could be restrained from attacking the American lines.

In the time of, and subsequent to the engagement, General Washington drew over to Long-Island, the greatest part of his army. After he had collected his principal force there, it was his wish and hope, that Sir William Howe, would attempt to storm the works on the island. These though insufficient to stand a regular siege, were strong enough to resist a coup de main. The rememberance of Bunker's-hill, and a desire to spare his men, restrained the British general from making an assault. On the contrary he made demonstrations of proceeding by siege, and broke ground within three hundred yards to the left at Putnam's redoubt. Though general Washington wished for an assault, yet being certain that his works would be untenable, when the British batteries should be fully opened, AUG. 30 he called a council of war, to consult on the measures proper to be taken. It was then determined that the objects in view were in no degree proportioned to the dangers to which, by a continuation on the island, they would be exposed. Conformably to this opinion, dispositions were made for an immediate retreat. This commenced soon after it was dark from two points, the upper and lower ferries, on East river. General M'Dougal, regulated the embarkation at one, and colonel Knox at the other. The intention of evacuating the island, had been so prudently concealed [302] from the Americans, that 1776 they knew not whither they were going, but supposed to attack the enemy. The field artillery, tents, baggage, and about 9000 men were conveyed to the city of New-York over East River, more than a mile wide, in less than 13 hours, and without the knowledge of the British, though not six hundred yards distant. Providence, in a remarkable manner favoured the retreating army. For some time after the Americans began to cross the state of the tide, and a strong northeast wind made it impossible for them to make use of their sail boats, and their whole number of row boats was insufficient for completing the business, in the course of the night. But about eleven o'clock, the wind died away, and soon after sprung up at south-east, and blew fresh, which rendered the sail boats of use, and at the same time made the passage from the island to the city, direct, easy and expeditious. Towards morning an extreme thick fog came up, which hovered over Long-Island, and by concealing the Americans, enabled them to complete their retreat without interruption, though the day had begun to dawn some time before it was finished. By a mistake in the transmission of orders, the American lines were evacuated for about three quarters of an hour, before the last embarkation took place, but the British though so near, that their working parties could be distinctly heard, being enveloped in the fog knew nothing of the matter. The lines were repossessed and held till six o'clock in the morning, when every thing except some heavy cannon was removed. General Mifflin, who commanded the rear guard left the lines, and under the cover of the fog got off safe. In about half an hour the fog cleared away, and the British entered the works which had been just relinquished. Had the wind not shifted, the half of the American army could not have crossed, and even as it was, if the fog had not concealed their rear, it must have been discovered, and could hardly have escaped. General Sullivan, who was taken prisoner on Long-Island, was immediately sent on parole, with the following verbal message from lord Howe to Congress,

1776

that though he could not at present treat [303] with them in that character, yet he was very desirous of having a conference with some of the members, whom he would consider as private gentlemen; that he with his brother the general, had full powers to compromise the dispute between Great-Britain and America, upon terms advantageous to both—that he wished a compact might be settled, at a time when no decisive blow was struck, and neither party could say it was compelled to enter into such agreement. That were they disposed to treat, many things which they had not yet asked, might and ought to be granted, and that if upon conference they found any probable ground of accommodation, the authority of Congress would be afterwards acknowledged to render the treaty complete.

Three days after this message was received, general Sullivan was requested to inform lord Howe,

that Congress being the representatives of the free and independent states of America, they cannot with propriety send any of their members to confer with his lordship in their private characters, but that ever desirous of establishing peace on reasonable terms, they will send a committee of their body, to know whether he has any authority to treat with persons authorised by Congress, for that purpose, on behalf of

America, and what that authority is; and to hear such propositions as he shall think fit to make respecting the same.

They elected Dr. Franklin, John Adams, and Edward Rutledge their committee, for this purpose. In a few days they met lord Howe on Staten-Island, and were received with great politeness. On their return they made a report of their conference, which they summed up by saying,

> It did not appear to your committee that his lordship's commission contained any other authority than that expressed in the act of parliament—namely, that of granting pardons, with such exceptions as the commissioners shall think proper to make, and of declaring America, or any part of it, to be in the king's peace, on submission: For as to the power of enquiring into the state of America, which his lordship mentioned to us, and of conferring and consulting with any persons the commissioners might think proper, and representing the result [304] of such conversation to the ministry, who, provided the colonies would subject themselves, might after all, or might not, at their pleasure, make any alterations in the former instructions to governors, or propose in parliament, any amendment of the acts complained of, we apprehended any expectation from the effect of such a power, would have been too uncertain and precarious, to be relied on by America, had she still continued in her state of dependence.

1776

Lord Howe, had ended the conference on his part, by expressing his regard for America, and the extreme pain he would suffer in being obliged to distress those whom he so much regarded. Dr. Franklin, thanked him for his regards, and assured him, ["]that the Americans would shew their gratitude, by endeavouring to lessen as much as possible, all pain he might feel on their account, by exerting their utmost abilities, in taking good care of themselves."

The committee in every respect maintained the dignity of Congress. Their conduct and sentiments were such as became their character. The friends to independence rejoiced that nothing resulted from this interview, that might disunite the people. Congress, trusting to the good sense of their countrymen, ordered the whole to be printed for their information. All the states would have then rejoiced at less beneficial terms than they obtained about seven years later. But

Great-Britain counted on the certainty of their absolute conquest, or unconditional submission. Her offers therefore comported so little with the feelings of America, that they neither caused demur nor disunion, among the new formed states.

The unsuccessful termination of the action on the 27th, led to consequences more seriously alarming to the Americans, than the loss of their men. Their army was universally dispirited. The militia ran off by companies. Their example infected the regular regiments. The loose footing on which the militia came to camp, made it hazardous to exercise over them that discipline, without which, an army is a mob. To restrain one part of an army, while another claimed and exercised the right of doing as they pleased, was no less impracticable than absurd.

1776

SEPT. 7

[305] A council of war, recommended to act on the defensive, and not to risque the army for the sake of New-York. To retreat, subjected the commander in chief to reflections painful to bear, and yet impolitic to refute. To stand his ground, and by suffering himself to be surrounded, to hazard the fate of America on one decisive engagement, was contrary to every rational plan of defending the wide extended states committed to his care. A middle line between abandoning and defending was therefore for a short time adopted. The public stores were moved to Dobbs' ferry, about 26 miles from New-York. 12,000 men were ordered to the northern extremity of New-York island, and 4500 to remain for the defence of the city, while the remainder occupied the intermediate space, with orders, either to support the city or Kingsbridge, as exigencies might require. Before the British landed, it was impossible to tell what place would be first attacked. This made it necessary to erect works for the defence of a variety of places, as well as of New-York. Though every thing was abandoned when the crisis came that either the city must be relinquished, or the army risqued for its defence, yet from the delays, occasioned by the redoubts and other works, which had been erected on the idea of making the defence of the states a war of posts, a whole campaign was lost to the British, and saved to the Americans. The year began with hopes, that Great-Britain would recede from her demands, and therefore every plan of defence was on a temporary system. The declaration of independence, which the

violence of Great-Britain forced the colonies to adopt in July, though neither foreseen nor intended at the commencement of the year, pointed out the necessity of organising an army, on new terms, correspondent to the enlarged objects for which they had resolved to contend. Congress accordingly determined to raise 88 battalions, to serve during the war. Under these circumstances to wear away the campaign, with as little misfortune as possible, and thereby to gain time for raising a permanent army against the next year, was to the Americans a matter of the last importance. Though the commander in chief abandoned those works, [306] which had engrossed much time and attention yet the advantage resulting from the delays they occasioned, far overbalanced the expence incurred by their erection.

SEP. 16

1776

The same shortsighted politicians, who had before censured general Washington, for his cautious conduct, in not storming the British lines at Boston, renewed their clamors against him, for adopting this evacuating and retreating system. Supported by a consciousness of his own integrity, and by a full conviction that these measures were best calculated for securing the independence of America, he for the good of his country, voluntarily subjected his fame to be overshadowed by a temporary cloud.

General Howe having prepared every thing for a descent on New-York island, began to land his men under cover of ships of war, between Kepps'-bay and Turtle bay. A breast work had been erected in the vicinity, and a party stationed in it to oppose the British, in case of their attempting to land. But on the first appearance of danger, they ran off in confusion. The commander in chief came up, and in vain attempted to rally them. Though the British in sight, did not exceed sixty, he could not either by example, intreaty, or authority, prevail on a superior force to stand their ground, and face that inconsiderable number. Such dastardly conduct raised a tempest in the usually tranquil mind of general Washington. Having embarked in the American cause from the purest principles, he viewed with infinite concern this shameful behaviour, as threatening ruin to his country. He recollected the many declarations of Congress, of the army, and of the inhabitants, preferring liberty to life, and death to dishonour, and contrasted them with their present scandalous flight.

SEP. 15

His soul was harrowed up with apprehensions that his country would be conquered—her army disgraced, and her liberties destroyed. He anticipated, in imagination, that the Americans would appear to posterity in the light of high sounding boasters, who blustered when danger was at a distance, but shrunk at the shadow of opposition. Extensive confiscations and numerous attainders presented, themselves in full view to his agitated mind. He saw, in imagination, new formed states, with [307] the means of defence in their hands, and the glorious prospects of liberty before them, levelled to the dust, and such constitutions imposed on them as were likely to crush the vigour of the human mind, while the unsuccessful issue of the present struggle would for ages to come, deter posterity from the bold design of asserting their rights. Impressed with these ideas he hazarded his person for some considerable time in rear of his own men, and in front of the enemy with his horse's head towards the latter, as if in expectation, that by an honourable death he might escape the infamy he dreaded from the dastardly conduct of troops on whom he could place no dependance. His aids and the confidential friends around his person, by indirect violence, compelled him to retire. In consequence of their address and importunity, a life was saved for public service, which otherwise from a sense of honour, and a gust of passion, seemed to be devoted to almost certain destruction.

On the day after this shameful flight of part of the American army, a skirmish took place between two battalions of light infantry and highlanders commanded by brigadier Leslie, and some detachments from the American army, under the command of lieutenant colonel Knowlton of Connecticut, and major Leitch of Virginia. The colonel was killed and the major badly wounded. Their men behaved with great bravery, and fairly beat their adversaries from the field. Most of these were the same men, who had disgraced themselves the day before, by running away[;] struck with a sense of shame for their late misbehaviour, they had offered themselves as volunteers, and requested the commander in chief to give them an opportunity to retrieve their honour. Their good conduct, at this second engagement, proved an antidote to the poison of their example on the preceding day. It demonstrated that the Americans only wanted resolution and good officers to be on a footing with the British, and inspired them with hopes that a little more experience would enable them to assume, not only the name and garb, but the spirit and firmness of soldiers.

The Americans having evacuated the city of New-York, [308] a brigade of the British army marched into it. They had been but a few days in possession, when a dreadful fire, most probably occasioned by the disorderly conduct of some British sailors, who had been permitted to regale themselves on shore, broke out, and consumed about a thousand houses. Dry weather, and a brisk wind, spread the flames to such an extent, that had it not been for great exertions of the troops and sailors, the whole city must have shared the same fate. After the Americans had evacuated New-York, they retired to the north end of the island, on which that city is erected. In about four weeks general Howe began to execute a plan for cutting off general Washington's communication with the eastern states, and enclosing him so as to compel a general engagement on the island. With this view, the greater part of the royal army passed through Hellgate, entered the sound, and landed on Frog's neck, in West-Chester county. Two days after they made this movement, general Lee arrived from his late successful command to the southward. He found that there was a prevailing disposition among the officers in the American army for remaining on New-York island. A council of war was called, in which general Lee gave such convincing reasons for quitting it, that they resolved immediately to withdraw the bulk of the army. He also pressed the expediency of evacuating Fort Washington, but in this he was opposed by general Greene, who argued that the possession of that post would divert a large body of the enemy, from joining their main force, and in conjunction with Fort Lee, would be of great use in covering the transportation of provisions and stores up the North-River, for the service of the American troops. He added farther, that the garrison could be brought off at any time, by boats from the Jersey side of the river. His opinion prevailed. Though the system of evacuating and retreating was in general adopted, an exception was made in favour of Fort Washington, and near 3000 men were assigned for its defence.

The royal army, after a halt of six days, at Frog's neck, advanced near to New-Rochelle. On their march they [309] sustained a

1776

OCT. 12
OCT. 14

OCT. 16

OCT. 18

considerable loss by a party of Americans, whom general Lee posted behind a wall. After three days, general Howe moved the right and centre of his army two miles to the northward of New Rochelle, on the road to the White Plains, and there he received a large reinforcement.

General Washington, while retreating from New-York island, was careful to make a front towards the British, from East-Chester, almost to White Plains, in order to secure the march of those who were behind, and to defend the removal of the sick, the cannon and stores of his army. In this manner his troops made a line of small detached and intrenched camps, on the several heights and strong grounds, from Valentine's hill, on the right, to the vicinity of the White Plains, on the left.

The royal army moved in two columns, and took a position with the Brunx in front, upon which the Americans assembled their main force at White Plains, behind intrenchments. A general action was hourly expected, and a considerable one took place, in which several

hundreds fell. The Americans were commanded by general M'Dougal, and the British by general Leslie. While they were engaged, the American baggage was moved off, in full view of the British army. Soon after this, general Washington changed his front, his left wing stood fast, and his right fell back to some hills. In this position, which was an admirable one in a military point of view, he both desired and expected an action; but general Howe declined it, and drew off his forces towards Dobbs' ferry. The Americans afterwards retired to North-Castle.

General Washington, with part of his army, crossed the North-River, and took post in the neighbourhood of Fort-Lee. A force of about 7500 men was left at North-Castle, under general Lee.

The Americans having retired, Sir William Howe determined to improve the opportunity of their absence, for the reduction of Fort Washington. This, the only post the Americans then held on New-York island, was under the command of colonel Magaw. The royal army made four attacks upon it. The first on the north [310] side, was led on by general Kniphausen. The second on the east by general Mathews, supported by lord Cornwallis. The third was under the

direction of lieutenant colonel Stirling, and the fourth was commanded by lord Piercy. The troops under Kniphausen, when advancing to the fort, had to pass through a thick wood, which was occupied by colonel Rawling's regiment of riflemen, and suffered very much from their well directed fire. During this attack, a body of the British light infantry advanced against a party of the Americans, who were annoying them from behind rocks and trees, and obliged them to disperse. Lord Piercy, carried an advance work on his side, and lieutenant colonel Stirling, forced his way up a steep height, and took 170 prisoners. Their outworks being carried, the Americans left their lines, and crouded into the fort. Colonel Rahl, who led the right column of Kniphausen's attack, pushed forward, and lodged his column within a hundred yards of the fort, and was there soon joined by the left column—the garrison surrendered on terms of capitulation, by which the men were to be considered as prisoners of war, and the officers to keep their baggage and side arms. The number of prisoners amounted to 2700. The loss of the British, inclusive of killed and wounded, was about 1200. Shortly after Fort Washington had surrendered. Lord Cornwallis, with a considerable force passed over to attack Fort Lee, on the opposite Jersey shore.   NOV. 18

The garrison was saved by an immediate evacuation, but at the expense of their artillery and stores. General Washington, about this time retreated to New-Ark. Having abundant reason from the posture of affairs, to count on the necessity of a farther retreat he asked colonel Reed—"Should we retreat to the back parts of Pennsylvania, will the Pennsylvanians support us?" The colonel replied, if the lower counties are subdued and give up, the back counties will do the same. The general replied, ["]we must retire to Augusta county, in Virginia. Numbers will be obliged to repair to us for safety, and we must try what we can do in carrying on a predatory war, and if overpowered, we must cross the Allegany mountains."

[311] While a tide of success, was flowing in upon general Howe,   1776
he and his brother, as royal commissioners, issued a proclamation, in which they commanded, "All persons assembled in arms against his majesty's government to disband, and all general or provincial congresses to desist from their treasonable actings, and to relinquish their usurped power." They also declared "that every person who within sixty days should appear before the governor, lieutenant

governor, or commander in chief of any of his majesty's colonies, or before the general, or commanding officer of his majesty's forces, and claim the benefit of the proclamation; and testify his obedience to the laws, by subscribing a certain declaration, should obtain a full and free pardon of all treasons by him committed, and of all forfeitures, and penalties for the same." Many who had been in office, and taken an active part in support of the new government, accepted of these offers, and made their peace by submission. Some who had been the greatest blusterers in favour of independence, veered round to the strongest side. Men of fortune generally gave way. The few who stood firm, were mostly to be found in the middle ranks of the people.

The term of time for which the American soldiers had engaged to serve, ended in November or December, with no other exception, than that of two companies of artillery, belonging to the state of New-York, which were engaged for the war. The army had been organized at the close of the preceding year, on the fallacious idea, that an accommodation would take place, within a twelve month. Even the flying camp, though instituted after the prospect of that event had vanished, was enlisted only till the first of December, from a presumption that the campaign would terminate by that time.

When it was expected that the conquerors would retire to winter quarters, they commenced a new plan of operations more alarming, than all their previous conquests. The reduction of Fort Washington, the evacuation of Fort Lee, and the diminution of the American army, by the departure of those whose time of service had expired, encouraged the British, notwithstanding the [312] severity of the winter, and the badness of the roads, to pursue the remaining inconsiderable continental force, with the prospect of annihilating it. By this turn of affairs, the interior country was surprised into confusion, and found an enemy within its bowels, without a sufficient army to oppose it. To retreat, was the only expedient left. This having commenced, lord Cornwallis followed, and was close in the rear of general Washington, as he retreated successively to New-Ark, to Brunswick, to Princeton, to Trenton, and to the Pennsylvania side of the Delaware. The pursuit was urged with so much rapidity, that the rear of the one army, pulling down bridges was often within sight, and shot off the van of the other, building them up.

1776

This retreat into, and through New-Jersey, was attended with almost every circumstance that could occasion embarrassment, and depression of spirits. It commenced in a few days, after the Americans had lost 2700 men in Fort Washington. In fourteen days after that event, the whole flying camp claimed their discharge. This was followed by the almost daily departure of others, whose engagements terminated nearly about the same time. A farther disappointment happened to general Washington at this time. Gates had been ordered by Congress to send two regiments from Ticonderoga, to reinforce his army. Two Jersey regiments were put under the command of general St. Clair, and forwarded in obedience to this order, but the period for which they were enlisted was expired, and the moment they entered their own state, they went off to a man. A few officers without a single private, were all that general St. Clair brought off these two regiments, to the aid of the retreating American army. The few who remained with general Washington were in a most forlorn condition. They consisted mostly of the troops which had garrisoned Fort Lee, and had been compelled to abandon that post so suddenly, that they commenced their retreat without tents or blankets, and without any utensils to dress their provisions. In this situation they performed a march of about ninety miles, and had the address to prolong it to [313] the space of nineteen days. As the retreating Americans marched through the country, scarcely one of the inhabitants joined them, while numbers were daily flocking to the royal army, to make their peace and obtain protection. They saw on the one side a numerous well appointed and full clad army, dazzling their eyes with the elegance of uniformity; on the other a few poor fellows, who from their shabby cloathing were called ragamuffins, fleeing for their safety. Not only the common people changed sides in this gloomy state of public affairs, but some of the leading men in New-Jersey and Pennsylvania adopted the same expedient. Among these Mr. Galloway, and the family of the Allens of Philadelphia, were most distinguished. The former, and one of the latter, had been members of Congress. In this hour of adversity they came within the British lines, and surrendered themselves to the conquerors, alledging in justification of their conduct, that though they had joined with their countrymen, in seeking for a redress of

1776

grievances in a constitutional way, they had never approved of the measures lately adopted, and were in particular, at all times, averse to independence.

On the day general Washington retreated over the Delaware, the British took possession of Rhode-Island without any loss, and at the same time blocked up commodore Hopkins' squadron, and a number of privateers at Providence.

In this period, when the American army was relinquishing its general—the people giving up the cause, some of their leaders going over to the enemy, and the British commanders succeeding in every enterprise, general Lee was taken prisoner at Baskenridge, by lieutenant colonel Harcourt. This caused a depression of spirits among the Americans, far exceeding any real injury done to their essential interests. He had been repeatedly ordered to come forward with his division and join general Washington, but these orders were not obeyed. This circumstance, and the dangerous crisis of public affairs, together with his being alone at some distance, from the troops

1776   which he commanded, begat suspicions that he chose to [314] fall into the hands of the British. Though these apprehensions were without foundation, they produced the same extensive mischief, as if they had been realities. The Americans had reposed extravagant confidence in his military talents, and experience of regular European war. Merely to have lost such an idol of the states at any time, would have been distressful, but losing him under circumstances, which favoured an opinion that, despairing of the American cause, he chose to be taken a prisoner, was to many an extinguishment of every hope.

By the advance of the British into New-Jersey, the neighbourhood of Philadelphia became the seat of war. This prevented that undisturbed attention to public business which the deliberations of Congress required. They therefore adjourned themselves to meet in eight

DEC. 12   days at Baltimore, resolving at the same time, "that general Wash-
20   ington should be possessed of full powers to order and direct all things relative to the department, and the operations of war."

The activity of the British in the close of the campaign, seemed in some measure to compensate for their tardiness, in the beginning of it.

Hitherto they had succeeded in every scheme. They marched up and down the Jersey side of the river Delaware, and through the country, without any molestation. All opposition to the re-establishment of royal government, seemed to be on the point of expiring. The Americans had thus far acted without system, or rather feebly executed what had been tardily adopted. Though the war was changed from its first ground, a redress of grievances to a struggle for sovereignty, yet some considerable time elapsed, before arrangements, conformable to this new system were adopted, and a much longer before they were carried into execution.

With the year 1776, a retreating, half naked army, was to be dismissed, and the prospect of a new one was both distant and uncertain. The recently assumed independence of the States, was apparently on the verge of dissolution. It was supposed by many, that the record of their existence would have been no more than that

> a fickle people, impatient of the restraints of regular government, [315] had in a fit of passion abolished that of Great-Britain, and established in its room free constitutions of their own, but these new establishments, from want of wisdom in their rulers, or of spirit in their people, were no sooner formed than annihilated. The leading men, in their respective governments, and the principal members of Congress, (for by this name the insurgents distinguished their supreme council) were hanged, and their estates confiscated. Washington, the gallant leader of their military establishments—worthy of a better fate—deserted by his army—abandoned by his country—rushing on the thickest battalions of the foe, provoked a friendly British bayonet to deliver him from an ignominious death.

1776

To human wisdom it appeared probable, that such a paragraph would have closed some small section in the history of England, treating of the American troubles, but there is in human affairs an ultimate point of elevation or depression, beyond which they neither grow better nor worse, but turn back in a contrary course.

In proportion as difficulties increased, Congress redoubled their exertions to oppose them. They addressed the states in animated language, calculated to remove their despondency—renew their hopes—and confirm their resolutions.

DEC. 10

They at the same time dispatched gentlemen of character and influence, to excite the militia to take the field. General Mifflin was, on this occasion, particularly useful. He exerted his great abilities in rousing his fellow citizens, by animated and affectionate addresses, to turn out in defence of their endangered liberties.

11 Congress also recommended to each of the United States "to appoint a day of solemn fasting and humiliation, to implore of Almighty God the forgiveness of their many sins, and to beg the countenance and assistance of his providence, in the prosecution of the present just and necessary war."

In the dangerous situation to which every thing dear to the friends of independence was reduced, Congress transferred extraordinary powers to general Washington, by a resolution, expressed in the following words:

1776

DEC. 27

[316] The unjust, but determined purposes of the British court to enslave these free states, obvious through every delusive insinuation to the contrary, having placed things in such a situation that the very existence of civil liberty now depends on the right execution of military powers, and the vigorous decisive conduct of these being impossible to distant, numerous, and deliberative bodies. This Congress, having maturely considered the present crisis; and having perfect reliance on the wisdom, vigour, and uprightness of general Washington, do hereby,

Resolve, That general Washington shall be, and he is hereby vested with full, ample, and complete powers, to raise and collect together, in the most speedy and effectual manner, from any or all of these United States, sixteen battalions of infantry, in addition to those already voted by Congress; to appoint officers for the said battalions of infantry; to raise, officer, and equip 3000 light-horse; three regiments of artillery, and a corps of engineers, and to establish their pay; to apply to any of the states for such aid of the militia as he shall judge necessary; to form such magazines of provisions, and in such places as he shall think proper; to displace and appoint all officers under the rank of brigadier general, and to fill up all vacancies in every other department in the American armies; to take, wherever he may be, whatever he may want, for the use of the army, if the inhabitants will not sell it, allowing a reasonable price for the same; to arrest and confine persons who refuse to take the continental currency, or are otherwise disaffected to the American cause; and return to the states, of which they are citizens, their names, and the nature of their offences, together with the witnesses to prove them: That the foregoing powers be vested in general Washington for and during the term of six months, from the date hereof, unless sooner determined by Congress.

In this hour of extremity, the attention of the Congress was employed, in devising plans to save the states from sinking under the heavy calamities which were bearing them down. It is remarkable, that, neither in the present condition, though trying and severe, nor in any other [317] since the declaration of independence, was Congress influenced either by force, distress, artifice, or persuasion, to entertain the most distant idea of purchasing peace, by returning to the condition of British subjects. So low were they reduced in the latter end of 1776, that some members, distrustful of their ability to resist the power of Great-Britain, proposed to authorise their commissioners at the court of France (whose appointment shall be hereafter explained) to transfer to that country the same monopoly of their trade, which Great-Britain had hitherto enjoyed. On examination it was found, that concessions of this kind would destroy the force of many arguments heretofore used in favour of independence, and probably disunite their citizens. It was next proposed to offer a monopoly of certain enumerated articles of produce. To this the variant interests of the different states were so directly opposed, as to occasion a speedy and decided negative. Some proposed offering to France, a league offensive and defensive, in case she would heartily support American independence; but this was also rejected. The more enlightened members of Congress argued, "Though the friendship of small states might be purchased, that of France could not." They alledged, that if she would risque a war with Great-Britain, by openly espousing their cause, it would not be so much from the prospect of direct advantages, as from a natural desire to lessen the overgrown power of a dangerous rival. It was therefore supposed, that the only inducement, likely to influence France to an interference, was an assurance that the United States were determined to persevere in refusing a return to their former allegiance. Instead of listening to the terms of the royal commissioners, or to any founded on the idea of their resuming their character of British subjects, it was therefore again resolved, to abide by their declared independence, and proffered freedom of trade to every foreign nation, trusting the event to Providence, and risquing all consequences. Copies of these resolutions were sent to the principal courts of Europe, and proper persons were appointed to solicit their friendship to the new formed states. These despatches fell into the hands of the British, [318] and were by them published. This was the very thing wished for by Congress. They well knew, that an apprehension of their making up all differences with Great-Britain was the principal objection to the interference of foreign courts, in what was represented to be no more than a domestic quarrel. A resolution adopted in the deepest distress, and the worst of times that Congress would listen to no terms of re-union with their Parent State, convinced those, who wished for the dismemberment of the British empire, that it was sound policy to interfere, so far as would prevent the conquest of the United States.

These judicious determinations in the cabinet, were accompanied with vigorous exertions in the field. In this crisis of danger 1500 of the Pennsylvania militia, embodied to re-inforce the continental army. The merchant, the farmer, the tradesman and the labourer, cheerfully relinquished the conveniences of home, to perform the duties of private soldiers, in the severity of a winter campaign. Though most of them were accustomed to the habits of a city life, they slept in tents, barns, and sometimes in the open air, during the cold months of December and January. There were, nevertheless, only two instances of sickness, and only one of death in that large body of men in the course if six weeks. The delay so judiciously contrived on the retreat through Jersey, afforded time for these volunteer reinforcements to join general Washington. The number of troops under his command at that time, fluctuated between two and three thousand men. To turn round and face a victorious and numerous foe, with this inconsiderable force was risquing much; but the urgency of the case required that something should be attempted. The recruiting business for the proposed new continental army was at a stand, while the British were driving the Americans before them. The present regular soldiers could, as a matter of right, in less than a week claim their discharge, and scarce a single recruit offered to supply their place. Under these circumstances, the bold resolution was formed of recrossing into the state of Jersey, and attacking that part of the enemy, which was posted at Trenton.

[319] When the Americans retreated over the Delaware, the boats in the vicinity were removed out of the way of their pursuers—this arrested their progress: But the British commanders in the security of conquest cantoned their army in Burlington, Bordenton, Trenton, and other towns of New-Jersey, in daily expectation of being enabled to cross into Pennsylvania, by means of ice, which is generally formed about that time. 1776

Of all events, none seemed to them more improbable, than that their late retreating half naked enemies, should in this extreme cold season, face about and commence offensive operations. They indulged themselves in a degree of careless inattention to the possibility of a surprise, which in the vicinity of an enemy, however contemptible, can never be justified. It has been said that colonel Rahl, the commanding officer in Trenton, being under some apprehension for that frontier post, applied to general Grant for a reinforcement, and that the general returned for answer. "Tell the colonel, he is very safe, I will undertake to keep the peace in New-Jersey with a corporal's guard."

In the evening of Christmas day, general Washington, made arrangements for recrossing the Delaware in three divisions; at M. Konkey's ferry, at Trenton ferry, and at or near Bordenton. The troops which were to have crossed at the two last places, were commanded by generals Ewing, and Cadwallader, they made every exertion to get over, but the quantity of ice was so great, that they could not effect their purpose. The main body which was commanded by general Washington crossed at M. Konkey's ferry, but the ice in the river retarded their passage so long, that it was three o'clock in the morning, before the artillery could be got over. On their landing in Jersey, they were formed into two divisions, commanded by general Sullivan, and Greene, who had under their command brigadiers, lord Stirling, Mercer and St. Clair: one of these divisions was ordered to proceed on the lower, or river road, the other on the upper or Pennington road. Col. Stark, with some light troops, was also directed to advance near to the river, and to possess himself [320] of that part of the town, which is beyond the bridge. The divisions having nearly the same distance to march, were ordered immediately on forcing the out guards, to push directly into Trenton, that they might charge the enemy before they had time to form. Though they marched different roads, yet they arrived at the enemy's advanced post, within three minutes of each other. The out guards of the Hessian troops at Trenton soon fell back, but kept up a constant retreating fire. Their main body being hard pressed by the Americans, who had already got possession of half their artillery, attempted to file off by a road leading towards Princeton, but were checked by a body of troops thrown in their way. Finding they were surrounded, they laid down their arms. The number which submitted, was 23 officers, and 885 men. Between 30 and 40 of the Hessians were killed and wounded. Colonel Rahl, was among the former, and seven of his officers among the latter. Captain Washington of the Virginia troops, and five or six of the Americans were wounded. Two were killed, and two or three were frozen to death. The detachment in Trenton consisted of the regiments of Rahl, Losberg, and Kniphausen, amounting in the whole to about 1500 men, and a troop of British light horse. All these were killed or captured, except about 600, who escaped by the road leading to Bordenton.

The British had a strong battalion of light infantry at Princeton, and a force yet remaining near the Delaware, superior to the American army. General Washington, therefore in the evening of the same day, thought it most prudent to recross into Pennsylvania, with his prisoners.

The effects of this successful enterprize were speedily felt in recruiting the American army. About 1400 regular soldiers whose time of service was on the point of expiring, agreed to serve six weeks longer, on a promised gratuity of ten paper dollars to each. Men of influence were sent to different parts of the country to rouse the militia. The rapine, and impolitic conduct of the British, operated more forcibly on the inhabitants, to expel them [323 (the original paging errs, skipping over 321–22)] from the state, than either patriotism or persuasion to prevent their overrunning it.

1776

DEC. 28

The Hessian prisoners taken on the 26th being secured, general Washington re-crossed the Delaware, and took possession of Trenton. The detachments which had been distributed over New-Jersey, previous to the capture of the Hessians, immediately, after that event, assembled at Princeton, and were joined by the army from Brunswick under lord Cornwallis. From this position they came forward towards Trenton in great force, hoping by a vigorous onset to repair the injury their cause had sustained by the late defeat. Truly delicate was the situation of the feeble American army. To retreat was to hazard the city of Philadelphia, and to destroy every ray of hope which had begun to dawn from their late success. To risque an action with a superior force in front, and a river in rear, was dangerous in the extreme. To get round the advanced party of the British, and by pushing forwards to attack in their rear, was deemed preferable to either. The British on their advance from Princeton, about 4 P.M. attacked a body of Americans which were posted with four field pieces, a little to the northward of Trenton, and compelled them to retreat. The pursuing British, being checked at the bridge over Sanpink creek, which runs through that town, by some field pieces, which were posted on the opposite banks of that rivulet, fell back so far as to be out of reach of the cannon, and kindled their fires. The Americans were drawn up on the other side of the creek, and in that position remained till night, cannonading the enemy and receiving their fire. In this critical hour, two armies on which the success or failure of the American revolution, materially depended, were crouded into the small village of Trenton, and only separated by a creek in many places fordable. The British believing they had all the advantages they could wish for, and that they could use them when they pleased, discontinued all further operations, and kept themselves in readiness to make the attack next morning. Sir William Erskine is reported to have advised an immediate attack, or at least to place a strong [324] guard at a bridge over Sanpink creek, which lay in the route the Americans took to Princeton, giving for reason that, otherwise, Washington if a good general, would make a move to the left of the royal army, and attack the post at Princeton in their rear. The next morning presented a scene as brilliant on the one side, as it was unexpected on the other. Soon after it became dark, gen. Washington ordered all his baggage to be silently removed, and having left guards for the purpose of deception, marched with his whole force, by a circuitous route to Princeton. This manoeuvre

1777

JAN. 2d

JAN. 2d

was determined upon in a council of war, from a conviction that it would avoid the appearance of a retreat, and at the same time the hazard of an action in a bad position, and that it was the most likely way to preserve the city of Philadelphia, from falling into the hands of the British. General Washington also presumed, that from an eagerness to efface the impressions, made by the late capture of Hessians at Trenton, the British commanders had pushed forward their principal force, and that of course the remainder in the rear at Princeton was not more than equal to his own. The event verified this conjecture. The more effectually to disguise the departure of the Americans from Trenton, fires were lighted up in front of their camp. These not only gave an appearance of going to rest, but as flame cannot be seen through, concealed from the British, what was transacting behind them. In this relative position they were a pillar of fire to the one army, and a pillar of a cloud to the other. Providence favoured this movement of the Americans. The weather had been for some time so warm and moist, that the ground was soft and the roads so deep as to be scarcely passable: but the wind suddenly changed to the northwest, and the ground in a short time was frozen so hard, that when the Americans took up their line of march, they were no more retarded, than if they had been upon a solid pavement.

JAN. 3

1776

General Washington reached Princeton, early in the morning, and would have completely surprised the British, had not a party, which was on their way to Trenton, [325] descried his troops, when they were about two miles distant, and sent back couriers to alarm their unsuspecting fellow soldiers in their rear. These consisted of the 17th, the 40th, & 55th regiments of British infantry and some of the royal artillery with two field pieces, and three troops of light dragoons. The center of the Americans, consisting of the Philadelphia militia, while on their line of march, was briskly charged by a party of the British, and gave way in disorder. The moment was critical. General Washington pushed forward, and placed himself between his own men, and the British, with his horse's head fronting the latter. The Americans encouraged by his example, and exhortations, made a stand, and returned the British fire. The general, though between both parties, was providentially uninjured by either. A party of the British fled into the college and were there attacked with field pieces which were fired into it. The seat of the muses became for some time the scene of action. The party which had taken refuge in the college, after receiving a few discharges from the American field pieces came out and surrendered themselves prisoners of war. In the course of the engagement, sixty of the British were killed, and a greater number wounded, and about 300 of them were taken prisoners. The rest made their escape, some by pushing on towards Trenton, others by returning towards Brunswick. The Americans lost only a few, but colonels Haslet and Potter, and capt. Neal of the artillery, were among the slain. General Mercer received three bayonet wounds of which he died in a short time. He was a Scotchman by birth, but from principle and affection had engaged to support the liberties of his adopted country, with a zeal equal to that of any of its native sons. In private life he was amiable, and his character as an officer stood high in the public esteem.

While they were fighting in Princeton, the British in Trenton were under arms, and on the point of making an assault on the evacuated camp of the Americans. With so much address had the movement to Princeton been conducted, that though from the critical situation of the two armies, every ear may be supposed to have been [326] open, and every watchfulness to have been employed, yet General Washington moved completely off the ground, with his whole force, stores, baggage and artillery unknown to, and unsuspected by his adversaries. The British in Trenton, were so entirely deceived, that when they heard the report of the artillery at Princeton, though it was in the depth of winter, they supposed it to be thunder.

That part of the royal army, which having escaped from Princeton, retreated towards New-Brunswick, was pursued for three or four miles. Another party which had advanced as far as Maidenhead, on their way to Trenton, hearing the frequent discharge of fire arms in their rear, wheeled round and marched to the aid of their companions. The Americans by destroying bridges, retarded these, though close in their rear, so long as to gain time for themselves, to move off, in good order, to Pluckemin.

So great was the consternation of the British at these unexpected movements, that they instantly evacuated both Trenton and Princeton, and retreated with their whole force to New-Brunswick. The

1776

American militia, collected and forming themselves into parties, waylaid their enemies, and cut them off whensoever an opportunity presented. In a few days they over-ran the Jerseys. General Maxwell surprised Elisabeth-town, and took near 100 prisoners. Newark was abandoned, and the late conquerors were forced to leave Woodbridge. The royal troops were confined to Amboy and Brunswick, which held a water communication with New-York. Thus, in the short space of a month, that part of Jersey, which lies between New-Brunswick and Delaware, was both overrun by the British, and recovered by the Americans. The retreat of the continental army, the timid policy of the Jersey farmers, who chose rather to secure their property by submission, than defend it by resistance, made the British believe their work was done, and that little else remained, but to reap a harvest of plunder as the reward of their labours. Unrestrained by the terrors of civil law, uncontrolled by the severity of discipline, and elated with their success, the soldiers of the royal army, and particularly [327] the Hessians, gave full scope to the selfish and ferocious passions of human nature. A conquered country, and submitting inhabitants presented easy plunder, equal to their unbounded rapacity. Infants, children, old men and women were stripped of their blankets and cloathing. Furniture was burnt or otherwise destroyed. Domestic animals were carried off, and the people robbed of their necessary household provisions. The rapes and brutalities committed on women, and even on very young girls, would shock the ears of modesty, if particularly recited. These violences were perpetrated on inhabitants who had remained in their houses, and received printed protections, signed by order of the commander in chief. It was in vain, that they produced these protections as a safeguard. The Hessians could not read them, and the British soldiers thought they were entitled to a share of the booty, equally with their foreign associates.

1776

Such, in all ages, has been the complexion of the bulk of armies, that immediate and severe punishments are indispensably necessary, to keep them from flagrant enormities. That discipline, without which an army is a band of armed plunderers, was as far, as respected the inhabitants, either neglected, or but feebly administered in the royal army. The soldiers finding, they might take with impunity what they pleased, were more strongly urged by avarice, than checked by policy or fear. Had every citizen been secured in his rights, protected in his property, and paid for his supplies, the consequences might have been fatal to the hopes of those who were attached to independence. What the warm recommendations of Congress, and the ardent supplications of general Washington could not effect, took place of its own accord, in consequence of the plunderings and devastations of the royal army.

The whole country became instantly hostile to the invaders. Sufferers of all parties rose as one man, to revenge their personal injuries. Those, who from age, or infirmities, were incapable of bearing arms, kept a strict watch on the movements of the royal army, and from time to time, communicated information to their countrymen [328] in arms. Those who lately declined all military 1777 opposition, though called upon by the sacred tie of honour pledged to each other on the declaration of independence, chearfully embodied, when they found submission to be unavailing for the security of their estates. This was not done originally in consequence of the victories of Trenton and Princeton. In the very moment of these actions, or before the news of them had circulated, sundry individuals unknowing of general Washington's movements, were concerting private insurrections, to revenge themselves on the plunderers. The dispute originated about property, or in other words, about the right of taxation. From the same source at this time, it received a new and forcible impulse. The farmer, who could not trace the consequences of British taxation, nor of American independence, felt the injuries he sustained from the depredation of licentious troops. The militia of New-Jersey, who had hitherto behaved most shamefully, from this time forward redeemed their character, and throughout a tedious war, performed services with a spirit and discipline in many respects, equal to that of regular soldiers.

The victories of Trenton and Princeton, seemed to be like a resurrection from the dead, to the desponding friends of independence. A melancholy gloom, had in the first 25 days of December overspread the United States; but from the memorable era of the 26th of same month, their prospects began to brighten. The recruiting service, which for some time had been at a stand, was successfully renewed, and hopes were soon indulged, that the commander in chief would be enabled to take the field in the spring, with a permanent regular force. General Washington retired to Morristown, that he might afford shelter to his suffering army. The American militia had sundry successful skirmishes with detachments of their adversaries. Within four days after the affair at Princeton, between forty and fifty Waldeckers were killed, wounded, or taken at Springfield, by an equal number of the same New-Jersey militia, which but a month before, suffered the British to overrun their country [329] without opposition. This enterprise was conducted by colonel Spencer, whose gallantry, on the occasion, was rewarded with the command of a regiment.

During the winter movements, which have been just related, the soldiers of both armies underwent great hardships, but the Americans suffered by far the greater. Many of them were without shoes, though marching over frozen ground, which so gashed their naked feet, that each step was marked with blood. There was scarcely a tent in their whole army. The city of Philadelphia had been twice laid under contribution, to provide them with blankets. Officers had been appointed, to examine every house, and, after leaving a scanty covering for the family to bring off the rest, for the use of the troops in the field; but notwithstanding these exertions, the quantity procured was far short of decency, much less of comfort.

The officers and soldiers of the American army were about this time inoculated in their cantonment at Morristown. As very few of them had ever had the small pox, the inoculation was nearly universal. The disorder had previously spread among them in the natural way, and proved mortal to many: but after inoculation was introduced though whole regiments were inoculated, in a day, there was little or no mortality from the small pox, and the disorder was so slight, that from the beginning to the end of it, there was not a single day in which they could not, and if called upon, would not have turned out and fought the British. To induce the inhabitants to accommodate officers and soldiers in their houses, while under the small pox, they and their families were inoculated gratis by the military surgeons. Thus in a short time, the whole army and the inhabitants in and near Morristown were subjected to the small pox, and with very little inconvenience to either.

CHAPTER XII

Three months, which followed the actions of Trenton and Princeton, passed away without any important military enterprise on either side. Major general Putnam was directed to take post at Princeton, and cover the country in the vicinity. He had only a few hundred troops, though he was no more than eighteen miles distant from [330] the strong garrison of the British at Brunswick. At one period 1777 he had fewer men for duty than he had miles of frontier to guard. The situation of general Washington at Morristown was not more eligible. His force was trifling, when compared with that of the British, but the enemy, and his own countrymen, believed the contrary. Their deception was cherished, and artfully continued by the specious parade of a considerable army. The American officers took their station in positions of difficult access, and kept up a constant communication with each other. This secured them from insult and surprise. While they covered the country, they harassed the foraging parties of the British, and often attacked them with success. Of a variety of these, the two following are selected as most worthy of notice. General Dickenson, with four hundred Jersey militia, and JAN. 20 fifty of the Pennsylvania riflemen, crossed Millstone-river, near Somerset courthouse, and attacked a large foraging party of the British, with so much spirit that they abandoned their convoy, and fled. Nine of them were taken prisoners. Forty waggons, and upwards of one hundred horses, with a considerable booty, fell into the hands of the general. While the British were loading their waggons, a single man began to fire on them from the woods. He was soon joined by more of his neighbours, who could not patiently see their property carried away. After the foragers had been annoyed for some time by these unseen marksmen, they fancied on the appearance of general Dickenson, that they were attacked by a superior force, and began a precipitate flight.

In about a month after the affair of Somerset courthouse, colonel FEB. 18 Nelson, of Brunswick, with a detachment of 150 militia men, surprised and captured at Lawrence's Neck, a major, and fifty-nine privates, of the refugees, who were in British pay.

Throughout the campaign of 1776, an uncommon degree of sickness raged in the American army. Husbandmen, transferred at once from the conveniencies of domestic life, to the hardships of a field encampment, could not accommodate themselves to the sudden change. The southern troops, sickened from the [331] want of salt provisions. Linen shirts were too generally worn, in contact with the skin. The salutary influence of flannel, in preventing the diseases of camps, was either unknown or disregarded. The discipline of the army was too feeble to enforce those regulations which experience has proved to be indispensably necessary, for preserving the health of large bodies of men collected together. Cleanliness was also too much neglected. On the 8th of August the whole American army before New-York, consisted of 17,225 men, but of that number only 10,514 were fit for duty. These numerous sick suffered much, from the want of necessaries. Hurry and confusion added much to their distresses. There was besides a real want of the requisites for their relief.

A proper hospital establishment was beyond the abilities of Congress, especially as the previous arrangements were not entered upon till the campaign had begun. Many, perhaps some thousands in the American army, were swept off in a few months by sickness. The country every where presented the melancholy sight of soldiers suffering poverty and disease, without the aid of medicine or attendance. Those who survived gave such accounts of the sufferings of the sick, as greatly discouraged the recruiting service. A rage for plundering, under the pretence of taking tory property, infected many of the common soldiery, and even some of the officers. The army had been formed on such principles, in some of the states, that commissions were, in several instances, bestowed on persons who had no pretensions to the character of gentlemen. Several of the officers were chosen by their own men, and they often preferred those from whom they expected the greatest indulgencies. In other cases, the choice of the men was in favour of those who had consented to throw their pay into a joint stock with the privates, from which officers and men drew equal shares.

The army, consisting mostly of new recruits and unexperienced officers, and being only engaged for a twelve month, was very deficient in that mechanism and discipline which time and experience bestow on veteran troops. General Washington was unremitting in his [332] representations to Congress, favouring such alterations as promised permanency, order and discipline, in the army, but his judicious opinions on these subjects were slowly adopted. The sentiments of liberty, which then generally prevailed, made some distinguished members of Congress so distrustful of the future power and probable designs of a permanent domestic army, that they had well nigh sacrificed their country to their jealousies.

The unbounded freedom of the savage who roams the woods must be restrained when he becomes a citizen of orderly government, and from the necessity of the case must be much more so, when he submits to be a soldier. The individuals composing the army of America, could not at once pass over from the full enjoyment of civil liberty to the discipline of a camp, nor could the leading men in Congress for some time be persuaded, to adopt energetic establishments. "God forbid, would such say, that the citizen should be so far lost in the soldiers of our army, that they should give over longing for the enjoyments of domestic happiness. Let frequent furloughs be granted, rather than the endearments of wives and children should cease to allure the individuals of our army from camps to farms." The amiableness of this principle, veiled the error of the sentiment. The minds of the civil leaders in the councils of America were daily occupied in contemplating the rights of human nature, and investigating arguments on the principles of general liberty, to justify their own opposition to Great-Britain. Warmed with these ideas, they trusted too much to the virtue of their countrymen, and were backward to enforce that subordination and order in their army, which, though it intrenches on civil liberty, produces effects in the military line unequalled by the effusions of patriotism, or the exertions of undisciplined valor.

The experience of two campaigns evinced the folly of trusting the defence of the country to militia, or to levies raised only for a few months, and had induced a resolution for recruiting an army for the war. The good effects of this measure will appear in the sequel.

The campaign of 1776 did not end, till it had been [333] protracted into the first month of the year 1777. The British had counted on 1777 the complete and speedy reduction of their late colonies, but they found the work more difficult of execution, than was supposed. They wholly failed in their designs on the southern states. In Canada they recovered what, in the preceding year, they had lost—drove the

Americans out of their borders, and destroyed their fleet on the lakes, but they failed in making their intended impression on the northwestern frontier of the states. They obtained possession of Rhode-Island, but the acquisition was of little service—perhaps was of detriment. For near three years several thousand men stationed thereon for its security, were lost to every purpose of active co-operation with the royal forces in the field, and the possession of it secured no equivalent advantages. The British completely succeeded against the city of New-York, and the adjacent country, but when they pursued their victories into New-Jersey, and subdivided their army, the recoiling Americans soon recovered the greatest part of what they had lost.

Sir William Howe, after having nearly reached Philadelphia, was confined to limits so narrow, that the fee simple of all he commanded would not reimburse the expence incurred by its conquest.

The war, on the part of the Americans, was but barely begun. Hitherto they had engaged with temporary forces, for a redress of grievances, but towards the close of this year they made arrangements for raising a permanent army to contend with Great-Britain, for the sovereignty of the country. To have thus far stood their ground, with their new levies, was a matter of great importance, because of them, delay was victory, and not to be conquered was to conquer.

Of Independence, State Constitutions, and the Confederation.

[334] IN FORMER AGES it was common for a part of a community   1777
to migrate, and erect themselves into an independent society. Since
the earth has been more fully peopled, and especially since the
principles of Union have been better understood, a different policy
has prevailed. A fondness for planting colonies has, for three preceding
centuries, given full scope to a disposition for emigration, and at the
same time the emigrants have been retained in a connexion with
their Parent State. By these means Europeans have made the riches
both of the east and west, subservient to their avarice and ambition.
Though they occupy the smallest portion of the four quarters of the
globe, they have contrived to subject the other three to their influence
or command.

The circumstances under which New-England was planted, would a few centuries ago have entitled them from their first settlement, to the privileges of independence. They were virtually exiled from their native country, by being denied the rights of men—they set out on their own expence, and after purchasing the consent of the native proprietors, improved an uncultivated country, to which, in the eye of reason and philosophy, the king of England had no title.

If it is lawful for individuals to relinquish their native soil, and pursue their own happiness in other regions and under other political associations, the settlers of New-England were always so far independent, as to owe no obedience to their Parent State, but such as resulted from their voluntary assent. The slavish doctrine of the divine right of kings, and the corruptions of christianity, by undervaluing heathen titles, favoured an opposite system. What for several centuries after the christian era would have been called the institution of a new government, was by modern refinement denominated only an extension of the old, in the form of a dependent colony. Though the prevailing ecclesiastical and political creeds [335] tended to degrade the condition of the settlers in New-England, yet there was always a party there which believed in their natural right to independence. They recurred to first principles, and argued, that as they received from government nothing more than a charter, founded on ideal claims of sovereignty, they owed it no other obedience than what was derived from express, or implied compact. It was not till the present century had more than half elapsed, that it occurred to any number of the colonists, that they had an interest in being detached from Great-Britain. Their attention was first turned to this subject, by the British claim of taxation. This opened a melancholy prospect, boundless in extent, and endless in duration. The Boston port act, and the other acts, passed in 1774, and 1775, which have been already the subject of comment, progressively weakened the attachment of the colonists to the birth place of their forefathers. The commencement of hostilities on the 19th of April, 1775, exhibited the Parent State in an odious point of view, and abated the original dread of separating from it. But nevertheless at that time, and for a twelve month after, a majority of the colonists wished for no more than to be re-established as subjects in their antient rights. Had independence been their object even at the commencement of hostilities, they would have rescinded these associations, which have been already mentioned and imported more largely than ever. Common sense revolts at the idea, that colonists unfurnished with military stores, and wanting manufactures of every kind, should at the time of their intending a serious struggle for independence, by a voluntary agreement, deprive themselves of the obvious means of procuring such foreign supplies as their circumstances might make necessary. Instead of pursuing a line of conduct, which might have been dictated by a wish for independence, they continued their exports for nearly a year after they ceased to import. This not only lessened the debts they owed to Great-Britain, but furnished additional means for carrying on the war against themselves. To aim at independence, and at the same time to transfer their resources to their enemies, could not have been [336] the policy of an enlightened people. It was not till some time in 1776, that the colonists began to take other ground, and contend that it was for their interest to be forever separated from Great-Britain. In favour of this opinion it was said, that in case of their continuing subjects, the Mother country, though she redressed their present grievances, might at pleasure repeat similar oppressions. That she ought not to be trusted, having twice resumed the exercise of taxation, after it had been apparently relinquished. The favourers of separation also urged, that Great-Britain was jealous of their increasing numbers, and rising greatness— that she would not exercise government for their benefit, but for her own. That the only permanent security for American happiness, was to deny her the power of interfering with their government or commerce. To effect this purpose they were of opinion, that it was necessary to cut the knot, which connected the two countries, by a public renunciation of all political connections between them.

The Americans about this time began to be influenced by new views. The military arrangements of the preceding year—their unexpected union, and prevailing enthusiasm, expanded the minds of their leaders, and elevated the sentiments of the great body of their people. Decisive measures which would have been lately reprobated, now met with approbation.

The favourers of subordination under the former constitution urged the advantages of a supreme head, to control the disputes of interfering

1777

colonies, and also the benefits which flowed from union. That independence was untried ground, and should not be entered upon, but in the last extremity.

They flattered themselves that Great-Britain was so fully convinced of the determined spirit of America, that if the present controversy was compromised, she would not at any future period, resume an injurious exercise of her supremacy. They were therefore for proceeding no farther than to defend themselves in the character of subjects, trusting that ere long the present hostile measures would be relinquished, and the harmony [337] of the two countries reestablished. The favourers of this system were embarrassed, and all their arguments weakened, by the perseverance of Great-Britain in her schemes of coercion. A probable hope of a speedy repeal of a few acts of parliament, would have greatly increased the number of those who were advocates for reconciliation. But the certainty of intelligence to the contrary gave additional force to the arguments of the opposite party. Though new weight was daily thrown into the scale, in which the advantages of independence were weighed, yet it did not preponderate till about that time in 1776, when intelligence reached the colonists of the act of parliament passed in December 1775, for throwing them out of British protection, and of hiring foreign troops to assist in effecting their conquest. Respecting the first it was said, "that protection and allegiance were reciprocal, and that the refusal of the first was a legal ground of justification for withholding the last." They considered themselves to be thereby discharged from their allegiance, and that to declare themselves independent, was no more than to announce to the world the real political state, in which Great-Britain had placed them. This act proved that the colonists might constitutionally declare themselves independent, but the hiring of foreign troops to make war upon them, demonstrated the necessity of their doing it immediately. They reasoned that if Great-Britain called in the aid of strangers to crush them, they must seek similar relief for their own preservation. But they well knew this could not be expected, while they were in arms against their acknowledged sovereign. They had therefore only a choice of difficulties, and must either seek foreign aid as independent states, or continue in the aukward and hazardous situation of subjects, carrying on war from their own resources both against their king, and such mercenaries as he chose to employ for their subjugation. Necessity not choice forced them on the decision. Submission without obtaining a redress of their grievances was advocated by none who possessed the public confidence. Some of the popular leaders may have [338] secretly wished for independence from the beginning of the controversy, but their number was small and their sentiments were not generally known.

1777

While the public mind was balancing on this eventful subject, several writers placed the advantages of independence in various points of view. Among these Thomas Paine in a pamphlet, under the signature of Common Sense, held the most distinguished rank. The stile, manner, and language of this performance were calculated to interest the passions, and to rouse all the active powers of human nature. With the view of operating on the sentiments of a religious people, scripture was pressed into his service, and the powers, and even the name of a king was rendered odious in the eyes of the numerous colonists who had read and studied the history of the Jews, as recorded in the Old Testament. The folly of that people in revolting from a government, instituted by Heaven itself, and the oppressions to which they were subjected in consequence of their lusting after kings to rule over them, afforded an excellent handle for prepossessing the colonists in favour of republican institutions, and prejudicing them against kingly government. Hereditary succession was turned into ridicule. The absurdity of subjecting a great continent to a small island on the other side of the globe, was represented in such striking language, as to interest the honor and pride of the colonists in renouncing the government of Great-Britain. The necessity, the advantages, and practicability of independence, were forcibly demonstrated. Nothing could be better timed than this performance. It was addressed to freemen, who had just received convincing proof, that Great-Britain had thrown them out of her protection, had engaged foreign mercenaries to make war upon them, and seriously designed to compel their unconditional submission to her unlimited power. It found the colonists most thoroughly alarmed for their liberties, and disposed to do and suffer any thing that promised their establishment. In union with the feelings and sentiments of the people, it produced surprising effects. Many thousands were convinced, and were led to approve [339] and long for a separation from the Mother Country. Though that measure, a few months before, was not only foreign from their wishes, but the object of their abhorrence, the current suddenly became so strong in its favour, that it bore down all opposition. The multitude was hurried down the stream, but some worthy men could not easily reconcile themselves to the idea of an eternal separation from a country, to which they had been long bound by the most endearing ties. They saw the sword drawn, but could not tell when it would be sheathed. They feared that the dispersed individuals of the several colonies would not be brought to coalesce under an efficient government, and that after much anarchy some future Caesar would grasp their liberties, and confirm himself in a throne of despotism. They doubted the perseverance of their countrymen in effecting their independence, and were also apprehensive that in case of success, their future condition would be less happy than their past. Some respectable individuals whose principles were pure, but whose souls were not of that firm texture which revolutions require, shrunk back from the bold measures proposed by their more adventurous countrymen. To submit without an appeal to Heaven, though secretly wished for by some, was not the avowed sentiment of any. But to persevere in petitioning and resisting was the system of some misguided honest men. The favourers of this opinion were generally wanting in that decision which grasps at great objects, and influenced by that timid policy, which does its work by halves. Most of them dreaded the power of Britain. A few, on the score of interest or an expectancy of favours from royal government, refused to concur with the general voice. Some of the natives of the Parent State who, having lately settled in the colonies, had not yet exchanged European for American ideas, together with a few others, conscientiously opposed the measures of Congress: but the great bulk of the people, and especially of the spirited and independent part of the community, came with surprising unanimity into the project of independence.

[340] The eagerness for independence resulted more from feeling than reasoning. The advantages of an unfettered trade, the prospect of honours and emoluments in administering a new government,

were of themselves insufficient motives for adopting this bold measure. But what was wanting from considerations of this kind, was
made up by the perseverance of Great-Britain, in her schemes of
coercion and conquest. The determined resolution of the Mother
Country to subdue the colonists, together with the plans she adopted
for accomplishing that purpose, and their equally determined resolution to appeal to Heaven rather than submit, made a declaration
of independence as necessary in 1776, as was the non-importation
agreement of 1774, or the assumption of arms in 1775. The last
naturally resulted from the first. The revolution was not forced on
the people by ambitious leaders grasping at supreme power, but
every measure of it was forced on Congress, by the necessity of the
case, and the voice of the people. The change of the public mind of
America respecting connexion with Great-Britain, is without a parallel. In the short space of two years, nearly three millions of people
passed over from the love and duty of loyal subjects, to the hatred
and resentment of enemies.

The motion for declaring the colonies free and independent, was   JUNE 7
first made in Congress, by Richard Henry Lee of Virginia. He was
warranted in making this motion by the particular instructions of
his immediate constituents, and also by the general voice of the
people of all the states. When the time for taking the subject under
consideration arrived, much knowledge, ingenuity and eloquence
were displayed on both sides of the question. The debates were
continued for some time, and with great animation. In these John
Adams, and John Dickinson, took leading and opposite parts. The
former began one of his speeches, by an invocation of the god of
eloquence, to assist him in defending the claims, and in enforcing
the duty of his countrymen. He strongly urged the immediate
dissolution of all political connexion of the colonies with Great-
Britain, from the voice of the [341] people, from the necessity of the   1776
measure in order to obtain foreign assistance, from a regard to
consistency, and from the prospects of glory and happiness, which
opened beyond the war, to a free and independent people. Mr.
Dickinson replied to this speech. He began by observing that the
member from Massachusetts (Mr. Adams) had introduced his defence
of the declaration of independence by invoking an heathen god, but

that he should begin his objections to it, by solemnly invoking the Governor of the Universe, so to influence the minds of the members of Congress, that if the proposed measure was for the benefit of America, nothing which he should say against it, might make the least impression. He then urged that the present time was improper for the declaration of independence, that the war might be conducted with equal vigor without it, that it would divide the Americans, and unite the people of Great-Britain against them. He then proposed that some assurance should be obtained of assistance from a foreign power, before they renounced their connexion with Great-Britain, and that the declaration of independence should be the condition to be offered for this assistance. He likewise stated the disputes that existed between several of the colonies, and proposed that some measures for the settlement of them should be determined upon, before they lost sight of that tribunal, which had hitherto been the umpire of all their differences.

After a full discussion, the measure of declaring the colonies free and independent was approved, by nearly an unanimous vote. The anniversary of the day on which this great event took place, has ever since been consecrated by the Americans to religious gratitude, and social pleasures. It is considered by them as the birth day of their freedom.

The act of the united colonies for separating themselves from the government of Great-Britain, and declaring their independence, was expressed in the following words:

1776

When, in the course of human events, it becomes necessary for one people to dissolve the political bands [342] which have connected them with another, and to assume among the powers of the earth, the separate and equal station to which the laws of nature and of nature's God entitle them, a decent respect to the opinions of mankind requires that they should declare the causes which impel them to the separation.

We hold these truths to be self-evident, that all men are created equal, that they are endowed by their Creator with certain unalienable rights, that among these are life, liberty, and the pursuit of happiness—That to secure these rights, governments are instituted among men, deriving their just powers from the consent of the governed; that whenever any form of government becomes destructive of these ends, it is the right of the people to alter or to abolish it, and to institute new government, laying its foundation on such principles, and organizing its power in such form, as to them shall seem most likely to effect their safety and happiness. Prudence, indeed, will dictate that governments long established should not be changed for light and transient causes; and accordingly all experience hath shewn, that mankind are more disposed to suffer, while evils are sufferable, than to right themselves by abolishing the forms to which they are accustomed. But when a long train of abuses and usurpations, pursuing invariably the same object, evinces a design to reduce them under absolute despotism, it is their right, it is their duty, to throw off such government, and to provide new guards for their future security. Such has been the patient sufferance of these colonies, and such is now the necessity which constrains them to alter their former systems of government. The history of the present king of Great-Britain is a history of repeated injuries and usurpations, all having in direct object the establishment of an absolute tyranny over these states. To prove this, let facts be submitted to a candid world.

He has refused his assent to laws, the most wholesome and necessary for the public good.

He has forbidden his governors to pass laws of immediate and pressing importance, unless suspended in their [343] operation till his assent should be obtained; and when so suspended he has utterly neglected to attend to them. 1776

He has refused to pass other laws for the accommodation of large districts of people, unless those people would relinquish the right of representation in the legislature, a right inestimable to them, and formidable to tyrants only.

He has called together legislative bodies at places unusual, uncomfortable, and distant from the depository of their public records, for the sole purpose of fatiguing them into compliance with his measures.

He has dissolved representative houses repeatedly, for opposing, with manly firmness, his invasions on the rights of the people.

He has refused, for a long time after such dissolutions, to cause others to be elected; whereby the legislative powers, incapable of annihilation, have returned to the people at large for their exercise; the state remaining in the mean-time exposed to all the danger of invasion from without, and convulsions within.

He has endeavoured to prevent the population of these states; for that purpose obstructing the laws for naturalization of foreigners; refusing to pass others to encourage their migration hither, and raising the conditions of new appropriations of lands.

He has obstructed the administration of justice, by refusing his assent to laws for establishing judiciary powers.

He has made judges dependent on his will alone, for the tenure of their offices, and the amount and payment of their salaries.

He has erected a multitude of new offices, and sent hither swarms of officers to harass our people, and eat out their substance.

He has kept among us, in times of peace, standing armies, without the consent of our legislatures.

He has affected to render the military independent of, and superior to, the civil power.

He has combined with others to subject us to a jurisdiction foreign to our constitution, and unacknowledged by our laws; giving his assent to their acts of pretended legislation:

1776

[344] For quartering large bodies of armed troops among us:

For protecting them, by a mock trial, from punishment for any murders which they should commit on the inhabitants of these states:

For cutting off our trade with all parts of the world:

For imposing taxes on us without our consent:

For depriving us, in many cases, of the benefits of trial by jury:

For transporting us beyond seas to be tried for pretended offences:

For abolishing the free system of English laws in a neighbouring province, establishing therein an arbitrary government, and enlarging its boundaries, so as to render it at once an example and fit instrument for introducing the same absolute rule into these colonies:

For taking away our charters, abolishing our most valuable laws, and altering fundamentally the forms of our governments:

For suspending our own legislatures, and declaring themselves invested with power to legislate for us in all cases whatsoever.

He has abdicated government here, by declaring us out of his protection, and waging war against us.

He has plundered our seas, ravaged our coasts, burnt our towns, and destroyed the lives of our people.

He is, at this time, transporting large armies of foreign mercenaries to complete the works of death, desolation and tyranny, already begun with circumstances of cruelty and perfidy, scarcely paralleled in the most barbarous ages, and totally unworthy the head of a civilized nation.

He has constrained our fellow-citizens, taken captive on the high seas, to bear arms against their country, to become the executioners of their friends and brethren, or to fall themselves by their hands.

He has excited domestic insurrections amongst us, and has endeavoured to bring on the inhabitants of our frontiers the merciless Indian savages, whose known rule of warfare is an undistinguished destruction of all ages, sexes and conditions.

In every stage of these oppressions we have petitioned [345] for redress in the most humble terms: our repeated petitions have been answered only by repeated injury. A prince, whose character is thus marked by every act which may define a tyrant, is unfit to be the ruler of a free people.

Nor have we been wanting in attention to our British brethren. We have warned them from time to time of attempts made by their legislature, to extend an unwarrantable jurisdiction over us. We have reminded them of the circumstances of our emigration and settlement here. We have appealed to their native justice and magnanimity, and we have conjured them, by the ties of our common kindred, to disavow these usurpations, which would inevitably interrupt our connections and correspondence. They too have been deaf to the voice of justice and of consanguinity. We must, therefore, acquiesce in the necessity, which denounces our separation, and hold them, as we hold the rest of mankind, enemies in war, in peace, friends.

We, therefore, the representatives of the United States of America, in General Congress assembled, appealing to the Supreme Judge of the world for the rectitude of our intentions, do, in the name, and by authority of the good people of these colonies, solemnly publish and declare, that these United Colonies are, and of right ought to be, FREE and INDEPENDENT STATES; that they are absolved from all allegiance to the British crown; and that all political connection between them and the state of Great-Britain is and ought to be totally dissolved; and that as free and independent states, they have full power to levy war, conclude peace, contract alliances, establish commerce, and to do all other acts and things which independent states may of right do. And for the support of this declaration, with a firm reliance on the protection of Divine Providence, we mutually pledge to each other our lives, our fortunes, and our sacred honour.

JOHN HANCOCK, President

New-Hampshire, Josiah Bartlett, William Whipple, Matthew Thornton. *Massachusetts-Bay*, Samuel Adams, John Adams, Robert-Treat Paine, Elbridge [346] Gerry. *Rhode-Island, &c.* Stephen Hopkins, William Ellery. *Connecticut*, Roger Sherman, Samuel Huntington, William Williams, Oliver Wolcott. *New-York*, William Floyd, Philip Livingston, Francis Lewis, Lewis Morris. *New-Jersey*, Richard Stockton, John Witherspoon, Francis Hopkinson, John Hart, Abraham Clark. *Pennsylvania*, Robert Morris, Benjamin Rush, Benjamin Franklin, John

Morton, George Clymer, James Smith, George Taylor, James Wilson, George Ross. *Delaware*, Caesar Rodney, George Read. *Maryland*, Samuel Chase, William Paca, Thomas Stone, Charles Carroll, of Carrollton. *Virginia*, George Wythe, Richard Henry-Lee, Thomas Jefferson, Benjamin Harrison, Thomas Nelson, jun. Francis Lightfoot Lee, Carter Braxton. *North-Carolina*, William Hooper, Joseph Hewes, John Penn. *South-Carolina*, Edward Rutledge, Thomas Heyward, jun. Thomas Lynch, jun. Arthur Middleton. *Georgia*, Button Gwinnett, Lyman Hall, George Walton.

From the promulgation of this declaration, every thing assumed a new form. The Americans no longer appeared in the character of subjects in arms against their sovereign, but as an independent people, repelling the attacks of an invading foe. The propositions and supplications for reconciliation were done away. The dispute was brought to a single point, whether the late British colonies should be conquered provinces, or free and independent states.

The declaration of independence was read publicly in all the states, and was welcomed with many demonstrations of joy. The people were encouraged by it to bear up under the calamities of war, and viewed the evils they suffered, only as the thorn that ever accompanies the rose. The army received it with particular satisfaction. As far as it had validity, so far it secured them from suffering as rebels, and held out to their view an object, the attainment of which would be an adequate recompense for the [347] toils and dangers of war. They were animated by the consideration that they were no longer to risque their lives for the trifling purpose of procuring a repeal of a few oppressive acts of parliament, but for a new organization of government, that would forever put it out of the power of Great-Britain to oppress them. The flattering prospects of an extensive commerce, freed from British restrictions, and the honours and emoluments of office in independent states now began to glitter before the eyes of the colonists, and reconciled them to the difficulties of their situation. What was supposed in Great-Britain to be their primary object, had only a secondary influence. While they were charged with aiming at independence from the impulse of avarice and ambition, they were ardently wishing for a reconciliation. But, after they had been compelled to adopt that measure, these powerful

1776

principles of human actions opposed its retraction, and stimulated to its support. That separation which the colonists at first dreaded as an evil, they soon gloried in as a national blessing. While the rulers of Great-Britain urged their people to a vigorous prosecution of the American war, on the idea that the colonists were aiming at independence, they imposed on them a necessity of adopting that very measure, and actually effected its accomplishment. By repeatedly charging the Americans with aiming at the erection of a new government, and by proceeding on that idea to subdue them, predictions which were originally false, eventually became true. When the declaration of independence reached Great-Britain the partisans of ministry triumphed in their sagacity. "The measure, said they, we have long foreseen, is now come to pass." They inverted the natural order of things. Without reflecting that their own policy had forced a revolution contrary to the original design of the colonists, the declaration of independence was held out to the people of Great-Britain as a justification of those previous violences, which were its efficient cause.

The act of Congress for dissevering the colonies from their Parent State, was the subject of many animadversions.

[348] The colonists were said to have been precipitate in adopting a measure, from which there was no honourable ground of retreating. They replied that for eleven years they had been incessantly petitioning the throne for a redress of their grievances. Since the year 1765, a continental Congress had at three sundry times stated their claims, and prayed for their constitutional rights. That each assembly of the thirteen colonies had also, in its separate capacity, concurred in the same measure. That from the perseverance of Great-Britain in her schemes for their coercion, they had no alternative, but a mean submission, or a vigorous resistance; and that as she was about to invade their coasts with a large body of mercenaries, they were compelled to declare themselves independent, that they might be put into an immediate capacity for soliciting foreign aid.

The virulence of those who had been in opposition to the claims of the colonists, was increased by their bold act in breaking off all subordination to the Parent State. "Great-Britain, said they, has founded colonies at great expence—has incurred a load of debt by

1776

wars on their account—has protected their commerce, and raised them to all the consequence they possess, and now in the insolence of adult years, rather than pay their proportion of the common expences of government, they ungratefully renounce all connexion with the nurse of their youth, and the protectress of their riper years." The Americans acknowledged that much was due to Great-Britain, for the protection which her navy procured to the coasts, and the commerce of the colonies, but contended that much was paid by the latter, in consequence of the restrictions imposed on their commerce by the former. "The charge of ingratitude would have been just," said they, "had allegiance been renounced while protection was given, but when the navy, which formerly secured the commerce and seaport towns of America, began to distress the former, and to burn the latter, the previous obligations to obey or be grateful, were no longer in force."

That the colonists paid nothing, and would not pay to the support of government, was confidently asserted, and [349] no credit was given for the sums indirectly levied upon them, in consequence of their being confined to the consumption of British manufactures. By such illfounded observations were the people of Great-Britain inflamed against their fellow subjects in America. The latter were represented as an ungrateful people, refusing to bear any part of the expences of a protecting government, or to pay their proportion of a heavy debt, said to be incurred on their account. Many of the inhabitants of Great-Britain deceived in matters of fact, considered their American brethren as deserving the severity of military coercion. So strongly were the two countries rivetted together, that if the whole truth had been known to the people of both, their separation would have been scarcely possible. Any feasible plan by which subjection to Great-Britain could have been reconciled with American safety, would at any time, previous to 1776, have met the approbation of the colonists. But while the lust of power and of gain, blinded the rulers of Great-Britain, mistated facts and uncandid representations brought over their people to second the infatuation. A few honest men properly authorised, might have devised measures of compromise, which under the influence of truth, humility and moderation, would have prevented a dismemberment of the empire; but these virtues ceased to influence, and falsehood, haughtiness and blind zeal usurped their places. Had Great-Britain, even after the declaration of independence, adopted the magnanimous resolution of declaring her colonies free and independent states, interest would have prompted them to form such a connexion as would have secured to the Mother Country the advantages of their commerce, without the expence or trouble of their governments. But misguided politics continued the fatal system of coercion and conquest. Several on both sides of the Atlantic, have called the declaration of independence, "a bold, and accidentally, a lucky speculation," but subsequent events proved, that it was a wise measure. It is acknowledged, that it detatched some timid friends from supporting the Americans in their opposition to Great-Britain, but it increased the [350] vigour and 1776 union of those, who possessed more fortitude and perseverance. Without it, the colonists would have had no object adequate to the dangers to which they exposed themselves, in continuing to contend with Great-Britain. If the interference of France was necessary to give success to the resistance of the Americans, the declaration of independence was also necessary, for the French expressly founded the propriety of their treaty with Congress on the circumstance, "that they found the United States in possession of independence."

All political connexion between Great-Britain and her colonies being dissolved, the institution of new forms of government became unavoidable. The necessity of this was so urgent that Congress, MAY 15 before the declaration of independence, had recommended to the respective assemblies and conventions of the United States, to adopt such governments as should, in their opinion, best conduce to the happiness and safety of their constituents. During more than twelve months the colonists had been held together by the force of antient habits, and by laws under the simple stile of recommendations. The impropriety of proceeding in courts of justice by the authority of a sovereign, against whom the colonies were in arms, was self-evident. The impossibility of governing, for any length of time, three millions of people, by the ties of honour, without the authority of law, was equally apparent. The rejection of British sovereignty therefore drew after it the necessity of fixing on some other principle of government. The genius of the Americans, their republican habits and sentiments, naturally led them to substitute the majesty of the people, in lieu of discarded royalty. The kingly office was dropped, but in most of the subordinate departments of government, antient forms and names were retained. Such a portion of power had at all times been exercised by the people and their representatives, that the change of sovereignty was hardly perceptible, and the revolution took place without violence or convulsion. Popular elections elevated private citizens to the same offices, which formerly had been conferred by royal appointment. 1776 The people felt an uninterrupted continuation of the blessings [351] of law and government under old names, though derived from a new sovereignty, and were scarcely sensible of any change in their political constitution. The checks and balances which restrained the popular assemblies under the royal government, were partly dropped, and partly retained, by substituting something of the same kind. The temper of the people would not permit that any one man, however exalted by office, or distinguished by abilities, should have a negative on the declared sense of a majority of their representatives, but the experience of all ages had taught them the danger of lodging all power in one body of men. A second branch of legislature, consisting of a few select persons, under the name of senate, or council, was therefore constituted in eleven of the thirteen states, and their concurrence made necessary to give the validity of law to the acts of a more numerous branch of popular representatives. New-York and Massachusetts went one step farther. The former constituted a council of revision, consisting of the governor and the heads of judicial departments, on whose objecting to any proposed law, a reconsideration became necessary, and unless it was confirmed by two thirds of both houses, it could have no operation. A similar power was given to the governor of Massachusetts. Georgia and Pennsylvania were the only states whose legislature consisted of only one branch. Though many in these states, and a majority in all the others, saw and acknowledged the propriety of a compounded legislature, yet the mode of creating two branches out of a homogeneous mass of people, was a matter of difficulty. No distinction of ranks existed in the colonies, and none were entitled to any rights, but such as were common to all. Some possessed more wealth than others, but riches and ability were not always associated. Ten of the eleven states, whose legislatures consisted of two branches, ordained that the members of both should be elected by the people. This rather made two co-ordinate houses of representatives than a check on a single one, by the moderation of a select few. Maryland adopted a singular plan for constituting an independent senate. By her constitution the members of that body [352] were elected for five years, while the members of the house of delegates held their seats only for one. The number of senators was only fifteen, and they were all elected indiscriminately from the inhabitants of any part of the state, excepting that nine of them were to be residents on the west, and six on the east side of the Chesapeak Bay. They were elected not immediately by the people, but by electors, two from each county, appointed by the inhabitants for that sole purpose. By these regulations the senate of Maryland consisted of men of influence, integrity and abilities, and such as were a real and beneficial check on the hasty proceedings of a more numerous branch of popular representatives. The laws of that state were well digested, and its interest steadily pursued with a peculiar unity of system; while elsewhere it too often happened in the fluctuation of public assemblies; and where the legislative department was not sufficiently checked, that passion and party predominated over principle and public good.

1776

Pennsylvania instead of a legislative council or senate, adopted the expedient of publishing bills after the second reading, for the information of the inhabitants. This had its advantages and disadvantages. It prevented the precipitate adoption of new regulations, and gave an opportunity of ascertaining the sense of the people on those laws by which they were to be bound; but it carried the spirit of discussion into every corner, and disturbed the peace and harmony of neighbourhoods. By making the business of government the duty of every man, it drew off the attention of many from the steady pursuit of their respective businesses.

The state of Pennsylvania also adopted another institution peculiar to itself, under the denomination of a council of censors. These were to be chosen once every seven years, and were authorised to enquire whether the constitution had been preserved—whether the legislative and executive branch of government, had performed their duty, or assumed to themselves, or exercised other or greater powers, than those to which they were constitutionally entitled. To enquire whether the public taxes had [353] been justly laid and collected, and in what manner the public monies had been disposed of, and whether the laws had been duly executed. However excellent this institution may appear in theory, it is doubtful whether in practice it will answer any valuable end. It most certainly opens a door for discord, and furnishes abundant matter for periodical altercation. Either from the disposition of its inhabitants, its form of government, or some other cause, the people of Pennsylvania have constantly been in a state of fermentation. The end of one public controversy, has been the beginning of another. From the collision of parties, the minds of the citizens were sharpened, and their active powers improved, but internal harmony has been unknown. They who were out of place, so narrowly watched those who were in, that nothing injurious to the public could be easily effected, but from the fluctuation of power, and the total want of permanent system, nothing great or lasting could with safety be undertaken, or prosecuted to effect. Under all these disadvantages, the state flourished, and from the industry and ingenuity of its inhabitants acquired an unrivalled ascendency in arts and manufactures. This must in a great measure be ascribed to the influence of habits, of order and industry, that had long prevailed.

The Americans agreed in appointing a supreme executive head to each state, with the title either of governor or president. They also agreed in deriving the whole powers of government, either mediately or immediately from the people. In the eastern states, and in New-York, their governors were elected by the inhabitants, in their respective towns or counties, and in the other states by the legislatures: but in no case was the smallest title of power exercised from hereditary right. New-York was the only state which invested its governor with executive authority without a council. Such was the extreme jealousy of power which pervaded the American states, that they did not think proper to trust the man of their choice with the power of executing their own determinations, without obliging him in many cases to take the advice of such counsellors as they thought proper to nominate. [354] The disadvantages of this institution far outweighed its advantages. Had the governors succeeded by hereditary right, a council would have been often necessary to supply the real want of abilities, but when an individual had been selected by the people as the fittest person for discharging the duties of this high department, to fetter him with a council was either to lessen his capacity of doing good, or to furnish him with a skreen for doing evil. It destroyed the secrecy, vigor and dispatch, which the executive power ought to possess, and by making governmental acts the acts of a body, diminished individual responsibility. In some states it greatly enhanced the expences of government, and in all retarded its operations, without any equivalent advantages.

New-York in another particular, displayed political sagacity superior to her neighbours. This was in her council of appointment, consisting of one senator from each of her four great election districts, authorised to designate proper persons for filling vacancies in the executive departments of government. Large bodies are far from being the most proper depositaries of the power of appointing to offices. The assiduous attention of candidates is too apt to biass the voice of individuals in popular assemblies. Besides in such appointments, the responsibility for the conduct of the officer, is in a great measure annihilated. The concurrence of a select few on the nomination of one, seems a more eligible mode for securing a proper choice, than appointments made either by one, or by a numerous body. In the former case there would be danger of favoritism, in the latter that modest unassuming merit would be overlooked, in favour of the forward and obsequious.

A rotation of public officers made a part of most of the American constitutions. Frequent elections were required by all, but several still farther, and deprived the electors of the power of continuing the same office in the same hands, after a specified length of time. Young politicians suddenly called from the ordinary walks of life, to make laws and institute forms of government, turned their attention to the histories of ancient republics [355] and the writings of speculative men on the subject of government. This led them into many errors and occasioned them to adopt sundry opinions, unsuitable to the state of society in America, and contrary to the genius of real republicanism.

The principle of rotation was carried so far, that in some of the

1776

states, public officers in several departments scarcely knew their official duty, till they were obliged to retire and give place to others, as ignorant as they had been on their first appointment. If offices had been instituted for the benefit of the holders, the policy of diffusing these benefits would have been proper, but instituted as they were for the convenience of the public, the end was marred by such frequent changes. By confining the objects of choice, it diminished the privileges of electors, and frequently deprived them of the liberty of choosing the man who, from previous experience, was of all men the most suitable. The favourers of this system of rotation contended for it, as likely to prevent a perpetuity of office and power in the same individual or family, and as a security against hereditary honours. To this it was replied, that free, fair and frequent elections were the most natural and proper securities, for the liberties of the people. It produced a more general diffusion of political knowledge, but made more smatterers than adepts in the science of government.

As a farther security for the continuance of republican principles in the American constitutions, they agreed in prohibiting all hereditary honours and distinction of ranks.

It was one of the peculiarities of these new forms of government, that all religious establishments were abolished. Some retained a constitutional distinction between Christians and others, with respect to eligibility to office, but the idea of supporting one denomination at the expence of others, or of raising any one sect of protestants to a legal pre-eminence, was universally reprobated. The alliance between church and state was completely broken, and each was left to support itself, independent of the other.

1776   The far famed social compact between the people and their rulers, did not apply to the United States. The [356] sovereignty was in the people. In their sovereign capacity by their representatives, they agreed on forms of government for their own security, and deputed certain individuals as their agents to serve them in public stations agreeably to constitutions, which they prescribed for their conduct.

The world has not hitherto exhibited so fair an opportunity for promoting social happiness. It is hoped for the honor of human nature, that the result will prove the fallacy of those theories, which suppose that mankind are incapable of self government. The ancients, not knowing the doctrine of representation, were apt in their public meetings to run into confusion, but in America this mode of taking the sense of the people, is so well understood, and so completely reduced to system, that its most populous states are often peaceably convened in an assembly of deputies, not too large for orderly deliberation, and yet representing the whole in equal proportions. These popular branches of legislature are miniature pictures of the community, and from the mode of their election are likely to be influenced by the same interests and feelings with the people whom they represent. As a farther security for their fidelity, they are bound by every law they make for their constituents. The assemblage of these circumstances gives as great a security that laws will be made, and government administered for the good of the people, as can be expected from the imperfection of human institutions.

In this short view of the formation and establishment of the American constitutions, we behold our species in a new situation. In no age before, and in no other country, did man ever possess an election of the kind of government, under which he would choose to live. The constituent parts of the antient free governments were thrown together by accident. The freedom of modern European governments was, for the most part, obtained by the concessions, or liberality of monarchs, or military leaders. In America alone, reason and liberty concurred in the formation of constitutions. It is true, from the infancy of political knowledge in the United States, there were [357] many defects in their forms of government. But in one 1776 thing they were all perfect. They left the people in the power of altering and amending them, whenever they pleased. In this happy peculiarity they placed the science of politics on a footing with the other sciences, by opening it to improvements from experience, and the discoveries of future ages. By means of this power of amending American constitutions, the friends of mankind have fondly hoped that oppression will one day be no more, and that political evil will at least be prevented or restrained with as much certainty, by a proper combination or separation of power, as natural evil is lessened or prevented by the application of the knowledge or ingenuity of man to domestic purposes. No part of the history of antient or modern Europe, can furnish a single fact that militates against this opinion, since in none of its governments have the principles of equal representation and checks been applied, for the preservation of freedom. On these two pivots are suspended the liberties of most of the states. Where they are wanting, there can be no security for liberty, where they exist they render any farther security unnecessary.

The rejection of British sovereignty not only involved a necessity of erecting independent constitutions, but of cementing the whole United States by some common bond of union. The act of independence did not hold out to the world thirteen sovereign states, but a common sovereignty of the whole in their united capacity. It therefore became necessary to run the line of distinction, between the local legislatures, and the assembly of the states in Congress. A committee was appointed for digesting articles of confederation between the states or united colonies, as they were then called, at the time the propriety of declaring independence was under debate, and some weeks previously to the adoption of that measure, but the plan was not for sixteen months after so far digested, as to be ready for communication to the states. Nor was it finally ratified by the accession of all the states, till nearly three years more had elapsed. In discussing its articles, many difficult questions occurred. One was to ascertain the ratio of [358] contributions from each state. Two principles presented themselves, numbers of people, and the value of lands. The last was preferred as being the truest barometer of the wealth of nations, but from an apprehended impracticability of carrying it into effect, it was soon relinquished, and recurrence had to the former. That the states should be represented in proportion to their importance, was contended for by those who had extensive territory, but they who were confined to small dimensions, replied, that the states confederated as individuals, in a state of nature, and should therefore have equal votes. From fear of weakening their exertions against the common enemy, the large states for the present yielded the point, and consented that each state should have an equal suffrage.

1776

It was not easy to define the power of the state legislatures, so as to prevent a clashing between their jurisdiction, and that of the general government. On mature deliberation it was thought proper, that the former should be abridged of the power of forming any other confederation or alliance—of laying on any imposts or duties that might interfere with treaties made by Congress—or keeping up any vessels of war, or granting letters of marque or reprisal. The powers of Congress were also defined. Of these the principle were as follows: To have the sole and exclusive right of determining on peace and war—of sending and receiving ambassadors—of entering into treaties and alliances,—of granting letters of marque and reprisal in times of peace.—To be the last resort on appeal, in all disputes between two or more states—to have the sole and exclusive right of regulating the alloy and value of coin, of fixing the standard of weights and measures—regulating the trade and managing all affairs with the Indians—establishing and regulating post offices—to borrow money or emit bills on the credit of the United States—to build and equip a navy—to agree upon the number of land forces, and to make requisitions from each state for its quota of men, in proportion to the number of its white inhabitants.

No coercive power was given to the general government, nor was it invested with any legislative power over [359] individuals, but only over states in their corporate capacity. As at the time the articles of confederation were proposed for ratification, the Americans had little or no regular commercial intercourse with foreign nations, a power to regulate trade or to raise a revenue from it, though both were essential to the welfare of the union, made no part of the federal system. To remedy this and all other defects, a door was left open for introducing farther provisions, suited to future circumstances.

The articles of confederation were proposed at a time when the citizens of America were young in the science of politics, and when a commanding sense of duty, enforced by the pressure of a common danger, precluded the necessity of a power of compulsion. The enthusiasm of the day gave such credit and currency to paper emissions, as made the raising of supplies an easy matter. The system of federal government was therefore more calculated for what men then were, under these circumstances, than for the languid years of peace, when selfishness usurped the place of public spirit, and when credit no longer assisted, in providing for the exigencies of government.

1776

The experience of a few years after the termination of the war, proved, as will appear in its proper place, that a radical change of the whole system was necessary, to the good government of the United States.

THE END OF THE FIRST VOLUME